STUDIA POST-BIBLICA
VOLUMEN UNDECIMUM

STUDIA POST-BIBLICA

ADIUVANTIBUS

J. BOWMAN . J. HOFTIJZER . T. JANSMA . H. KOSMALA
K. H. RENGSTORF . J. COERT RIJLAARDSDAM
G. SEVENSTER . D. WINSTON THOMAS
G. VAJDA . G. VERMES

EDIDIT

P. A. H. DE BOER

VOLUMEN UNDECIMUM

LEIDEN
E. J. BRILL
1966

A HISTORY OF
THE JEWS IN BABYLONIA

II. THE EARLY SASANIAN PERIOD

BY

JACOB NEUSNER

Associate Professor of Religion
Dartmouth College

LEIDEN

E. J. BRILL

1966

For Suzanne

By the same author:

A Life of Rabban Yohanan ben Zakkai

 E. J. Brill, Leiden, 1962: Studia Post-biblica VI.

 Awarded The Abraham Berliner Prize in Jewish History of The Jewish Theological Seminary of America, 1962.

Fellowship in Judaism: *The First Century and Today*

 Vallentine, Mitchell & Co. Ltd., London, 1963.

A History of the Jews in Babylonia, I. The Parthian Period

 E. J. Brill, Leiden, 1965: Studia Post-biblica IX.

History and Torah: *Essays on Jewish Learning*

 Vallentine, Mitchell & Co. Ltd., London, 1965, and Schocken Books, N. Y., 1965.

CONTENTS

V Rabbinic Judaism in Early Sasanian Babylonia (II):
Theology and Liturgy 151
  i.   Ideas about God 151
  ii. Contributions to Liturgy 159
  iii. Prayer and Fasting 168
  iv. Blessings 170
  v.   Laws Pertaining to Synagogue Worship 177
  vi. Rav's Theology 180

VI Rabbinic Judaism in Early Sasanian Babylonia (III):
Biblical Exegesis and History 188
  i.   The Pentateuch 188
  ii. The Prophetic Books 199
  iii. The Writings 217
  iv. Heroes of Torah in Biblical Times 222
  v.   Tannaitic History 229
  vi. Rav and Samuel as Heirs of R. Akiba and R. Ishmael . . 232
  vii. Exegesis and History. 236

VII Geography and Population 241
  i.   Jewish Settlements in Babylonia 241
  ii. A Population-Estimate 246

VIII The People and the Law 251
  i.   The Problem 251
  ii. Agricultural Offerings 260
  iii. Transfers of Property, Torts, and Damages 262
  iv. Laws of Personal Status 268
  v.   Laws on Religious Life. 274
  vi. The Rabbis' Influence 282

Appendix: Further Exegeses on Exodus and Esther. 288

Supplementary Bibliography. 291

Addenda et Corrigenda ad Volumen I. 302

Index of Biblical and of Talmudic Passages 308

General Index 322

LIST OF MAPS

PREFACE

No brief period in Jewish history so permanently impressed its mark upon all subsequent ages as did the four decades under study. Every aspect of Jewish cultural and religious life, the conduct of civil affairs in the diaspora, the formulation of political policy both within the Jewish community and toward the outside world, the elaboration of theological, historical, and biblical motifs—all continue to reveal the enduring imprint of these years. And if this is so, the reason must be found in the towering personalities of Rav and Samuel, who form the center of interest in the history of this period, and the abiding importance of whose achievements renders it consequential for succeeding generations. Ismar Elbogen noted that the influence of Rav and Samuel may be discerned upon every page of the Jewish prayerbook. The same may be said of many another central institution and idea of Judaism. These two men provide, therefore, the chief foci around which our study centers. At the same time, I must emphasize that we shall by no means exhaust all aspects of their legacy, or even note everything of interest in it. My effort is to provide more than a joint biography of two important men, but rather, through a study of their sayings and those of their adult contemporaries,[1] to recover some clear, sequential, and well-organized ideas about the history of Babylonian Jewry and Judaism in this age. We have a number of biographical studies of both men, including those by David Hoffman, Y. S. Zuri, and others of lesser value. We even have a full compendium of Rav's sayings, compiled by Berthold Jeiteles. The structure of the literary remains of the period was revealed in the researches of both classical Talmudic commentators, and such modern scholars as Y. N. Epstein, H. Albeck, S. Lieberman, and others. Many have contributed to the study of law, philology, and literature of the early 'Amora'im. Apart from rather brief, superficial, and methodologically unsophisticated works, however, we do not have *history*. And that is what I propose to provide.

Two major themes, one external, the other internal, dominate Babylonian Jewish history in the period of the first two Sasanian emperors (226-272). Ardashir brought to an end a fortunate time in Jewry's life,

---

[1] I am postponing study of sources relevant to the students of Rav and Samuel to Volume III, which will be devoted to the period from ca. 265 to ca. 300, except for those sayings clearly to be dated during the lifetimes of the first Babylonian 'Amora'im, or directly pertinent to their affairs.

and the Jews dreaded the new and far less accommodating rulers who had overthrown the Parthians. Jewish leaders consequently had to find a new basis for their community's politics, to explain to the people exactly what the cataclysmic events meant within the framework of redemption, and to respond to the rich ferment in regional cultural and religious life characteristic of this period. An equally significant event was the great expansion of the rabbinic movement in Babylonia, marked by the return from Palestine of Rav, Levi ben Sisi, and other teachers, the foundation of new academies, and the application to Babylonian Jewish affairs of the Mishnah of Rabbi Judah the Prince.

The first three chapters focus upon the first, external challenge, that of political events, and religious responses to them. The third chapter forms a transition, for, as we shall see, the exilarch was strengthened, in his quest for a new political basis for existence by the services of well-trained judges, teachers, and lawyers, who constituted at the same time the core of the rabbinic movement. Chapters Four, Five, and Six concentrate on religious and cultural matters, specifically, the nature of rabbinic leadership, theology, and Scriptural commentary. Since Bible study played a substantial part in rabbinic Judaism, a detailed survey of exegetical literature is provided in Chapter Six. The final two chapters are concerned with sociological questions, in particular the character of Babylonian Jewry, its population, and the ways in which society was influenced by the rabbis' traditions and laws. The impact of political history upon rabbinic Judaism is further discussed in Chapter Five, sections ii and vi, Chapter Six, section vii, and Chapter Eight, section vi. The relationship between the law and popular practice is additionally treated in Chapter Two, section vii, Chapter Three, sections v, vi, and vii; Chapter Four, sections ii and iv, and Chapter Five, sections iv and v.

The period at hand forms a perfectly natural division in both Jewish and Iranian history. The rise of the Sasanians under Ardashir, and the consolidation of their power by Shapur, both strong emperors, represent the first and most glorious chapter in their history. Shapur's successors, a series of weak emperors until Shapur II, merely maintained, as best they could, the legacy of the first two rulers. Rav and Samuel, similarly, stand by themselves. Their students and heirs spent many decades studying, preserving, and realizing the legacy of the first generation of Amoraim.

In volume I of this study, I was forced, by the paucity of sources dealing with both Babylonian Jews and Parthians, to offer numerous

conjectures and hypotheses based upon limited evidence. Here the
problem is the very opposite. We have extensive primary literature
dealing with aspects of Jewish culture. For Sasanian Iran, archaeological and numismatic evidence now supplements a relatively rich and
well-established literary-historical tradition, rather than constituting
almost the whole of historical evidence (apart from the classical
histories) as it does for the Parthian period. If the first volume relied
far too much on the augmentative, but never certain, resources of the
historical imagination, the second required the exercise of the faculty
to select and discriminate, to select important problems, and to discriminate in favor of subjects heretofore neglected or only partially
studied. Little will be achieved by detailed rehearsals of well-known
facts of Sasanian history, chronology, culture, religion, and politics.
I am not qualified to enter the much-vexed problems of that history,
being mainly interested in it for its capacity to illumine Jewish affairs.
In Chapter One I have tried, as before, to offer a modest summary of
the accepted facts of Iranian history and culture, with references
provided for those interested in further pursuing these matters. I have
not, however, offered an opinion on such matters as, e.g., the chronology of Shapur's wars, or cast an uninvited, and never to be counted,
ballot on the scholarly issues inhering in the study of third century
Mazdaism, the work of Tosar and Kartir in establishing the state-
church, the history of Zurvanism, or similar matters. I believe the
Jewish sources may illumine many problems in Sasanian studies, just
as these studies offer fundamental information for Babylonian Jewish
history. In this work, nonetheless, only Jewish history is at issue.

   Jewish history in this period has been much discussed, yet, as I said,
I do not believe we have an adequate, detailed, and informed account
of it. What we have, and what I depend upon, are mainly literary and
legal studies of Babylonian-Talmudic matters, but these are not meant
as history, and certainly they are not. Issues most commonly discussed
pertain to the later history in Babylonia of the Mishnah, Tosefta, and
other Tannaitic documents, to the state of Jewish academies and law in
the early Amoraic period, and to the exposition of Talmudic materials
in situ. Literary and legal scholars do not provide sequential and well-
organized historical information, though their commentaries contribute greatly toward its recovery. For my part, I must emphasize that
this work is not intended as either legal or literary history. The reader
interested in literary aspects of the Talmudic sources should look
elsewhere, beginning in such works as Y. N. Epstein's *Introductions to*

Amoraic Literature (in Hebrew, Jerusalem, 1962), and his *Introduction to the Text of the Mishnah* (in Hebrew 2nd ed., Jerusalem, 1964), H. Albeck's *Introduction to the Mishnah* (in Hebrew, Jerusalem, 1959), A. Weiss's various works, listed in the bibliography, on the literary history of the Talmud, the monumental commentaries of L. Ginzberg and S. Lieberman on the Palestinian Talmud, and, of S. Lieberman, on the Tosefta, and similar studies. Moreover, this is not legal history, nor could a history of Jewish law be composed on such a narrow chronological and geographical basis as one small region and half of a single century. It is possible that legal historians may find useful some of the suggestions on cultural and social history which are offered here, but in no case have I attempted to reduce complex legal questions to sociological, political, or extrinsic, cultural terms unless the 'Amora'im themselves did so. If therefore the reader is looking for novellae on issues of literary or legal interpretation of the Babylonian Talmud, he will be disappointed in the pages that follow. Here the Babylonian Talmud and other relevant sources are being read from the perspective of the history of political, social, and cultural-religious realities, and not, except as part of that history, of law or literature, however penetrating such perspectives may be. On the other hand, one very important question is, To what degree did the law actually describe the life of the people? What impact did the legal and ethical dicta of Rav, Samuel, and their fellow Amoraim make upon popular affairs? To answer these questions, I have had to pay close attention to the evidences of the enforcement of Jewish law, and to the influence of that law upon Jewish life and society.

One of the chief difficulties in using essentially legal and exegetical texts for historical purposes is the necessity to break the natural continuities which the texts exhibit in the original. The sayings of Rav and Samuel most commonly are preserved within the framework of fundamentally scholastic, dialectical discussions. That framework did not originate with Rav and Samuel, who engaged mainly in *ad hoc* exposition of law and doctrine, but, as I shall argue in a subsequent volume, with the generation of Rabbah, Rava, and Abaye, who, having exhausted the hermeneutical possibilities of inherited tradition, struck out in bold, new directions indicated by their own dialectical genius. The fact is that many of the sayings of Rav and Samuel are preserved in utterly non-historical settings. The result is that one uses them for historical purposes only by violently detaching them from their legal context, or by diverting attention from the history of their age to the history of law, neither a desirable alternative.

A second major problem, likewise not satisfactorily solved here, is posed by the need to assess the reliability of historical information provided by the Talmud. The texts which preserve this information were finally edited about two and a half centuries later, and though it is likely that notes, and even brief, organized tractates, existed before that time, we have no way of knowing how accurately the actual words of the rabbis were reported in the final recension. At first I had assumed that the one solid rock upon which to build was the sayings ascribed to the sages. A number of stories explicitly state however that the words of Rav or Samuel, cited in a clear-cut legal formula, were not actually said by them at all, but were rather formulated in their names by students who, observing their actions, presumed to generalize on such a basis, and to offer what they thought was the master's abstract, legal opinion. If this is so in several cases, as it is, one cannot be certain how much else is, in fact, pseudepigraphic. I cannot offer a general law for verifying the reliability of Talmudic materials, although my assumption is that legal dicta were actually stated by the rabbis to whom they are credited unless contrary evidence denies it. I have come to a number of *ad hoc* decisions. If one has no final certainties, that is what makes research interesting.

It will be useful for the reader to know the chief scholarly influences upon my research. Among the Iranists, I have relied upon the judgment, both written and oral, of my teacher Richard N. Frye, and upon that, generously given when solicited, of W. B. Henning, upon the philological studies of Telegdi, both Geigers, Kohut, de Menasce, Henning, and others; upon the historical and religious-cultural insights of Geo Widengren, the only Iranist to make a direct contribution to our subject; and upon other studies cited where relevant. The works most commonly cited on Babylonian Jewish matters are those of Funk and Obermeyer. Obermeyer's geographical researches are universally and rightly accepted as the foundation for all study, superseding all their predecessors and never themselves rendered obsolete. The pioneer work of Babylonian Talmudic history was S. Funk's *Die Juden in Babylonien* (Berlin 1902). Like Graetz, Funk had the merit of offering valid generalizations. But like Graetz, he covered the whole period too briefly. Graetz's brief chapter was adequate for his purposes. It is unfortunate that others have used it when in need of more than a very superficial summary. J. Newman's small volumes *Agricultural*

Life of the Jews in Babylonia and *Commercial Life* are likewise widely
cited, particularly by Iranists, far more than their slender value would
have warranted, while F. M. Heichelheim's economic survey has
yet to receive requisite attention. The works of Yavetz and Halevi
have continued to guide me in many ways, as did the several volumes
on Talmudic history, and the biography of Rav, by Y. S. Zuri. Zuri's
work has been unaccountably ignored by most recent students of
Talmudic history, partly because of the prolix and repetitious manner
of his presentation, partly because of the very uneven standard of his
research. For this period, Zuri's work supersedes in usefulness that of
Yavetz and Halevi. Halevi in particular was mainly intent upon
demonstrating the antiquity of the Oral Torah in Babylonia, but
having done so, he found relatively little of interest in the period under
study. In specific matters it will be seen that his thought continued, as
in volume I, to exert a strong influence upon my own. As earlier, I
found the historical insights of J. H. Weiss vastly overrated, and those
of S. Dubnow inconsequential. Samuel Krauss and A. Kohut provided
research which had to be consulted at every step. Kohut's edition, with
the supplements of Geiger and others, of the *Arukh* remains of value.
Krauss's many articles and books on Talmudic archaeology and history
likewise proved invariably fruitful. Among those now specializing in
the history of the Talmudic period, M. Beer and Hugo Mantel have
greatly enriched my knowledge and understanding through each of
their several contributions, correspondence, and criticism of my work.
I learned much from the unpublished doctoral dissertation (Hebrew
Union College, Cincinnati, Library) of Professor Ezra Spicehandler.
The relevant chapters and notes in the first two volumes of Salo
Baron's *Social and Religious History of the Jews* offered important guidance. At specific points in the discussion, I shall, of course, cite many
other works of great value. While this account by no means exhausts
the collegial contributions to my research, as the notes, bibliography,
and supplementary bibliography make abundantly evident, it will
serve to indicate the scholarly context in which this work is intended
to find a place.

Citations of Talmudic literature are included in the text, rather than
in notes, to facilitate reading.

Most translations of Babylonian Talmudic texts follow those edited
by Dr. I. Epstein, and those of Midrash Rabbah, that edited by Dr. H.
Freedman and Maurice Simon, both published by the Soncino Press,
London, in 1948 and 1939 respectively. Rabbi William Braude's trans-

lation of the Midrash on Psalms, published by Yale University Press, New Haven, in 1959, was followed throughout. While I have checked these translations against the original texts, and, where possible, against variant readings as well, and have altered some of them, in the main I have found it satisfactory to make use of the available translations, since this is not a work of philology, text-criticism, or commentary. Texts are here cited mainly for illustration, rather than extended analysis, except where relevant to a strictly historical question.

In the appendix, I have included corrections and additions to volume I.

Professor Richard N. Frye read and offered helpful comments on the first three chapters, and Professor Seymour Siegel did the same for the entire manuscript. Professors W. B. Henning, Saul Lieberman, and Morton Smith provided, in correspondence, invaluable comments. I am deeply grateful to these generous teachers for their continuing contributions to my research. Its failings are mine alone.

It is my pleasant task, also, to acknowledge gratefully the assistance of the following: Miss Linda Lutz, formerly Reference Librarian of Baker Library, Dartmouth College, who procured numerous books and articles otherwise unavailable to me; the Committee on Research of Dartmouth College, which made numerous grants, large and small, for research and typing expenses; the Penrose Fund of the American Philosophical Society, which supported parts of my research expense in the summer of 1965; Mrs. Margaret Sanders, secretary of the Departments of Philosophy and Religion at Dartmouth College, who typed part of the manuscript; and Dr. Lawrence Marwick, Head of the Hebraic Section of the Library of Congress, who provided important bibliographical assistance.

My thanks are due also to Professor Jes P. Asmussen, who gave helpful criticism on Iranian matters, and to Mr. David Goodblatt, who prepared the indices and assisted in reading and correcting proofs, and to whom I am indebted for valuable help in seeing the manuscript through the press.

To my wife, who has brought to fulfillment in my life the blessings described in Proverbs 31: 10-31, these pages are offered in homage.

JACOB NEUSNER

Hanover, New Hampshire
25 Kislev 5726
December 19th, 1965.

CHRONOLOGY

I. *Political Events in Early Sasanian Times: Foreign Policy*

229 – Ardashir demanded Alexander Severus return territories once ruled by the Achemenids.

231 – Attack of Alexander Severus.

232 – Romans repulsed, peace restored.
– Xosroes assassinated, Ardashir conquered Armenia, Trdat son of Xosroes fled to Rome.

240 – Shapur crushed revolts in Armenia, took Hatra.

241 – Outbreak of First War with Rome against Philip the Arab.
– Shapur attacked via Nisibis and Carrhae, Romans retook Carrhae and (according to their account) threatened Ctesiphon[1].

244 – Peace of Shapur and Philip. Iran kept Armenia, Romans retook part of Mesopotamia.
– Bactria entered direct relations with Rome.

256 – Outbreak of Second War with Rome. Shapur took Nisibis, Carrhae, Edessa, and Antioch. Valerian hastened east, retook Antioch.

260 – Valerian captured, Shapur put up his own candidate for the Roman throne against Macrianus and Gallienus, Miriades/Cyriades of Antioch. Shapur retook Antioch, installed his candidate as Caesar, invaded Cilicia and Cappadocia, took Tarsus, Cilicia Campestris, passes of the Taurus, besieged and took Caesarea Mazaca.

261/2 – Shapur returned home, checked at Emesa, and harried by Odenathus of Palmyra.

262-3 – Odenathus attacked Carrhae and Nisibis, drove down to gates of Ctesiphon, ravaged central Babylonia, and retired to Palmyra.

263-272 – Shapur occupied himself with construction of great works, including new city of Shapur, dike at Shuster, memorials at Hadji-Abad, Nakhš-i Radjab, Nakhš-i Rustam, and Darabgerd.

273 – Shapur died, succeeded by his son.

II. *Jewish Aspects of Political Events*

226-242 – Jews lost their former political and religious autonomy, had to accomodate themselves to more vigorous rule, establish-

---

[1] See Richard N. Frye, Review of Ensslin, *Zu den Kriegen, Bibliotheca Orientalis* 8, 1956, 103-106.

ment of state-cult, by Sasanians. R. Shila, R. Kahana, and Rav
were unable to formulate realistic policy, and reconcile themselves
to the change effected by the new regime.

242-263 – Samuel succeeded in reconciling the Jews to Persian rule,
in alliance with the new emperor, Shapur I, who proclaimed a
policy of cultural and religious toleration.

253-256 – Dura Jews supported Rome against Persian conquest.

260 – Samuel refused to lament the slaughter of Jews of Caesarea
Mazaca by Shapur's army.

263 – Samuel's Daughters made captive, sent to Palestine for ransom,
probably in siege and destruction of Nehardea by Palmyrene
army. Samuel's academy destroyed.

Ca. 272 – Reaction, led by Kartir, against Shapur's policy of toleration.

LIST OF ABBREVIATIONS

I. Journals

AJSL	=	American Journal of Semitic Languages and Literatures
AO	=	Acta Orientalia
ArcO	=	Archiv Orientalni
BOR	=	Babylonian and Oriental Record
BSOS	=	Bulletin of the School of Oriental (and African) Studies
CAH	=	Cambridge Ancient History
HUCA	=	Hebrew Union College Annual
IA	=	Iranica Antiqua
IEJ	=	Israel Exploration Journal
JA	=	Journal Asiatique
JaJGL	=	Jahrbücher für Jüdische Geschichte und Literatur
JaJLG	=	Jahrbuch der jüdisch. Literatur-Gesellschaft
JAOS	=	Journal of the American Oriental Society
JBL	=	Journal of Biblical Literature
JE	=	Jewish Encyclopedia
JJS	=	Journal of Jewish Studies
JNES	=	Journal of Near Eastern Studies
JQR	=	Jewish Quarterly Review
JR	=	Journal of Religion
JRAS	=	Journal of the Royal Asiatic Society
JSS	=	Journal of Semitic Studies
MGWJ	=	Monatschrift für die Geschichte und Wissenschaft des Judenthums
MO	=	Monde Oriental
MWJ	=	Magazin für die Wissenschaft des Judenthums
PAAJR	=	Proceedings of the American Academy for Jewish Research
Pope	=	A. U. Pope, *Survey of Persian Art*, N.Y. 1938, vol. I.
REJ	=	Révue des Études Juives
RHR	=	Révue de l'Histoire des Religions
RSO	=	Revista degli Studi Orientali
ZDMG	=	Zeitschrift der deutschen Morgenländischen Gesellschaft
ZWN	=	Zeitschrift für Neutestamentliche Wissenschaft

II. Talmudic Literature

b.	=	Babylonian Talmud	Mak.	=	Makkot
y.	=	Palestinian Talmud	Meg.	=	Megillah
R.	=	Rabbah	Men.	=	Menaḥot
A.Z.	=	ʿAvodah Zarah	Ned.	=	Nedarim
B.B.	=	Bava Batra	Nid.	=	Niddah
B.M.	=	Bava Meẓiʾah	Pes.	=	Pesaḥim
B.Q.	=	Bava Qamma	Qid.	=	Qiddushin
Bekh.	=	Bekhorot	R.H.	=	Rosh Hashanah
Ber.	=	Berakhot	Sanh.	=	Sanhedrin
Bik.	=	Bikkurim	Shab.	=	Shabbat
ʿEruv.	=	ʿEruvin	Shev.	=	Shevuʿot
Git.	=	Gittin	SOZ	=	Seder ʿOlam Zuta
Ḥag.	=	Ḥagigah	Suk.	=	Sukkah
Ḥul.	=	Ḥullin	Yev.	=	Yevamot
Ket.	=	Ketuvot	Zev.	=	Zevaḥim
M.Q.	=	Moʿed Qatan			

III. Biblical Books

Gen.	= Genesis	Ezek.	= Ezekiel
Ex.	= Exodus	Ez.	= Ezekiel
Lev.	= Leviticus	Ps.	= Psalms
Num.	= Numbers	Prov.	= Proverbs
Deut.	= Deuteronomy	Song	= Song of Songs
Jud.	= Judges	Lam.	= Lamentations
Sam.	= Samuel	Koh.	= Kohelet
Is.	= Isaiah	Dan.	= Daniel
Jer.	= Jeremiah	Chron.	= Chronicles
		Est.	= Esther

IV. Other Abbreviations

(N.B. Bibliographical data are given in the bibliography, Vol. I, 191-213, and in the Supplementary Bibliography, below, pp. 291-301).

Vol. I	= A History of the Jews in Babylonia, I. The Parthian Period
Life	= A Life of Rabban Yohanan ben Zakkai
Arukh	= Arukh HaShalem, ed. A. Kohut
Bacher, *Agada*	= W. Bacher, Die Agada der babylonischen Amoräer
Christensen, *L'Iran*	= A. Christensen, L'Iran sous les Sassanides
Dik. Sof.	== R. Rabbinovicz, Dikdukei Soferim, I-XV
Duchesne-Guillemin, *La Religion*	= J. Duchesne-Guillemin, La Religion de l'Iran Ancien
Frye, *Heritage*	= Richard N. Frye, Heritage of Persia
Funk, *Juden*	= Salomon Funk, Die Juden in Babylonien
Ginzberg, *Perushim*	= Louis Ginzberg, Perushim veḤiddushim baYerushalmi
Halevi, *Dorot*	= I. Y. Halevi, Dorot HaRishonim
Jastrow	= M. Jastrow, Dictionary of Talmud Babli, Yerushalmi, Midrashic Literature, and Targumim
Krauss, *Paras*	= Samuel Krauss, Paras veRomi baTalmud uvaMidrashim
KZ	= Kaʿab-i Zaradusht
Lieberman, *Yerushalmi*	= Saul Lieberman, HaYerushalmi Kifshuto
Levy, or, Levy, Wörterbuch	= Jacob Levy, Wörterbuch über die Talmudim und Midraschim
Obermeyer, or Obermeyer, *Landschaft*	= Jacob Obermeyer, Die Landschaft Babylonien im Zeitalter des Talmuds und des Gaonats. Geographie und Geschichte nach Talmudischen, Arabischen, und anderen Quellen
Pigulevskaja, *Villes*	= N. Pigulevskaja, Les Villes de l'État Iranien aux Époques Parthe et Sassanide
Rawlinson, *Monarchy*	= George Rawlinson, Seventh Great Oriental Monarchy
Weiss, *Dor*	= J. H. Weiss, Dor Dor veDorshav
Yavetz, *Toldot*	= Ze'ev Yavetz, Sefer Toldot Yisrael
Zaehner, *Dawn*	= R. C. Zaehner, Dawn and Twilight of Zoroastrianism
——, *Zurvan*	= Zurvan, A Zoroastrian Dilemma

CHAPTER ONE

THE IRANIAN BACKGROUND

I. The Rise of the Sasanian Dynasty

By the time they fell from power, with astonishing suddenness in the brief period from the rise of the Sasanians in 211-212, to the coronation of Ardashir in September, 226,[1] the Arsacids had held the throne of Iran for four and a half centuries. The last of these, from the time of Trajan, had proven most critical, for the Romans, mounting three major invasions of Mesopotamia-Babylonia, had captured Ctesiphon twice, under Trajan, and, again, under Avidius Cassius, and seriously threatened to do so still a third time in the last decade of the second century. The Parthians successfully repulsed each attack, however, sometimes by force of arms, mostly by force of circumstance. As a consequence, the Arsacid throne must have seemed more secure at the turn of the third century than it had for generations. Moreover, during the first two decades of that century, the last Arsacid, Ardavan V, achieved remarkable victories over Rome, completely nullifying Caracalla's earlier gains and forcing his successor to pay a humiliating ransom in exchange for the peace of Nisibis in 218. The Parthians had long retained the loyalty of their Semitic subjects, including the series of Semitic petty-states which marked the perimeter of their western frontier; the Jews and Greeks of central Babylonia fully accepted the easy yoke of the Arsacids. The dogged local resistance against repeated Roman invasions indicates how successfully the Parthians had cultivated the minority groups in their western satrapies.

It is, therefore, not easy to explain the rapid turn in events, for the dynasty fell not at a moment of weakness, but in an hour of success in world politics. No wars raged on the frontiers, nor were the subject peoples discontented with their lot, when the Arsacids suddenly fell from power. The incessant dynastic struggle, which in this period pitted Ardavan V against his brother Vologases V, certainly diverted the attention of the court at Ctesiphon from the incipient threat posed by the rise of its vigorous, rebellious satrap, Ardashir, in Persia.

---

[1] I follow the chronology of S. H. Taqizadeh, "The Early Sassanians", *AO* 18, 1940, 260f., in particular, 285, 294-299. Compare H. Lewy, "Le Calendrier Perse", *Orientalia* 10, 1941, 45-51.

Ardavan made a feeble response to Ardashir's original advances, which he regarded as mere insolence, and only aroused himself to assemble an army when the vassal achieved notable successes in Kerman, east of Persia, and Media to the north. The Persians overcame Ardavan's forces in several battles, finally killing the last Parthian ruler in April of 227. Ardavan's sons fought on in the north and in Armenia, both of which continued to be ruled by cadet branches of the Arsacid dynasty, but by 228-229, Ardashir had successfully established his rule over the greater part of the Parthian empire, and, moving his court from Fars to Ctesiphon, turned his attention westward, toward the Roman Orient (section II, below).

The precipitous course of events has been variously explained. Some have held that the Persians, rebelling on account of the dissatisfaction of the Magi with their position under the eclectic Parthians, quickly won the loyalties of the other Iranian peoples for religious reasons; others have held that the Persians were motivated by national pride, which had been severely damaged in the preceding centuries; or that the Arsacids were greatly weakened by the exertions of the second century; or that the feuds and civil wars, characteristic of the feudal system by which the Parthians had loosely governed their great empire, in the end brought about their fall. The Magi, however, were not powerful throughout the Iranian empire but, in this period, possibly only in Persis itself, and did not exert sufficient influence either to overthrow a government that ignored them, or to preserve one that favored them, although later on the Sasanians altered this state of affairs. The pride of the Persians in their own glorious past may explain why they followed Papak and Ardashir[1] to battle, but not why they won. Regarding reverses in foreign affairs, the Arsacids lost power not when Rome held Ctesiphon, but as undisputed rulers of most of the Mesopotamian valley. As to the alleged weakness of their government, while their administration was not efficient, they were able to muster

---

[1] For the course of Ardashir's revolt, see George Rawlinson, *Seventh Great Oriental Monarchy* (London, 1876), 1-15, 30-39, and Arthur Christensen, *L'Iran sous les Sassanides* (1st edition, Copenhagen and Paris, 1936) 79-91. Rawlinson cites classical and Armenian sources, Christensen adds oriental and numismatic evidence. R. Ghirshman, *Iran: Parthians and Sassanians* (London, 1962), 119, notes that the change in dynasty is no longer regarded as an 'oriental' reaction against the Philhellenism of the Parthians, and Christensen stresses that widespread anarchy preceded the fall of the Arsacids. I do not believe that such anarchy alone led to their fall, however, since the middle of the first century witnessed a general collapse of government in all of Babylonia without similar result.

strong armies for their third effort against the Persians, after two
successive and damaging defeats, which would suggest that they
managed to rally their feudal supporters with considerable success.
So it seems to me that the Persians, fighting for whatever motive, or
group of motives, may seem plausible, won for essentially military,
rather than political, cultural, or sociological reasons. They fought
better, probably because of greater enthusiasm. Since both sides employed similar tactics, and since the sources do not indicate a great
disparity in numbers, we may suggest that the Persians, like the Mos-
lem Arabs who brought down their dynasty four centuries later, fought
with superior élan, on account of religious inspiration, than did those
accustomed to power and unable sufficiently to fear an upstart foe,
their own subject, to take early and sufficiently effective action. Iranian
tradition looked upon the cataclysmic events as the will of the deity,
and modern explanations, though in naturalistic idiom, need not
greatly diverge.

Sasan, eponymous ancestor of the new dynasty, was said to have
been a priest in the Zoroastrian clergy, which was powerful in Persis,
and served at the Istakhr temple. His son, Papak, born about 150, held
no higher post, but Papak's son, Ardashir, born about 180, was raised
as the protege of Tire, argabadh of Darabgird, and in 197-8 or 201-2
succeeded to his 'throne', that is to say, to the post of commandant of
the garrison and fortress of the town.[1] The year 208 or 211[2] is the date
of the commencement of the Sasanian reckoning, and Taqizadeh
suggests, most plausibly in my view, that it was then that Ardashir
began to struggle for the supremacy of his district, or achieved a major
success. (Whatever claims the Sasanians later laid to be heirs of the
Achemenids, descended from Darius, the only evidence we have is
that before 226, they never said so, or probably had reason to.)

Ardashir spent most of his life engaged in foreign struggles, mainly
in securing his throne against intervention from Armenia, Bactria, and
Rome. His domestic history may be conveniently summarized here.
He married a daughter, or cousin, of Ardavan, so as to legitimize his
dynasty by marriage to an Arsacid, though Christensen regards this

[1] M.-L. Chaumont, "Recherches", *JA* 250, 1962, 11-22, on the title and function
of the *argapat* and *dizpat*; see also her discussion in *JA* 249, 1961, p. 305; and vol.
I, pp. 102, 108.
[2] Taqizadeh, *op. cit.*, 294, holds to 211-212, Chaumont, "Papak, roi de Staxr
et sa cour", *JA* 247, 1959, 175-191 gives the date at 208. Taqizadeh cites Tabari
who says that Ardashir "sprang" in the Seleucid year 523=211-212.

story as merely folklore.[1] Crowned at Istakhr, where his successors for four centuries were invested, in September, 226, he made Babylonia the center of his interest, settling his capital at Veh-Ardashir (formerly, Seleucia-on-the-Tigris), across the river from Ctesiphon. Full of vigor, he embarked upon an expansive policy of construction, building canals, temples, and other public works, founding numerous new towns, and developing the economy. While war occupied most of his attention, the empire prospered, and when he died, in October of 241,[2] his son Shapur inherited a flourishing régime. At his death the frontiers stretched from the Euphrates to Merv, Herat, and Seistan, and Shapur further extended them. We shall consider Shapur's reign in our review of foreign affairs, because, like his father, he spent most of his life in establishing a powerful and secure empire at his neighbors' expense.[3]

II SASANIAN FOREIGN POLICY UNDER ARDASHIR AND SHAPUR

The Sasanians' foreign policy[4] had to take account of three major geographical frontiers, that with Rome on the west and northwest,

---

[1] Christensen, 83-9.

[2] Following Taqizadeh. According to him, Papak died between 214 and 223, but it was Ardashir, and not Papak, who led the revolt. He dates the coronation of Shapur at April, 243, and his death in 273. See also R. N. Frye, *Heritage of Persia* (N.Y. — Cleveland, 1963), 199.

[3] Other accounts of early Sasanian history include the following: Ferdinand Justi, *Geschichte des Alten Persiens* (Berlin, 1879), 176-89; A. von Gutschmid, *Geschichte Irans* (Tübingen, 1888), 154-72; A. Christensen in *CAH* XII, 109-114; M.-L. Chaumont, "Le Culte d'Anahita et les Premiers Sassanides", *RHR* 153, 1958, 154-75, on the role of Papak as magus, *artestar* (warrior), *advenpat* (master of ceremonies), and *patixsai* (director of the revenues of the temple); E. Herzfeld, *Paikuli* (Berlin 1924), 35-51; T. Nöldeke, *Aufsätze zur Persischen Geschichte* (Leipzig, 1887), 86f.; T. Nöldeke, ed. and trans., *Geschichte der Perser und Araber zur Zeit der Sasaniden, Aus der Arabischen Chronik des Tabari* (Leiden, 1879); Frye, *op. cit.*, 198-223; E. Herzfeld, *Archaeological History of Iran* (London, 1935), 76-108; R. Ghirshman, *Iran* (Baltimore, 1954), 290-1; Martin Sprengling, *Third Century Iran. Sapor and Kartir* (Chicago, 1953); and Jean Gagé, *La Montée des Sassanides et l'Heure de Palmyre* (Paris, 1964). Further references are provided in the bibliography and supplementary bibliography.

[4] Iranian, classical, and archaeological sources present a confused picture of Shapur's wars. My account follows the views, in general, of Alföldi, Ensslin, Rostovtzeff, and Maricq, and most especially of W. B. Henning, against those of Olmstead and Christensen. (*CAH* XII pp. 126-137 and *L'Iran* 213-221). The Jewish sources make no contribution whatever to clarifying the picture, but rather (see below, Chap. II section III) themselves must be elucidated by the course of events revealed here.

See Glanville Downey, *History of Antioch in Syria from Seleucus to the Arab Conquest* (Princeton, 1961), 252-264, who holds that Antioch was taken twice,

with Armenia on the north, with the nomad peoples, first the Kushans, and then the Ephthalites on the northeast and east. Ardashir's first major problem concerned Armenia. Like the Arsacids, the Sasanians had to secure their hold over Armenia against both indigenous opposi-

---

once in 256, the year of Dura's fall to the Persians, the second time in 260. Downey (587-96) reviews the relevant sources and scholarly opinion to the present time. Compare A. T. Olmstead, "The Mid-Third Century of the Christian Era", *Classical Philology* 27, 1942, and following him, Saul Lieberman, "Palestine in the Third and Fourth Centuries", *JQR* n.s. 37, 1, 1946, 31-41, and contrast M. Rostovtzeff, "Res gestae divi Saporis and Dura", *Berytus* 8, 1943, 17-60, and the full bibliography, to that date, of the *KZ*, provided there. Olmstead thinks that there was an invasion of Syria in 251, following his own interpretation of the Thirteenth Sybilline Book; Rostovtzeff in 253; and Ensslin (cited below) holds that the city was captured only once, in 260. Downey's view is that Shapur made two campaigns, and took Antioch twice, in 256 and 260. With reference to Shapur's siege of Caesarea Mazaca, we must emphasize that there was only *one* campaign in which Shapur reached so far west into Asia Minor, which took place in 260. Whether Shapur took Syria or not before 260, he *never* before that date reached Cappadocia.

Further bibliography includes the following: J. Gagé, "Les Perses à Antioche et les courses de l'hippodrome au milieu du IIIe siècle, à propos du 'transfuge' syrien Mariades", *Bulletin de la Faculté des Lettres de Strasbourg* 31, 1935, 301-324; N. Pigulevskaja, *Les Villes de l'État Iranien*, (Paris, 1963). 124-7; H. M. D. Parker, *History of the Roman World from A.D. 138 to A.D. 337* (London, 1958, 2nd rev. ed.) 148-152, 163-171, 389-390; Giovanni Pugliese-Caratelli, "Res Gestae Divi Saporis", *La Parola del Passato* 5, 1947, 232f.; A. Alföldi, in *CAH* XII, 174-180; G. Mattingly in *CAH* XII, 301-4; F. Justi, *Geschichte des Alten Persiens*, (Berlin, 1879) 182-9; Frye, *Heritage*, 202-8 and 273 n. 16; David Magie, *Roman Rule in Asia Minor to the End of the Third Century after Christ*, (Princeton, 1950, I-II), I, 694-6, II, 1560 n. 12; R. Ghirshman, *Iran*, (Baltimore, 1954), 289-290; Rawlinson, *Seventh Great Oriental Monarchy*, 42-53; P. Asdourian, *Die politischen Beziehungen zwischen Armenien und Rom von 190 v. Chr. bis 142 n. Chr.*, (Venice, 1911) 120-9; Nöldeke, trans., *Tabari*, 14-5, 409f.; T. Nöldeke, *Aufsätze zur Persischen Geschichte*, (Leipzig, 1887) 86f.; R. Ghirshman, *Iran: Parthians and Sassanians*, (London, 1963) 292-4; and M. Sprengling, *op. cit., passim*.

On the Palmyrenes in Syria, see Downey, *Antioch*, 262-9; Parker, *History*, 173-5, 198-205, 392, 395; M. Rostovtzeff, *Caravan Cities*, (Oxford, 1932) 91-119, and his "Res Gestae", *Berytus* 8, 54. Parker holds that Sasanian policy changed, and no longer encouraged the caravan trade to Palmyra; by taking Characene, Shapur began to find his own routes. He suggests, therefore, that it was partly economic necessity that led Odenathus to make war on Shapur, and partly the opportunities of the hour. Rostovtzeff suggests, very hypothetically, that Odenathus' earliest actions antedated 260. He began as an ally of Rome, but very quickly pursued his own interest exclusively. In any event, I follow W. B. Henning (in a personal communication, Aug. 4, 1964), "Odenathus has been most overrated, and most of what is said about his exploits against the Persians is patently absurd."

On the *KZ*, bibliography is extensive. Here are cited only those works consulted to determine the question of Shapur's invasion(s) of Cilicia-Cappadocia, and the more important general introductions to the inscription. See Rostovtzeff in *Berytus* 8; Frye, *Heritage*, 272 n. 1; Parker, *History*, 391f.; A. Maricq, *Syria*, 1958, 295-360, who gives a particularly full bibliography; A. T. Olmstead, *op. cit.*;

tion and Roman intervention. For Rome, Armenia was an important means of securing a route to the Orient to bypass the Iranian-Babylonian entrepôts, and, additionally, served as a major invasion route to threaten the Iranians, just as Armenia might endanger the Roman Orient when in Persian hands. Furthermore Armenia was ruled by a cadet branch of the Arsacid dynasty, and thus posed particular danger to the new dynasty. Since the Armenian Arsacids had Roman support, a clash with the west and north was inevitable. Ardashir himself precipitated it, for, as Dio Cassius says, he had boasted that he would win back everything held by ancient Persia, claiming it all as the rightful inheritance from his forefathers.[1] He invaded Mesopotamia, which fell easily, and threatened Syria. When Alexander Severus reminded him of the Parthian victories of Augustus, Trajan, Lucius Verus, and Septimius Severus, Ardashir replied with an order that Rome evacuate Syria and Western Asia.

In the autumn of 231, Alexander Severus reached Antioch, with a force gathered from the eastern legions. Ardashir likewise fielded a large army, mainly of heavy and light cavalry, as was the Iranian custom. The Romans crossed the Euphrates, and in the spring of 232 recovered the province of Mesopotamia. Alexander then divided his armies into three parts, one to move north, via Armenia to attack Media, the second to threaten Persia from the southern Babylonian marches, and the third, led by Alexander himself, to move between the pincers. The first and second units moved forward, but Alexander's held back, so that the army advancing by the line of the Euphrates

---

W. B. Henning, "The Great Inscription of Sapur I," *BSOS* 9, 1939, 823f.; Martin Sprengling, "From Kartir to Shahpuhr I", *AJSL* 57, 1940, 330f.; "Shahpuhr I The Great on the Kaabah of Zoroaster (KZ)," *ibid*, 341f. and "Pahlavi Notes", *ibid*, 58, 1941, 169f.; Ernest Honigmann and André Maricq, *Recherches sur les Res Gestae Divi Saporis*, Brussels, 1953; and Wilhelm Ensslin, *Zu den Kriegen des Sassaniden Schapur I*, Munich, 1949, *Sitzungs. d. Bayerischen Ak. d. Wissensch., Phil.-Hist. Kl.*, 1947, 5.; W. B. Henning in *Asia Major* 6, 1957, 119; and M. Sprengling, *Third Century Iran, Passim*.

The most important work on Palmyra is that of J. G. Février, *Essai sur l'Histoire Politique et Economique de Palmyre*, Paris, 1931, and *La Religion des Palmyreniens*, Paris, 1931, where full bibliography to that date will be found. See also J. Gagé, *op. cit.*

On Shapur's campaigns and problems of Roman-Iranian relations generally, see also L. Dilleman, *Haute Mésopotamie Orientale et Pays Adjacents* (Paris, 1962), 207-210, and most recently, Karl-Heinz Ziegler, *Die Beziehungen zwischen Rom und dem Partherreich, Ein Beitrag zur Geschichte des Völkerrechts* (Wiesbaden, 1964), especially 141-154. Compare also Krauss, *Paras* 253-7, and O. Klima, *Manis Zeit und Leben*, Prague, 1962, 192-202.

[1] *Roman History* LXXX, trans. E. Cary, N.Y. 1927, IX, 483.

suddenly confronted the Iranian forces at the heart of the great plains, whose terrain was highly suited to cavalry warfare, and was destroyed by the Persians' superior cavalry and bowmanship. Alexander signaled the retreat to the forces in Media, as well as to the ravaged force on his right. As winter came, the troops in the Median highlands suffered from the harsh climate, while those with Alexander were reduced by disease, an enemy that had devastated the forces of Trajan and Lucius Verus as well. The result was not wholly disastrous, however, for Ardashir was made to understand that Rome would not easily be driven from the Middle East. Matters returned to *status quo ante bellum*, though it is not clear whether this was by treaty or merely by tacit consent.

Ardashir thereupon turned to the final subjugation of Armenia. The Armenian shah, Xosroes, had cooperated with the Romans. Without Roman help, Xosroes could not hope to hold off the Persians. Ardashir hastened matters by arranging for his assassination, and immediately afterward, in the spring of 233, invaded and defeated the Armenian satraps with their Roman allies. Xosroes's son, Trdat, escaped to Rome. For the next seven years, Ardashir spent his time in peaceful pursuits, particularly in the reorganization of Iranian Mazdaism (see below, p. 14f.).

Shapur probably came to the throne in 241, and was crowned in 243. In the next thirty years, before his death in 273, Shapur almost achieved the boast of Ardashir, recovering for a brief time practically the ancient limits of the Achemenids in the west, excluding only the Ionian coast beyond Cappadocia, Palestine, and Egypt. His armies pillaged almost at will in Syria and much of eastern Asia Minor, including not only Armenia, but also Cilicia and Cappadocia. Like the Parthians, Shapur never attempted to establish permanent rule over the Roman Orient, but, as the *KZ* states (1. 12), "Shapur, the king of kings, with his horse, pillaged, burned, and devastated." He established his rule over Iranian and non-Iranian peoples alike, ruling with grand tolerance and sagacity. He could have added to his empire the western territories of Mesopotamia, Syria, and Asia Minor, but he was not a great organizer[1] and did not have the administrative resources to take and hold such vast territories, far beyond those he had inherited.

Shapur's first task was to crush incipient revolts, first in Armenia,

---

[1] Frye, *Heritage*, 206.

and then in Hatra. He easily subdued the Armenians. Shortly afterward the king of Hatra, south of Armenia, refused to bow to Shapur, and assumed the rule over considerable territories around the city. Shapur took Hatra, whose walls had withstood the assault of Trajan and Severus, according to tradition with the treasonable connivance of the king's daughter, whom he beguiled with a promise of marriage, and afterward put to death. Hatra's independence calls to mind the tendency of Middle Eastern principalities, from Characene, Nabataea, Armenia, and Herodian Judea in the second and first centuries B.C., to Palmyra in the third A.D., to exploit troubled times to good advantage. Under Shapur, no Iranian-ruled satrapy made such an effort; only Palmyra, client-state of Rome, did so. Shapur turned next to the eastern frontier, and seized Peshawar, the Indus Valley, over-whelmed the Bactrian Kushans, took the area about Samarkand and Tashkent, and deposed the Kushan dynasty.

Having pacified his own territories and strengthened his eastern frontier, Shapur turned west. At this time, Roman politics was in great disarray. Alexander had been murdered in 235 by Maximin, who himself was overthrown in 238. M. Antonius Gordianus, proclaimed emperor in 238, seemed an inconsiderable foe. Shapur advanced west-ward by way of Nisibis, which offered prolonged resistance before its walls were breached. The taking of Nisibis represented the first major Iranian success in a siege operation involving extensive mining and other engineering procedures. The Parthians had never successfully besieged a great fortress, nor had the Persians been able to prevail against Hatra except by guile. The eastern legions of Rome were thus forewarned that they faced a more formidable adversary than ever before. Gordian gathered a large army to attempt to retrieve the disastrous situation, and, accompanied by an able general, Timesi-theius, defeated Shapur near Reasina, recovering Nisibis and returning to the banks of the Tigris in the north. To the changing destinies of Mesopotamia, R. Yoḥanan applied the Scripture (Daniel 7.5) "And behold, another beast, a second one, like a bear. It was raised up on one side; it had three ribs in its mouth between its teeth; and it was told, Arise, devour much flesh. . ." R. Yoḥanan said (b. Qid. 72a) that the three ribs refer to Hulwan, Adiabene, and Nisibis, "which Persia sometimes swallowed and sometimes spit out. [The Jews invariably interpreted the bear of Daniel to refer to Persia.]" Shapur retired across Mesopotamia, and the Romans according to their account threatened Ctesiphon before retiring northward, forced to retreat not by Iranian prowess, but by discontent within the army. Gordian was murdered by the prefect, Philip, near Circesium, and Philip made peace with Shapur, leaving the east in 244, with Armenia in Persian hands, and Mesopotamia safely in Roman possession, an inherently unstable situation.

For more than a decade (the exact chronology becomes very difficult to establish[1]), Shapur kept the peace with Rome, probably because of troubles in the east. He finally provoked a second war in the west, again hoping to take advantage of Roman weakness. After Philip, six weak emperors intervened, four of whom died violent deaths, and the western Roman provinces were threatened by Alemanni, Goths, and Franks. Sometime between 253 and 256, Shapur again moved against the Roman Orient, and retook Nisibis, Carrhae, and Edessa, finally surprising and seizing Antioch, and setting up his headquarters there. The Roman emperor, Valerian, moved eastward, retook Antioch, and his chief prefect Macrianus maneuvred the Roman army into Mesopotamia. These maneuvres were disastrous, and the army found itself surrounded. Unable to break through the siege lines, Valerian surrendered, and his army was mostly captured, and resettled in the east, where it was set to work on great engineering projects. Shapur thereupon proposed an obscure Antiochan as his candidate for the Roman throne, against Gallienus, Valerian's son, and Macrinus, his prefect, and, to support him, seized Edessa again, in 260, and recaptured Antioch. There he installed as Roman emperor his own candidate, and turned north and westward, into Cilicia and Cappadocia. He took Tarsus, Cilicia Campestris, the Taurus gates, and besieged Caesarea Mazaca, the greatest city of Asia Minor, capturing it after a prolonged struggle.

Shapur could probably have held all of Asia Minor, but he turned back to the Mesopotamian frontier. His object, however, had not been to build an empire in the west, but to destroy one, and he pursued a scorched-earth policy from central Asia Minor to the Euphrates-Tigris frontier. He left the occupied regions in ruins, and while the stories of his excessive cruelty may be exaggerated, he does seem systematically to have attempted the depopulation of part of the Roman Orient, just as Shapur II did in Armenia later on. Laden with plunder, he besieged one more town, Emesa, but without success. On his return home, he was met by an embassy from Odenathus, the

---

[1] *Ibid.*, 256.

semi-independent ruler of Palmyra, who offered Palmyrene loyalty in exchange for Shapur's friendship. Shapur spurned this offer and the accompanying gifts. Odenathus thereupon trailed the withdrawing army, and at suitable opportunities, fell upon it with a large force of irregulars, until Shapur found safety behind his own frontiers. Odenathus's inroads have been much exaggerated. Shapur certainly returned home with the larger part of his army and booty intact, including great numbers of slaves. The Palmyrenes probably inconvenienced him, rather than posing a serious threat. But Odenathus became a major problem in time. Trying to exploit the weakness of Rome and the temporary inattention of Shapur, who seems to have been occupied with problems in the east, Odenathus crossed the Euphrates in 263, took Carrhae and Nisibis, and besieged Ctesiphon. Odenathus's chief interest, Syria, Palestine, and Mesopotamia in the north, was thus neglected, as he moved eastward. Reenforcements from other parts of the Iranian empire came to the defense of the western capital, and Shapur threw the Palmyrene army out of central Babylonia. The Palmyrenes held Mesopotamia until the capture of his queen and successor, Zenobia, and the destruction of Palmyra by the Romans under Aurelian, in 273.

After the repulse of the Palmyrene threat, Shapur enjoyed his remaining years in peace. Palmyra was kept busy by Rome, the east seems to have been pacified, and Shapur was able serenely to live out his last years undisturbed by war on any front.

III. NEW CITIES

Ardashir and Shapur were the greatest city-founders of the Sasanian dynasty,[1] founding, renaming, or reviving urban centers throughout the empire. Some of those renamed were merely increased in size, but most received new political status as well. The former city-states of Seleucid and Arsacid times greatly impeded the formation of a strong central government, for they retained rights and privileges from the earlier period. It was imperative to revise their political status, which was done through 'refounding' them, and to develop new cities in a different and more subservient relationship to the central regime. N. Pigulevskaja maintains that Ardashir, having achieved power and unified the state with the support of the military nobility, moved against the feudal class through his policy of urbaniza-

---

[1] Frye, *Heritage*, p. 202-4, and Pigulevskaja, *Villes*, 97-8, 119-23, 127-8.

tion, attempting in so doing to win new sources of support for the throne. (She holds likewise that the same intention lay behind his strengthening of the status and privileges of the Zoroastrian clergy.) In the third and fourth centuries, autonomous cities, whose rights dated from Seleucid or Arssacid times, disappeared, as formerly free states now served as residences for members of the royal family. (Thus in *KZ* 1. 19 we read of 'the royal city and its province.') Ardashir himself founded six new towns (according to Tabari, eight). Shapur resettled the captive troops of Valerian in new towns, and further transferred both monetary and demographic resources from the ravaged Roman Orient into his own empire, for this purpose building a number of new cities. In Mesene, Shapur founded a city, and it is thought that a number of obscure lines in the Shapur inscription refer to the names of other cities founded by him. Besides city-building, the early Sasanians greatly increased the number of fire-temples, of which Ardashir established several, and Shapur even more, which he listed in his inscription in his own name and in the names of members of his family, of his three sons, Hormizd Ardashir, king of Armenia, Shapur, king of Mesene, and Narseh, king of Sakhastan and Tokharistan, and in honor of his many victories.

The new towns served economic, as well as political, purposes. A. Leo Oppenheim points out that the lateness and swiftness of the Euphrates' flood results in the deposit of mud far less fertile than that carried by the Nile.[1] This mud could not be immediately deposited on the fields, but clogged the canals, silted the watercourses, and increased the soil's salinity. It became imperative to redig canals, or to dig new ones, and to resettle population on new land. Oppenheim calls this "an essential part of the economic and political program of a responsible sovereign, rivaling in importance the maintenance of the dikes." The new cities or villages would certainly have produced richer crops, at a smaller investment of seed, than the old. The Sasanians, coming into power with intention to reform the government of their empire, thus brought with them far more prosperous agricultural conditions than had formerly prevailed, as Adams points out.[2] Their policy of founding new towns is reflected in the following:

> Rava b. Meḥasia in the name of R. Ḥama b. Goria in the name of Rav said: A man should always seek to dwell in a city only recently populated, for since it is recently populated, its sins are few, as it is

[1] A. Leo Oppenheim, *Ancient Mesopotamia* (Chicago 1964), 41-2.
[2] Robert McC. Adams, *Land Behind Baghdad* (Chicago, 1965) 69-84.

said, 'Behold now this city is *near* (KRWBH) to flee to, and it is a little one (Gen. 19.20)'. What is meant by near and small? Surely they could see that for themselves! Rather, because its settlement was *recent* (YŠYBTH KRWBH) its sins are few.

(B. Shab. 10b)[1]

Rav observed new villages and towns to be more prosperous, a condition he naturally ascribed to the spiritual merits of its inhabitants. A town is prosperous because the accumulated sins of its inhabitants are few. His observation, as we have seen, was quite sound, for the new towns *were* more prosperous, their canals bringing more water, their soil containing less salinity, and their crops drawing sustenance from virgin land. One must suppose that the policy of urbanization and of opening new territories greatly affected the lives of Jewish merchants and farmers alike. When people moved to new places, uprooting themselves from old lands and old ways, they became more willing likewise to consider new challenges and to respond to the demands of those who, like the early 'Amora'im, sought to revise their former way of living. It stands to reason therefore that the reforms effected by the rabbis were facilitated by the fact that numbers of Jews were living in new places.

IV. SOCIAL-STRUCTURE

The Sasanians divided their empire into a pyramidal class structure, in which there was little mobility across class lines and none among ethnic groups. Society was split into four estates, ecclesiastical, warrior, bureaucratic, and the fourth estate, by far the most numerous, of farmers and artisans. Each class was further divided into subgroups, the clergy into judges, priests (of fires and sacrifices), teachers, and inspectors. The head of the clergy was known as *Mobadhan Mobadh*, the head general, *Eran Spahbadh*, the head of the bureaucracy, *Eran Dibherbadh*, and the head of the fourth estate, *Vastryošansalar*. The princes of the empire (*Shahrdaran*), chiefs of the great families (*Vaspuhran*), and knights or free men (*Azadhan*) were all members of the first class of state. The second order included chiefs of clans, of the seven great families dating from Parthian times, and so on. The four classes were, of course, unequal in size; the great families held whole provinces, collecting taxes and serving the crown when called upon. By fostering the growth of bureaucracy, creating high officers of state, heads of

---

[1] Compare the variants in *Dik. Sof.* II, 15, which do not affect the sense of the passage.

administrative offices and other royal officials acting upon the authority of the crown, the emperor sought to curb the power, so vast under the Arsacids, of the great nobility. Under the Sasanians, the number of local dynasties did in fact decline.

The empire was divided into provinces according to the point of the compass, and united by good roads with frequent way stations, and a far-reaching civil administration. The army, commanded by a hereditary general-in-chief of royal blood, was based on heavily armed cavalry, protected by light cavalry, archers, elephants, and a rear guard. The infantry was the weakest element, consisting of poorly armed peasants. But as we have noted, the Sasanians developed engineering skills unavailable to the Parthians.

The priests administered justice and education. Their authority extended beyond the cult, but pertained to the legalization of births and marriages, purification rites, and so forth. They owned enormous territories, possessed resources far beyond their regular revenues of tithes and gifts, and represented a state within the state, governed, like the state itself, by a minutely regulated and graduated hierarchy. Under the Sasanians the great law collections, the Erpatestan, the Nirangastan, and the Husparan Nask, ecclesiastical and ritual codes, were completed. The priests were well treated and highly regarded. They settled many public questions, and the Armenian historian Agathias reported that among the Persians, "nothing is considered lawful and just unless it had been approved by a Magus." The Magi lived by their own laws. The Magus (*Mogh*) was under the authority of the *Herpat* (chief of fire), and *Mobad* (chief of Magi), headed at the top of the pyramid by the *Herpatan Herpat* (chief justice) and *Mobadan Mobad* (high priest). In addition to their priestly duties, the Magi dominated law and culture, decided law cases, taught reading, writing, and arithmetic to townsmen and merchants, and offered ethical guidance.

Taxes applied to land, while non-property-owners paid a head tax. They were collected by the estates, or, among the minorities, who paid heavier imposts, by communities. Thus the Nazarenes paid through their own bishops. Tax collection was strictly supervised; farmers could not harvest until land taxes, proportionate to the crop, were collected. Customs were paid, and crown lands produced revenues in addition; there was considerable indirect taxation, and corvées were common as well. Trade was very strictly regulated, and, of course, taxed. For its part, the government improved the roads, provided water supplies along them, developed caravanseries and frontier posts and ports, imported mulberry trees and silk worms from China, and in other ways increased investment in the economy.[1]

Although in Iranian culture, agriculture was the most honored profession, and farmers were assured of rich rewards in the world to come, the hard life of the farmer was recognized by Rav, who strongly advised his sons to enter commerce and avoid agriculture. The following stories reveal his attitude:

> Rav once entered among growing ears of wheat. Seeing that they were swaying, he called out to them, Swing as you will, engaging in business brings more profit than you can.   (B. Yev. 63a)

> [Rav advised his son, Aibu]: I have labored over your studies without success, so come and I shall teach you worldly wisdom. Sell your wares while the sand is still on your feet. Everything you may sell and regret [should the price rise] save wine, which you may sell without regret [for it might go sour]. Untie your purse and then open your sacks [Pocket payment before delivery] . . . When dates are in your bag, run to the brewery.
>   (B. Pes. 113a)

> [To Rav Kahana he said], Even if you merely ascend to the roof, take food with you. Even if a hundred pumpkins cost but a zuz in town, let them be under your skirts [stock up].
>   (B. Pes. 113a)

While many of the 'Amora'im were in trade or crafts, nonetheless, the bulk of the Jewish population, like the Iranians and other groups in the Persian empire, engaged in agriculture.[2]

v. The Sasanian State-Church

As we shall see below, the Jews knew very little about Sasanian Zoroastrianism, except for some of the external manifestations of

---

[1] Relevant works include Frye, *op. cit.*, 200-202, 206-7, and for a list of the officers of Ardashir's court, 201, and of Shapur's, 206-7; Rawlinson, *Monarchy*, 60-62; Christensen in *CAH* XII. 114-118; in *L'Iran* 92-136; Ghirshman, *Iran*, 308-14; on the reorganization of the army, see Ghirshman, *op. cit.*, 291-2; on the growing sophistication of economic practice, 342; on taxes, Christensen, *L'Iran* 117-121, Ghirshman, 311, 345; on the organization of the empire into classes, Christensen, *L'Iran*, 92-110, of the army, 124-7, of the bureaucracy 127-31; on industry and commerce, 121-124.

[2] See J. Newman, *Agricultural Life of the Jews in Babylonia*, London 1932; Louis Jacobs, "The Economic Conditions of the Jews in Babylon in Talmudic Times compared with Palestine", *JSS* II 1957 349-59. M. Beer's *Ma'amadam Ha kalkali vehaHevrati shel 'Amora'ei Bavel* (Ramat Gan, 1963) provides a singularly thorough account of the economic position of the 'Amora'im throughout the Talmudic period.

the faith. We shall, therefore, survey briefly only those aspects of Sasanian religion relevant to this study, the most important of which are the development of a state-cult under Ardashir, and the modulation of religious militancy by Shapur.

The Sasanians associated themselves with the cult of Anahita and Ohrmazd throughout their rule, although in time Anahita like Mithra was relegated to second place in the state cult.[1] While Ardashir made Mazdaism the state cult, this did not take place in one year, nor was the process completed by one emperor alone. First of all, even among the Iranian peoples there was much syncretism, with many local cults flourishing. Second, the minority peoples, though influenced by Mazdaism, never abandoned their ancestral gods. The Jews, Christians, and probably, Mandeans, took no part whatever in the state religion, nor were these groups willing to abandon their faith even under persecution. In fact, we may discern three successive stages in the establishment of Mazdaism and consequent attitudes towards other religions, first, the earliest establishment by Ardashir and his chief priest, Tosar, second, the development of a policy of toleration by Shapur, and finally, the beginnings of a period of reaction toward the end of Shapur's reign and afterward, led by Kartir.

Under Ardashir, just as the royal court was reorganized, to centralize under its bureaucracy the actual government of the empire, so the state church was created for very much the same purpose.[2] Ardashir established a hierarchy of church officials with the Magi at the bottom, as we have noted, and *Mobads* over each ecclesiastical district. The chief of the *Herpats*, teaching priests, was Tansar or Tosar,[3] charged by Ardashir with the actual reorganization of the church. The church officials vigorously persecuted other religions, were exceptionally intolerant, and would allegedly imprison and catechize one who sinned against the faith, and, if the sinner refused to confess his error, would put him to death. How far such activities extended within the Jewish

---

[1] Ghirshman, *Iran*, 314-8. See also J. Duchesne-Guillemin, *La Religion de l'Iran Ancien* (Paris 1962), 276-308; J. C. Puech, *Le Manichéisme* (Paris 1949). 38f, 120f; on the popularity of Anahita, Pigulevskaja, *Villes, op. cit.*, 234f.; on widespread syncretism, Christensen, *L'Iran*, 110-117.

[2] See Richard N. Frye, "Notes on the Early Sassanian State and Church", *Studi Orientalistici in onore di Georgio Levi Della Vida* I, Rome, 1956, 314-35. See also H. Lewy, *op. cit. Orientalia* 10, 1940, 56-62.

[3] On Tosar, see Pigulevskaja, *Villes.*, 100-102; J. Darmesteter, "Lettre de Tansar au Roi de Tabaristan", *JA 9th ser. III* 1894, 185-250, 502-555; Duchesne-Guillemin, *La Religion*, 64, 279f.; Christensen, "Abarsam et Tansar", *Acta Orientalia* X, 1936, 43-55; Frye, 209.

community we do not know for certain. We do not have a single explicit instance of forced conversion or religiously motivated capital punishment of Jews in this period, and since the Jewish sources do not hesitate to record whatever religious persecutions actually were directed against Jews, it is entirely reasonable to suppose that Jewry, for one, was not terribly troubled by the Mobads and Herpats (but they were by the *hazarpats*, see below p. 27f.); it is equally sure that later the Armenian and Adiabenian Christians were.[1] According to the Denkart, Tosar was also charged with collecting the 'scattered teachings', and canonizing the sacred writings of the faith. He decreed:

> The interpretation of all the teachings from the Religion of the worshippers of Mazdah is our responsibility: for now there is no lack of certain knowledge concerning them.[2]

Thus, as we have noted, just as administration was centralized, so also was the interpretation of the faith. Whether Tosar actually codified the Avesta or not is a question I cannot claim the competence to discuss; but it is probable, following the view of de Menasce, that he and his fellow Herpats reestablished the Avestan tradition. [3]

Under Shapur, the policy of persecuting minority cults was abrogated completely. If both Ardashir and Shapur hoped to unify their empire through religion, Shapur found that realities would not permit its achievement through Mazdaism. According to Elisaeus Vardapet[4] Shapur forbade the Magi to persecute Christianity:

---

[1] See Darmesteter, *op. cit.*, 524. Compare R. C. Zaehner, *Zurvan*, 3.

[2] Translation cited is by R. C. Zaehner, *Dawn* 175-6. See the very full discussion of J.-P. de Menasce, *Une Encyclopédie Mazdéenne, Le Denkart* (Paris, 1958) 56f.

[3] *Le Denkart* 57. Compare W. B. Bailey, *Zoroastrian Problems in the Ninth Century Books* (Oxford 1943). 149-77, S. H. Taqizadeh in *BSOS* 9, 1939, 133, and J. Duchesne-Guillemin, "La Fixation de l'Avesta" in *Indo-Iranica* and his *La Religion* 179f. De Menasce and Duchesne-Guillemin hold that Tosar codified the Avesta. Bailey argues that the Denkart tradition, that Ardashir with Tosar's help recovered the scattered writings, while Shapur restored to the Avesta books scattered in India and Rome, is not historically reliable. He points out that no single account of the transmission of the texts had been uniformly accepted by the ninth century A.D. There was no wide distribution of copies of the text. Bailey says that the first complete writing down of the Avesta could not have taken place before the middle of the 6th century. Before that time the tradition was handed on orally. Duchesne-Guillemin (in "La Fixation") says that in Arsacid times, there was a *written* Avesta, deposited in the royal treasury, and that Shapur assembled the recited texts, as well as the religious books on medicine etc, with the final text being fixed in the 4th century by Shapur II. See also Widengren, *Die Religionen* 245-257, who accepts this view.

[4] Cited by Christensen, *CAH* XII 112.

Magi, Manichaean, Jew, Christian, and all men of whatever religion should be left undisturbed and at peace in their belief in the several provinces of Persia.

Shapur encouraged Mani to expound a syncretistic doctrine capable of bringing together Christian, Buddhist, and Iranian under one cult, probably hoping in such a way to achieve religious unification. He likewise added to the Zoroastrian canon elements from other cultures:

> He collected those writings from the Religion which were dispersed in India, the Byzantine Empire, and other lands, and which treated of medicine, astronomy, movement, time, space, substance, creation, becoming, passing away, qualitative change, logic, and other arts and sciences. These he added to the Avesta ... and he examined the possibility of basing every form of academic discipline on the Religion of the Worshippers of Mazdah.[1]

Zaehner holds that in so doing, Shapur added the whole corpus of philosophical and scientific learning of Roman Orient and India alike. His cultivation of the friendship of Jewish subjects was quite consistent with such a broad and accomodating policy.

Kartir, a leading priest under Shapur, and chief priest in the reigns of his successors, reversed this policy of tolerance. We do not know when he achieved sufficient power to do so, though it was most likely after Shapur's death, for it was then that he put to death the prophet Mani, whom Shapur had protected as long as he lived, and pursued the reform of the body of Magi, the purification of the doctrine and cult, the elimination of foreign religions so far as possible, the encouragement of consanguineous marriages, and the advancement of the faith.[2] Kartir's establishment of new fire temples was

---

[1] Translation of Zaehner, *Dawn*, 185. See his *Zurvan*, 10. On Shapur's religious policy see, in addition to Zaehner, on the Indian books of Shapur, J. de Menasce, "Notes Iraniennes", *JA* 237, Herzfeld, *Archaeological History* 101; *CAH* XII, 112 n. 3 and the works cited in connection with Kartir, below.

[2] On Kartir's career and Shapur's liberal religious policies, see J. de Menasce, "La Conquête de l'Iranisme et la recuperation des Mages Hellénisés", *École Pratique des Hautes Études Annuaire* 1956-1957 (Paris, 1956), 1-12, M. Sprengling, "Kartir, Founder of Sasanian Zoroastrianism", *AJSLL* 57, 1940, 197f.; W. B. Henning in *BSOS* X 1940-42, 947f.; J. de Menasce, *Škand Gumanik Vičar* (Fribourg, 1945), 243-4; E. E. Herzfeld in *BSOS* 8, 1937; M. Sprengling, "Shahpuhr I, the Great, on the Kaabah of Zoroaster (KZ)", *AJSLL*, 57, 1940, 341-420; M.-L. Chaumont, in *RHR* 153, 2, 1958, 163-74, who holds that Kartir "Zoroastrianized" the cult of Anahita;; N. Pigulevskaja, *Villes.*, 100-101; Zaehner, *Zurvan*, 34-54; and his *Dawn* 175-192, 284-302; M.-L. Chaumont, "L'Inscription de Kartir à la Ka'abah de Zoroastre", *JA* 248, 3, 1960, 339-380, and W. B. Henning, "Notes on the Inscription of Sapur", in *Jackson Memorial Volume* (Bombay

not limited to Iranian (including of course Babylonian) lands for he specifically says in his famous inscription that he established fire temples in non-Iranian ones as well. De Menasce holds that it was at Shapur's initiative that Kartir centralized the organization of the clergy, but it was only under Bahram I and Bahram II that he achieved really substantial authority. Of special interest is Kartir's boast that among others, the Jews "were opposed" by him, probably after 273 when he got the power to do so. He boasted (in Sprengling's translation):

> And in kingdom after kingdom, and place after place throughout the whole empire, the services of Ohrmazd and the gods became superior, and to the Mazdayasnian religion and the Magi-men in the empire great dignity came, and the gods and water and fire and small cattle in the empire attained great satisfaction, while Ahriman and the devs attained great beating and hostility, and the teachings of Ahriman and the devs departed from the empire, but there [within the empire] were left uncultivated. And Jews and Buddhist Sramans and Brahmins, for Brahmins and Nasoreans and Christians and Maktak and Zandiks in the empire became smitten, and destruction of idols and scattering of the stores of the devs were left uncultivated. And in kingdom after kingdom, and place after place, many divine services in magnificence, and many Varahran fires, were established, and many Magi-men became happy and prosperous, and many fires and Magi were imperially installed.[1]

The lines (KZ 1. 9-10) relevant to the Jews are thus translated by Chaumont:

> Les doctrines d'Ahriman et des demons, de l'Empire furent écartées: Juifs, Shamans, Brahmanes, Nazaréens, Chrétiens, Maktiks(?), Zandiks dans l'Empire furent abattus.[2]

1954) 53-4; Chaumont, "Recherches sur le clergé Zoroastrien; Le Herbad", *RHR* 158, 1, 1960, 55-80; A. Christensen in *CAH* XII, 119-121; E. E. Herzfeld, *Archaeological History of Iran* 99-103; J. Duchesne-Guillemin, *Ohrmazd et Ahriman* (Paris 1948) 135-9; A. V. W. Jackson, *Zoroastrian Studies*, 173-4; R. N. Frye, *Heritage*, 209-212 and 275 n. 31; A. Christensen, *L'Iran*, 136-173; Widengren, *Die Religionen* 9-10, 277-83.

[1] Trans. M. Sprengling, cit. above, *AJSLL* 57, 1940, 51.

[2] Trans. Chaumont, *JA* 238, 1960, 358. See also 371-2, 377 notes 70-75, on the identification of the several groups mentioned here; also see Zaehner, *Dawn*, 24-5 and 184; de Menasce, *Škand*, 206-9 Frye *Heritage*, 209-10 and 275 n. 31. Note also that the Marcionites were called Christians in later Persian Christian sources, see Arthur Vööbus, *History of Asceticism in the Syrian Orient* (Louvain, I, 1958, II, 1960), I, 48. If Kartir meant by Christians, Marcionites, then Nazarenes were probably Orthodox Christians, and not Mandaeans, since there were certainly sufficient Orthodox Christians in Babylonia and the Iranian empire generally to warrant his attention. See also M. L. Chaumont, "Les Sassanides et la Christianisation de l'Empire iranien au IIIe Siècle", *RHR* 165, 1964.

We know that Shapur had devoted some effort to reconciling the
Jews, among others, to his reign. I do not believe that Shapur would
at the same time have allowed Kartir to engage in persecutions of the
Jews, and the Jewish evidence does not indicate that he did. (In
vol. III we shall consider evidence of anti-Jewish policies between
Shapur's death in 273 and the rise of Shapur II). Shapur certainly
benefitted the Magi and set up many fires, but he did not prevent
others from doing honor to their gods. Under Shapur, Kartir was
called[1] simply Herpat (in Greek, Magus), while later on, in the Nakhš-i
Rajab and Sar Mashad inscriptions, he was called "Kartir the soul-
savior of Bahram and Ahuramazda's Mobad." The higher honors
accorded to Kartir doubtless represent increasing power, and it was
then, but not earlier, that he used this power, by his own word, to
persecute the Jews among others. If, as Ardashir said, "Religion and
Kingship are two brothers,"[2] then for Shapur, it must be added that
the king also found some useful, if distant cousins.[3]

VI. OTHER RELIGIONS

Although the Mazdean religion was the dominant one under the
Sasanians, early and late, other religions and cults flourished in Babylonia in this period, including those listed by Kartir, the Brahmans and
Shamans, whom Chaumont identifies as mendicant, itinerant Hindus
and Buddhists, Nazareans and Christians, difficult to differentiate,
though de Menasce holds, on good grounds, that the former were
orthodox Christians and the latter Marcionites; Maktiks, whom no
one can identify; and Zandiks, who, it is generally supposed, were
Manichaeans. In the Tigris-Euphrates valley, the Manichaeans,
Christians and Mandaeans were most numerous, although as I
emphasized above, apart from Judaism and Christianity, no religion
or cult held the exclusive loyalty of its communicants, and many cults
flourished, in both the Greco-Oriental and Iranian idoms, which do
not require specification here.

No religious leader in antiquity was more closely associated with

---

[1] On Kartir's titles, see especially Duchesne-Guillemin, *La Religion*, 294, and
Frye, "Early Sassanian State and Church", cited above.

[2] *Dawn* 284.

[3] We shall discuss the relationship between Judaism and Mazdaism below,
pp. 72-91. See especially, for a brief but comprehensive statement, Z. Frankel,
"Zur Geschichte der jüdischen Religionsgespräche", *MGWJ* 4, 1855, 410-13.

Babylonia than Mani,[1] who was born of distinguished Iranian parentage in the time of Ardashir's rise to power and died at the hand of his grandson. The Manichaean tradition regarded Mani's mother as a member of the Arsacid royal family; his father had migrated from Hamadan to Mesene, where he associated with 'baptizers,' a gnostic-type sect Puech regards as "analogous to Mandaeism." Born in 215-6, in his youth Mani studied the various religious systems of the day, in particular Zoroastrianism, Christianity, and the gnostic systems of Bardesanes of Edessa and Marcion. From Marcion he derived a negative view of Judaism and the Hebrew Scriptures and the idea of how to organize his disciples. His basic ideas, though Iranian in orientation, were phrased in the language of the Mesopotamian gnostic with Christian sympathies, according to Geo Widengren. In time he received his own revelation, and announced himself as the successor of Buddha, Zoroaster, and Jesus, and as the prophet of the God of truth and the seal of prophecy. To Shapur he said:

> Wisdom and deeds have always from time to time been brought to mankind by the messengers of God. So in one age they have been brought by the messenger called Buddha, to India; in another by Zaradusht, to Persia; in another by Jesus, to the West. Thereupon this revelation has come down, this prophecy in this last age, through me, Mani, messenger of the God of truth to Babylonia.[2]

Shapur showed favor to Mani, as we have noted, and the faith flourished. Mani formed a church of five ranks, including twelve

---

[1] The literature on Mani and Manichaeism is enormous. For our purposes the following proved most useful: Christensen, *L'Iran*, 174-200; Frye, *Heritage*, 210-13; Ghirshman, *Iran*, 315-8; Pigulevskaja, *Villes* 238-41; Prosper Alfaric, *Les Écritures Manichéennes* (Paris, 1918); A. V. W. Jackson, *Researches in Manichaeism* (N.Y. 1932); F. C. Burkitt, *Religion of the Manichees* (Cambridge, 1925); S. H. Taqizadeh, "Dates of Mani's life", translated, introduced, and concluded by W. B. Henning *Asia Major*, 6, 1, 106-21; Geo Widengren, *Mani und der Manichäismus* (Stuttgart, 1961), and his *Religionen*, 299-307; Alfred Adam, "Manichaeismus", in B. Spuler ed., *Handbuch der Orientalistik* VIII, *Religion*, ii. *Religionsgeschichte des Orients in der Zeit der Weltreligionen* (Leiden, 1961), 102-19; Geo Widengren, *Mesopotamian Elements in Manichaeism* (Uppsala, 1946); and mainly H. C. Puech, *Le Manichéisme* (Paris, 1949). Citation to Widengren is in *Mesopotamian Elements*, 179. See also A. V. W. Jackson, "Traces of Biblical Influence", *JAOS* 56, 1936, 198-207, who points out that Mani may have known Hebrew, and certainly knew the New Testament. For Jewish influence on Mani, Jackson cites J. C. Bauer, *Das Manichäische Religionssystem* (Göttingen, 1831), 356-68; I. Scheftelowitz, *Die Enstehung der Manichäischen Religion* (Giessen, 1922), 34-40. See also H. J. Polotsky, "Manichäismus", *PW* Suppl. VI ,265-7, and O. Klima, *Manis Zeit und Leben*, Prague, 1962.

[2] Quotation from Shapuhragan, cit. by F. C. Burkitt, *Religion of the Manichees*, 37.

masters in the first class, seventy-two bishops in the second, and
360 presbyters. The last two classes were unlimited in numbers,
the final group, auditors, being believers who did not take upon
themselves the more severe disciplines imposed upon the other classes.
All followers observed frequent fasts, tithing, and prayer. Mani's
church made great progress, not only in Babylonia but in Iran Proper,
and, protected by the king of kings, on whose coronation day Mani
proclaimed the faith, Mani was able to convert members of the royal
family, including Shapur's brothers, Mihrshah, governor of Mesene,
and Peroz. Mani's great success was based upon the universal appeal
of his message. One could emphasize the worship of Mazdah, and
Buddha in the east, or Jesus in the west. Mani carried the faith to
the east himself, preaching in India and Sogdia, before he returned to
Ctesiphon, and martyrdom in 274. He left a great body of literature,
which was preserved and circulated by his church. His successor as
head of the Manichaeans was Sis, or Sisin, also domiciled in Babylonia,
though the large-scale persecutions organized by the Mazdean clergy
and led by Kartir, continuing into the reigns of Narseh and Ohrmazd II, resulted in flight to the east, where the faith grew strong,
especially in Sogdia.

For the third century, the "Zandik," or heretic, par excellence
was the Manichaean. His faith, based upon the opposition between
light and darkness, good and evil, the spirit and the body, aimed at
the liberation of the soul from the body, and laid stress on celibacy,
vegetarianism, and other ascetic practices among the clergy, and much
fasting among the laity. Manichaean doctrines were deeply influenced
by gnostic forms; the hymns were Babylonian in inspiration; Mani
stressed ethics as did Zoroaster; and special place was reserved for
Jesus, the trinity, and the Christian gospels, the Buddhist idea of
metempsychosis, and Syrian angelology. All these varied elements
reflected a successful synthesis of every religion present in the Sasanian
empire save one, Judaism.[1] Moses and the prophets were considered

---

[1] W. A. Wigram, *History of the Assyrian Church* (London, 1907), 24f. points
out that when the Sasanians came to power, they found Christianity wide-spread
and well organized on apostolic lines, constituting a legally recognized entity.
Before the conversion of Constantine, Christianity suffered infrequent persecution in the east, though that of Kartir cannot be ignored. See also Eduard
Sachau, *Die Chronik von Arbela* (Berlin 1915). Both Sachau and Wigram comment
on the strange fact that Seleucia-Ctesiphon was so lately evangelized, a fact I
believe satisfactorily explained here, and in vol. I. On the deportations of Christians, see also Downey, *Antioch*, 261; *Tabari*, ed. Nöldeke, 32-3, 40-1. See also

to be devils, and Judaism the creation of the lord of darkness. It is puzzling that a peculiarly Babylonian development, aiming at an international and cosmopolitan audience, should have so utterly omitted Judaism from the approved cults, on the one hand, and abhorred its doctrines, on the other. Obviously, Judaism as we know it was a highly intractable tradition, incapable of participating in a syncretistic structure. Yet Christianity, at least in its gnostic and Marcionite forms, found a place in Mani's thought. Some Jews, likewise, might have been won over by inclusion of Moses. Two factors may be discerned to explain this anomaly. First, Mani himself, raised in the anti-Jewish climate of Mandaeism (following Puech), could not have found in Judaism anything useful or worthwhile for his theology, never having heard anything but evil about it. Second, the Jews themselves may have appeared hopelessly impervious to Mani's teaching to warrant inclusion of their prophets and teachings, so far as they might fit, into his system. One may suppose that these prophets and teachings could never have been accomodated by *any* syncretistic system, though the evidence of Dura, Alexandria, and elsewhere denies it. Though Jews lived in substantial numbers in Mesene, where Mani grew up, and in still greater numbers in Babylonia, where he preached, they must have incurred his wrath, and I can suppose one reason only, namely by actively opposing him and his message within their community, or, less likely, by complete indifference to his message to begin with. Why were the Jews uniquely impervious to that message? I think the obvious reason is the growing

---

F. C. Burkitt, *Early Christianity outside the Roman Empire* (London, 1899), and J. Labourt, *Le Christianisme dans l'Empire Perse* (Paris 1904). Labourt points out (16) that as early as 270 there were Christian-Manichaean disputations in Charax Spasinu. Other relevant works include A. Harnack, *Mission and Expansion of Christianity* (repr. N.Y. 1961), 312-18; Johannes Leipoldt, "Frühes Christentum im Orient" in B. Spuler, *op. cit.*, 3-17; Frye, *Heritage*, 214; Herzfeld, *Archaeological History*, 102-4; Christensen, *L'Iran*, 34f, 186f., and especially 261-310. Christensen points out that the situation of the Christians was different from that of the Jews, for Zoroastrian intolerance was political rather than propagandistic; for this period, I do not see significant differences in the situations of the two communities. See especially Arthur Vööbus, *History of Asceticism in the Christian Orient*, (Louvain I, 1958, II, 1960), and Felix Haase, *Altchristliche Kirchengeschichte* (Leipzig, 1926) 94-111, who holds (p. 102) that Nisibis and Seleucia-Ctesiphon did not have bishops *for fear of the pagans*, a 'reason' that apparently did not apply in Edessa, Arbela, and many other places, and hence that explains nothing! Further bibliography and discussion will be found in Haase, p. 94-6, n. 3; vol. I, pp. 166-9, and in my "Conversion of Adiabene to Christianity", *Numen* XIII, 2, 1966.

influence of the Tannaitic-Amoraic tradition in Babylonia. I have noted (Vol. I pp. 166-9) that Christianity made its greatest and earliest advances across the Euphrates precisely in those cities which possessed large Jewish communities, specifically Edessa and Arbela, *not* under Tannaite influence, while it made little progress, for at least a century and a half, in Babylonian and Mesopotamian communities (Nehardea, Nisibis) where Tannaite influence was well established. We may reasonably infer therefore that Tannaitic Judaism effectively halted the spread of Christianity among the earliest audience for the Christian gospel, diaspora Jews. If this is the case, then one must consider it likely that in Central Babylonia in Mani's time, Tannaitic-Amoraic ideas on the proper relationship to paganism in all its forms, which we shall consider below, had by the middle of Shapur's reign begun so to predominate, that Mani's ideas could gain no hearing whatever. Having been predisposed to an antipathy to Judaism from his youth, Mani never found a reason to reconsider his earlier views.

In early Sasanian times, Christianity, well established in Adiabene, and struggling for a foothold in Babylonia itself, received a considerable impetus with the deportation of large numbers of Christians, along with other Roman Orientals, from Antioch to Persia.[1] These formed the nucleus of the Christian church in Persia. (H. J. Schoeps holds that there were Jewish-Christians in Babylonia.[2] In any event, as we have noted, there was no bishop in Ctesiphon before 300, although seventy-five years earlier bishoprics and apostolic sees existed throughout northern Mesopotamia, and Christianity in heretical forms obviously enjoyed widespread influence in Babylonia, long before the foundation of the Ctesiphon see. Further, there must have been a local Christian community in Babylonia before Sasanian times, for the church could not easily have established itself afterward. The progress of the faith was slow, quiet, and steady, marred neither by organized persecutions, before Kartir's, nor by major schism known to us. With the advent of state Mazdaism, as we have seen, conversion of a Zoroastrian to Christianity was made a capital crime for both disciple and master, and progress must have slowed in the center of the western empire. As late as 270 only a few Christians lived there.

Settled near the Persian Gulf, in the alluvial land where the Tigris

---

[1] See p. 21, n.l.

[2] This was certainly true in 270-310, as I shall show in vol. III chap. one.

and Euphrates meet and in the lowlands along the Karun, the Mandeans preserved a gnostic, highly syncretistic religion, like Manichaeism a hybred embracing Babylonian astrology, Iranian dualism, Hellenistic speculative theology, and the Hebrew and Christian Scriptures.[1] Lady Drower hypothesized that *Nasirutha* germinated in the Jewish colonies in Parthia, Media, and Babylonia; the Nasoreans, by their own account, had fled from both Jews and Christians to Parthia and Media, and under Parthian protection into Babylonia. According to the *Haran Gawaita*, they had escaped from persecution in Jerusalem before 70, and found refuge in Carrhae in the north and Media in the east. (Their persecutors were finally punished, they believed, by the destruction of Jerusalem.) Finally, in Haran, they found co-religionists of an earlier settlement and, under Ardavan, established themselves in lower Mesopotamia. Oral tradition likewise holds that they reached their present home from Haran, and, before that, from Palestine, though this may represent merely a typological reversal of Abraham's movement. Though the origins of the Mandeans are by no means clear, it is quite apparent that they, like the Manichaeans, were very negatively disposed toward Judaism. It has been supposed that the anti-Jewish polemic was caused by the persecution, in Hasmonean times, or during the war of 66-73 against Rome, of an aberrant or fringe group on the periphery of Judaism. For the Mandeans, as for the Manichaeans, the Jewish God was an evil spirit, the law was given by the evil *ruha* and the seven planets, and the Hebrew Bible was read with a particularly critical eye. "Adonai" the God of the Jews possessed a negative signification, according to

---

[1] See E. S. Drower, *The Secret Adam* (Oxford, 1960), xi-xv, 99f., on Mandean origins; her edition of the *Haran Gawaita and Baptism of Hibil Ziwa* (Vatican City, 1953), ixf.; and her *Mandaeans of Iraq and Iran* (Leiden, 1962), xv-xxv and 1-19. See also Mark Lidzbarski, *Das Johannesbuch der Mandäer* (Giessen, 1915), xvi-xxx, and Kurt Rudolph, *Die Mandäer* (Göttingen, 1960), I, 80-101. On Mandean origins in Judaism, see also Geo Widengren, "Die Mandäer" in B. Spuler ed., *op. cit.*, 83-102, esp. 83 and J. Doresse, *Secret Books of Egyptian Gnostics* (N.Y. 1960) 315-6. This is not the place to enter into the complicated questions of Mandean origins, dating and so forth. I regard Rudolph's view as definitive, that the Mandeans, whenever and wherever they took shape, were originally half-Jews on the periphery of Judaism. It is this which explains their antipathy toward traditional Jewish theological motifs. But I can find nothing that reflects knowledge of Talmudic-Midrashic literature or ideas, clearly understood, and the Jewish elements seem to me to be mainly biblical, apart from the echoes of Judaism in the magical texts cited by Rudolph from Montgomery, Stube, and Blau. A very good discussion of the Mandean problem as relevant to NT studies will be found in Wayne Meeks, *King and Prophet in the Fourth Gospel* (Leiden, 1967).

Rudolph; biblical creation material was used, but reworked. Mandean magic texts reveal many affinities for the Jewish ones and the Mandean world-view is built upon that of the Bible. The reason for the Man-deans' revulsion against Judaism seems to have had historical and political, rather than religious, roots, unlike that of Mani, but by the time the Mandeans settled down in southern Babylonia, it hardly mattered so far as Judaism was concerned, for both Manichaeism and Mandaeism, religious communities within the gnostic idiom, found nothing of interest in contemporary Judaism.

We do not know much about other religions' influence upon Judaism. On the one hand, the Talmudic sources speak of *minim*,[1] usually understood to refer to Jewish heretics, in Babylonia, and it is reasonable to suppose that some Jews did apostasize to religions, such as Mandaeism, Manichaeism, and Christianity, which made some use of their Scriptures. On the other hand, these same rabbinic sources exhibit no significant influence, during this period at least, emanating from other contemporary religions, and, more interestingly, very little direct knowledge of them. Archaeological information from the Dura synagogue, and, relating to a later period, from the Nippur magical bowls, quite to the contrary, indicates tremendous alien influence upon the ordinary Jew, at least in matters pertaining to decorative art and magic. This much therefore seems to me quite evident: whatever the state of practices among the masses, the *doctrines* of competing cults made no impact whatever upon those of the Judaism known to us from the Talmud and cognate literature. Moses is praised and never reviled; Adam is no hero; the Hebrew Bible is never viewed as the origin of lies or deceit; the dualism of body and soul, evil and good, and the like which is so characteristic of Mandaeism and Manichaeism never occurs in Jewish settings, except, as in Dura, in a highly conventional way. Magic, astrology, and other occult sciences, on the other hand, were as attractive to Jews as they were to pagans and Christians; these were regarded as advanced sciences, and to reject them, the Jews, and their leaders, would have had to ignore the most sophisticated technological attainments of contemporary civilization.[2] It was quite natural for Jews

---

[1] See Frankel, *op. cit.*, 412-3.

[2] See S. Lieberman, *Greek in Jewish Palestine* (N.Y. 1942). 115-143, and especially 98-9.

to borrow from, and contribute to, the cultural resources of the region. Such borrowing does not, standing by itself, prove more than that the Jews shared in the occult practices of the common life of Babylonia.[1]

---

[1] See below, pp. 72-91 for further discussion. Note especially that the rabbis preached sermons against the Jews who not only neglected their religious obligations, but celebrated pagan festivals, saying that the Persians exhumed [the Jewish] dead because they [the Jews] "rejoiced on their festivals". Likewise, they lived in close physical contact with the other peoples, and entertained them, and accepted entertainment in their homes. Samuel and other rabbis did so as well; Samuel maintained friendship with a "Persian sage", Avlat. This question cannot, however, be evaluated in such a narrow context as the present volume, but requires a full and comprehensive study of its own. Here we shall consider only the limited evidence directly relevant to the period of Ardashir and Shapur. Note also the view of Eric Peterson, "Urchristentum und Mandäismus", *ZNW* 27, 1928, 93f. "The sharp polemic of Babylonian Judaism against the Jews of Mesene and the prohibition of marriage with them is best understood if there was among the Jews in Mesene real syncretism with the Mandaeans." We shall consider the passage Peterson refers to (b. Qid. 72a) below, p. 240-242. See also I. Scheftelowitz, "Die Mandäische Religion und das Judentum", *MGWJ* 73, 1929, 211-32, and the general view of Gilles Quispel, "Christliche Gnosis und jüdische Heterodoxie", *Evangelische Theologie* 14, 1954, 474-84.

CHAPTER TWO

THE SASANIANS AND THE JEWS

I. ARDASHIR AND THE JEWS

The Jews did not welcome the change in dynasty. They had enjoyed cordial relations with the Arsacids, whose rule had marked for them a long period of peace and political autonomy. Moreover, to intensify the Jews' dismay, the Sasanians burst into power full of reforming energies, determined to unify their disparate empire by cultural and religious means, to honor their divinity, which had guided their fortune in such an amiable manner, by erecting a state-church, and in any event to intervene, in the interest of their cult and state, as they thought proper, into the affairs of the subject-peoples of the Mesopotamian valley. As a result, the Jews' thoughts turned to Rome, under whose rule Palestinian Jewry lived at the time in peace and relative freedom,[1] and whose dominion appeared infinitely preferable to that of the zealous Mazdeans. Only after Shapur's coronation were the Jews conciliated to the new state.[2]

Rav had enjoyed particularly close relations with the Arsacid government. I have maintained[3] that he was related to the exilarch, who served the Parthian government as Jewish ethnarch, and carried forward its interests both among Babylonian Jews and, where possible, in Palestine as well, and who, in partnership with the Palestinian patriarchate, advanced the Parthian economic eterprise in the Roman Orient. Rav quickly recognized the inauspicious meaning of the upheaval, allegedly lamenting the death of Ardavan:

---

[1] Despite the contrary view of A. Marmorstein and others, this has been amply demonstrated for the 3rd century by S. Lieberman, "Palestine in the Third and Fourth Centuries", *JQR* n.s. 36, 329-70. See in particular 342, 365, and 370. There were no Roman religious or political persecutions in this period, and no policy directed against the welfare of Jewry in particular can be discerned. The Persians' attitude was therefore particularly resented by those who had earlier prided themselves in the fact that they enjoyed conditions superior to those of their brethren in Palestine.

[2] Lieberman, *op. cit.*, *JQR* n.s. 37, 1, 34. We shall treat this matter further, pp. 64-72.

[3] Vol. I, 23-31, 50-58, 97-113.

> Antoninus served Rabbi [Judah the Prince]. Ardavan[1] served Rav.
> When Antoninus died, Rabbi lamented, The bond is snapped. When
> Ardavan died, Rav lamented, The bond is snapped.[2]

(b. A.Z. 10b-11a)

No doubt, Ardavan served Rav just as "Antoninus" served Rabbi
Judah the Prince, that is to say, not at all. The latter in each case
ably served the interests of the former. Nonetheless, the saying
attributed to Rav was appropriate, for the 'bond,' or bundle, indeed
fell apart, that had joined Jewry and the Arsacid regime,[3] and an
ancient alliance had come to an end. Palestinian Jews for their part
entertained no doubt whatever that the change was catastrophic:

> When R. Yoḥanan was informed that the Magi [ḤBRY] had come
> to Babylonia, he reeled and fell. When he was told that they accepted
> bribes, he recovered and sat down again.

(b. Yev. 63b)

Likewise, the later editors of the Talmud interpreted R. Ḥiyya's
saying, that God had driven the Jews to Babylonia because he knew
that they could not endure Roman persecution, to apply to the period
before the Magi came to power in Babylonia, but afterward, conditions
changed, so that the exclamation of Rabbah b. Bar Ḥana applied,
"O merciful, either in thy shadow or in that of the son of Esau
[=Rome]."[4]

Before attempting to assess just how severe were Sasanian persecutions of the Jews or Judaism in this period, we may usefully recall
their general policy toward minorities at the outset of their rule.
Ardashir's government actively sought the conversion of religious
minorities to the Mazdean faith. According to the Arbela Chronicle,
Ardashir established in each satrapy not only a political officer, but
also a *mobad*, to foster the interests of the faith. He ordered the

---

[1] Texts reads 'DRKN, however, see R. Rabbinovicz, *Dikdukei Soferim* [Hence-
forward, *Dik. Sof.*] (repr. N.Y. 1940), XII, 26, *ad loc.* There can be no doubt that
the reference is to Ardavan V, and no other, for the parallel is intended to show
that just as R. Judah was friendly with the Roman emperor, so Rav was friendly
with the equivalent, Parthian figure. Efforts to identify this Ardavan with some
'otherwise unknown local official' are silly.

[2] Jastrow: the bond of friendship (between the two nations) is severed. Levy:
Der Bund ist aufgelöst.

[3] Note b. Ber. 57b, where Rav comments on the equivalent importance of R.
Judah and "Antoninus". Samuel on the other hand took a different view of the
relationship between Rome and the House of Rabbi Judah the Prince (b. A.Z.
16a). For Rav's difficulties with local Roman officials in the Galilee, see y. Ber. 9.1.

[4] b. Git. 17a. But this may refer to Kartir's times. See vol. III, ch. One.

construction of fire-temples throughout the realm, and encouraged, probably by force, the conversion of many men of other religions to the service of 'the sun and fire.'[1] Likewise, as we have seen, Kartir reported that he had created many fire-temples and established many Magi in non-Iranian areas which belonged to the king of kings.[2] There can be no doubt that religion was one important means by which the Sasanians attempted to strengthen their hold on the empire, and their repeated efforts to convert Armenia, Georgia, and other areas, to Mazdaism illustrate this fact. (In later reigns, in particular, Christians suffered, for the conversion of Byzantium to Christianity rendered their political position particularly vulnerable.)[3] If the militancy of the Mazdean clergy had political implications, however, their faith was, to begin with, an exclusivist one, whose adherents regarded those of other faiths as possessors of evil and lying doctrines. The building of fire-temples, the zealous opposition to other cults and religions, the encouragement of consanguineous marriage and enforcement of Zoroastrian laws on burial were all expressions of conviction of the truth of their faith, a belief which could not have boded well for other cults, including Judaism, under the new regime. As we have noted, under Shapur matters greatly improved, which accounts for the evidences of toleration of Judaism later on.[4] But in the time of Ardashir, the Jews, among others, faced a serious political and religious crisis.

This crisis, however, must be understood as part of the trauma of governmental upheaval, and not as the result of a policy of persecution directed especially against Jewry. It was rather a direct consequence of the beginnings of the Sasanians themselves. Originating in the Zoroastrian clergy, closely associated with the Istakhr temple, the Sasanians' politics was founded upon the conviction that they were to be the means by which the religion and cult of ancient Iran might once again predominate in both Iranian and non-Iranian lands, and, as I have suggested, it was this very conviction which inspired their

---

[1] Ed. Sachau 62-3, ch. VIII, Ḥairan.

[2] See Geo Widengren, *Die Religionen Irans*, (Stuttgart 1965) 274-83, esp. 275.

[3] Christensen, *L'Iran*, 261.

[4] For discussion of the later policy toward the Jews, see Nöldeke, *Tabari*, 68 n. 1; Labourt, *Le Christianisme dans l'Empire Perse*, (Paris, 1904) 7-9, and especially, S. Krauss, *Paras*, 90-93, whose judgment, contrary to Labourt and Christensen, is, as I have held, that the early years of Ardashir marked a period of considerable difficulty for the Jews. We shall examine below evidences of exactly what these difficulties were. See also David Hoffmann, *Mar Samuel* (Leipzig 1873), 37-42.

earliest victories. By contrast, the Parthians associated themselves
with no particular cult, but from the beginning, constituted a military
aristocracy intent upon building and maintaining a great empire,
and they needed, in order to do so, to conciliate whatever groups
they found in it, as best they could. They never exhibited particular
loyalty to a single cult, though for reasons mainly political,[1] they
emphasized, from time to time, their loyalty to their Achemenid
'ancestors,' ancestors whom they first discovered in the first century
A.D. Greeks, Babylonians, Syrians, and Jews alike found that they
could cultivate their traditions, and govern themselves, without
significant interference from the Parthian court, which exercised
authority mainly through semi-independent, local satraps. Without
a religious mission and preferring decentralized government, the
Parthians naturally appeared to be more tolerant than the Sasanians,
who, espousing the cult of Istakhr long before they aspired to the
throne of Iran, recognizing the disastrous consequences of excessive
decentralization, and not faced with the kinds of necessities, both
political and cultural, which had originally led the Parthians to such
an accommodating policy, were, under Ardashir, exceptionally
intolerant. Among other groups, the Jews discovered the difficulty
of living under a government which assigned central importance to a
specific cult, and determined not only to rule, but actually to supervise
the day-by-day affairs of its empire, and which created a vast bureaucracy in order to do so. Here we emphasize the political implications
of the Sasanians' religious and cultural policies. Below (p. 35-9) we
shall consider the consequent repression of Judaism. It suffices now
to note that the cultic beginnings of the dynasty determined its
attitude toward the minority peoples whose government it inherited
when it captured Babylonia.

The new regime, first of all, annulled Jewish legal autonomy, and
made it clear that the government would supervise the activities of
Jewish courts as the Parthians never had. Formerly, these courts had
exercised complete authority over the Jews, so far as we can tell from
the slender evidence available to us, perhaps including the right to
inflict capital punishment.[2] The change under the Sasanians was
immediate and far-reaching, according to the following:

---

[1] See my "Parthian Political Ideology", *IA* 3, 1963, 40-59, and Richard N.
Frye, "The Charisma of Kingship in Ancient Iran", *IA* 4, 1964, 36-54.
[2] See, for example, b. Git. 14b and y. Git. 1.5, cited in Vol. I, 94-5. But compare
R. Shila's sayings below, p. 32.

A certain man who desired to reveal another's straw [for taxation?] appeared before Rav, who said, Do not show it! Do not show it! He replied, I certainly will show it! Rav Kahana, who was then sitting before Rav, tore his windpipe out of him [lit.; Jastrow: forced him to give up the threatened information against his neighbor]. Rav thereupon cited the Scripture, 'Thy sons have fainted, they lie at the heads of all the streets as a wild bull in a net' (Is. 51.20). Just as a wild bull falls into a net and none has mercy upon it, so when the property of an Israelite falls into the hands of pagan oppressors, no mercy is shown towards it. Rav thereupon said to him, Kahana, until now, the Greeks[1] who did not punish bloodshed were [here] but now the Persians, who punish bloodshed are [here] and (they will certainly cry, Rebellion, rebellion!)[2] Arise, therefore, and go up to the land of Israel . . . . .

(b. B.Q. 117a)

This story poses numerous difficulties. First, the court procedure is unprecedented in Talmudic law, and the penalty of death for exposing one's neighbor's property to confiscation has no legal standing whatever. At worst, the man would have had to make restitution. However, according to *Dik. Sof.* the phrase "his windpipe out of him" does not appear in all recensions, and the word שמטיה standing alone would mean nothing in such a context. If we read שמתיה then we might understand that Rav Kahana declared the man to be excommunicated, an action the Persians would certainly regard as impeding the administration of taxes, and hence as rebellion. In such a context, one should understand מרדון to derive from the Semitic 'rebellion' rather than from the Iranian 'murder.'[3] On the other hand, Rav's saying that the Persians now paid attention to capital punishment (lit., shedding of blood) in Jewish courts supports the reading in the printed text, that Rav Kahana actually tore out the man's windpipe, which would similarly be regarded by the government as rebellion. In any event, the account poses far more severe difficulties, for the story goes on to relate perfectly fabulous

---

[1] Printed texts reverse the order, Persians then Greeks, but MS. variants support this reading, which is historically the only possible one, contrary to the view of the Tosafist, s.v. *Hashta.* See *Dik. Sof.* VIII 297.

[2] Some MS omit the phrase in parenthesis.

[3] *Arukh* IX 268 supports this explanation, contrary to Krauss, *Paras* 257. The clear meaning is that Rav Kahana was to flee because of supporting the evasion of taxes, which is precisely the meaning of the word in other contexts. Compare *Arukh* V 242, where a different view is set forth. In any event, whether Rav Kahana actually killed the man, or merely excommunicated him, the meaning of MRD is unaffected.

events which took place after Rav Kahana reached the academy of
R. Yoḥanan, including his death and resurrection. Moreover, it
explicitly states that at this time, R. Yoḥanan was a very old man.
We know that Rav died long before R. Yoḥanan, and was hence
not alive in the latter's dotage. The story moreover clearly indicates
that Rav referred to a very recent change in regime ("until now...").
It is not possible that the account, even without its folkloristic
elements, corresponds to a historical situation we can identify.[1]
It preserves, I believe, only two reasonable facts, first, that Rav Kahana
fled from Babylonia, early in Sasanian times, for political reasons,
and second, that Jewish courts were no longer so free as they had
been under the "Greeks" [=Parthians]. The second conclusion is
reenforced by the following, far more reliable, story:

> R. Shila administered lashes to a man who had intercourse with a
> gentile woman. The man went and informed against him to the
> government, saying, There is a man among the Jews who executes
> judgement without the permission of the government [בלא הרמנא
> דמלכא].[2] A messenger[3] [פריסתקא] was sent to him. He said to him,
> when he came, what is the reason that you flogged this man? He
> replied, Because he had intercourse with a she-ass. He said to him,
> Do you have witnesses? He replied to them, Yes. Elijah came and
> appeared in the form of a man, and gave testimony. They said to him,
> If so, he was worthy of being put to death. He replied, Since we have
> been exiled from our land we do not have authority [רשותא] to execute.
> They said, Do with him as you like. While they were considering the
> case, R. Shila began to say, 'Yours, O Lord, is the greatness and the
> power' (I Chron. 29.11). What are you saying? they asked him. He
> replied, What I am saying is this: Blessed is the All-merciful who has
> made earthly loyalty on the model of heavenly royalty, and has invested
> you with dominion, and made you lovers of justice. They said to him,
> Are you so solicitous of the honor of the government? They gave
> him a staff [קולפא][4] and said to him, You may act as judge. When he

---

[1] Funk, *Juden*, I, 68, ignores these difficulties, as have all others who cite this
text.

[2] *Arukh* III 245-6, anordnung, Befehl=command of the king.

[3] Frestaghan=messengers, see Christensen, *L'Iran* 188. The word appears in
pre-Sasanian Jewish texts but in this context certainly indicates a government
official of the Sasanian regime. On hermana=firman, and frestak, see H. S.
Nyberg, *Hilfsbuch des Pahlevi* (Uppsala, 1931), s.v., 72, 76.

[4] *Arukh* IX 364, Geiger derives the Aramaic word from the Persian *kopāl*. One
notes that in the Kartir Inscription, the priest Kartir emphasizes that he received
the *kumar* and the *kulaf*, honorary sash and tiara of office. But the kulpa here
cannot have been a tiara, because R. Shila used it to strike the man, and hence the
Aramaic meaning stands. I am grateful to Professors Richard N. Frye and Baruch
Levine for their comments on kulaf/kulpa. Professor Levine notes that since

went forth, that man said to him, Does the All-Merciful do miracles
for liars? Thus he replied, Evil man! Are they not called asses? For it
is written, 'Whose flesh is as the flesh of asses' (Ezek. 23.20). He
noticed that the man was about to inform them that he had called
them asses, and said, This man is a pursuer, and the Torah has said,
'If a man comes to kill you, rise early and kill him first' (Ex. 22.1). So
he struck him with the staff and killed him. Then he said, Since a
miracle has been wrought for me through this verse, I will expound it.
'Thine O Lord is the greatness'—refers to the Works of Creation.[1]
And so it says, 'Who doeth great things past finding out' (Job 9.10).
'And the power'—This refers to the Exodus from Egypt, as it says,
'And Israel saw the great works' (Ex. 14.31). 'And the glory'—this
refers to the sun and moon which stood still for Joshua, as it says,
'And the sun stood still and the moon stayed' (Joshua 10.13). 'And
the victory'—this refers to the fall of Rome, as it says, 'And their life
blood is dashed against my garments' (Is. 63.3). 'And the majesty'—
this refers to the valley of the Arnon, as it says, 'Wherefore is it said.'
(Num. 21.14). 'For all that is in heaven and earth'—this refers to the
war of Sisera, as it says 'They fought from heaven, the stars in their
courses fought against Sisera' (Jud. 5.20). 'Thine is the kingdom O
Lord'—this refers to the war against Amalek, for so it says, 'The hand
upon the throne of the Lord, the Lord will have war with Amalek
from generation to generation' (Ex. 17.16). 'And thou art exalted'—
This refers to the war of Gog and Magog, and so it says, 'Behold I
am against thee, O Gog . . .' (Ezek. 38.3).

(b. Ber. 58a)

This story poses no significant historical difficulties, but, on the
contrary, reveals accurate knowledge of Persian legal terminology
(firman, frestak); the exchange with the government agent rings
true; and the account conforms to the fact that R. Shila did exert
considerable authority among the Jews in the early part of Sasanian
rule.[2] That the new regime supervised the activities of Jewish courts is
beyond question, and that an aggrieved party would complain to the
higher authority seems quite reasonable. As 'Elijah' is frequently
identified with otherwise unknown, friendly intervention, one may
suppose that a Jew came in the nick of time, and testified against the
accused party, and that this perjury was interpreted as a miracle.
Of considerable interest is R. Shila's sermon. The great event of the

---

kulpa derives from KLP, meaning a leather strap, it may be that R. Shila was
given a headband, emblem of judicial office here as in the case of Kartir. In this
context, however, I think it was a staff, a judgment supported by the variant;
קולפא דפרזלא that is, a staff of iron.

[1] See Chap. V section vi.
[2] See p. 108-111.

Sasanians' rise to power was naturally interpreted by the Jews in the light of biblical history, and required that the Jewish exegete find a place for this new empire in the pattern of sacred history. In his sermon, R. Shila referred to the Exodus, the conquest of the land, the wars against several enemies, but most especially the war against Amalek, a paradigm of Israel's enemies, and Gog and Magog, who may, in R. Shila's mind, have been associated with the Sasanians. In all, R. Shila emphasized his original conviction, that power and dominion belonged to the God of Israel, and that whatever vicissitudes history might bring, in the end, the God of Israel would reign. His reference to the fall of Rome probably signified the Persian victories in the time of Ardashir. In the light of this story, moreover, one may reconsider the strange punishment inflicted by R. Kahana, for, in both instances, the rabbis took extra-legal and extreme action in defense of Jewish self-government, against Jews whose actions endangered it, in each case by 'informing against' the Jewish leadership to the new government, an action the aggrieved party would have naturally called an appeal to higher authorities.

The earliest political response of the Jewish authorities reveals considerable ineptitude. The officials sought to maintain their earlier freedom of action through subterfuge, hoping by *force majeure* to keep the Jews in line, and, at the same time, by dissimulation to hoodwink the Sasanian bureaucracy. Such a policy, which would have been both successful and unnecessary under the Parthians, proved impossible under the new authorities, who quite clearly intended to impose very effective control of all their subjects, and who had no very good reason to conciliate the Jewish autonomous government by reaffirming its traditional prerogatives. The Parthians had created that government for their own purposes[1] and the Sasanians, owing nothing to the Jews, and finding, at first, no use for it, and seeing no great need to maintain it, at best were prepared to tolerate it. A more realistic policy for the Jews required formulation. It could not come, however, from Rav, who was thoroughly compromised by his close association with the Arsacid throne, nor, quite obviously, from R. Shila, who could only repeat the ancient hope that the Sasanians would, like earlier world-empires, pass from the scene. However vivid such a hope may have been, and however convincingly others might calculate the date of the messianic arrival,[2] in the

---

[1] Vol. I, 50-8.
[2] See p. 52-57.

meanwhile, something more constructive had to be devised than a retrogressive and sterile policy of political and religious irredentism. It was, as we shall see, Samuel who correctly assessed the situation, and carried through a realistic, constructive, and mutually profitable program of reconciliation with the new regime. Before he succeeded, however, the Jews suffered from the lack of understanding between themselves and the Sasanian authorities.

II. ARDASHIR AND JUDAISM

The change in the political status of the Jewish community in the early decades of Sasanian rule was accompanied by a similarly disastrous modification of the position of Judaism. The Arsacids certainly never persecuted the Jewish religion, even though in the unrest of the first century C.E., Jewish political figures, such as Zamaris, Anileus, and Asineus, suffered a fall from favor. Whatever the religious attitudes of the Parthian government, Jews never found difficulty in exercising their religion in the four centuries of Arsacid rule. Under Ardashir, by contrast, they complained very bitterly against the government's decrees concerning their religion, decrees which were, as we have seen, part of a broader policy of repression of competing cults in favor of the Mazdean state-church. One must therefore keep in mind the profound contrast between the former and the new regime, in order to appreciate how grave a crisis confronted Jewry.

What the Mazdean Mobads did was simply to forbid those Jewish religious practices which offended their sensibilities:

> They decreed thrice on account of three things. They decreed concerning meat because of the priestly gifts. They decreed concerning the baths on account of ritual immersion. They exhumed the dead, because they [the Jews] rejoiced on their festivals, as it is said (I Sam. 12.15): 'Then shall the hand of the Lord be against you and against your fathers [RSV: king].' For Rabbah b. Samuel said, That [against the fathers] referred to exhumation of the dead, for the master said, 'For the sins of the living are the dead exhumed.'

> (b. Yev. 63b)[1]

The context of the prophet Samuel's speech, exhorting the Jews not to follow the ways of the gentiles, suggests that we are dealing with a sermon, rather than a strictly historical report. In each instance the sin of the Jews was contrasted with the appropriate decree of the

---

[1] Compare Yalkut Shimo'ni II 115, 770.

Mazdeans, an attitude expressed by Samuel, for instance, when he taught that the pagan government can enact an oppressive measure effectively only when Israel disregards the words of the Torah (Lam. R. Proem II). One cannot, nonetheless, deny that the Persians in fact prohibited ritual preparation of meat, use of ritual baths, and burial of the dead, for the homily depends upon the existence of such prohibitions, taking them for granted, and building upon the peoples' reaction to them.[1] There can be no doubt moreover that the Persians made decrees to protect the sanctity of fire:

> Rav was asked, Is it permitted to move the Hanukah lamp on account of the Magi (ḤBRYM) on the Sabbath, and he answered, It is well.
>
> (b. Shab. 45a, compare Git. 17a)

The Jewish practice, to kindle the Hanukah lamp near the street, would now have to change. Significantly, the Talmudic tradition regarded Rav's ruling as one for a time of troubles only, which may reflect the liberalization of Sasanian religious and cultural policies under Shapur and afterward. (The Ge'onim had a tradition that "the Persians" forbade the reading of a prophetic lesson on the afternoon of the Sabbath, but this was certainly not in the early period, for Rav discussed the practice without indicating that it was threatened or prohibited, and there is no clear evidence to indicate when such a decree was issued.[2])

The Persians nonetheless made life miserable for the Jews, for not only did they impose petty inconveniences, such as those noted above, but in fact destroyed synagogues, probably in the first flush of conquest:

> Rav said, Persia will fall into the hands of Rome. Thereupon R. Kahana and R. Assi asked Rav, Shall builders [of the Second Temple] fall into the hands of the destroyers [thereof]? He said to them, Yes, it is the decree of the king. Others say, he replied to them, They too are guilty, for they destroyed synagogues. It has also been taught by a Tanna: Persia will fall into the hands of the Romans, first, because they destroyed synagogues, second, because it is the king's decree that the builders shall fall into the hands of the destroyers. Rav further

---

[1] That the Persians left the dead to the vultures, later burying the bones, is well known, but despite their honoring water, I cannot understand the 'prohibition against the baths' if that is what it was, nor decrees concerning ritual slaughter.

[2] b. Shab. 24a, and Rashi *ad loc.* Compare b. Shab. 116b, and Ismar Elbogen, *Der jüdische Gottesdienst in seiner geschichtlichen Entwicklung* (repr. Hildesheim, 1962), 118, who holds that it happened before the 9th century. But we have no more exact date.

said, The son of David will not come until the wicked kingdom of
Rome will have spread over the whole world for nine months, as it is
said (Micah 5.2), 'Therefore will he give them up until the time that
she who travaileth hath brought forth, then the residue of his brethren
shall return with the children of Israel.'

(b. Yoma' 10a, compare Sanh. 98b)[1]

Rav, who likewise described the horrible fate of R. Akiba as the
king's decree which must not be challenged, here clearly stated that
the Persians destroyed synagogues. Further, there may have been
specific public persecutions directed against individual Jews, for
Rav warned (b. Sanh. 74b) that if it is a royal decree to transgress the
faith, one must not even change his shoelace.[2] The Magi, likewise,
were described by Levi b. Sisi to R. Judah the Prince, probably before
their political establishment by the Sasanians, as "destroying angels"
(b. Qid. 72a). Further, Rav stated:

Rava b. Meḥasia in the name of R. Ḥama b. Goria in the name of
Rav said: Under an Ishmaelite but not under a Roman [Edomite],
under a Roman but not under a Magus, under a Magus but not under
a scholar, under a scholar but not under a widow or an orphan . . . . .
If all the seas were ink, all the reeds were pens, all the heavens parch-
ment, and all men were scribes, they would not suffice to write down
the intricacies of the government.

(b. Shab. 11a)[3]

The preference for the rule of Rome rather than that of the Magi
reflects the fact that in this period, the Jews in the Roman Orient
lived at peace, as we have noted, by contrast with the unhappy
condition of their Babylonian brothers. Rav's reference to the intricacies of government recalls that the Sasanians built a very

---

[1] See the variants, *Dik. Sof.* V 21. I have followed the printed text. MS variants
omit "it is the king's decree", which may be an echo of the comment of Rav on
R. Akiba's martyrdom, see below, Chap. VI section 5. Likewise 'they too destroyed" etc. is omitted in some MSS, and one may conjecture that Rav's only saying
was that Persia would fall into the hands of Rome, and that the subsequent comment were added by others. The *beraita* would indicate that both of the statements,
allegedly said by Rav, were harmonized into a single teaching later on.

[2] Compare the prayer of Mordecai, *Esther R.* 8. 6, "It is fully known before thy
glorious throne . . . that it was not from pride of heart . . . that I refused to bow
down to Haman, but through fear of thee . . . For who am I that I should not
bow down to Haman for the salvation of thy people Israel? *For that I would even
kiss his shoe-latchet.*"

[3] See *Dik. Sof.* II 15, I have followed the variant, 'Edom'=Rome, rather than
'Nakhri'. On the expression "If all the seas were ink" etc. see my *Life*, 26-7, and
27 n. 1. This expression was used by R. Johanan b. Zakkai and R. Eli‘ezer b.
Hyrcanus his student.

elaborate administration for the government of their empire. Rav thus reflected upon the change from the former easy and lax administration of the Arsacids. That these sayings are congruent to the earliest conditions of Sasanian rule cannot be doubted. Rav died in 247, according to Ge'onic tradition, and in any event he could not have lived beyond the time of Shapur. Shapur's reign was marked by a thorough revision of earlier policies, in favor of a more tolerant attitude toward all religions, including Judaism. Rav could not have made such comments, therefore, with reference to the reaction of Kartir, but only to the original policies of Ardashir and his court.

We have already noted that the repression of Judaism and other religions reflected the priestly origins of the Sasanian dynasty and its conviction that Persian success revealed the grace of Ohrmazd. Since Shapur shared that belief, but nevertheless pursued a very different policy, we must take account of a second important factor, namely, the political naiveté of the Sasanians and their lack of knowledge of the western satrapies in which many minority groups lived. Without experience in governing a heterogeneous population, the Sasanians could well conceive that the best policy was to repress minority cults in favor of their own, and to reward adherence to the state-church. If the minority groups had been very small and weak, such a policy of forced conversion would doubtless have won its goal, probably without too much bloodshed. Babylonia was not, however, a land of Iranian cultural predominance, for in it had flourished for centuries Greeks, as well as Syrians, Babylonians, Jews, and other Semites. The Iranian element, though powerful, confronted significant and numerous competing traditions. The unwillingness of these groups to submit to Mazdaism, and the inconvenience of pursuing a repressive policy over many generations, required a revision of the earliest attitudes, and this was, as we have seen, undertaken by Shapur. Yet Shapur himself revealed considerable inexperience when he took control of alien territories, for while invading Asia Minor and Syria, he behaved in such a cruel and destructive manner toward the local populations that he created allies for Rome and enemies for himself. If he had intended to build a permanent government in these territories, destroying the cities and enslaving the people would have thwarted such a policy. As it was, he wanted nothing more than plunder. At home, on the other hand, he sought to accommodate the minority cults and communities, and learning from the failure of his father's policies and impressed by the intransigence of the local communities, he sought and found another way. But he acted in Asia Minor just as did his father in Babylonia, and with just as little wisdom.

III. BABYLONIAN JEWS AND PERSIAN FOREIGN AFFAIRS

The Jews, who, in Parthian times, had participated in international affairs in ways highly useful to the Iranian government, became under the Persians mainly passive observers of events which affected them,

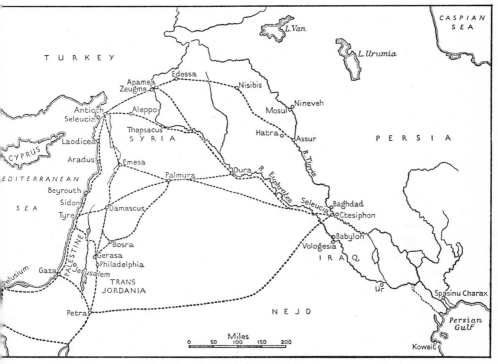

III. Trade routes of the Near East

but which they could not influence. So far as we know, the Sasanian chancellery never attempted to use Jewish influence in Syria and Palestine, either to stir up trouble in preparation for an invasion, or to subvert the existing government for long-term political purposes. The Parthians had certainly done the former, and probably the latter as well, not once but many times, in particular in the second century A.D. Three facts account for the change. First of all, as we have noted, the Jews themselves could not have wanted to be so employed, at least under Ardashir, because of both their hostility to the new regime, and its malevolence toward them. Second, the Sasanians, even under Shapur, did not engage in long-term preparations, over a period of years, for war with Rome. Their attacks, in annual campaigns, consisted of quick forays, mainly to seize booty and throw the Romans off balance, and for which extended preparations, including guerilla activity across the frontier, were thought unnecessary. The Persians' intention was not, as we have said, to establish a new empire west of the Euphrates, but to destroy an old one. They were uninterested in local public opinion. Their greatest successes were allowed to dissipate. The intricacies of international intrigue, at which they proved adept enough in Hatra, Antioch, Armenia, and elsewhere, interested them only for transient, military and tactical reasons. By contrast, the Parthians had attempted to stir up trouble in the west, including Palestine long before they mounted an invasion, and invariably used Jews for that purpose.

I think one may understand this contrast by recalling that the Parthians, in the first century B.C., had actually taken Jerusalem and intervened in domestic politics there. They therefore continued to interest themselves in Palestinian affairs, and understood how useful the Jews there, in Babylonia, and in Egypt as well, might be. In Babylonian politics, too, the Arsacids found, some to their profit, how significant was Jewish support. Ardavan III, for example, negotiated with the Jewish satrapy under Anileus and Asineus, and found timely, loyal friendship in newly-Judaized Adiabene, when he was pressed by his rival Gotarzes. Vologases I may well have established (or re-established) the exilarchate as a means of arranging the political affairs of his Jewish subjects. In the second century, the Jews of Babylonia, Mesopotamia, possibly Palestine, and certainly Egypt,[1] arose at a critical time to save the Parthians when the Romans stood at the gate of Ctesiphon, and several crises, later in the century, found the Jews actively engaged in support of the Arsacid throne. A third fact thus emerges, that the Parthians had a long tradition of dealing with the Jews, who constituted a major factor in western Asian politics in their day, and their experience led them most naturally to consider how they might make use of Jewish support in international affairs, and, when the throne was disputed, in local politics as well.

---

[1] See Y. Gutman, "Milḥemet HaYehudim bimei Trayanus", *Sefer Assaf* (Jerusalem 1953) 149-184.

For their part, as I said, the Sasanians could not have known a great deal about the Jews, or other peoples, in western Asia; they relied at the outset solely on Iranian, mainly Persian, armies, and probably did not have adequate knowledge of regional politics, as shown in the abortive effort to crown their own pretender in Antioch as Roman emperor, a gauche and futile gesture. It was, in the end, probably ignorance of international politics, rather than clear-headed decisions *not* to make use of potentially helpful groups in the west, which led to the neglect of the former alliance with the Jews. In local politics, the Sasanians did not need to depend upon the support of groups outside their own government to help them settle dynastic or local political questions, as had the Arsacids. As a result, while the Jews, along with others in the western satrapies, suffered from the economic and political unrest accompanying the wars of Ardashir and Shapur, and most grievously during Odenathus's invasion of Babylonia in 263, and while they witnessed and reflected upon great events, the movement of large armies, and the fall of ancient cities, they themselves were bystanders, and not actors, in decades of high drama.

The massing of armies and skirmishes of war created constant unrest on the western (Euphrates-Tigris) frontier, which was in any case always open to the incursions of Beduin, but particularly vulnerable in times of international unrest. A revealing example of what the arrival of armies, even friendly ones, meant for the local populace is provided by Samuel's report that when the king's forces came to town, they disturbed the rabbis, who in consequence could not say their prayers.[1] He added that the incident was a rare event, however, saying that in his entire life, he had never omitted a certain part of the liturgy,

---

[1] b. Ber. 30a-b, compare y. Ber. 4.6, where Samuel reports another such singular event when the exilarch's son died. See esp. L. Ginzberg, *Perushim veHiddushim Ba Yerushalmi* (N.Y. 1941, henceforward, *Perushim*) III, 410, who gives the text as follows: "In all my days I did not pray the Musaf prayer by myself in Nehardea excepting that day on which an army came to Nehardea, and everyone was distraught, and I prayed [it] by myself." Ginzberg holds that this came toward the end of Samuel's life, before the destruction of Nehardea by the Palmyrenes, though he accepts the date of R. Sherira for Samuel's death, a date I shall discuss below, pp. 48-51. He prefers the above reading to "the king's force", for Samuel and Shapur had good relations, and therefore it seems unreasonable to him to suppose that Shapur's troops would have disturbed the Jews. It is not unlikely, however, that whatever the attitude of the shah-an-shah to the Jews, his troops, wherever they went, would cause considerable commotion. The y. Ber. 4.6 reading in any event cannot be reconciled with that of b. Ber. 30a-b. See also S. Krauss, *Synagogale Altertümer* (Berlin, 1922), 218.

except on that one day, which was obviously particularly well remembered and widely known, as well as the day on which the exilarch's son died.

One should not, however, conclude that in Babylonia, times were peaceful, and punctuated only rarely by the tumult of war, for a number of legal discussions suggest that it was, in fact, quite a common occurrence for Jews to be taken captive, and held for ransom, by pagans. In the unrest accompanying constant foreign invasions, and the massing of armies, along a disputed frontier, the personal safety of individuals could not have been assured. Further, lying near the desert, Babylonia was always open to incursions from the west, and now, when the government's attention was diverted elsewhere, it may have been fairly easy for a raiding party to seize and hold captives for ransom. In any case, the legal implications of kidnapping were discussed in language reflecting the matter-of-fact quality of such events. For example, Rav and Samuel discussed how an adult, taken captive by pagans and isolated from Jewry, could know when the Sabbath day ought to be observed, one holding that he should count six days, from any one, and then observe the Sabbath, the other that the captive should observe any day as the Sabbath and then count six days.[1] Likewise both interpreted the Mishnah concerning one who forgets the very principle of Sabbath observance to apply to a child taken captive by gentiles, or to a proselyte who converted in the midst of gentiles.[2] It is reasonable to suppose that the former, if not the latter, was a relatively frequent event, justifying the application of a general Mishnaic law to such a specific, and in normal conditions, remote circumstance.[3] Furthermore, Rav and Samuel frequently discussed legal issues posed by the captivity of men, women, and children. If, for instance, a man was taken captive, his next of kin was authorized to enter his estate, according to Samuel, but not Rav, though Samuel held that if he left home voluntarily, on a commercial venture, and was afterward taken captive, his next-of-kin was not so authorized.[4] Samuel possessed a slave, moreover, who was carried off and ransomed.[5] His father, Abba b. Abba, who took charge of the ransoming of slaves in Nehardea (a regular communal

---

[1] Y. Shab. 7.1.
[2] b. Shab. 68a. See also b.Yev. 16a, and Obermeyer 133.
[3] Compare b. Ket. 26b.
[4] b. B. M. 38b, 39a.
[5] b. Git. 38a

office), discussed with Rav, according to the following source, the status of Jewish women who had been ravished by their captors:

> Samuel's Father ruled, The wife of an Israelite who had been outraged is forbidden to her husband, since the act begun under compulsion may have terminated with consent. Rav objected to Samuel's Father, [Is it not written in the marriage contract] 'If you are taken captive I will ransom you and take you again as my wife'? He remained silent. Rav thereupon applied to Samuel's Father the text (Job 29.9), 'The princes refrained from talking and laid their hand on their mouth.'
>
> (b. Ket. 51b)

That these discussions were not merely theoretical, but were elicited by circumstance, is suggested by the fact that Samuel's own daughters were taken captive and carried away to Palestine, according to the following source:

> Certain women were brought as captives to Nehardea. Samuel's Father placed watchmen over them [to guard them until they might be ransomed]. Samuel said to him, Who watched over them until now? He replied, If they had been your daughters, would you have spoken of them so lightly? It was 'as an error which proceeds from before the ruler' [Koh. 10.5]. The daughters of Mar Samuel were taken captive, and brought to the land of Israel. They had their guards remain outside, and entered the academy of R. Ḥanina. One said, I was taken captive, but I am pure [undefiled], and the other said, I too was taken captive, but am pure. So they permitted them [to marry]. Then the captors entered [to claim ransom]. R. Ḥanina thereupon said, They are the children of a sage [for they knew how to state a claim which would be accepted, for she who testifies to her own injury and claims further to be undefiled is believed]. It became clear that they were the daughters of Mar Samuel. R. Ḥanina thereupon said to R. Shaman b. Abba, Go and take care of your relatives [marry one of them, R. Shaman may have been son of Abba b. Abba, and hence uncle of the daughters of Samuel]. Said he to R. Ḥanina, But there are witnesses abroad [to testify that they were in captivity, and hence their own testimony is not decisive] . . .
>
> (b. Ket. 23b)

It stands to reason that Samuel's daughters were taken captive at a time in which they would have been brought to Palestine, rather than to their home in Babylonia, for ransom. The captors would have done so because, in fact, they could not do business in Babylonia. It seems to me that these conditions prevailed in the Palmyrene invasion. Having invaded the region in 263, Odenathus held on to it only briefly, as part of his ephemeral empire stretching from the Euphrates to the Nile. When he took and destroyed Nehardea, he doubtless held many captives for ransom, including Samuel's daughters, who lived there. Shortly afterward, however, Shapur drove the Palmyrenes out of the capital region. Hence they would have brought Jewish captives to Palestine for ransom, not to Babylonia, and among them were Samuel's daughters. (The earlier incident, to which the source refers, should be dated before ca. 235, when Samuel's Father died.) Abba b. Abba's discussions with both Rav and Samuel suggest that captivity of Jews, among others, by marauders, could not have been uncommon, while Samuel's reference to 'that day' implies that actual military operations took place in Babylonia only very seldom. Both facts conform to the situation of Babylonia in this period. On the one hand, from earliest times there was continuous infiltration from the western wilderness,[1] and it was not uncommon for small bands to cross over briefly, seize booty, and retreat to the desert. In times of trouble, this frontier was lightly defended, and easily accessible, for theaters of war were in the north and west. On the other hand, except for Severus Alexander's abortive invasion of 231, and again Odenathus's of 263, Babylonia itself was not a battleground.

While the Babylonian Jews did not easily reconcile themselves to Sasanian rule, on the other hand, they clearly favored the Iranians over the Romans, a very ancient attitude, and, moreover, in Shapur's time, the government began to solicit their support. The reason for preferring Iranian to Roman ascendancy has nothing to do with local patriotism. Rome remained associated in the Babylonian Jewish mind with the destruction of Jerusalem and its Temple in 70, with the devastation of Judea in 132-135, and with the maintenance of pagan rule over the Holy Land. Babylonian Jewish opinion was not affected by the comparative benevolence of the 3rd century Palestinian regime, nor by the influence of the patriarchate, which in Palestine itself sedulously supported the Roman regime, and ruled the Jews with the support of the Roman provincial administration. Divorced from local circumstances as they were, Babylonian Jews could see in Rome only the destroyers of the Temple. According to Saul Lieberman,[2] R. Abbahu, a contemporary Palestinian, enigmatically announced that the 'Jewish account' with Edom (Rome) would be settled by Natrona, basing his comment on Ex. 12.6, and playing on the name Shapur (ŠMWR/ŠBWR). The same rabbi held that God would take

---

[1] See A. Leo Oppenheim, *Ancient Mesopotamia* 37 f. for the earlier period.
[2] S. Lieberman, in *JQR* n.s. 37, 1, 1946, 32-4.

vengeance on Bozrah for supplying Rome with a new emperor after
kingship had been uprooted from 'Edom,' referring to the Philippi.
Likewise, according to N. Krochmal, the following passage indicates
that Shapur solicited Jewish support:

> King Shapur said to Samuel, You maintain that the Messiah will
> come upon an ass (Zech. 9.7). I will rather send him a white horse of
> mine! He replied, Have you a steed of a hundred colors?
>
> (b. Sanh. 98a)[1]

One cannot determine whether this story has a historical basis.
It conforms, however, to what Shapur should have done. Coming
to power after the zealous enthusiasm of the early years of conquest
had worn off, Shapur came to a more perceptive assessment of the
ethnic realities of his empire than had the earliest Sasanian government
under his father. Part of his policy, as we have seen, was to encourage
a great variety of cultures and religions to flourish within his empire.
Likewise he cultivated in Manichaeism a faith which might serve as a
unifying force within his disparate empire. In dealing with the Jews,
while he did not, apparently, make extensive use of their trouble-
making potential on the Roman side of the frontier, Shapur determined
to conciliate the Jews to his regime, and successfully did so. Evidence
of this is to be derived from the following:

> ... When they informed Samuel that King Shapur had slain 12,000
> Jews in Caesarea-Mazaca, he did not rend his clothes .... And is it
> a fact that King Shapur killed Jews? For King Shapur said to Samuel,
> May evil befall me if I have ever slain a Jew! For there it was they [the
> Jews] who had brought it upon themselves, for R. Ammi said, The
> noise of the harpstrings of Caesarea-Mazaca burst the wall of Laodicea.
>
> (b. M.Q. 26a)

While, of course, we cannot know whether Shapur said any such
thing to Samuel, it is quite certain that the Jews believed he did, and
equally certain that Shapur and his government attempted to win
over the support of their Jewish subjects, and succeeded in the effort.
Samuel, for his part, would not have permitted public mourning in
memory of the enemies of Persia, in the hour of Shapur's greatest
triumph. Such mourning, had it taken place, would have permanently
estranged Jewry from the Sasanian government, and placed the Jews
in a position similar to that of the Christians under Shapur II, a
group thought to be allied to the empire's greatest enemy. On the
other hand, I am not convinced that Shapur's alleged attempt to

---

[1] HeHaluz I, 83.

'assist,' or at least exploit Jewish messianic hopes had any basis in fact. As I have noted, the Sasanians ignored, or knew nothing about, the possible support to be derived from elements of Palestinian Jewry, and neither prepared the road for their armies by subversion across the frontier, except by temporary, tactical devices, nor were seriously interested in building a permanent empire across the Tigris-Euphrates frontier. There is no precedent, therefore, for such an effort to ingratiate themselves to the Jews by taking action in support of Jewish messianism, the political importance of which had been demonstrated time and again. Moreover, Samuel, for his part, tended to 'spiritualize' the messianic hope, as we shall see below. The story of offering a white steed in place of a humble ass, and of Samuel's rather sarcastic reply, has a very different point from that which Krochmal discerned. It demonstrated, rather, the foolishness and incomprehension of a pagan emperor like Pharaoh or Ahasueros. One does not honor the Messiah by improving upon biblical precepts, and only a naive monarch would try. (We shall return to Samuel and Shapur's relationship below, section vi.)

The date of the siege of Caesarea-Mazaca has been much discussed.[1]

---

[1] See especially W. B. Henning, "The Great Inscription of Sapur I", *BSOS* 9, 1939, 823-49, esp. 835-41. Compare A. Christensen, *CAH* XII, 128-137, who holds (133-4) that the siege was in 256, but that the city was taken only after the capture of Valerian, following the *KZ*. See also Krauss, *Paras*, 214-5, H. Graetz in *MGWJ* 1852, 512, D. Hoffmann, *Mar Samuel*, 48, Salo Baron, *Social and Religious History*, II, 397, n. 7; G. Alon, *Toldot HaYehudim* II, 166-7; David Magie, *op. cit.*, Appendix I, 1560, n. 12; A. T. Olmstead, "The Mid-Third Century of the Christian Era", *Classical Philology* 37, 1942, 241-62, 398-420, who holds that the first invasion was in June, 251, and extended to Caesarea Mazaca, but that that particular attack was not by Shapur himself, and hence Olmstead s views cannot be cited in support of the Talmudic account as we have it. See also Saul Lieberman, *op. cit.*, 34-6. Lieberman points out that R. Yoḥanan, in Palestine, did in fact rend his garments at the tragic news from Cappadocia. He remarks (35 n. 323) that the story about the splitting of the wall of Laodicea is a legend; as to the dream of Shapur which Samuel interpreted, Lieberman says that it sounds like an echo of what, in fact, Shapur did to Valerian. In any event, since Shapur took Caesarea Mazaca in 260, Lieberman states, "We probably have here a pseudepigraphic anecdote", while in the text he states, "Since Samuel died in 254 . . . the event must have taken place before that year, and there is no reason to doubt the information provided by the rabbis." In a letter (November 24, 1961), Professor Lieberman wrote me that he regards it as unlikely that in the earlier invasion of Cappadocia, Shapur took Caesarea-Mazaca, but "It is most probable that the Roman army fought Shapur at that time near Caesarea. It appears that many Jews from Caesarea took part in the battle. Since in this respect the report of Rav Sherira can hardly be questioned there is no alternative but to come to the conclusion I came to."

Christensen and Olmstead hold that Shapur invaded Asia Minor in ca. 251, and besieged, but did not take, the city at that time. W. B. Henning states that the invasion of Cilicia and Cappadocia took place, and only could have taken place, after the defeat of Valerian and consequent collapse of Roman power in the Middle East, in 260. At that point, and then alone, Shapur made a violent attack upon Syria and Asia Minor, devastated Antiochia, ravaged Cilicia and Cappadocia, took Tarsus, and, after a protracted siege, Caesarea (*KZ* 1.23). The Cappadocian capital did not surrender, and, during the months-long siege, Shapur sent raiding parties into the surrounding country as far as Tyanitis and Lycaonia to the northeast. The reason the date is important for our study is that Ge'onic sources, both the *Letter of R. Sherira* and the *Seder Tanna'im ve'Amora'im*, date Samuel's death at 254/5. Some historians have therefore held that the account of his comment on the siege is pseudepigraphic, or that (preferably) it refers to "some earlier battle at Caesarea-Mazaca," following the chronology of Olmstead and Christensen.[1] I find the latter alternative impossible, for even though one admits that Shapur besieged Caesarea-Mazaca in 251, or at any time before 260, such a siege, which did not succeed in breaching the walls of the town, even according to those who hold there was such a siege in the first place, could not have resulted in the massive slaughter of Jews, among others, such as Samuel refused to mourn. Only capturing the city could have led to great carnage among the inhabitants. It is, on the other hand, equally unsatisfactory to postulate that Samuel's words are pseudepigraphic, for they conform to everything we know of his attitude and policy toward the Persians, and are most reasonably to be ascribed to him. The date of R. Sherira for this and other 3rd century matters has long stood inviolable. I believe it must be rejected, if, as in this instance, it contradicts evidence of literary and archaeological sources far closer in time to the events under study than R. Sherira himself. (R. Sherira's date for the fall of Nehardea to "Papa bar Naẓer," 259, is equally impossible, for the Palmyrene siege, the only invasion of Babylonia during these years by a very large force which could have destroyed a major town, took place at the earliest in 263. We shall return to this matter below, p. 49-51). G. Alon argues[2] that the Talmudic tradition is "additional proof" of a Persian invasion

---

[1] Cited above, p. 46 n.1.
[2] *Toldot HaYehudim* II 167.

in 251. But the Talmud contains no such tradition; it states only that
Samuel refused to mourn the Fall of Caesarea-Mazaca. It does not
say *when* Samuel died. A Ge'onic responsum six centuries later does.
That hardly constitutes proof of anything at all, and under the circumstances, must be rejected. I have no doubt whatever that Samuel
said the words ascribed to him, of an event in 260, and probably
lived for a short time afterward, perhaps to the invasion of Odenathus
in 263, when he would have perished and his daughters been made
captive.

In any event, while the Babylonian Jews by Shapur's time favored
victory for their sovereign, they were mostly excluded from international political life, except as onlookers and occasionally as victims.
The peoples of the Roman Orient, including the Jewish diaspora,[1]
were forced by the character of the Iranian invasions to fight for
their lives, and hence for Rome, and whether it was out of love for
Rome or fear of Persia hardly matters. It seems fair to conclude
that the original failure of Ardashir to win over his Jewish subjects,
if only because of their past and potential usefulness, deprived the
Sasanians of the counsel and the support of a very effective group.
For one thing, the Jews might have helped the Sasanians to see their
western razzias as something more than mere invasions for booty;
they might have fostered at Ctesiphon a greater conception of western
empire than prevailed there, with the result that the Sasanian armies
might have behaved in a manner calculated to win local support,
instead of driving the local peoples, however disaffected from Roman
rule, as some most certainly were, back into the arms, and armies,
of Rome. On the other hand, Shapur's effort to win over the Jewish
group was merely part of a broader policy of cultural and religious
accomodation, necessitated by the ethnic facts of the western satrapies,
and facilitated by the cooling of the fiery religious enthusiasm of the
early years. But it was not, any more than the early persecutions,
directed specifically toward the Jews, and produced at best a more
satisfactory accommodation, rather than a vigorous alliance as under
the Parthians.

As Shapur retreated from Asia Minor to Babylonia, he was harassed
by Odenathus of Palmyra, but, as we noted, this harassment could
not have seriously impeded him, for he brought back a great number
of prisoners and vast stores of booty, as well as his army. His successful

---

[1] *Ibid.*

return indicates how vastly exaggerated are the accepted accounts of Odenathus's exploits against the Persians in their desert retreat.[1] Odenathus, however, mounted a major invasion down the Euphrates, intending to take and hold Characene, and thereby to open the Indian and Far Eastern markets to Palmyrene trade.[2] Not merely a raid, Odenathus's campaign followed the usual invasion route, via Edessa, Carrhae, and Nisibis. Odenathus proceeded southeastward, pillaged the neighborhood of Ctesiphon, and besieged, but did not take, the capital, probably in 263 but no earlier than 262. He was forced to turn to other fronts, and at the same time, Shapur rallied his forces and relieved the siege of Ctesiphon. As we noted, according to R. Sherira,[3] Papa b. Nazer, who is identified with Odenathus[4] destroyed the town of Nehardea, and consequently Samuel's students were forced to establish their academy elsewhere. While it is possible that the razing of Nehardea was merely an act of brigandage, I think it was not accidental but quite intentional, for Nehardea was the center not only of Jewish religion and culture, but also of the activities of Jewish merchants. Samuel's Father, for instance, who made his home in Nehardea, was a trader in silk, and took his place in the international pattern of commerce in that commodity, and probably others as well.[5] Gagé points out (p. 149) that toward 235, Palmyra lost the special protection of Roman emperors and at the same time, was deprived by Ardashir of its lower Mesopotamian trading facilities:

> On a pu supposer que ces diverses raisons expliquaient justement, la brusque militarisation des institutions de Palmyre, qui se révèle à partir de 261 avec le pouvoir local d'un Odeïnath ...

Since their invasion of Babylonia was motivated by economic, perhaps more than political, reasons, it is quite likely that the Palmyrenes, who lived by commerce, and competed with Jewish merchants, among others, took the occasion of their temporary military ascendancy in Babylonia to wipe out the competition of Babylonian Jewish merchants.

We have noted the difficulty in R. Sherira's date for the destruction of Nehardea. He says that 'Papa bar Nazer' destroyed the town in

---

[1] Henning, *BSOS* 9, 842.
[2] Février, *Politique*, 80-88.
[3] Ed. Levin 82.
[4] Alon, *op. cit.* II 170 n. 40. See also Lieberman, *op. cit.*, 38 n. 345.
[5] See Vol. I, 88-94.

Ann. Sel. 570 (=258/9). The conventional view, which we have no reason to challenge, associates Bar Naẓer with Odenathus, as that name was carried by Odenathus's eponymous ancestor. Graetz emends Sherira's letter to *Seleucid year* 572 (= 261). Alon keeps to the earlier date, but rejects the identification of Odenathus with Papa b. Naẓer, though holding that the family would have been the same. Alon here follows the view of S. Funk,[1] who thinks that the reason for the destruction of the Jewish town was the friendship of its inhabitants for Shapur's army, on the basis of the following:

> An army once came to Nehardea, and R. Naḥman [a student of Samuel] told his disciples, Go out into the marsh and prepare an embankment, so that tomorrow [the Sabbath] we may go there and sit on them.

(b. ʿEruv. 34b)

All that the above account indicates is that the scholars expected that they should be unable to meet in their usual place, and hence prepared in advance of the Sabbath an alternate place for their studies. It proves absolutely nothing about the attitude of the students to the otherwise unspecified army, nor of course do we know whose 'army' it was to begin with, nor when it came to Nehardea. In any event, I think it completely impossible for a Palmyrene army to have destroyed a large town in Babylonia before 260, in which year the Palmyrenes besought Persian friendship, and at which time the Persian armies were at the height of their power and prestige. It was one thing for marauding bands to snatch a few people for ransom, but quite another to invade a territory at the heart of the western satrapies and destroy a major population center in it. This could have happened only when the Palmyrenes mounted a full-scale invasion, with a large army, and at a propitious time, and that invasion took place, all sources agree, in 263 and no earlier. Hence the view of Funk and Alon must be rejected, for it ignores the military and political realities of the Sasanian empire at this time, the known policy of the Palmyrenes before 260, and the accepted chronology of events, merely in order to retain a date from a very late and otherwise hardly reliable Ge'onic tradition. Whether Papa bar Naẓer was in fact Odenathus, or was a relative of his, of course we cannot say for certain, but it does not affect the facts as we have them.

---

[1] *Die Juden*, 75-6. Compare H. Graetz, "Die talmudische Chronologie und Topographie", *MGWJ* 1, 1852, 509f., in particular 519-20: Rav founded Sura in 219, died in 247; Samuel died in 257, Papa b. Naẓer dates to 259.

Odenathus's rule extended over Palestine as well. One might have expected that he would have been well received there, for Palmyra had a significant Jewish population, and Odenathus's wife, Zenobia, was reputed by Christians to favor Judaism. However the Jews rejected his rule so far as they could, and compared Odenathus to the little horn in the vision of Daniel, to which reference was repeatedly made in the exegesis of this period:

> 'And behold, there came up among them another horn, a little one' (Dan. 8.9)—this refers to Ben Naẓer, 'before which three of the first were uprooted'—this refers to Macrianus, Carus, and Cyriades.
>
> (Gen. R. 76.6)

Professor Saul Lieberman points out that the Jews regarded Odenathus as an agent of Rome, "My brother that advances upon me on behalf of Esau."[1] If I am correct in my interpretation of the Palmyrene destruction of Nehardea, then one may discern a second factor in the Jewish antipathy toward Odenathus. His actions in Babylonia would have adversely affected the economy of those Palestinian Jews who were in partnership with the Babylonians. In any event, Palestinian Jewry rejoiced at the downfall of Odenathus and Zenobia, whom they reviled.[2]

It is quite possible that the Palmyrene invasion of Babylonia produced a major religious-legal change, for, Halevi[3] suggests, as a

---

[1] *JQR op. cit.* 37 n. 341.

[2] See M. Avi-Yonah, *Bimei Roma uVizantion* (Jerusalem, 1952) 81-3. On the Jewish view of Odenathus and Zenobia, see for example b. Ket. 51b, where Ben Naẓer is referred to as a highwayman by comparison to a great king, but as king by comparison to robbers; b. Yev. 16a-17a, R. Yoḥanan's view on whether proselytes from Tadmor (Palmyra) may be accepted or not. See also Z. Yavetz, *Toldot*, VII, 112-3; Ensslin, *op. cit.*, 73-85; Herzfeld, *op. cit.* 83-4; C. Clermont-Ganneau, "Odeinat et Vaballat", *Revue Biblique* 29, 1920, 382f.; H. Graetz, *Die Königreich Mesene* (Breslau 1873), 32f., who points out that the Jews regarded Palmyra as a settlement of slaves, dating from the time of Solomon, and accused its inhabitants of having profited from the destruction of Jerusalem. See also Baron, *op. cit.*, II, 397, n. 7, 407, n. 43; and S. Ochser, "Zenobia and Septimia", *JE* XII, 660, and his "Palmyra", *JE* IX, 507; and J. Février, *Essai sur l histoire politique et économique de Palmyre* (Paris 1931) 79f.; A. Alföldi, *CAH* XII 174f. and J. Starcky, *Palmyre* (Paris 1952) 53f.; also K. H. Ziegler, *Beziehungen*, 143-4; Gagé, *op. cit.*, 157f.

[3] I. Y. Halevi, *Dorot* I, v. 698-704. Halevi holds that from the exile in 586, Babylonian Jews separated the necessary offerings. He cites the following saying of R. Yoḥanan (y. Ḥallah 4.4):
Our rabbis in the Exile used to separate heave-offerings and tithes until the *RWBYN* came to Babylonia and suspended them. Who are the *RWBYN*? TRGMWNY'.

result of their depredations, Babylonian Jewry was so impoverished that it became necessary to annul the separation of heave-offerings and tithes, and to permit common people to keep the portion of their depleted crops which formerly had been given to the priests.

IV. JUDAISM AND THE SASANIANS: (A) MESSIANISM

Judaism's response to historical events of a cataclysmic character normally takes two forms, first, renewed messianic speculation, and second, a search in Scripture for relevant ideas, attitudes, and historical paradigms. Between the destruction of the Jerusalem Temple in 70 and the rise of Islam six centuries later, no event bore greater significance, nor made a deeper impact upon the Babylonian Jews' consciousness, than the rise of Sasanian power and the concomitant establishment of Mazdaism. Hence we shall consider third century Messianic sayings, and below (section v) examples of Scriptural exegesis, to examine aspects of how Judaism met the challenges of this period.

Believing that the end of days, which must surely come, will be hastened by the advent of a new world-empire, the Jews' attention turned once again to the character of the Messianic age, the conditions that would precurse its coming, and the time of its arrival. In Palestine, in the second and third centuries, the Messianic hope underwent a radical transformation;[1] formerly offering an activist, military

---

The explanation of this passage may depend upon the variant, DWBYN, that is, bears, to whom the Persians were repeatedly compared (as b. Qid. 72a). Thus R. Yoḥanan held the Persians responsible for the abrogation of the agricultural offerings, just as he regarded their advent in general as calamitous (b. Yev. 63b, cited above p. 28). Halevi, however, cites discussion among the Amoraim about giving such offerings, and he holds these discussions indicate that they were separated after the advent of the Persians. He proposes that TRGMWNY' be read TRMWDY', Tadmorites, or Palmyrenes. He also explains 'rubin' from 'archers' (RWBH QŠT), on the basis of descriptions of the Palmyrenes which include reference to their ability as archers, rather than Dubin, Persians. He holds that the great destruction brought by the Palmyrene invasion necessitated a liberalization of agricultural taxes, though afterward the practice of tithing was restored. I find his conjecture quite reasonable, though I doubt that the offerings were restored later on. On the *rubin* as Palmyrenes, see also Ber, *op. cit.*, 11 n. 366; compare Zuri, *Rav.*, 92 n. 57; Ginzberg, *Perushim*, I, xxiii, the cessation of terumot was due to the third century wars, and compare III, 65, on the annulment of tithing, where Ginzberg accepts the identification of rubin/Tadmoraya with the Palmyrene invasion. See also S. Funk, I. 50.

[1] See N. N. Glatzer, "The Attitude toward Rome in Third-Century Judaism", *Politische Ordnung und Menschliche Existenz. Festgabe für Erich Vögelin* ed., Alois Dempf et al. (Munich 1962), 243-57. See also my "Religious Uses of History", *History and Theory* V, 2, 1966, 153-171.

program of subversion of Roman rule, it now constituted an irenic and spiritualized, mostly passive expectation. In the new formulation, as evidenced in the sayings of R. Yoḥanan, Roman power was seen as irresistible; her dominion would continue indefinitely; and those who undertake to oppose her rule prematurely and disastrously hasten the redemption, in a form no one could really desire. Such a formulation, running quite counter to the political and military realities of the middle third-century, was in its way just as hopelessly unrealistic as the former one. Rav and Samuel both tended to encourage a quietistic policy, with far better reason. Babylonian Jews could not have sustained a war against the Sasanian regime; as a minority, they could not long dominate any substantial territories, nor did they possess natural allies in the region. Moreover, there was no reason, in current messianic thought, for a diaspora community to rebel against its pagan ruler; such an action could have no bearing whatever upon the messianic process. Neither politics nor religion, therefore, justified a contrary attitude. Both Rav and Samuel interpreted temporal disasters in such a way as to bank the fires of messianic fervor, and mainly direct the attention of Israel to prayer, and to its own spiritual condition as the means for meriting, and thus hastening, the coming of the messiah. This attitude had characterized Pharisaic-Tannaitic Judaism from the time of R. Yoḥanan ben Zakkai, who held, after the destruction of the Temple, that if Israel obeyed the will of their father in heaven, then no nation or race could rule over them, and that the means of reconciliation in the new age, replacing the destroyed sanctuary and its sacrifices, was prayer, study of Torah, and pursuit of deeds of loving kindness.[1] By the early third century, these ideas met no significant competition in rabbinic circles, though as we have noted (volume I pp. 73-82) in the second century, messianic expectations were directed by R. Simeon b. Yoḥai (as formerly, by R. Akiba) into more violent paths.

An example of the spiritualization and ethicization of messianism is found in the following saying of Samuel:

> 'And the host was given over to it together with the continual burnt-offering through transgression' (Dan. 8.12) . . . Through the transgression of the Torah. 'And truth was cast to the ground.' When Israel cast the words of Torah to the ground the pagan kingdom decrees and succeeds [in carrying out its decree]. What is the reason? 'And truth was cast down to the ground, and the horn acted and

---

[1] See my *Life* 129-146.

prospered.' And truth is none other than Torah as it is said (Prov.
23.23) 'Buy the truth and sell it not.'

(y. R.H. 3.8, compare Lam. R. Proem II)

The reference to the 'little horn' and its growing prosperity recalls
the saying, cited above, of R. Yoḥanan that the 'little horn' refers
to Odenathus, from whose depredations the Jews suffered grievously.
Assuming that Samuel understood the image of Daniel in a similar
way, we may discern here a sermon to the stricken Jews of Babylonia,
that the prosperity of the 'little horn' is accounted for by the failure
of the Jews satisfactorily to hearken to the 'words of Torah.' It is
striking, if this interpretation is valid, that the Jews were more
disturbed by the Palmyrene success, which directly affected their
welfare, than by that of the Sasanians, to whom no similar references
were made. (This would, furthermore, be an additional indication
that Samuel was alive after 254, the date ascribed to his death by
Ge'onic tradition, for not before 262-263 was Palmyra a major
threat to Babylonian Jewry.) The only direct reference to Sasanian,
success, that of R. Shila cited above, contained no such specific
reference to suffering at the hands of pagans but caused by Jewish
wrong-doing, but rather a generalized 'scheme of history' intended
merely to reassure the people that in the end, things would work out.
The saying of a later teacher, R. Papa (ca. 300-375), conveys the spirit
of Samuel's dictum:

> When the haughty cease to exist in Israel, the Magi shall cease.
> When the judges cease to exist in Israel, the *gezirpati*[1] [= chiliarchs
> or, court-officers] shall cease.

(b. Shab. 139a, Sanh. 98a)

This saying, based on Zephaniah 3.15, transformed an unconditional
messianic promise into a conditional one: if this will happen, then
the other shall surely come. Likewise Rav explained that it was the
sins of the people that caused them to lose their property to the state,
rather than any metaphysical disjuncture, and hence it would be
better to improve their moral life if they wished to alter their historical
condition.[2] In these teachings, the natural longing of the people for a
better age was diverted from political to moral realities, and so

---

[1] On *Gezirpati* as *Hazarapat*, see Christensen, *L'Iran*, 314-7, and compare
Krauss, *Paras*, 146-7, and *Arukh* 9, 118-9, Geiger explains it as gendarme, with
several subsidiary meanings, but mainly, in Talmudic contexts, as agents of a
court, sheriffs or bailiffs. Compare Sprengling, *Third Century Iran*, 31.

[2] b. Suk. 29b.

divested of any subversive potentialities. Likewise, Rav and Samuel debated what would bring the Messiah:

> Rav said, All the predestined dates [for redemption] have passed and the matter [now] depends only on repentance and good deeds. But Samuel maintained, It is sufficient for a mourner to keep his mourning.
>
> (b. Sanh. 97b)

Samuel's saying meant that living in exile warrants redemption, regardless of repentance. What is important here is that for neither teacher is repentance dependant on the coming of a specific 'day of the Lord,' but rather upon simply continuing, in penitence or not, to *endure*. The exchange is, moreover, an echo of a dispute between R. Eli'ezer b. Hyrcanus and R. Joshua a century and a quarter earlier:

> R. Eli'ezer said, If Israel acts penitently, they will be redeemed, and if not, they will not be redeemed, and R. Joshua said to him, If they do not act penitently, they will not be redeemed, but [nonetheless] the Holy One blessed be He, will set up for them a king whose decrees will be as harsh as those of Haman, and Israel will do penance and he will restore their fortune.
>
> (b. Sanh. 97b, presented as the basis of the above discussion)

It is no accident that Rav and Samuel should pursue this conversation, available to them from Tannaitic tradition, for the reference to setting up a king as harsh as Haman adumbrates the view, which we shall offer below, that the Book of Esther, about an earlier 'Ardashir' and how the Jews were saved from his hand, possessed particular relevance for the Jews of this period, and that they read it in order to find out the meaning of their own day.

Samuel warned, moreover, that the Messiah's coming would be heralded by great catastrophes:

> R. Zera said that R. Jeremiah b. Abba stated, In the generation in which the son of David will come, there will be a persecution of the scholars. When I repeated this statement before Samuel, he exclaimed, Test after test, for it is said (Is. 6.13), 'And if there be yet a tenth part of it, it shall again be eaten up.'
>
> (b. Ket. 112b)

Samuel's teaching emphasized that the Messianic time would come only after great suffering, and hence ought not to be too eagerly awaited. At the same time he taught that the difference between this world and the Messiah's time would only be in respect to subjugation to [pagan] governments.[1] This saying, based on Deut. 15.11, that

---

[1] b. Pes. 68a, Shab. 63a, based on Deut. 15.11, and b. Ber. 34b.

the poor shall never cease out of the land, underlined his view that the "golden age" would not be an age of either economic abundance or miraculous healing. By contrast, Rav's sayings on the Messianic age emphasized that conditions of life would radically change for the better. Thus he said that the wild trees in the land of Israel will bear fruit (basing his saying on Joel 2.22);[1] that the Jews are destined to eat their fill in the days of the Messiah;[2] and that the future world will be utterly different from the present one:

> A favorite saying of Rav was, The future world is not like this world. In the future world there is no eating nor drinking, nor procreation, nor business, nor jealousy, nor hatred, nor competition, but the righteous sit with their crowns on their heads feasting on the brightness of the Divine Presence, as it says, 'And they beheld God and did eat and drink' (Ex. 24.11).
>
> (b. Ber. 17a)

Likewise, the righteous would resurrect the dead in that day.[3] Samuel discouraged public fasts, besides the 9th of Av,[4] for such fasts aroused the longing of the people for a better age and their hope that they might somehow act to achieve it. Rav for his part speculated on who the Messiah might be:

> If he is of the living, it would be Our Holy Master [= R. Judah the Prince], if of the dead, it would have been Daniel, the most desirable man. R. Judah said in the name of Rav: The Holy One, blessed be He, will raise up another David for us, as it is written, 'But they shall serve the Lord their God and David their king whom I *will* raise up unto them' (Jer. 30.9). Not, 'I raised up', but 'I will raise up.'
>
> (b. Sanh. 98b)

Here Rav emphasized that the Messiah would surely come, that he would be of the Davidic line, and that if he was alive, he was in fact R. Judah the Prince, scion of the Davidic line in Palestine. He would thus have excluded two other possibilities, first, that the Messiah was anyone other than a Davidide, living or dead, and second, that he was, if alive, anyone other than the patriarch himself. One recalls that Rav's uncle, R. Ḥiyya, had likewise applied to R. Judah the Prince a Scripture normally understood as referring to the

---

[1] b. Ket. 112b.

[2] b. Sanh. 98b.

[3] b. Pes. 68a. Zuri (*Rav*, 182) suggests that Rav's saying about no eating, drinking, etc. in the world to come represented a criticism of the Magi who said the contrary, but he does not cite such a saying from sources contemporary to Rav's life.

[4] b. Pes. 54b. Such is my interpretation, but it may have been for merely legal reasons.

Messiah.[1] We do not know who else was claiming to be the Messiah in this time. Specifically, there is no evidence that the Exilarch, to whom Rav and R. Ḥiyya were related, issued such a claim, or that messianic-zealots were the objects of Rav's saying. Nonetheless, I find it curious that Rav and R. Ḥiyya, both of whom had difficulties with the patriarch, should identify him as the Messiah. Rav certainly did *not* believe that the conditions pertaining to the Messianic age were present, for self-evidently eating, drinking, and the other activities supposed to cease later on were actually going on quite normally. Hence I cannot conclude that he actually believed the patriarch to be the Messiah, nor did anyone else. That some Jews, in both Palestine and Babylonia, accepted the Christian view that Jesus, another Davidide, was the Messiah is beyond doubt; Rav's saying may be part of a polemical tradition directed against Christianity[2] (though not against Mani, quite obviously, who never claimed to be 'the Messiah' in terms the Jews would find it necessary to refute).

The worldly relevance of Messianic aspirations cannot have escaped either teacher. In guiding Jewry toward a policy of passive acceptance of Sasanian rule, the drastic revision of messianic speculation in favor of a wholly uneschatological, nonapocalyptic, ethically-oriented formulation would certainly have served the purposes of Samuel, at the very least, who publicly cast doubt upon the desirability and imminence of the great age.

v. JUDAISM AND THE SASANIANS:
(b) PHARAOH AND AHASUEROS IN BABYLONIA

The biblical accounts of the early years of Moses (Exodus 1-3) and of the salvation of Israel in the time of Ahasueros were among the most important texts for Babylonian Judaism in this period. This fact is suggested by both literary and archaeological sources. On Exodus 1-3 and on Esther Rav and Samuel produced connected commentaries. The walls of the Dura synagogue indicate concentration of interest in these two narratives as well.

The Scroll of Esther tells the story of an earlier Ardashir[3] and of how he gave the Jews into the hands of Haman, a malevolent agent, just as Ardashir permitted the Magi under Tosar to mistreat the Jews.

---

[1] Vol. I, 106.
[2] See b. Taʿanit 20a, Jerusalem will be reinstated. Compare below p. 72.
[3] Ahasueros = Artaxerxes = Ardashir.

I could, at first, see no similarly striking relationship between Exodus 1-3 and events of this period, except for the obvious one that it is the account of the catastrophes that followed the rise of a 'new pharaoh' who knew not Joseph, just as the new *shahanshah*, who, so to speak, knew not Rav, persecuted Israel until they looked for salvation. A more direct connection between the two stories was discerned by Brevard S. Childs,[1] and it seems to me that the midrashic traditions dating from this period indicate that the rabbis saw a similar connection. Childs points out that a secondary development of the birth story of Moses applies the threat of Pharaoh to the whole people, as in Esther.[2] God does not appear in the story; everything has a natural cause, "Yet it is clear that the writer sees the mystery of God's providence through the action of the humans involved."[3] Pharaoh, like Haman, is a wicked fool, whose "cleverness misfires and reveals him as incredibly stupid." Like the mother of Moses, the Jews in the Esther story remained passive, with faith in the ultimate benevolence of God.

In the Dura synagogue, likewise, two important panels concern the birth of Moses and the Esther story.[4] The Esther story (Kraeling, Panel WC2) occupied a central place in the synagogue, at the left of the Torah shrine in the center of the west wall. The composition consists of two scenes, to be read from left to right, the first showing Mordecai mounted on Haman's steed, as a reward for having saved the life of Ahasueros, in the style of the imperial triumph and similar, Kraeling points out, to the triumph of Shapur later depicted at Nakhš-i Rajab. The second scene shows the king seated upon his throne, at the left the queen, and from his right a courtier advances holding an important document. These figures are identified by Aramaic tituli. Kraeling holds, correctly in my view, that the scene represents the action depicted in Esther 9.11-14, in which Esther asks for another day on which to punish the enemies of the Jews and the sons of Haman in Sushan itself. This would represent, also, the authorization of the festival of Purim. The scene Kraeling calls "Pharaoh and the Infancy of Moses" takes up the largest part of the

---

[1] B. S. Childs, "The Birth of Moses", *JBL* 84, 2, 1965, 109-122.

[2] See S. Talmon, "Wisdom in the Book of Esther", *Vetus Testamentum* 13, 1963 419f.

[3] Childs, *op. cit.*, 120.

[4] See Carl H. Kraeling, *The Synagogue* (N.H. 1956), in particular 151-164, 169-178.

north half of Register C on the west wall of the synagogue. In four scenes, in a single panel, is portrayed the entire story of the miraculous rescue of Moses. The group comprising the king and his courtiers is similar to that in the Esther panel; the king appears in the same apparel as Ahasueros and Mordecai, differently colored; two courtiers who appeared in the Mordecai and Esther panel reappear here, with other parallel representations. Kraeling holds that since the man at the left of Pharoah's throne is identical in pose and position with the comparable figure in the Esther panel, the two should represent one and the same official.[1] Other poses show analogies to the Esther panel as well. E. R. Goodenough[2] offers full interpretation of the paintings at hand. That interpretation, while of great interest, does not affect the subject of importance to us, for there is no question whatever about the identification of the figures in both panels.

The only comment on Exodus[3] which is directly germane to our inquiry is the following:

> Abitol the hairdresser in the name of Rav said, Pharoah in the time of Moses was a cubit tall, with a beard a cubit long, and his shock of hair (or, phallus[4]) was a cubit and a span, justifying what is said, 'And he setteth up over it the lowest of men' (Dan. 4.14). And he further said, Pharaoh in the time of Moses was a Magus, because it is said, 'Get thee unto Pharaoh in the morning, lo he goeth out into the water' (Ex. 7.15).
>
> (b. M.Q. 18a)

The reference to 'the lowest of men' was made, in Daniel, to Nebuchadnezzar. As we shall see, the rabbis compared Ahasueros to the same monarch, and quoted Isaiah 14, a passage referring to the 'king of Babylonia' who boasted arrogantly only to be brought low.

The immediate relevance of the Book of Esther is quite obvious. At every point, it stood as a testimony toward the new age, in which the fate of Jewry hung in the balance. Rav made this quite explicit:

> Rav opened his discourse [on the Scroll of Esther] with the text, 'And thy life shall hang in doubt before thee (Deut. 28.66).' Rav

---

[1] 171

[2] See E. R. Goodenough, *Jewish Symbols in the Greco-Roman Period*, IX. *Symbolism in the Dura Synagogue* (N.Y. 1964), 177-87, 197-227.

[3] A survey of other comments on these chapters is provided in Appendix I.

[4] Rav refers also to the PRMSTQ of Pharoah, here translated 'shock of hair". PRMSTQ=N. P. PRMASTK, see Levy IV, 118 and 229, *Arukh* VI, 430, IX 340. Geiger holds that the word is Iranian but after reviewing several explanations, says that its origin is unknown. The context of M. Q. would favor the meaning of *Arukh* VI 430.

interpreted the text as applying to [Israel in the time of] Haman. 'Thy life shall hang in doubt before thee'—this was for the twenty-four hours from the removal of the ring (Est. 3.10). 'And thou shalt fear night and day'—this was at the time when the letters sped forth. 'And thou shalt have no assurance of thy life'—this was when [the enemies of the Jews were told] that 'they should be ready against that day (Est. 3.14).'

(Esther R., Proem, 1, trans. Maurice Simon, [London, 1939], 1-2)

Likewise, Samuel interpreted the message of Esther:

Samuel opened with the text: 'And yet for all that when they are in the land of their enemies, I did not reject them, neither did I abhor them to destroy them utterly, to break my covenant with them, for I am the Lord their God' (Lev. 26.44). 'I did not reject them'—in Babylonia. 'Neither did I abhor them'—in Media. 'To destroy them utterly'—when subject to Greece. 'To break my covenant with them' —when subject to the wicked kingdom [Rome]. For I am the Lord their God'—in the Messianic era.

(Esther R. Proem 4, compare b. Meg. 11a)

Similarly, they interpreted Scripture to apply to the Persian crisis:

Rav and Samuel took each his text. Rav said, All the words of the Holy One blessed be He had reference to him [Ahasueros]. It is written, 'I will cut off from Babylon name and remnant and offshoot and offspring' (Is. 14.22). 'Name' refers to Nebuchadnezzar. 'Remnant' refers to Evil-merodach. 'Offshoot' refers to Belshazzar. And 'offspring' refers to Vashti . . . Samuel said, All the words of the Holy One, blessed be He, refer to him [Ahasueros]. It is written, 'And I will set my throne in Elam, and will destroy from thence king and princes' (Jer. 49.38). 'King' refers to Vashti. 'Princes' refers to the seven princes of Media and Persia.

(Esther R. Proem 11)

While earlier, the Scroll of Esther had not been easily admitted to the canon, nor was it cited by the community of Qumran, the Babylonian rabbis maintained that it was written under the inspiration of the holy spirit, at the request of Esther herself to the sages.[1] Samuel offered a proof of that fact from Esther 9.27, "They confirmed and took upon them," interpreting the text, "They confirmed *above* what they took upon themselves *below*."[2] There can be no doubt, moreover, that a coherent, continuous commentary by Rav and Samuel covered much of the book. Rav taught that it is permitted to exposit the text of the Scroll of Esther,[3] (as he said elsewhere that

---

[1] b. Meg. 7b.
[2] Ibid. see also Ruth R. 4.5, Esther was written on Mt. Sinai, and y. Ber. 9.5.
[3] y. Meg. 1.1.

the Book of Chronicles was given only for purposes of midrashic exposition, the obvious implication being that some thought neither book should be exposited). Relevant comments on the Esther-Scroll include the following:

And it came to pass [Wayehi] in the days of Ahasueros (1.1).

Rav said, The word *wayehi* is equivalent to *wai* and *hi*, woe and mourning.[1] With reference to this it is written, 'And there ye shall sell yourselves unto your enemies for bondmen and women and no man shall buy you' (Deut. 28.68).

(b. Meg. 11a)

Ahasueros: Rav said, He was [as name implies] the brother of the head and the counterpart of the head.

The brother of the head—brother of Nebuchadnezzar the wicked who was called head, as it is written, 'thou art the head of gold' (Dan 2.38). And the counterpart of the head—one slew, the other sought to slay, one laid waste, the other sought to lay waste, as it is written, 'And in the reign of Ahasueros, in the beginning of his reign, they wrote an accusation against inhabitants of Judah and Jerusalem' (Ezra 4.6). Samuel said, his name indicates that the face of Israel was blacked in his days like the sides of a pot (Hushharu).

(b. Meg. 11a)[2]

Who reigned—Rav said, This indicates that he *raised himself* to the throne [For it does not say, 'who was king']. From Hodu to Kush— Rav and Samuel, one said, Hodu is at one end of world, Kush at the other, and the other said, Hodu and Kush adjoin one another, and that the meaning is this, as he ruled over Hodu and Kush so he ruled from one end of the world to the other.

(b. Meg. 11a)

'On the 7th day, when the kings heart was merry with wine' (1.10). Was his heart not merry with wine until then? Rav said, The 7th day was the Sabbath when Israel eat and drink. They begin with discourse on the Torah and with words of thanksgiving. But the nations of the world, idolaters, when they eat and drink, only begin with words of frivolity. And so at the feast of that wicked one, some said, Median women are the most beautiful, and others said, Persian women are most beautiful. Said Ahasuerus to them, the vessel that I use is neither Median nor Persian but Chaldean. Would you like to see her? They said, Yes, but she must be naked.

(b. Meg. 12b, Compare Esther R. 3.13)

Another comment on 'Also Vashti the Queen' (1.9): Samuel opened with the text, 'With their poison [*behuman*, lit. 'their heat'] I will prepare their feast' (Jer. 51.29). Said the Holy One, blessed be He:' When

---

[1] See Vol. I, 157. This was an ancient Babylonian exegesis.

[2] See Bacher, *Agada*, 30 n. 197.

they come to warm themselves up with monarchy, I will destroy their foundations. And I will make them drunken with their troubles'. 'Because they exulted': because they rejoiced at the destruction of the Temple.' Said the Holy One, blessed be He: 'The Temple is in ruins and this wretch makes carousal!' The wicked Vashti also made carousal, as it is written, 'Also Vashti the Queen made a feast for the women' (1.9).

(Esther R. 3.3.)

'The Seven Princes of Persia and Media' (1.14). Rav and Samuel gave different explanations. Rav said that the text speaks of the kingdom of Ahasueros, whereas Samuel said that it speaks of the kingdom of Belshazzar. If we accept the view of Rav that it speaks of the kingdom of Ahasueros, there is no difficulty. But if we take the view of Samuel, who said that it speaks of the kingdom of Belshazzar, we have to ask, how could they have lived all those years? R. Huna said: It was because these abstained from making use of the vessels of the Sanctuary. So it is written, 'Belshazzar, while he tasted the wine, commanded to bring the . . . vessels.' (Dan. 5.2), and it was on that account that 'In that night Belshazzar the Chaldean king was slain' (*ib.* 30).

(Esther R. 4.3)

'And this day will the princesses of Persia and Media say . . . so will there arise enough contempt and wrath' (1.18). Rav and Samuel joined issue here. Rav said: The contempt shown fully merited the wrath displayed. Samuel said, The wrath displayed was fully equal to the contempt shown. R. Ḥanina said, The contempt shown by her father for the vessels of the Sanctuary fully merited the wrath visited upon her through which she was slain.

(Esther R. 4.8)

'Throughout all his kingdom, great though it be' (1.21). Rav and Samuel gave different interpretations. One said, This kingdom is great for this offence; the other said, This offence is great for this kingdom. 'All the wives will give to their husbands honour.'

(Esther R. 4.10)

'And Esther called Hatakh one of the king's eunuchs' (4.5). Rav said, Hatakh is the same as Daniel.[1] Why was he called Hatakh? Because he was degraded from his high position. Samuel said, 'Because all affairs of state were decided by his voice.'

'And Mordecai passed and did everything as Esther had ordered him' (4.17). Rav said, This indicates that he made the first day of Passover to pass as a fast day. Samuel said, This means that he crossed a stream on that day.[2]

(b. Meg. 15a, Compare Esther R. 8.6, on the prayer of Mordecai)

---

[1] See also b. B.B. 4a.

[2] Obermeyer, *Landschaft* 214 points out that the Jews of Susa were separated from the main city by a stream.

'And Haman recounted unto them ... and the multitude of his children' (5.11). How many? Rav said, Thirty, ten died, ten were hung, and twenty [sic] were reduced to beggary.

(b. Meg. 15b)

Another instance [of the twofold 'he said'] is, 'Then said the king Ahasueros and said unto Esther the queen' (Est. 7,5). Why is 'said' repeated? Rav said in the name of R. Ele'azar: Before the king detected that she was a Jewess, he used to speak with her in public; but when he became aware of it, he spoke to an intermediary and the latter spoke to Queen Esther.

(Lamentations R. 1.13.41)[1]

The converts to Judaism of Esther's day were held by Rav to be true proselytes, who should be accepted and won over to Judaism.[2] Many of the sayings on the Scroll of Esther bear more than exegetical significance, but rather represent comments, in an exegetical guise, upon the events of the day. Rav thus emphasized that the lives of the Jews were insecure, and called their attention to the Scriptures which place the blame for such suffering on the failure of the people 'to do all the words of this law which are written in this book.' Samuel, like R. Shila, emphasized the other part of the conditional contract, that no matter what might happen, the people must be assured that God has not rejected them, but should take heart. Ridiculing the anti-Semitic Ahasueros, they repeatedly compared him to the 'king of Babylonia' of Isaiah 14, who arrogantly threatened to climb to the heavens, and in the end was brought down to Sheol:

Those who see you will stare at you and ponder over you:
Is this the man who made the earth tremble, who shook kingdoms,
Who made the world like a desert and overthrew its cities,
Who did not let his prisoners go home?

(Is. 14.16)

Just as R. Yohanan ben Zakkai took comfort in Isaiah's ridicule of pagan pretentions at the time of the destruction of the Temple in 70,[3] so Rav saw this newest 'king of Babylon' as one who would, in the end, not even have an honorable burial nor a memorial afterward. Samuel, for his part, compared Ardashir/Ahasueros to the king of Elam, whose armies would be scattered and terrified before their enemies. Ardashir/Ahasuerus was further to be compared to Nebu-

---

[1] Compare Lev. R. 26.8 and Meg. 16a.
[2] y. Qid. 4.1.
[3] See my *Life* 98-9. This was a Scripture in the *Shi'ur Qomah* tradition, see below.

chadnezzar, his 'brother,' who in Daniel 2.38 dreamed a dream which signified that another kingdom, inferior to his, would arise after him, a third of bronze, and a fourth of iron which would crush the former ones. Eventually God would set up a kingdom which will never be destroyed, and which would itself destroy the former kingdoms. In the beginning of his reign, Israel was terribly frightened. That contemporary conditions played a part in their interpretations is indicated by Rav's emphasizing Ahasuerus' humble origins. He raised himself to the throne, just as the new shahanshah had raised himself to the throne, and ruled 'the whole world' though not of noble birth. The contrast between Israel and the heathen, and between the piety of the one, and the coarse, licentious behavior of the other, was contemptuously drawn, just as the failure of the heathen to mourn the destruction of the Temple was noted. These sayings differ in spirit from the admiration expressed in former generations for the modesty and good manners of the "Persians," who were then the Parthians. That the Book of Daniel was believed to have taken place in an earlier time of troubles, and that its vision and message applied with special clarity in the new age[1] are quite obvious.

One may note, finally, that Rav and Samuel made several references to Lev. 26 and Deut. 28, chapters devoted to the punishments which would overtake Israel in exile in consequence of their violating the covenant. Rav cited Deut. 28.66, and Samuel, Lev. 26.44, in their sermons on the Scroll of Esther. So they underlined their view that breaking the covenant in Esther's time had brought about the persecutions of Haman, clearly implying that in their own day as well Israel's prosperity depended upon penitence, prayer, and reconciliation with God. As we shall see (Chapter Five, section ii), the rabbis were not offering idle advice, but composed prayers which would, if heard and answered, bring about a more satisfactory situation.

VI. SAMUEL AND SHAPUR

It was one thing to exegete angrily about a dreadful turn of events, and to leaf through Scriptures in search of verses which might both bring comfort to the troubled synagogue and show the imminence of divine wrath against Israel's troubler. It was quite another accurately

---

[1] By contrast to R. Tarfon's application of verses of Daniel to the affairs of the Tannaitic court at the end of the first century, see Sifré Num. 118, b. Zev. 57a, and my *History and Torah* (London 1965) 89-90.

to assess the new situation and realistically to cope with it. For Babylonian Jews, this was an extraordinarily new situation. For four
centuries and more, they had lived under adaptable and accommodating rulers, the Parthians, who, as I said, had brought them into
an alliance and given them a major role in both domestic and international politics. Before them, under the Seleucids, the Babylonian
Jews had known a period of peace, and were favored by the regime,
like the Jews in other diaspora communities, as a means of keeping
the peace in revolted regions. And before the Seleucids, the Achemenid
Persians had restored the Jerusalem Temple, a fact, as we have seen,
to which Rav referred. Having put forward a foolish policy under
the same Ahasueros (from the third century perspective, the same as
the foolish monarch of the Esther Scroll), they had learned the lesson
that the Jews were a group not to be trifled with. We cannot, therefore,
locate an adequate precedent for the new situation, which found
Babylonian Jews at odds with a powerful, central government, not
easily swayed (despite R. Yohanan's belief that the bureaucrats took
bribes) from its purposes, and pursuing goals inimical to the welfare
of Jewry. All that Scripture could say, as we have seen, was that
the new empire would pass, as others had, and that God had not
forsaken his covenant with Israel, but would honor it, and eventually
bring the Messiah; for the rest, nothing.

Nor could Palestinian Jews provide a helpful policy. Their attitude
toward Rome, in times of oppression and otherwise, was based upon
the firm conviction that Rome had no rightful place in Palestine,
because pagans should not rule the holy land. Palestinian Jewry
could never regard Roman rule as wholly legitimate, nor reconcile
themselves to it, even though in R. Judah the Prince's day and afterward tensions were relaxed, and calm was restored. From Babylonian
Jews, however, no such conviction of the essential wrongness of
Sasanian rule could emerge. Although the Jews' settlement long
antedated the advent of the new Persian ruler, they themselves had
no special claim on Babylonia, nor did they ever think that they did.
They were sojourners in a land not their own, though not possessed
by anyone else either. Throughout the more than eight centuries
preceding Sasanian domination, however, Babylonian Jews had always
found it possible to get along quite well with the ruling empire,
even to find a place of special favor in the politics of the region. No
wonder it seemed to Rav and Samuel that theirs was a generation marked
out for punishment, because the people had set aside 'words of Torah'.

Within the Pharisaic tradition inhered a quietist, renunciatory attitude toward politics, which proved remarkably appropriate for the new situation, and which was discovered, and enunciated, by Samuel. It was based in part upon the necessities of the aftermath of 70, when, with the Temple destroyed and autonomous government, which had been based upon it, dispersed, R. Yohanan ben Zakkai came to an agreement with the Roman government. That agreement called for Jewish acquiescence to Roman rule in Palestine, in exchange for the right to pursue the legal, religious, and social policies of the Pharisaic party without interference. It represented, on the face of it, a turning away from aspirations toward worldly power, and was based on a still older attitude of Pharisaism, from the time of the Hasmoneans, that Palestine would be better off with neutral, pagan rulers, who would allow the Pharisaic party to dominate the country, than with wrong-headed Jewish rulers, who would not. Out of the experience of R. Yohanan ben Zakkai, emerged a fully articulated policy of political quietism, illustrated by the second-century saying that Rome's rule in Palestine was of divine origin. Quite obviously, not all Jews accepted the new politics, and the agreement with Rome itself proved meaningless when the leader of the Pharisaic-Tannaitic group, R. Akiba, recognized in Ben Koziba the messiah, and the whole country followed his leadership in a disastrous and terribly destructive war. After the country was pacified, however, Rome returned to her original, and now more successful, policy of making use of influential native leaders in keeping the population peaceful, and, as we have noted, by the time of R. Judah the Prince, most Jews accepted the status quo.

R. Yohanan ben Zakkai himself had based his politics upon prophetic teaching. From Jeremiah he learned that submission to the rule of the pagan emperor was the price the Jews would have to pay for their disloyalty to the covenant, and that through exile lay their road to reconciliation. From Hosea he learned that in a time of crisis, such as that of Northern Israel in its last years, the most important quality was compassion, and the most important activity, doing deeds of lovingkindness. From Ezekiel he learned that God transcended the sanctuary, and that the earthly triumph of the pagan did not signify a heavenly vindication of his god. He himself not only contemplated the visions of Ezekiel as a source for his own theological and mystical enterprise, but behaved exactly as had Jeremiah before 586, and the descriptions of his activities leave no doubt that the prophetic paradigm was very much in the mind of those who observed, and recorded his deeds.

One recalls the viewpoint of both Rav and Samuel, in discussing the coming of redemption. Samuel held that merely living in exile was sufficient to merit redemption, and Rav, that repentance and good deeds were called for. Likewise the 'sins of the living' caused the exhumation of the dead. 'Through transgression of the Torah' the pagan kingdom 'decrees and carries out its decrees.' Similarly when the haughty depart from Israel, then the court-officers will disappear too. Rav and Samuel's discussion was, we noted, a direct continuation of that of two of R. Yoḥanan ben Zakkai's greatest students, R. Joshua and R. Eliezer, and the presupposition of their argument was, in fact, that of R. Yoḥanan ben Zakkai himself: Israel, if obedient to the will of their father in heaven, would enjoy every blessing, but if not, the least among the nations would rule over them (paralleled by Rav's saying that Ahasueros/Ardashir was a parvenu.) Until the advent of the Sasanians, however, it was unnecessary for Babylonian heirs of the Pharisaic-Tannaitic tradition to lay stress on these ideas, or to spell out and apply their political implications.

The time was ripe for a reconciliation. As we have seen, Shapur pursued a policy of cultural and religious syncretism, bringing to the corpus of Iranian scriptures the wisdom of west and east, encouraging Mani to proclaim a religion capable of unifying the empire, and assuring the Christians and Jews that none would molest them any further. In pursuing such a policy, Shapur was coming to grips with the realities of his empire, which, east and west alike, possessed large and important groups who had still to be won over to the new regime, and who, in Ardashir's time, were deeply distraught by the change from an accommodating to a zealous and hostile administration. For his part, Shapur must have realized that the success of his policy of military aggressiveness, east and west, depended upon the stability of his own empire. The western satrapies, with which we are concerned, lay immediately adjacent to an unfriendly frontier, and across the border lived the kinsmen of his own disaffected population. If these groups could be won over by the Romans, as earlier the Parthians had solicited the support of the brethren, in the Roman Orient, of their own minority populations, then the western satrapies would, like Armenia, pose a serious threat to his regime. At the very least, Shapur had to make certain that success in the west would not jeopardize his throne, that, for example, the massacre of Jews, as took place in Caesarea-Mazaca, would not result in a rebellion within his own empire. Whatever his strength in international affairs, matters were such that a petty principality, such as Hatra or Palmyra, could greatly inconvenience the Sasanian state. In this fluid and potentially dangerous situation, it would no longer be possible to ignore the feelings and loyalties of groups antagonized by Ardashir, nor to permit such groups, including Jews and Christians, to remain alienated, since, in a foreign invasion, they might ally themselves to the enemies of the state. (Indeed, one wonders whether behind the exegeses of Exodus lay the thought that Jews in the new empire would, indeed, do what the Egyptians had long ago feared they might, by joining the forces of an invading army. Perhaps the exegetes were reconsidering the ancient lesson with just such an eventuality in mind. If this was the case, however, we do not have direct evidence that the Sasanians knew about it.)

We do not know who took the initiative, Samuel or Shapur. We have already noted how Samuel declined to mourn the disaster in Asia Minor. Likewise, he minimized casualties among the civilian population at home:

> Samuel said, A government which kills only one out of six is not punished, for it is said, 'My vineyard, which is mine, is before me. Thou, O Solomon, shalt have the thousand'—for the kingdom of heaven—and 'two hundred for these that keep the fruit thereof'—for the kingdom on earth (Song of Songs 8.12)'.
>
> (b. Shev. 35b)

Here Samuel drastically reinterpreted earlier exegetical treatment of the verse, which had applied it to study of the Torah, in order to stress the insignificance of casualties accruing from the wars of the day. He expressed hostility to Rome, saying that the city was founded the day Solomon married Pharoah's daughter.[1] He emphasized, for the Jews, the power of the throne:

> If royalty says, I will uproot mountains, it will uproot them and not go back on its word.
>
> (b. B.B. 3b)

Such an attitude, if sufficiently widespread, would encourage the people to submit to the regnant authorities.

---

[1] b. Shab. 56b.

Of greatest importance, Samuel and the exilarch both decreed that the law of the government is law.[1] This saying, which has a long history in the development of Jewish law, and has been subjected to many varying interpretations throughout that history, meant originally that Persian law must be observed among the Jews, a meaning emergent in the several contexts in which the saying is cited. In consequence Persian law could not be ignored or evaded, as R. Shila had tried to do; Persian taxes must be paid; Persian rules on land tenure and transfer must be observed; all bills and conveyances drawn up by Persian courts had to be accepted by the Jews, even though they could not read Pahlavi (although they understood it when it was spoken). One can hardly overestimate the importance of this dictum, both for Samuel's lifetime and in the following generations. It was, first of all, a *politically* significant statement. Under the Parthians, the Jews were, so far as we can ascertain, governed by their own courts and under their own laws. In saying that the 'law of the land is law,' Samuel instructed the Jewish courts to conform to the new circumstances, and to accept the overlordship of the Iranian officials. Second, it represented the recognition that the Iranians *did* possess just courts and just laws, and should not be regarded as barbarians. It regularized, moreover, the status of such laws in Jewish communal affairs, and prevented Jews from claiming that by rights they should attempt to evade taxes and obedience to the government, contrary to the Palestinian view. By this dictum, subsequent Jewries accepted the legal authority of their respective governments, and thus quite directly conformed to the policy of Samuel enunciated when the Babylonian Jews confronted for the first time a government that was both hostile and insistent upon supervising their internal affairs.[2]

---

[1] b. B.B. 54b. Here Samuel's saying is cited by Abaye in contradiction of a ruling which R. Judah gave in Samuel's name, that heathen property is on the same footing as desert, hence ownerless. The circumstance is that in which a Jew purchases heathen land, and another acquires it by means recognized in Jewish law. That the exilarchate pursued exactly the same policy as Samuel is seen in b. B.B. 55a; see below, ch. III.

See also b. Git. 88b, Ned. 28a, and B.M. 108a, etc. See also J. Newman, *Agricultural Life* 187-193; Krauss, *Paras* 94; Funk, *Juden*, i, 57, 70-1; Yavetz *Toldot*, VII, 431.

[2] The history in Jewish law of this sentence of Samuel would fill several volumes. That history, while interesting, has no direct bearing upon our subject, nor do the various interpretations of Samuel s intent, normally constructed in the light of subsequent circumstance. For a recent article on the subject, see Shabtai Ben-Dov, "Dina' deMalkhuta' Dina'", *Talpioth* 9, 1964, 230-8.

According to Talmudic sources, Samuel and Shapur cultivated one another's friendship, which proves beyond doubt that the Jews firmly believed such was the case, certainly because the improved relations they enjoyed with the Persian state made it credible. Samuel's willingness to collaborate with the emperor, whose father had so embittered the lives of the Jews, must have taken considerable courage, and, as we shall see, he did not escape criticism. Shapur, for his part, allegedly paid attention to Jewish religious law in conciliating Jewry:

> Mar Judah and Bati b. Tovi were sitting with King Shapur and a citron was set before them. The king cut a slice and ate it, and then cut a slice and handed it to Bati b. Tovi. After that, he stuck the knife ten times into the ground [to render it ritually fit], cut a slice of the citron, and handed it to Mar Judah. Bati b. Tovi then said to the king, Am I not an Israelite? He replied, Of him I am certain that he is observant, but not of you . . .

(b. A.Z. 76b.)

We do not know how to verify such a story; it may be merely an example of a homily urging the Jews to indicate their piety in public. It does signify, however, that the Jews believed Shapur would honor their faith and those who kept it, and if this is folklore, then the *policy* of Shapur was thus reflected in the popular imagination.[1] Samuel allegedly entertained him by juggling eight glasses of wine,[2] interpreted his dreams for him like Joseph for Pharoah,[3] and so identified himself with Shapur that subsequent generations referred to him as 'King Shapur.'[4] Samuel also told stories about how the patriarch in Palestine was forced to contribute to the celebration of the Roman festivals, and how the concession of exemption from direct contribution to the pagan sacrifices had to be bought at a cost of 120,000 denarii,[5] a story which certainly contradicts what we know about the relationship of the patriarch with the Antonines, and which clearly was intended to enlist support for Persia against Rome.

---

[1] His interest in Jewish customs appears in b. A.Z. 76b. His name was proverbial, also, for great wealth (b. B.M. 85a, 'as rich as King Shapur'), and with his own age (b. Ned. 25a, Shev. 29b, etc.). But this may be Shapur II.

[2] b. Suk. 53a. This was a skill apparently passed on among the rabbis, see my *Life* 43.

[3] b. Suk. 56a, compare Midrash HaGadol on Genesis, Yalkut II 1060, etc. But the form of this story is identical with that preceding it, about 'the Roman emperor' and R. Joshua b. Hananiah, and may signify merely a Babylonian parallel to a Palestinian legend.

[4] b. B Q 96b, B.M. 119a, B.B. 115a. See Krauss, *Paras*, 94-6.

[5] b. A.Z. 16a.

For his part, Rav did not approve Samuel's friendship with the monarch. He never reconciled himself to the change in dynasty. He accused Shapur of taking money unjustly from the Jews, and giving it to the pagans:

> He that by usury and unjust gain increaseth his substance he shall gather it for him that pitieth the poor (Prov. 28.8)'. What is meant by 'for him that pitieth the poor'? Rav said, King Shapur.
>
> (b. B.M. 70b)[1]

He held that Daniel was punished only for having given good advice to Nebuchadnezzar,[2] with the obvious implication that anyone such as Samuel who consorted with the new 'king of Babylonia' had better watch out too. Having spent many years in Palestine, and there having acquired a very different view of the legitimacy of pagan authority over Jews, Rav never accepted the change in political life which took place in his later years. Samuel, who knew no other home than Babylonia, appears in retrospect to have been better able to accommodate himself to the changing course of events and to conform to the needs of the new day. Accepting the realities of diaspora life, regarding as enemies the enemies of his government, prepared to foster good relations with the regime for the benefit of the Jews, Samuel found, in Shapur, a willing collaborator, who, for his purposes and in his own way, was just as eager as the Jewish leader for reconciliation.

We must stress, in conclusion, that this was a *strictly* political policy, and does not by any means reveal the whole of the rabbis' response to Sasanian rule. As we shall see, contrary to their outward, political quietism, the rabbis wrote prayers laying great stress upon the Messianic hope, and since they believed that God, who ruled history, heard and answered prayer, we cannot ignore the political implications of their liturgy. While, as we have seen, they sought a political accommodation with Shapur, they undertook to hasten the Messianic resolution of history, and the fall of worldly empires, both by making Israel worthy of redemption, and by stressing, in their address to the divinity, its pressing timeliness. Professor Yohanan Muffs points out, in this connection, that Jeremiah's response to the Babylonian conquest was here, again, paradigmatic, for just as he

---

[1] Compare Ex. R. 31.11. This interpretation is based on Rashi, ad. loc., and see also W. Bacher, *Agada*. 23, who sees Rav's words as ironic.
[2] b. B.B. 4a.

advised the Palestinian Jews to submit to, and the Babylonian Jews to accept, the exile and not to rebel, so too he predicted the fall, in 70 years, of Babylonia itself, and issued fearful curses and dire predictions to that end, which are recorded in Jer. 51. Moreover, he "wrote in a book all the evil that should come upon Babylonia," sent it to the exile, and ordered the book symbolically to be cast into the Euphrates River, with the words, obviously of magical or theurgic weight, "Thus shall Babylon sink to rise no more, because of the evil that I am bringing upon her." Professor Muffs sees in Jer. 51 the necessary concommitant of Jer. 28-29, and points out the parallel between Jeremiah's political and religious doctrines and those of the third-century rabbis. While we have, therefore, emphasized the political consequences of the rabbis' policy of public passivity, we ought to keep in mind the religious program, equally significant to their way of thinking, which they also undertook. The rabbis could offer quietistic advice precisely because they believed they had another, better way to meet the problem. In addressing the people however, they did not reveal it, for Samuel emphasized, as we have noted, that not too much should be hoped for in the age to come. In their biblical exegeses, as we shall see, they similarly added ethical conditions to eschatological Scriptures, or more commonly simply either avoided such Scriptures, or interpreted them in a wholly non-eschatological way. This too followed the example of Jeremiah, whose public message was to submit but to take heart, but who *acted* in a manner calculated to employ supernatural powers to restore Israel's prosperity and destroy Babylonia. (We shall return to this subject in Chapter Five section ii and Chapter VI section vii.)

VII. JUDAISM AND OTHER RELIGIONS

The political rapprochement between Samuel and Shapur did not comprehend a reconciliation between Judaism and other religions in the Sasanian Empire. What Samuel and Shapur negotiated, if anything, was an accommodation between a minority group and its government. Judaism was, and remained, engaged in a struggle with other religions, and neither peace nor respite was possible. Here we shall examine the attitudes and practices of Judaism in relationship to other religious groups.

Faith in Jesus as Christ was present in Babylonia among two groups (apart from Mani's followers), the Mandeans, whose anti-

Jewish attitudes we have touched on above, and other, 'orthodox' Christians. Christians were abhorred by the rabbis, if we accurately understand the following saying:

> Rav could not enter a BY ʾBYDN and certainly not a BY NZRPY. Samuel would not enter a BY NZRPY but he would enter a BY ʾBYDN.[1]

(b. Shab. 116a)

Likewise, R. Abbahu was asked whether one might save the books of a *Be Abedan* from a fire or not, there being no question whatever that those of a *Be Nizrefe* might not be saved. The *Be Abedan*, according to Kohut, included a library of sacred writings of many faiths, and hence might contain Jewish Scriptures which should be saved from a fire even on the Sabbath. Krauss[2] regards both words as referring to a 'special Persian temple,' holding that *NZRP* is a play on *NSRP*, hence, a "place where things are burned." My judgment is that BY ʾBYDN refers to an *āpētān*, BY NZRPY to a 'Nazarene' Church,[3] and that the attitude of Rav, regarding the Christians as more

---

[1] Be ʾBYDN has been variously explained as an *apadana*, or Bet Mobadhan, house of a chief Magus. Levi (III, 432) explains *Nizrefi* as a gathering place of Nazareans, Jewish-Christians. Jastrow likewise regards *ZRP* as "a cacophemistic disguise of Nozri, a Christian place of worship." Kohut (II, 46) says that NZRPY may refer to Zurvan (ZRPN); ʾBYDN refers to Ophites and, more likely, NZRPY to 'another Christian gnostic sect.' His discussion seems far-fetched to me. S. V. ʾPDN (I 209) Kohut defines the word as a courtyard in the palace (hof).
See also Felix Kanter, *Beiträge* (Berlin, 1895), 30-1. He interprets BY ʾBYDN as "das Haus wo der Vater disputirte", reading BY ʾBY DN (sic!). Krochmal, in *HeHaluz* II 100, interprets the phrase as applying to a gathering place of Nazarenes. See below, n. 3 for Henning's view of Be Abidan.

[2] S. Krauss, *Synagogale Altertümer* (Berlin 1922) p. 31. Compare L. Ginzberg, *MGWJ* 77, 23, and S. Funk, *op. cit.*, II, 53, n. 5 "haus der Gottesknechte, kloster", who cites Nöldeke, *Tabari* 24, "abad heissen die christlichen Einwohner der Stadt". Compare J. Newman, *Commercial Life*, 24, Be Abidan was a public meeting place for discussions on various kinds of subjects, *Be Nizrife*, places of discussion of specifically religious questions, by reference of A.Z. 48a (= ʿEruv. 79b). But that passage refers to the setting aside of dates for a *be nizrefe*, which dates were distilled, and the liquor drunk on feast days. This does not necessarily refer to idolatrous practice, however. See b. Shab. 152a,

[3] In Kartir *KZ* we find NʿʿČRʿʿY = Nazarenes. Since the Mandeans called their doctrine *nasirutha*, however, I am not certain whether the antipathy of the rabbis was directed toward orthodox Christians, Jewish-Christians, or Mandeans. The attitude of the rabbis toward the second group was first expressed at the end of the first century by R. Tarfon. (b. ʿArakhin 16b) see my *History and Torah* 96-7, and 101 n. 54 (compare H. J. Schoeps, *Theologie und Geschichte des Judenchristentums* (Tübingen, 1949), 140, who holds that Jewish-Christianity did, in fact, reach Babylonia). See also D. Hoffmann, *Mar Samuel*, pp. 40-1, n. 4, *Be Avidan* is a place of religious disputation. Professor W. B. Henning offers the following: "*Abidan*

reprehensible than the (pagan) Mazdeans, reflected the Palestinian view, first enunciated by R. Tarfon, that the Christians had known the faith but denied it.[1] Samuel likewise abhorred the Christians, but held, consistently with other attitudes we have noted, that one might consort with, and learn from, Mazdeans. Moreover, Samuel probably regarded the Christians as idolaters.[2] Rav likewise held that *minim*, in this case most likely Jewish-Christians, must be prevented from *leading* public worship in the synagogue.[3] He left a saying which probably formed part of a polemical argument:

> 'While the king sat at his table my spikenard gave up its fragrance' (Song of Songs 1.12), that is, while the king was at Sinai, Israelites lost their fragrance through sin. Said Rav, Yet his love was still with us, for 'gave' is written, not 'made noisome.'

(b. Shab. 88b)

Since the Christians held that Israel had been rejected by God, and that the destruction of the Temple in 70 was a sign of this rejection, it was important to emphasize, as did Rav above and elsewhere,[4] that however Israel may have sinned in its past, it had not, and could never have, lost the love of God, nor been rejected from the covenant of Abraham.

The Jews regarded the pagans as utterly estranged from God and his blessings. Rav, for example, stated:

> He who puts his faith in a battered idol shall not behold God's goodness, for it is said (Ps. 31.20) 'O How abundant is thy goodness, which thou hast laid up for them that fear thee.'

(Midrash on Psalms, trans. W. Braude, I, 397)

---

cannot possibly constitute a descendant of O. Pers. *appadan* ("apadana" so-called). The actual forms are in *Trans. Philol. Soc.* 1944, 110 n. 1. Kohut is no guide for this sort of thing. There is a Pahlavi word *āpētān*, which would be pronounced *abedan*, which refers to places, but the meaning is obscure."

[1] b. Shab., 116a, Tosefta Shab., 14.5, compare b. Git. 88b. "They know and deny God while the pagans never knew him to deny him".

[2] b. A.Z. 7b, see also 6a. My interpretation is based on *Dik. Sof.* XII 9 n. 20. But Samuel may simply mean that, since no business is done on the Sabbath, according to R. Ishmael, who forbids business three days before, and after a holiday, one will never be able to do business on a Sunday.
Rashi understands Samuel to mean that Sunday is forbidden, as well as the preceding and following days. On this basis I have interpreted Samuel's saying to indicate that he regarded Christians as idolaters. See also E. E. Urbach, "Laws Regarding Idolatry", cited below p. 77 n. 4, for the same view. Marmorstein sees Rav's saying, that Israel had not been forsaken even though they had worshipped the golden calf, as a reply to Paul's reference to Hosea 2,25, see *Studies*, 193.

[3] b. Ber. 29a. See also b. A.Z. 17a, *Minim* go to gehenna, cited below, p. 103.

[4] See b. Sanh., 104a. etc.

They regarded pagan rites as abominations, and ridiculed the immorality they thought was involved in serving pagan gods:

> R. Judah in the name of Rav: A gentile woman once fell sick. She vowed, If I recover, I will go and serve every idol in the world. She recovered and proceeded to serve all the idols. On reaching Pe'or she asked its priests how it is worshipped. They replied, people eat beets, drink strong drink, and then uncover themselves before it. She replied, I would rather fall sick again than serve an idol in such a manner. But you, O house of Israel, were not so, for it is written (Numbers 25.5), 'Slay you every one his men that were joined unto Baal Pe'or'—You were attached to it like an airtight lid.
>
> (b. Sanh. 64a)[1]

Whether Rav's sermon had contemporary application or not we do not know, though we shall suggest below that it may have.

Rav likewise made fun of the gods of the pagans:

> R. Judah in the name of Rav said: 'And the men of Babylon made Sukkot-benot (II Kings 17.30)'. What is this?—a fowl [that is to say, they worshipped the image of a fowl]. 'And the men of Cuth made Nergal'. What is it?—A cock. 'And the men of Hamath made Ashima'. What is that? A bald buck. 'And the Avites made Nibhaz and Tartak'. What are these? A dog and an ass. 'And the Sepharvites burned their children in fire to Adrammelekh and Anammelekh, the gods of Sepharvaim'. What are these? The mule and the horse: Adram-melekh meaning that it honors its master [hadar, to honor, melekh, king] with its load. Anamellekh meaning that the horse responds to its master in battle ['n', to respond]. The father of Hezekiah king of Judah wished to do likewise to him [burn him in fire] but his mother anointed him [with the blood of the] salamander [which made him fireproof, see b. Hag. 27a].
>
> R. Judah in the name of Rav said, The Israelites knew that the idols were nonentities, but they engaged in idolatry only that they might openly satisfy their incestuous lusts.
>
> (b. Sanh. 63b)

Rav's 'rationalization' of Israelite paganism in the early period recalls the view of Euhemerus, which enjoyed a revival in the second century, that the gods were really no more than earthly kings, worshipped after their death for their benefactions or prowess in life. Revealing a kind of neo-Euhemerism, Rav ridiculed the pagans' images and made it clear that the Israelites never really took the whole matter very seriously, except as a license for sexual immorality.

---

[1] See also Sifré Num. 131, which, Büchler holds, refers to contemporary, not merely historical, events. Compare Rav, Sanh. 63a and 81b.

Rav regarded it as Israel's task to make known 'their father who is in heaven,' and recognized that where the nations know Israel, they knew about Israel's God, but where Israel had not settled, there God was unknown. He held that Israel's God was known, therefore, from Tyre to Kurdistan, but not west of Tyre nor east of Kurdistan.[1] Likewise, stories were told, like those of Hillel and Shammai, about how Rav and Samuel confronted pagans and taught them 'the Torah':

> 'And the patient in spirit is better than the proud in spirit' (Eccles. 7.8). A Persian came to Rav and said to him, Teach me the Torah. He told him, Say 'aleph.' The man remarked, Who says that this is an aleph. There may be others who say that it is not. Say 'bet,' to which he remarked, Who says that this is a bet? Rav rebuked him and drove him out in anger. He went to Samuel and said to him, Teach me the Torah. He told him, Say 'aleph.' The man remarked, Who says that this is 'aleph?' Say 'bet,' to which he remarked, Who says that this is 'bet?' The teacher took hold of his ear and the man exclaimed, My ear! my ear! Samuel asked him, Who says that this is your ear? He answered, Everybody knows that this is my ear. The teacher replied, In the same way everybody knows that this is 'aleph' and that is 'bet.' Immediately the Persian was silenced and accepted instruction. Hence 'And the patient in spirit is better than the proud in spirit'—better is the forbearance which Samuel displayed with the Persian than the impatience which Rav showed towards him, for otherwise the Persian might have returned to his heathenism.
>
> (Koh. R. 7.8.1)

This story is obviously copied from the similar one about Hillel and Shammai,[2] and one has no reason to regard it as historically authentic. Though as we have seen, Samuel did take a consistently more tolerant view of the Persians than Rav, in this case the point of the story is not Samuel's greater forbearance (despite the editor's comment) but rather his greater cleverness at disputation. Nonetheless there can be no doubt that Jews did conduct a polemic against paganism, and sought wherever possible to win the pagan to Judaism.[3]

---

[1] b. Men. 110a. Neubauer, *Géographie* 294 holds that one must transpose the geographical reference, from Tyre eastward and from Carthage westward the nations know neither Israel nor their father who is in heaven. But Obermeyer, 135, more reasonably understands it to mean from Tyre to Karduchene=Kurdistan.

[2] b. Shab. 31a.

[3] See, for example, b. B.B. 91a:

R. Ḥanan b. Rava in the name of Rav stated: The name of the mother of Abraham was Amathlai the daughter of Karnebo [Lamb of Nebo]; the name of the mother of Haman was Amathlai the daughter of Oravti (raven); and your mnemonic is,

While the Jews were not hostile to Persian culture, they looked for the biblical roots of that culture. Rav, for example, regarded the Persian word for scribe, DBYR (dipir) as based on Judges 1.11, just as R. Ashi, in later time, found the basis for the Persians' calling a menstruous woman 'dashtana' in Gen. 31.35.[1] R. Joseph likewise insisted that in Babylonia, Jews should speak either Hebrew, or Persian, but not Aramaic.[2] Rav and Samuel held that the Scroll of Esther might be read in Greek to Jews who do not speak Hebrew, and an external tradition added, likewise, in Coptic to the Copts, Hebrew to the Hebrews, Elamite to the Elameans, and Greek to the Greeks.[3] What is meant by "Elamite" to the "Elameans" is by no means clear to me, but the force of the *beraita* is that there were Jews, in Egypt, the Roman Orient, and the Iranian Empire, to whom Hebrew was unintelligible, and that these Jews might carry out their obligation to hear the *Megillah* on Purim in a language known to them, most universally, according to Rav and Samuel, Greek.

It is perfectly clear that some Jews assimilated into Oriental-Greek culture even in Babylonia, and that a great many did not meet the high standards of separation from paganism in all forms demanded by the rabbis. The Amoraic view cannot have prevailed without opposition or exception. Those Jews who remained within the community, and these are the only ones known to us, were by no means uniform in their beliefs and practices. The literature we have deals only with the groups responsive to rabbinic authority. Yet even here we have noted evidence that the rabbis were not entirely satisfied with their religious standards. Moreover, we know that at the synagogue in Dura-Europos were Jews who did not hesitate to decorate the walls of their synagogue in a manner contradictory to rabbinic law.[4] Similarly, in the time of Rav and Samuel there was a statue (andarta) in the synagogue 'which moved and settled' in

---

unclean to unclean, clean to clean. The mother of David was named Nizbeth the daughter of Adael. The mother of Samson was Zlelponith, and his sister, Nashyan. In what respect do they matter? In respect of a reply to the heretics [minim]. [Perhaps the failure of Scripture to identify the mothers of important figures would be regarded as a proof of its incompleteness, hence these are provided by oral tradition.]

[1] b. A.Z. 24b.

[2] b. Sotah 49b.

[3] b. Meg. 18a. See my "Škand Miscellanies", *JAOS*.

[4] Compare the view of E. E. Urbach, "The Rabbinical Laws of Idolatry in the Second and Third Centuries in the Light of Archaeological and Historical Facts", *IEJ* 9, 3-4, 1959, 149f. See below, Chapter VIII Part V, for further discussion.

Nehardea, and Rav, Samuel, and Samuel's Father prayed there, though they could not have approved of the *andarta*.[1] In fact, Samuel explicitly interpreted the Mishnah (A.Z. 3:1) to prohibit such a thing! Rav refrained from prostrating himself in a synagogue in Babylonia (Obermeyer says it was at Sura[2]) because there was a stone pavement (clearly, a mosaic) on the floor, which contradicted his understanding of Leviticus 26.1 "Neither shall ye place any figured stone in your land to bow down to it." Although Rav did not approve, he could not force the removal of the mosaic floor.[3] Moreover, R. Judah, Samuel's student, thought that it was permitted to have a figured seal which others had made, and Samuel required him to disfigure it by putting out (marring) the eye of the seal's figure, a means of neutralization used at Dura also. (The Talmud distinguished between a seal which projected, and one which was embedded, in the former case, one may not wear it but may use it as a seal, in the latter, one may wear it but not use it as a seal.) More seriously, Samuel held that Jews who married gentile women produced heathen children,[4] and one assumes that in specifying localities where such was the case, he was indicating that there Jews were leaving the community through such marriages.

One certainly must agree with Urbach[5] that there was no Jewish idolatry as such (yet see below, on Jews' worshipping bricks!). Nor can one disagree with his contention that the laws relating to idolatry fluctuated. For that reason we shall examine the laws attributed to this particular period, to find in them the general attitude toward pagan artifacts which characterized third-century Babylonian Judaism. Urbach holds, however, that for economic reasons, Jewish craftsmen were forced to manufacture appurtenances for idolatry. He does not cite, nor have I found, evidence that Jews were permitted, to begin with, to make use of mosaic floors in their synagogues or otherwise to make use of plastic, representational art as they did at Sura, Dura, Nehardea, and elsewhere in this very period. Synagogue art had nothing whatever to do with the economic requirements of Jewish

---

[1] b. R. H. 24b. See Meg. 29a, and b. A.Z. 41a.

[2] Obermeyer, *op. cit.*, 306.

[3] b. Meg. 22b. See also b. A.Z. 41a. Compare Targum Yonatan to Lev. 26.1, "But a mosaic pavement of designs and forms you may set in the floor of your places of worship, so long as you do not do obeisance to it."

[4] b. Yev. 16b-17a, compare b. Qid. 68b.

[5] *Op. cit.*, 155.

craftsmen. The rabbis, second and third century alike, were not the source of inspiration for this art. That Rav, Samuel, and Samuel's Father objected to the figures in the Nehardea and Sura synagogues is beyond question. That their objection meant nothing to the Jews who prayed there regularly is also beyond question. The necessity to preach sermons against those who did not pay sufficient heed to 'the words of the Torah,' and to blame such people for the misfortunes of the new age, signifies, at the very least, that the rabbis were not wholly satisfied with the religion of the masses, nor were they able to do much about it.

The Jews had to work out regulations to deal not only with paganism, but with the pagans, in whose midst they lived in the closest, workaday relations. Jews and gentiles lived in the same quarters, and visited one another on holidays. It became necessary for Rav to announce, therefore, that the law of *ḥaẓar* (in connection with the 'eruv) does not apply to the pagan.[1] Samuel visited a Persian on the Sabbath, and was careful not to make use of the light the pagan kindled until he saw that it was for the pagan's own use, not for his benefit.[2]

In the view of some, including both Rav and Samuel, one need not return an article which a pagan has lost, for this was regarded as ownerless property, and Samuel held likewise that it was permissible to benefit from a pagan's mistake in trade, and he so acted.[3] Rav taught quite explicitly:

> Whence can we learn that the lost article of a heathen is 'permissible'? Because it says, 'And with all lost things of thy brother' (Deut. 22.3) —it is to your brother that you make restoration, but you need not make restoration to a pagan.
>
> (b. Sanh. 76b)[4]

One need not excuse or defend an ethical view inconsistent with one's own. Suffice to say that the view of the rabbis, whether based on exegesis or social policy (and clearly, although Rav regards it as an exegetical necessity, he likewise approved it, as did Samuel) was hardly congruent with the attitudes of the people who lived in close contact with pagans, who shared the great events of their lives,

---

[1] y. 'Eruv. 6.10.

[2] y. Shab. 16.9, compare b. Shab. 122b, where the name is given as Abin of Toran, or MS. M. Abitoran.

[3] b. Sanh. 76b, B.Q. 113b.

[4] See also b. B.Q. 113b.

and who must have come to a sounder view of inter-group ethics
than did the rabbis.

The close daily ties between gentiles and Jews led to the rabbis'
taking a strict view, where possible, of those laws which separated
the two groups. Thus, while the stringent laws on the preservation
of the ritual purity of wine, by keeping it from pagans' touch, were
rigidly enforced by the early 'Amora' im, we have, to the contrary, a
case (b. A.Z. 56b) in which, in Nehardea, an Israelite and a heathen
pressed out wine together. Rav held that even a pagan child one day
old can render wine unfit[1] though if a pagan touched wine accidentally
with a branch, the wine might be sold to heathen (thus though Jews
may not consume the wine, they may derive benefit from it).[2] Likewise,
Samuel held that slaves purchased from a heathen, though both
circumcized and baptized, render wine prohibited until 'idolatry is
entirely banished from their lips,' which a later authority held was
a period of twelve months. He regarded mixing Jewish with pagan
wine as equivalent of a libation.[3] Even wine *casks* which had been
seized, and later returned, by pagans under a high army officer, were
subject to question.[4] Naturally, food prepared by a pagan was subject
to severe restrictions. Raw food was permitted, but cooked food was
not.[5] In this period, controversy raged about pagan oil and beer.
Rav held that although the beer prepared by a pagan was permitted,
he would still not allow his son to drink it.[6] The reason was not
religious, but hygienic, however, for both he and Samuel held that
the pagans did not properly protect their food from contamination by
reptiles and vermin.[7] Likewise Rav warned against employing pagan
physicians.[8] In the last years of R. Judah the Prince, he and his court
voted to permit the oil of gentiles.[9] Rav refused to accept the ruling,
even though it was preached in R. Judah's name, both in Nisibis
and in Nehardea, by R. Simlai and Samuel, respectively. Samuel

---

[1] b. A.Z. 57a, compare the view of Samuel, 56b, on wine prepared by a Jew
and gentile together. Compare b. A.Z. 58a.

[2] *Ibid.*

[3] b. Git. 52b *re* the explanation of the Mishnah.

[4] b. A.Z. 33b, 61b. GZRPTY PRZK means high chiliarch (thus chief gendarme)
(PRZK probably to be read PZRK, hence *bozorg*). Compare Funk, *Juden*, I, 33.

[5] b. Beẓah 16a, A.Z. 38a, 40a, 59a, Yev. 46a.

[6] b. A.Z. 31b. As for Shatita, a kind of beer, Rav permitted while Samuel's
father prohibited it. B. A.Z. 38b. See *Arukh* S. V. Shemen.

[7] *Ibid.* Compare A.Z. 30a.

[8] B. Niḍ. 55b.

[9] See b. A.Z. 36a, 37a, y. A.Z. 2.6, 2.8; b. Git. 76b, y. Shab. 1.4, b. Ket. 2b.

threatened to declare Rav a 'rebellious elder' if he persisted in his opposition, and in a trip to Palestine, Rav investigated the matter, but remained adamantly opposed to the ruling. Rav regarded the decree against pagan oil as having been made by Daniel, who was reckoned a prophet, and held that the decree against gentile bread, wine, oil, and women was reenforced among the 'eighteen decrees' enacted before the outbreak of the war in 66. Why Samuel was so eager to accept the liberalization cannot be explained with any certainty. It is reasonable to regard his attitude as consistent with his general view that Jewish-pagan relations should be relatively unencumbered, where the law permits, for his eagerness to accept the ruling of R. Judah's court, over the opposition of Rav who had substantial ties with Palestine, leads one to suppose the presence of a motive not obviously based upon the authority responsible for the decree. On the other hand, Samuel forbade the sale of geese to pagans, lest they commit bestiality with them, as he had a tradition from R. Ḥanina that such an act had taken place.[1] Regarding the Mishnaic teaching that one may not do business on the three days preceding idolatrous festivities, Rav called such festivities "'YD," testimony, and Samuel "'YD," calamity.[2] But no differing evaluation of the pagan festivals can be uncovered in this difference over spelling and pronunciation.

That gentiles were influenced by the Jews in their midst is suggested, for this period, by the fact that a 'Persian' asked Rav about blessing bread,[3] and from Rav's discussion of the status of heave-offering separated by a heathen.[4] For their part, the rabbis discouraged commerce of all kinds with heathen, holding that a slave sold to a heathen cleric (=*frahang*[5]) goes free, that one should not say (following Deut. 7.2), 'How beautiful is that idolatress,' and the like.[6] Rav would not cross a bridge upon which a heathen was sitting, 'lest judgment be visited upon him, and I be seized together with him;' Samuel would cross only when a heathen was upon it, saying 'Satan has no power over two nations

---

[1] b. A.Z. 22b.

[2] y. A.Z. 1.2, the dispute being based on Is. 53.9 and Deut. 32.35. Compare y. Ber. 8: 6. ʿEruv. 6: 1.

[3] y. Ber. 6.2.

[4] b. ʿArakhin 6a.

[5] PRHNG=frahang, teacher, see H. S. Nyberg, *Hilfsbuch des Pehlevi* (Uppsala 1931), 70.

[6] b. Git. 44a.

simultaneously;' and R. Yannai would examine the bridge and then
cross.[1] Likewise, Rav held that one may not hoe with heathens in
the Sabbatical year, nor give a 'double-greeting' (using the divine
name) to heathens.[2] Samuel for his part did not regard it necessary
to rend one's garments upon hearing the divine name blasphemed by
a gentile. Of Samuel it was reported:

> A Persian woman once cursed her son with one syllable of the
> Ineffable Name. Samuel heard her and said, Go prepare shrouds for
> him.
>
>   (Koh. R. 3.11.3 = y. Yoma' 3.7)

The Yer. version reports that the Persian woman said, "I have lost
two things, my son [and the secret of the Name for] someone heard
from me the Ineffable Name." It stands to reason that the Jews,
like other groups, were regarded, as possessing sources of magical science, which others would want to exploit without thereby
becoming Israelites. The names of gods, in particular, were believed
to contain great potency, and since the Jews regarded the name of
their God in such a way, as we shall see below (p. 84) the pagan
neighbors were likely to agree. Despite the theoretical severity of the
law, one must take account of the attitudes of individuals, and their
natural tendency to recognize exceptions to the law. For example,
R. Judah, student of Rav and Samuel, sent a gift to a friend, Abidarna,
on his festival, saying, "I know that he does not worship idols."[3]
Doubtless other Jews, not so close to the rabbinical circles, followed
suit without similar scruple.

Two main issues concerning pagan artifacts were discussed in this
period, first, How does a pagan artifact cease to be prohibited? And
second, How does the action of an Israelite render an object forbidden
by making it an object of worship? Urbach points out[4] that in Palestine
Jews made casual use of scraps or fragments of objects bearing the
figures of gods, and of statues intended for idolatry. The same situation
applied in Babylonia, for Rav and Samuel both discussed when
objects made for idolatrous purposes might be permitted for Jewish
use. Rav held[5] that a statue of Mercury, even though its parts were
scattered, was never annulled, and might never be used by Jews.

---

[1] b. Shab. 32a.
[2] b. Git. 62a.
[3] b. A.Z. 64b.
[4] *Op. cit.*, p. 229.
[5] y. A.Z. 4.1.

He and Samuel debated whether any *other* kind of statue might be annulled. Rav held that if the finder of an idol shattered it limb by limb, the sherds might be used, and Samuel held that they might never be used.[1] The general rule was that if an idol was abandoned by its worshippers, it might be regarded as having lost its former status, and could be used, while otherwise, it might not:

> R. Jeremiah b. Abba in the name of Rav: The Temple of Nimrod is to be regarded as the same as an idol whose worshippers abandoned it in time of peace and is permitted, for although due to the fact that the All-Merciful dispersed them, it was like a time of war, if they had wished to return they could have returned, but since they did not they must have annulled them.
>
> (b. A.Z. 53b)

Both men held that a damaged pedestal was prohibited.[2] Samuel thus explained the rule of annulment of an idol:

> It is written, 'Thou shalt not covet the silver or gold that is on them', and it continues, 'Thou shalt take it unto thee' (Deut. 7.25). How is this [apparent contradiction] to be understood? When the idolater fashions it into a god, do not covet it, but when he has annulled it, so that it is no longer a god, you may take it for yourself.
>
> (b. A.Z. 52a)

Still, Rav held that an idol belonging to an Israelite must be kept out of sight. He referred specifically to an *'asherah*, the meaning of which was discussed:

> How is an *'asherah* which is not so specified [to be recognized]? Rav said, Any tree beneath which heathen priests sit but of whose fruits they do not partake. Samuel said, Even if they say, These dates are for a *Be Nizrefe*, the tree is prohibited, because they brew an intoxicating liquor from them which they drink on their feast days.
>
> (b. A.Z. 48a)[3]

The second question concerning pagan artifacts was, How the worship of an Israelite affected them? The answer was quite unequivocal: he prevented their use by any other Jew at any time. If a Jew prostrated himself to a house, he prohibited it.[4] Furthermore, both Samuel and Rav held that if an Israelite set up a brick for worship

---

[1] y. A.Z. 3.2. But compare b. A.Z. 41a, Samuel permits fragments.

[2] b. A.Z. 53b.

[3] See also b. 'Eruv. 79b. Compare Sanh. 17b, the law follows Samuel's view.

[4] This is Rav's opinion, undisputed by any other authority, y. A.Z. 3.6. See also b. A.Z. 47b. Compare y. Shab. 9.1.

but did not do so, and an idolator did, the brick is prohibited because of the original intent of the Israelite.[1] Likewise:

> R. Judah in the name of Rav: If an idol is worshipped [by tapping before it with a stick] and an Israelite broke a stick in its presence, he is liable [of punishment for idolatry], but if he threw a stick in front of it, he is free of penalty.
>
> (b. A.Z. 50b-51a)

In the light of the attention paid to these questions, it seems reasonable to suppose that some Jews tried their hand at pagan forms, perhaps to mobilize whatever powers inhered in them, just as pagans did with Jewish magic. That great numbers did so cannot be proved; yet that some did is incontrovertible, and also entirely natural. In a great and mixed population, not all of the Jews were, as I said, so deeply aware of rabbinic attitudes and interpretations of the law as the rabbis wanted, and some of them may have seen nothing terribly amiss in an occasional experiment with something that may have seemed merely magical. The kinds of pagan or idolatrous actions described in these sources are general and innocuous; they do not relate to any specific cult (though we noted Rav's vigorous prohibition of even sherds of a statue of Mercury, which may indicate that such objects were made into talismans by common people). Likewise, Rav prohibited[2] using the divine name as a magical formula which suggests that some people did, as did pagans who imitated Jews.

No one doubted, furthermore, that astrology was a science.[3] The issue debated in this generation, as earlier, was whether astrological phenomena affected the destiny of Israel.[4] Both Rav and Samuel firmly denied it:

> R. Judah in the name of Rav: The Holy One blessed be He said to our father Abraham, 'Walk before me and be thou perfect' (Gen. 17.1). He was thereupon seized with trembling. Perhaps, he said, there is still something shameful in me, but when He added, 'And I will make my covenant between me and thee,' his mind was appeased. 'And he brought him forth abroad' (Gen. 17. 4). Abraham had said to him, Lord of the Universe, I have gazed at my star [= the constellation which rules my destiny] and seen that I am not fated to beget children. God replied, 'Go forth'—from your astrological speculations

---

[1] b. A.Z. 53b. Samuel held the same view, 46a.
[2] b. Sanh. 101a.
[3] See S. Lieberman, *Greek in Jewish Palestine* (N.Y. 1942) 98-9.
[4] See vol. I 130, 162-3.

(ʾYZTGNYNWT). Israel is not subject to planetary influences
[Lit. = Israel has no star.]

(b. Ned. 32a)

Rav too holds that Israel is immune from planetary influence, for
R. Judah in the name of Rav said: How do we know that Israel is
immune from planetary influence? Because it is said, 'And he brought
him forth from abroad'. Abraham pleaded . . . (as above). What is thy
calculation? Because Zedek (Jupiter) stands in the west? I will turn
back and place it in the east, and thus it is written, 'Who hath raised
up Zedek from the east, he hath summoned it for his sake' (Is. 41.2).

(b. Shab. 156a-b)[1]

That God should be believed to know Abraham's horoscope and
to have altered it to achieve his own purposes indicates beyond
doubt that rabbis accepted the validity of astrology in general,
doubting, as I said, only whether or not it applies to Jewry in particular. Furthermore, Rav cited a teaching of Yosi of Huzal, to
prove that one must not consult astrologers,[2] indicating not only
that some Jews did, but that they thought it was not improper.
Rav and Samuel differed on the value of the Magus's learning. One
held that it was merely sorcery, the other, that it was blasphemy.
Rav, who had said that anyone who learns a single thing from a
Magus is worthy of death, regarded it as blasphemy, not merely
sorcery, while Samuel consistently took the more lenient view, as
one might expect.[3]

Sources relevant to the early Sasanian period yield some insight
into what Jews knew, and thought about, specific pagan phenomena
in their day. As we have noted above, the general laws on the subject
reveal almost no precise information about known cults, forms of
worship, or magical rites, but only produce examples of petty feti-
shism. We know of only one direct contact between the ʾAmoraʾim
of this period and Iranian sages, that between Ablat and Samuel and
Levi, of which Rav's saying is probably a direct criticism. One discussion between Samuel and Ablat concerned whether astrological influences governed Israelites, which Samuel denied, 'proving'
that one's fate depended upon his special merit achieved through

---

[1] The story involving Samuel and Ablat is cited in vol. I, 160.

[2] b. Shab. 113b.

[3] b. Shab. 75a. The exegesis is on Deut. 18.9, one should not learn *to do*, but
to understand is permitted. See Hoffmann, *Mar Samuel* pp. 78f., whose interpretation of the passage is followed here.

philanthropy, rather than upon his star.[1] Levi and Ablat discussed Sabbath law, and Levi offered a justification for a detail of the law through an analogy, afterwards bolstering his viewpoint by reference to a Scriptural exegesis for the benefit of his students.[2] Samuel and Ablat discussed medical traditions:

> Ablat found Samuel sleeping in the sun. He said to him, O Jewish sage [Or, Wisest of the Jews], can that which is injurious be beneficial? It is a day of bleeding [and I need the heat], he replied. Yet it is not so, but there is a day when the sun is beneficial for the whole year, the day of the Tammuz (summer) solstice, and he said to himself, I will not reveal it to him.
>
> (b. Shab. 129a)

Samuel regarded his medical traditions as peculiarly private, not to be revealed to gentiles. For his part, Ablat was very careful not to render unfit kosher wine:

> Samuel and Ablat were sitting together, when boiled wine was brought up for them, and he (Ablat) withdrew his hand [not to touch the wine and render it unfit]. But Samuel said, Behold it has been said that boiled wine is not to be suspected of idolatrous use.
>
> (b. A.Z. 30a)

One recalls that Shapur allegedly knew about the laws regarding the fitness of kitchen utensils (above, p. 70). There can be no doubt that these rules, which were obvious and striking to the outsider, were known to the surrounding peoples, as were the Sabbath laws.[3] But the pagans knew little more than these, so far as we can tell, and Jewish occult science. I doubt that the Jews had a very detailed idea of what the gentiles' religious practices actually were, apart from Rav's polemical exaggerations; at Dura, it is clear that they did, on the other hand. We have noted the most generalized prohibitions of actions and artifacts involved in 'pagan' worship, and have found no evidence whatever that such 'pagan' practices were identified with one or another particular cult. The conversations with Ablat, on astrology and medicine, indicate that these sciences, part of the common legacy which all who lived in Babylonia inherited from the earlier civilization of the region, interested both Jewish and Iranian sages, and formed the basis of conversation between them. But if the sages

---

[1] b. Shab. 152a-b.

[2] y. Shab. 3.3, for a similar distinction between analogical and exegetical replies to difficult questions, see my *Life* 61-2, 169-171.

[3] Vol. I, 155-56.

talked of substantive theological or philosophical issues, we have
no record of it, and I do not believe that they did. What the Iranian
sage and king knew was a peculiarity of Jewish practice (specifically
regarding the Sabbath and eating), which required, and elicited,
special consideration. What little the Jewish sages knew about
Iranian religion we shall see below.

According to Professor Saul Lieberman's interpretation of the
following sources, Samuel knew about the *ludi Saeculares* [of 248]:

> R. Judah in the name of Samuel said: They observe yet another
> festival in Rome once every seventy years. Then a healthy man is
> brought and made to ride on a lame man, he is dressed in the attire of
> Adam, on his head is placed the scalp of R. Ishmael, and on his neck
> are hung pieces of fine gold to the weight of four zuz. The market
> place is paved with onyx stones, and the proclamation is made before
> him, The reckoning of the ruler is a forgery. The brother of our lord
> [is] the forger! Of what avail is his deceit to the deceiver and his
> forgery to the forger! He who sees it sees it; he who does not see it
> now will never see it.
>
>   (b. A.Z. 11b)

Professor Lieberman comments[1] that the information about events
in Rome in Philip's reign would have been known to the Persian court,
particularly the games, which symbolized Roman patriotism. He
explains the strange language "The reckoning of the master is a
fiction" to refer to the plans of Shapur, and he regards the passage
as an anti-Persian saying. He does not cite, nor provide explanation
for, the Jewish details of Samuel's report, concerning the attire of
Adam, the use of the scalp of R. Ishmael (who was believed to have
been scalped and martyred) and so on. Rashi's interpretation, that the
lame man refers to Jacob, and the healthy man riding on his back, to
Esau, is doubtless completely correct, in which case we are dealing
with a Jewish view of what a pagan holiday would have been like,
based not on direct witness but on the fragmentary report of an
eye-witness, which subsequently would have been elaborated by the
sage's imagination or by that of his informant. It seems far-fetched,
in any event, to assume that the Persians thus described the festival
to the Jewish sage, in order to win his support, and that of his people,
against the Romans. Though we have some evidence that Shapur
did indeed attempt to win Jewish support, and succeeded, I do not
believe the Persians were sufficiently well-informed of rabbinic

---

[1] S. Lieberman, *JQR* 37, 1, 39-40. See also Baron, *op. cit.*, II, 396.

attitudes to embellish the story they gave out with such details as reference to midrashic typologies about Jacob and Esau, or rabbinic memories of the martyrdom of Tanna'im in the Hadrianic period.

In his commentary on the Mishnah ("These are the festivities of the idolaters: Kalenda, Saturnalia, Kratesis"), Samuel explained Kratesis as the day on which Rome extended her dominion (over the Greeks).[1]

The Talmud cites the following Persian festivals: Mutardi, Turyaski, Muharneki, Muharin; Babylonian festivals: Muharneki, Aknaya, Bahnani, and the 10th of Adar; Median festivals: Musardi, Triaski, and Moharneki. Rav gave them as follows: for Babylonia, Mahur, Kanuni, and Banauta; for Media, Nosardi, Tiriaski, and Meninkna. The names of these festivals are mutilated, and the information they provide garbled. In fact, as S. H. Taqizadeh showed, Nusardi refers to Nausard, new year; Triaski[2] to Tiraghan, 13th of the 4th month; and Moharneki to Mihragan, 16th of the 7th month; likewise, Mutardi yields Musardi, again, Nausard; Turyaski Tiraghan; Muharnekai, Mihrakan; and Muharin must be a mutilated form of Nauruz. In the Yer. passage, Nauruz is said to fall on the 2nd of Adar in Persia, and the 20th of Adar in Media. This was not the Persian New Years' day, which did not begin in Adar but in September (Tishri). Taqizadeh points out that if Nauruz was used in the sense of the beginning of the religious and fixed Persian year, then the Yer. saying must be dated at 261 or 264, when the 2nd day of Adar corresponded with the 1st day of Shahrevar, Feb. 19, 261 or Feb. 18th, 264.

What is most striking in the above, first of all, is the absence of information on the correct names of the various festivals, all of which are given in mutilated forms indicating lack of precise knowledge. Second, the Jewish sayings indicate little or no knowledge about the *meaning* of the festivals. Third, they knew nothing, or said nothing, about such other, important holidays as Spandarmad, the 5th day of the 12th month, a feast of farmers; about the six days following the Farvardigan; about the 1st of Atur; about the 1st and 16th of Dadr, days which were new year festivals (apart from Nauruz). In each month of the Sasanian calendar, the day which bore the name of the month was celebrated, thus, the 13th of Tir (Tiraghan, cited above), the 7th of Shahrevar, the 9th of Atur, the 15th of Dadv, the

[1] b. A.Z. 8b.
[2] His transliterations.

5th of Spandarmad, etc. None of this is clear in the Jewish sources. Moreover, two of those which they knew, specifically Nauruz and Mihragan, were days on which additional taxes were paid, and their knowledge was thus based on civil rather than religious realities. Furthermore the division of good Mazdean festivals among Babylonia, Media, and Persia is unfounded. It is quite possible that Babylonians celebrated festivals handed on in their old tradition, in addition to Iranian ones. But the Persian festivals are, in fact, identical with the Median ones, as Taqizadeh showed. We learn from these sayings, some attributed to Rav, less about the Mazdean festivals than about Jewish knowledge of them, which from the evidence considered here was spotty and limited at best.[1] Just as the pagans knew little

---

[1] See b. A.Z. 11b, y. A.Z. 1.2. The authoritative treatment of these festivals, which were widely discussed before his time, is by S. H. Taqizadeh, "The Iranian Festivals Adopted by the Christians and Condemned by the Jews", *BSOS* 10, 1940-42, see especially pp. 632-9. The Syrian Christians adopted the Iranian calendar, the Nestorians doing so in 485. (See also A. Kohut, "Les fêtes Persanes et Babyloniennes dans les Talmuds de Babylon et de Jerusalem", *REJ* 24, 256-71.) Taqizadeh points out that both Mutardi and Musardi mean New Year (Nusardi, Nauruz), one for the sprinkling of water, the other for the first fruit of dates, both falling at the end of July or in early August. On the Mazdean Calendar, see also Christensen, *L'Iran* 119, 164f. On Nauruz and Mihrakan, additional taxes were paid, which is probably why the Jews knew about these holidays. On Mihrakan, compare Andreas-Henning, *Mitteliran. Manichaica*, 1932, 189 n. 1. On Tiraghan, the custom was to wash, and to taste cheese and fruit dishes. Like the Jewish New Year, Mihrakan included cosmogonic and eschatological themes. See also David Oppenheim, "Die Namen der persischen und babylonischen Feste im Talmud", *MGWJ* 3, 1854, 347-52; S. Funk in *A. Schwarz Festschrift* (Berlin 1917) 430; N. Pigulevskaja, *Villes*, 242-4; J. Duchesne-Guillemin, *La Religion*, 118-124; G. Widengren, *Die Religionen* 182f. Note also that in the Dura synagogue, the days are given according to the Iranian calendar, "In the month of Fravartin in the year 15 [of Shapur] on the day Rashnu"; "in the month of Mihr in the year 14 on the day of Sathrevar"; "in the month of Mihr in the year 14"; "in the month Mihr in the year 14 and on the day Fravartin"; "in the month Mihr in the year 14 on the day Mahrspand"; "month Amurdat and the day Fravartin"; "month Sathrevar, day Mahrspand"; "month Mihr and day Rashnu"; "month [Urt-Vahisht?] day Hormazd". See B. Geiger in Kraeling, *The Synagogue*, pp. 300-16. There, all the *dipirs* had typical Zoroastrian names, and were doubtless better informed about the Iranian calendar than the rabbis, as the good knowledge of Iranian dating indicates. I should not presume to suggest the meaning of the specifically Babylonian festivals, referred to by both the anonymous *beraita* and Rav, Aknaya, Bahnani, the 10th of Adar, or, Kanuna and Banauta. We do find *nubattu*, a night vigil; *Akitu* was of course the New Year, but what these would have been called in the third century C.E. cannot be ascertained from Babylonian sources, the most recent of which dated to the first century A.D. See Edouard Dhorme, *Les Religions de Babylonie et d'Assyrie* (Paris 1949) 234-9. As to Rav's distinction between Persia and Media, I have found no evidence that the Mazdean holidays of these satrapies differed from one another. It may be

about Judaism, other than a few obvious features, so the Jews knew only those Iranian holidays which impinged upon their lives.

Rav referred to five temples of idolatry: in Babylon, the Temple of Bel; in Kursi, of Nebo; in Mapug, of Tar'ata; in Ashkelon, of Zerifa; and in Arabia of Nishtra. The references are to the Temple of Marduk, which was in ruins long before Rav's time; Nebo in Kursi probably refers to Gerasa, in Palestine; Tarata in Magub to Hieropolis; Zerifia may mean Venus, or following Kohut, Serapis; and Nishtra must have been a deity resembling an eagle. Rav likewise offered an explanation of Kalendes:

> The First Man established [Kalendes]. When night fell, he said, Woe is me, perhaps he of whom it is written, "he will smite thee by his head, and you him by your heel (Gen. 3.15)—perhaps he will come and bite me .... When the day broke, he exclaimed, Kalendes— Kalon deo [praise God].

(y. A.Z. 1.2)

It should not be thought that Jews had no genuine knowledge of, or interest in, paganism. Considerable evidence exists, as we have seen, that some Jews took a keen interest in paganism, greatly displeasing the rabbis not only by their indifference to whom they married, but also by their exploitation of non-Jewish magical formulae. Krauss points out, for example that while the Jews hated the Magi, and were hated by the Mandeans, Mandaeism was the source of many Jewish beliefs and magical practices; magical bowls were used in common by

---

that the Jewish sources preserved variants in the names, which, as we have seen, apply, in fact, to the *same* festivals. I think, however, that the biblical idiom, in which the Medes and the Persians are frequently joined together as allies, but not as a single united empire, led the Jews in the later period to regard the two satrapies as more separate in culture, religion, and politics than they actually were. Since the names themselves are so garbled, it would indicate that the Jews, knowing very little, in any event, about Mazdean holidays, simply assumed that the holidays of the Medes would differ from those of the Persians or Babylonians, and vice versa, and so signified by the separate categories by which they listed them. See also A. Kohut, *AJSLL* 14, 1897, 186f. He holds that the reference to Media in fact means Persia. The Babylonian festivals of which the Talmuds speak, he says, are "actually references to Persian festivals celebrated in Babylonia in the Sasanian period." He understands by MWTYRR' Medyarem, one of the six Gahanbars; Tiriski means Tiragan, Mihrkani, Mihrgan, MWHRWZ Nauruz etc. He cites Abu Othman al Gahiz (d. 869), that the Exilarch had to pay on Nauruz 4,000 dirhams into the royal treasury. See also Kohut in *REJ* 24, 256-71; *Arukh* Supplement, 11, 15, 16, 42, 52, 55, 56, 69; Perles, *Etymologische Studien*, 101; Krauss, *Talmudische Archaeologie*, III, 123, 127-30, and 298 n. 366-80. On *Kalendes*, see S. Lieberman, *Hellenism in Jewish Palestine* (N.Y. 1950), 10, Kalendae was thus connected to a primitive sun festival, in Rav's view.

Christians, Mazdeans, Jews, and Mandeans, and, as we have noted, considerable credence was placed by both Jews and pagans in one another's traditions on astrology, medicine, and magic. What we learn from our consideration of Talmudic accounts of Mazdean festivals is that the rabbis knew very little, apart from holidays on which taxes were paid, about them. But that tells us nothing about what other Jews knew or did not know. The great emphasis on laws calculated to separate the Jews from the gentiles suggests that the masses of the people actually lived in close touch with their pagan neighbors, and required frequent admonitions from the rabbis to keep separate from them. What the actual proportions of adherents to the different sorts of Judaism present in third century Babylonia were we cannot guess but certainly the proportion of gnostics and other kinds of, from the rabbis' viewpoint, heretics was assuredly much larger than is their proportion in their preserved remains; in the literary sources, we know mainly about the condemnation of their rabbinical enemies.[1]

---

[1] See S. Krauss, "Babylonia", JE II 405-6 on Mandean influence; on mixed marriages, b. Qid. 71b-72b. James A. Montgomery, *Aramaic Incantation Texts from Nippur* (Philadelphia, 1913) holds that archaeological evidence shows "the absolute community of ideas and terms and practice between Jewish and Gentile [Hellenistic] sorcery." In almost every Jewish house at Nippur was found an incantation bowl, and some were in cemeteries as well. Thirty of the forty bowls published by Montgomery are in language similar to, or precisely the same as, Babylonian-Talmudic Aramaic. We do not know how early these bowls were used; the latest possible dating is 7th century. The bowls were (p. 43) primarily a domestic phylactery, guarding the home against evil spirits. Some were love charms or served other positive functions. This is, as I said above, not the place for a detailed discussion of Jewish magic in Babylonia. An excellent recent discussion of the magical bowls will be found in Edwin Masao Yamauchi, *Mandaean Incantation Texts* (Ann Arbor, 1964: Microfilm of Brandeis University Dissertation). See also Wilfred L. Knox, *St. Paul and the Church of the Gentiles* (Cambridge, 1961), 208-212, Jewish influences on magical literature, and of interest also in his note on the Mandeans, 212-219.

CHAPTER THREE

JEWISH SELF-GOVERNMENT IN
EARLY SASANIAN BABYLONIA

i. The Legacy of Arsacid Times

In my view,[1] the exilarchate as we know it was organized by the regime of Vologases I, ca. 70 C.E., to solve two important problems. First of all, he and his government had to take account of the anarchy prevailing in Babylonia after the dynastic struggles of the preceding half-century. Among other groups, the Jews required attention. They had established their own state, under Anileus and Asineus,[2]

---

[1] See volume I, 50-58, 97-112. See M. Beer, "The Exilarchs in Talmudic Times" (in Hebrew) *Ziyyon* 28, 1963, 3-33. Beer cites (3-5) the sources applying to Arsacid times to prove that the exilarchate enjoyed "Persian" support throughout its history, but at the same time properly criticizes earlier historians for anachronisms. See also Jacob Roifman, "The Exilarch" (in Hebrew) *Bikkurim* I, 1864, 36-49.

[2] In volume I, 50-55, I discussed the 'Jewish state' of Anileus and Asineus. Here I should like to call attention to the penetrating remarks of Professor Hildegard Lewy on the same matter, in "The Genesis of the Faulty Persian Chronology" *JAOS* 64, 1944, 197-214. She points out a possible connection between the struggle of Gotarzes and Ardavan and the fate of the 'Jewish state' of Babylonia. As I noted, Ardavan accepted the fait-accompli of the Jewish brothers, and recognized their state. Lewy points out that Ardavan was actually *using* the Jews as a counter-balance against his unreliable satraps in Babylonia. Lewy, noting other instances of such a Jewish alliance, states:

> This marked friendship between Ardavan and his Jewish subjects makes it clear that, if Gudarz [Gotarzes] wanted to weaken his father's influence in favor of his own ambitious plans, he had to break the power of Ardawan's Jewish supporters, a task which must have appeared to him all the more imperative since, under the leadership of the brothers Asinaeus and Anilaeus, the Jewish state had engulfed large parts of Babylonia and Mesopotamia.

Lewy notes that although Josephus does not speak of any political implications connected with this campaign, the date—35 or 36 A.D.—clearly indicates that Ardavan's internal adversaries used, for the annihilation of his Jewish supporetrs in Mesopotamia, "precisely the time when the founder of the new dynasty had fled to his eastern provinces in order to gather a new army with which to reconquer his empire from the Ashkanian prince Tiridates." I had missed such a connection because Josephus speaks of Ardavan's son-in-law as leader of an action against the Jews. Lewy holds that this was merely 'the first battle,' (perhaps for curbing an ally's excesses?) while the leader who actually destroyed the Jewish forces is unnamed. Lewy holds that the Persian tradition, according to which that leader was Gotarzes, is valid, and adds (p. 212 n. 145) that the massacre of Babylonian Jews may be one of the 'bloody deeds' which Tacitus (Ann. 11.8.3) ascribed to Gotarzes.

between 20 and 35, and after its collapse, had suffered from the depredations of the Greeks and Babylonians. A numerous group, the Jews could clearly not be ignored, nor could their government be satisfactorily entrusted to a territorial regime, for just as their rule over Greeks and Babylonians had proved unacceptable, so the latter could not effectively govern them. At the same time, the Parthians could make good use of Jewish officials, who both at home and abroad might win the support of their brethren for the Arsacid government. It was necessary, therefore, for domestic political reasons to establish an institution charged with the government of the Jews, and the normal means, within the highly feudalized structure of the Arsacid empire, was to appoint a feudatory power, owing direct responsibility and loyalty to the throne, in this case ruling a minority group settled over a large region, rather than a circumscribed territory.

Second, the destruction of the Temple in Jerusalem, in 70 C.E., posed a serious problem to the Parthian government. In former times, Babylonian Jewry, like that in other parts of the diaspora, was deeply loyal to the Temple. Pilgrims went up to Jerusalem, and Temple collections of a half-shekel were gathered regularly in Nehardea, in the south, and in Nisibis, in the north, and forwarded in armed caravans to the Temple. The Temple authorities, for their part, sent

---

On two points I cannot follow Lewy's conclusions. First, I believe it unlikely that the 'Jewish state' actually 'engulfed' vast stretches of Babylonia and Mesopotamia. Lewy's citation here is inconclusive. It seems to me incredible that 'the Jews', a minority, could have held such vast territories, but more likely, the core of the Jewish state consisted, in fact, of the region around Nehardea, where Jews probably constituted a majority of the local population. The inclusion of distant Nisibis as a center of refuge does not necessarily indicate it was formerly a center of political power. Second, her treatment of the Edessa legend is far-fetched. Lewy holds that Abgar V, allied with Gotarzes, campaigned against the Jews in Nisibis, which "fact" led later Christian historians to assume he was Christian, "a conclusion which enticed them to transfer upon him the historic story of the conversion of Abgar IX." While there may be a kernel of historical truth in the story of Abgar IX's conversion to Christianity, the details of that legend are so extraordinary as to preclude our acceptance of them as simple historical facts. Furthermore, I see no reason to assume, with Lewy, that Abgar V collaborated with Gotarzes in a campaign against the Jews. In any event there is more than one way to read Moses of Khorene's account of Abgar's 'expedition to Palestine,' assuming that that account has a historical foundation at all, a very difficult step for me to take.

In any event, I believe Lewy's interpretation of the place of the Babylonian 'Jewish state' in Parthian politics to be fruitful and provocative, even though some of the details may be require further study.

letters to Babylonia, as did the Pharisaic party, to advise the Jews on matters of calendrical regulation and other religious issues. After the destruction, the authority of the Temple was assumed by the remnants of the Pharisaic party at Yavneh, where, with Roman approval, the powers formerly exercised by the Temple administration became vested in R. Yoḥanan ben Zakkai and R. Gamaliel II after him. The Parthians enjoyed the services of an excellent intelligence bureau, and must have known that the Palestinian Jewish authority would no longer be exercised by quasi-independent officials, but would, quite naturally, be very closely supervised by the Romans, as was the case. If the Parthians were willing to allow limited, and on the whole politically neutral, authority to be exerted from Jerusalem over their subjects, they would never permit a Roman function- ary to do the same. Quite to the contrary, just as the Romans sought to mobilize Jewish support, and to use Jewish officials for their own purposes, so the Parthians exploited the fact that within their here- ditary enemy's territories, flourished a large religious-ethnic group, with strong ties across the Euphrates, and a deep sense of grievance against Rome. They always tried to foment unrest among minority groups within the Roman Empire. (The Romans, for their part, were keenly aware of the danger of leaving a substantial ethnic group to straddle their borders, and for this reason, invaded Britain, and attempted to retain Armenia in the preceding century and a half. They were, moreover, deeply concerned about Jewish public opinion in Parthia, and therefore hired Josephus to convey their view of war guilt across the Euphrates, as he explicitly stated.) The exilarchate in Parthian Babylonia, like the patriarchate in Roman Palestine, was the most convenient means to manage a potentially useful ethnic group's affairs at home, and, perhaps, to exploit its connections abroad. It was most certainly a way of annulling whatever influence Jewish functionaries of Rome might exert over Babylonian Jewry, by providing an alternate, home-born authority, supported and closely supervised by the government. Both the exilarchate and patriarchate were backed up by imperial troops, R. Judah having a detachment of Goths at his command, the exilarch an armed retinue, and both eventually achieved great spiritual influence over their respective Jewish communities. Each saw the other as its natural counterpart, as was very much the case, for both were, in fact, created because of the destruction of Jerusalem, the patriarchate as a means of governing internal Jewish affairs in which the Romans had no special interest and at the same time of keeping the peace in Palestine, the exilarchate to do the same in Babylonia. At the same time both were supposed to prevent aliens from influencing Jews under their control, and to exert malevolent influence across the frontier where possible.

In the second century, the exilarchate developed into a powerful instrument of government. Its agents enjoyed the perquisites of the Iranian nobility. It inflicted the death penalty, and governed the Jews by its own lights, enforcing its judgment with military force when it chose. If, moreover, the several Jewish revolts against Rome, at times highly propitious from the Parthian viewpoint, were in fact instigated by its agents, and if the support given to the Arsacid throne in the crisis of Trajan's invasion was in a measure the result of exilarchic influence, as seems quite plausible, then the Parthians must have judged the exilarchate to be a great success indeed. By the end of the 2nd century, the exilarch R. Huna[1] was regarded with a mixture of respect and apprehension in Palestine, where his claim to Davidic ancestry in the male line, superior to R. Judah's, allegedly in the female line, was recognized. Among the Jews and Parthians alike, the exilarchate played a major political and administrative role.

The advent of the Sasanians changed all this. The political foundations of the exilarchate were swept away, for Ardashir had no need, as we have seen, to reaffirm existing political institutions or patterns of action, nor did he do so. He owed nothing to the Jews. The Jews lost, therefore, the legal autonomy they had enjoyed under the Parthians, and, as we have noted, their courts at first possessed no legal standing whatever in Sasanian law, but were supervised by Persian agents. What other changes were made we may only surmise from the fact that while Parthian legal forms never affected the administration of justice among the Jews, so far as we know, numerous references attest not only to the keen interest of the Persians in Jewish court procedures, but to Jewish knowledge of Persian law. Samuel's dictum that the law of the land was law expressed grudging acceptance of this new and disagreeable circumstance. The exilarchate continued, nonetheless, to exist. This much is certain in the contemporary sources. What its functions were, how it effected the government of the Jews under the new regime, how it achieved a rapprochement with the government—these are questions for which we shall seek answers, mainly by inference from inadequate evidence. We shall

---

[1] On R. Huna, see esp. Yavetz, *Toldot* VII, 23.

first consider this evidence, and then attempt a more general description of the development of the exilarchate in the first forty years of
Sasanian rule.

II. THE GE'ONIC TRADITIONS

R. Sherira,[1] who lived in Pumbedita in the 9th-10th century, and
had access to the ancient archives of its academy, provided the following information:

> In the days of Rabbi [Judah the Prince] Rav Huna the First was
> exilarch in Babylonia.
>> ('*Iggeret R. Sherira Gaon*, ed. B. Levin [Haifa 1923] 76 1. 3)
> And after Rav Huna, Mar Rav 'Ukba was appointed in Babylonia.
>> (*ibid.* 77 1. 15)
> And here was R. Shila the Head of the House of the Rabbis [ריש רבנן
> בירבנן]. And they called the Resh Sidra [ריש סידרא] in Babylonia
> the Resha de Rabbanan [ריש דרבנן].[2]
>> (*ibid.* 78 1. 9)

What is important here is that Rav Sherira thought that "Mar
Rav 'Ukba" was exilarch in the period after the death of R. Judah
the Prince in Palestine, hence ca. 220 C.E. His information, he himself
states explicitly, was based upon b. Shab. 55a, which we shall consider
below.

The *Seder Olam Zuta* provides the following:

> In the 166th year of the Destruction of the Temple [= 236 C.E.] the
> Persians came upon the Romans. And Shekheniah died and after him
> arose his son, Hezekiah, and the sages directed him.[3] And Hezekiah
> died and was buried in the land of Israel in the valley of Arabel, which
> belongs to Judah b. Sharaf the Priest eastward of the city. And after
> him arose his son, and the sages directed him. When he died, Nathan
> was still in his mother's womb, he is Nathan of Zuzita. And Nathan
> died and after him arose Rav Huna, his son, and the sages directed him.
> And 'Akov died, and Nahum his son arose, and the sages directed him.
> Rav Huna, Rav Hanina, Rav Mattenah, Rav Hananel were his sages.

---

[1] See Y. N. Epstein, *Introductions to Amoraic Literature* (in Hebrew) (Jerusalem
1962) 610-15.

[2] On 'rabbanan deve resh galuta' see b. Shab. 58a.

[3] The meaning of "and the sages DABRUHU" (דברוהו), about which I was
formerly uninformed (Vol. I, 100), was definitively stated by S. Krauss, "Notizen
zur 'kleinen Chronik' ", *MGWJ* 61, 1917, 7-25. Providing a full analysis of the
matter, Krauss concludes that the meaning was "die Gelehrten hatten ihn ein-
gesetzt". Compare Y. L. Zunz, *Sermons in Israel* (in Hebrew), trans. and ed.
H. Albeck (Jerusalem 1954) 307 n. 72, Epstein, in *MGWJ* 63, 1919, 253f; and
M. Beer, *op. cit.*, 23-4, particularly 24 n. 164.

And Nahum died and Yoḥanan arose, and the sages directed him
Rav Ḥananel was his sage. And Shefet died, and there arose after him
ʿAnan his son, and the sages directed him. And Rav Samuel was his
sage. There went forth Pasa [sic] b. Naẓer and destroyed Nehardea.
And Rav Huna died and was buried in the land of Israel near R. Ḥiyya
the Great. And Nathan his son arose, and the sages directed him.
R. Judah b. Ezekiel and R. Sheshet were his sages.

(*Seder ʿOlam Zuta*, ed. M. Grosberg [London 1910] 34-40)

Zunz's judgment[1] is that the author of Seder ʿOlam Zuta, who lived
in the 8th century at the earliest, had no valid information whatever
about the exilarchs before the time of Samuel, but the names dating
from 240 to 470 are more reliable. In any case, in the *SOZ* list, Huna is
not mentioned. Rather, Nahum was followed by his brother Yoḥanan,
and then his son Shafat (compare I. Chron. 3: 22-4), who was succeeded by Anan. W. Bacher[2] identifies ʿAnan with Huna, known in
Talmudic sources to have been a contemporary of R. Judah the
Prince, for, he says, "at the time of his successor Nathan ʿUkban
occurred the fall of the Arsacids," which he finds referred to by the
SOZ date of 236. He holds that Nathan ʿUkban was none other than
Mar ʿUkba, contemporary of Rav and Samuel. His successor,
following Bacher, was his son Huna (= Huna II), 'advised' by Rav
and Samuel. His son and successor was Nathan, called also Mar ʿUkban II. The Geʾonic traditions on this period are therefore as follows:

SOZ	*R. Sherira*
ʿAnan	Huna
Nathan ʿUkban	Mar ʿUkba
[= Nathan of Ẓuẓita, following	
b. Shab. 56b and Sanh. 31b]	
Huna	

Of the two traditions, R. Sherira's is clearly preferable, being based
upon his own investigation of the Talmudic sources as well as of his
academy's traditions. The *SOZ* was mainly concerned to prove,
first, the Davidic origin of the early exilarchs, and second, the submission of these same exilarchs to the will of the sages. From it
we learn more about the Geʾonic period than about that under study.
For the rest, we shall have to review the Talmudic evidence.[3]

---

[1] Zunz-Albeck, 65-6, 307-8, ns. 73-8,

[2] *JE* V, 289.

[3] See also Felix Lazarus, "Die Häupter der Vertriebenen", *JaJGL* 10, 1890,
1-183; Halevi, *op. cit.*, III 38f.

III. MAR ʿUKBA

It is impossible to regard all sources, in which the name Mar ʿUkba appears, as applying to a single individual. It is therefore necessary at the outset to consider the sources according to the natural divisions into which they fall.

The first, and smallest group of sources deals with an exilarch called Mar ʿUkba. These I have isolated quite mechanically by reference to the known functions of the exilarch, including the declaration of the calendar and the administration of Jewish government. The most important of these sources is the following:

> Rav said, There was no greater penitent than Josiah in his generation, and a certain person in ours, and who is that? Abba father of R. Jeremiah b. Abba. Some say, Aḥa the brother of Abba the father of Jeremiah b. Abba . . . . R. Joseph said, And there is yet another in *our* generation, and who is he? ʿUkban b. Nehemiah the Resh Galuta. And he is Nathan of Zuzita. R. Joseph said, I was sitting at the session and dozing, and saw in a dream how one stretched out his hand and received him.
>
> (b. Shab. 56b, see 140a)

This passage normally is interpreted to mean that ʿUkban b. Nehemiah and Mar ʿUkba were one and the same, the exilarch referred to in the Geonic passage cited above. Yet that interpretation poses difficulties, for R. Joseph specifically refers to a great penitent of his *own* generation, which is that of R. Judah of Pumbedita, Samuel's student, and R. Huna of Sura, Rav's student, thus ca. 260-300. Since R. Joseph studied with the students of Rav and Samuel, he cannot in any case be dated in the early part of that generation. I fail therefore to see how his saying concerning ʿUkban b. Nehemiah the exilarch has anything at all to do with the Mar ʿUkba who was contemporary of Rav and Samuel.

A passage on MarʿUkba suggests that he made a circuit of the Jewish communities, but failed to impress them with his learning:

> Mar ʿUkba chanced to come to Gazaca, and he was asked, Is fasting for a number of hours considered a fast or not? He was unable to reply. Are wine-jars belonging to idolaters prohibited for us or not? He was unable to reply. In which [garments] did Moses perform the service in the Tabernacle during the seven days of consecration? And he was unable to reply. He went and asked at the school and was told, The law is that fasting for a matter of hours is considered a fast . . . .
>
> (b. Taʿanit 11b)[1]

---

[1] Compare b. A.Z. 34a, R. Akiba visited the same town.

A parallel passage in A.Z. reads 'R. Akiba'; it is known that R. Akiba did visit Gazaca (Ginzak). In any event the readings are confused.[1] One thing is certain, and that is, that Mar ʿUkba was one of the leading authorities of his generation, and such a story as this would suggest that while the Mar ʿUkba who was Rav and Samuel's contemporary was a sage, the MarʿUkba (if it *was* Mar Ukba) who made a circuit to Ginzak was *not* learned, but had to resort to the guidance of the school house. This theme frequently occurs in the rabbis' denigrating stories about the exilarch's ignorance and dependence on their learning, even for obvious and uncomplicated matters such as these.

That Mar ʿUkba had dealings with calendar regulation is clear from the following:

> Mar ʿUkba found two letters. In one was written, It is well in my sight and in the sight of my colleagues to add to the year thirty days, and in one, It is well in our sight (etc.).
>
> (y. Meg. 1.5)
>
> Mar ʿUkba sent a letter to the exilarch . . .
>
> (y. Meg. 3.2)[2]
>
> They sent (from Palestine) to Mar ʿUkba saying, The Adar which precedes Nisan is always defective . . .
>
> (b. R.H. 19b)

Since the Palestinians wrote letters to the Babylonian exilarchate[3] it stands to reason that the Mar ʿUkba, who found such letters, found them in the archives of his court; likewise, the evidence that such letters were sent *to* him is beyond question. The latter passage was discussed by R. Ḥisda and Rav Kahana, presumably of the generation after 260, however, and proves nothing whatever about the contemporary of Samuel. As to the letter sent, according to the Yer. *by* Mar ʿUkba *to* the exilarch, this proves very little. It may have been sent before Mar ʿUkba himself became exilarch; or it may have been sent by a Mar ʿUkba who was not, and never became, exilarch, as Beer plausibly points out. The above evidence therefore yields only one firm conclusion, that *a* Mar ʿUkba was probably exilarch; but if so, it was probably a Mar ʿUkba/ʿUkban b. Nehemiah of the generation after Samuel, that is to say, in the end of the third century and beginning of the fourth.

The second natural division of Mar ʿUkba sayings is marked by

[1] See *Dik. Sof.* VI 60.

[2] See Epstein, *Introductions to Amoraic Literature* 342-3, n. 38.

[3] See *Life* 40-2, and vol. I, pp. 41-43.

the fact that R. Ḥisda transmitted them. R. Ḥisda, of the generation at the end of the third century, reported sayings of Mar ʿUkba which are not recorded in the name of any other, earlier tradent, and it stands to reason that these sayings do not date before R. Ḥisda's time. They include the following:

> Our rabbis taught, One may not wash barley on Pesaḥ, and if one did and they split, they are forbidden, but if they did not split, they are permitted. R. Yosi said, He can soak them in vinegar and vinegar binds them. Samuel said, The law is not as R. Yosi. R. Ḥisda in Mar ʿUkba's name said, It does not mean literally split. But Samuel said, It means literally split. Samuel acted in the vicinity of the home of Bar Hashu [BDWRʾ DBY BR HSW) on the view that split is meant literally.

(b. Pes. 40a)

If, as we shall see below, Samuel submissively accepted the legal dicta of a Mar ʿUkba, then it is difficult to understand how he *acted* as described here, for it is clear that however he may have *taught* the law, he followed the view, when it was enunciated, of the Mar ʿUkba of *his* time. I think it likely therefore that the citation of R. Ḥisda concerns another, later, Mar ʿUkba. Other sayings of Mar ʿUkba cited by R. Ḥisda concern the interpretation of Song of Songs 5.11, which 'teaches that it is possible to pile up mounds of expositions on every single stroke (of the letters of the Torah)';[1] on the law concerning gifts in anticipation of death,[2] the provision of food and clothing for the family of an insane man,[3] and other matters.[4] None of these sayings yields specific historical information. (We know, further, of a Mar ʿUkba who came before R. Naḥman, Samuel's student, for the confirmation of his possession of property.[5] This particular Mar ʿUkba could not have been either a contemporary of Samuel,[6] or the Exilarch.)

The third natural division of the Mar ʿUkba sayings concerns the Mar ʿUkba with whom Samuel and Rav had dealings. These sources reveal *unequivocally* that in their time, there was a Mar ʿUkba who was a judge or *av bet din*.[7] The relevant sources on Mar ʿUkba and Rav

---

[1] b. ʿEruv. 21b.

[2] b. Ket. 70a.

[3] b. Ket. 48a.

[4] b. Nid. 52a, Ber. 10b, 29b, Sotah 5a, Sanh. 38a, 70a, Shab. 54b, 116b, 119b, Git. 70a, 88a, see also Ket. 87a, R. Zakkai to Mar ʿUkba.

[5] b. Ket. 94b.

[6] But compare b. Ket. 78b-79a, see below.

[7] Beer points out that the title, *av bet din*, is used very seldom in sources relevant

show only that Mar ʿUkba cited Rav.[1] Mar ʿUkba appears in connection with Samuel, or as an important judge, in the following sources:

R. Judah was sitting before Samuel when a woman came and cried before him, but he ignored her. Said he to him, Does not the Master agree (Prov. 21.13), 'Whosoever stoppeth his ears at the cry of the poor he shall also cry but not be heard'? O Keen scholar, he replied, Your superior [I] will be punished with cold water, but your superior's superior with hot [That is, there is a higher court than mine to take up the matter]. Surely Mar ʿUkba the *Av Bet Din* is sitting, for it is written, 'O House of David, thus saith the Lord, Execute judgment in the morning' (Jer. 21.12).

(b. Shab. 55a)[2]

Mar ʿUkba did not attend court on a day of severe south wind.
(b. ʿEruv. 65a)

A message was once sent [from Palestine] to Mar ʿUkba: To him whose lustre is like that of the son of Bithia [= Moses], Peace be with thee. ʿUkban the Babylonian has complained to us saying, My brother Jeremiah has obstructed my way. Speak therefore to him and see that he meets us in Tiberias.

(b. Sanh. 31b)

It has been stated, If a minor is betrothed without her father's knowledge, Samuel said, She requires both *get* and *miʾun*. Said Karna, This is intrinsically objectionable: If a *get*, why *miʾun*, and vice versa. They said to him, But there is Mar ʿUkba and his court at Kafri [whom we should ask] . . . .

(b. Qid. 44b)

The above sources indicate, first of all, that Mar ʿUkba the contemporary of Samuel was a judge, whose court at Kafri was regarded by Samuel as of a higher status than his own. This Mar ʿUkba was, second, believed to maintain very high standards of law.[3] They indicate, third, that Palestinians treated respectfully with Mar ʿUkba's

---

to this period. For an exceptionally comprehensive study of the term, the specific sense of which cannot have been much different in Babylonia, see H. Mantel, *op. cit.*, 102-140.

[1] y. ʿEruv. 8.5. Rav cited Mar ʿUkban in y. Shev. 3.3. There can be no doubt that *this* Mar ʿUkba was a learned man, who would assuredly have known the answers to such simple questions as those posed in Ginzak!

[2] The reference to the "house of David" proves that the Mar ʿUkba to whom Samuel made reference was a Davidide, as we know the exilarch in fact claimed to be.

[3] See for example b. Ket. 105b, even a common courtesy was regarded by Mar ʿUkba as sufficient to disqualify himself from judging a case. See also b. Sanh. 28b-29a, which shows that this Mar ʿUkba was well-informed about the law, by contrast to the passage on Ginzak cited above.

court (though we do not know which Mar ʿUkba was here referred
to). The same source indicates that the name ʿUkba was not uncommon; since it was a diminutive of Jacob (Yaʿakov) there is no reason
why it should have been. Therefore they indicate that Mar ʿUkba's
court in Kafri was held to have appellate status, and that his court
possessed excellent knowledge of the law. The following suggests
that Samuel's chief function was regarded as instructional, while
Mar ʿUkba's was judicial:

> And our [= rabbis'] reproof, how long [is its disability]? One day
> only as in the case of Samuel and Mar ʿUkba. When they were sitting
> together [at the school house] Mar ʿUkba sat before him at a distance
> of four cubits, and when they sat together at a judicial session, Samuel
> sat before him at a distance of four cubits, and a place was dug out
> for Mar ʿUkba where he sat on a matting so that he should be heard.
> Every day Mar ʿUkba accompanied Samuel to his house. One day he
> was engrossed in a suit, and Samuel walked behind him. When he
> had reached his house Samuel said to him, Have you not been rather
> a long time at it [lit. Is it not yet clear to you]? Now take up my case!
> He then realized that [Samuel] felt aggrieved and submitted himself to
> 'reproof' for one day.
>
> (b. M.Q. 16b)

The ʿMar Ukba who was Samuel's contemporary cited Samuel's
sayings, particularly his medical teachings,[1] laws on preparation of
the ʿeruv,[2] on judicial procedure,[3] and other matters.[4] For his part,
Samuel acted as guardian for the children of Mar ʿUkba after his
death.[5] There can be no doubt whatever, therefore, that the Mar ʿUkba
who was Samuel's contemporary and friend was a judge, of a higher
rank in the Jewish judiciary than Samuel, and at the same time a
student of Samuel in matters of Jewish law. He not only accepted
Samuel's teachings, but also transmitted many of them. But nothing
here explicitly indicates that this particular Mar ʿUkba was anything
more than a high judge, though surely an important one.

A fourth group of sayings cannot easily be analyzed historically,
as they contain no marks of having originated in a given generation.

---

[1] b. Shab. 108b-109a, on the use of an eye salve on the Sabbath. Here Mar
ʿUkba cites several other medical sayings as well. See also y. Qid. 3.8, three sayings
of Samuel cited by Mar ʿUkba, on family law and judicial procedure, and compare y. M.Q. 3.5.

[2] b. ʿEruv. 81a.

[3] b. B.Q. 112b.

[4] y. M.Q. 3.5. Gen. R. 100.7, b. B.B. 144b, b. Yev. 12a, 76a.

[5] b. B.M. 70a.

They add to our knowledge of *a* Mar 'Ukba, and I am inclined to think it is the contemporary of Samuel. The following saying indicates that Mar 'Ukba's father was a very pious man:

> Mar 'Ukba said, On this matter [cheese and meat] I am as vinegar to wine when compared to my father, for he waited twenty-four hours, and I wait to the next meal.
>
> (b. Ḥul. 105a)

The same comparison is made by Samuel between himself and his father, and it stands to reason that the sayings originated in the same generation, and were cast together for purposes of transmission, because of the similarity of filial sentiments they contained. Likewise, Mar 'Ukba and R. Mattenah, holding different views, both advanced them in the names of Samuel's Father and R. Levi (b. Sisi). [1] Of a Mar 'Ukba, we are told stories of great generosity and consideration for the poor. This same man was very wealthy, for at his death his account totaled seven thousand 'Sijan' denarii.[2] We do not know which one. There is ample precedent for the very good reputation that this particular Mar 'Ukba enjoyed in the stories we have considered above. On the other hand, we have a saying which obviously belongs in the R. Ḥisda category of stories:

> 'The horse-leech hath two daughters, Give, give.'
> (Prov. 30.15). What is meant by 'Give, give.'? Said Mar 'Ukba, It is the voice of the two daughters who cry from Gehenna calling to this world, Bring, bring! And who are they? *Minut* and the Government. Some report, R. Ḥisda in the name of Mar 'Ukba said, It is the voice of Hell crying and calling, Bring me the two daughters who cry and call in this world, Bring, bring.
>
> (b. A.Z. 17a)

We cannot closely categorize the above sayings, for we cannot be certain that those which do not have a chain of tradition attached to them do *not* belong to the Ḥisda-group;[3] and hence apply to Mar 'Ukba II. Other such sayings include the following:

> An inquiry was once addressed to Mar 'Ukba: Where does Scripture tell us that it is forbidden to sing? He replied [with the following quotation written on lines]: 'Rejoice not O Israel unto exultation like the peoples, for thou hast gone astray from thy God (Hos. 9.1)'. The

---

[1] b. M.Q. 26b, compare B.B. 54a.
[2] b. Ket. 67b, compare b. B.B. 10b.
[3] Other such unclassified sources are found in the following places: y. Ber. 2.3, 'Eruv. 5.3 (cited by R. Zera), B.Q. 8.1, Mak. 2.7 (cited by R. Zera='Eruv. 5.3), Meg. 4.11 (in the name of 'the Babylonian rabbis'); Qid. 3.12; b. Shab. 32a, 75b.

Exilarch said to R. Huna, On what ground is based the prohibition of garlands? He replied, This was imposed by the rabbis on their own authority . . .

(b. Git. 7a)

I can think of no more striking example of our problem. If Mar 'Ukba of the first clause were the Exilarch, then it is astonishing that while he could explain the former question, he had to inquire of a colleague the answer to the latter, which closely relates to it. It seems to me quite clear that the Mar 'Ukba of the earlier clause is not, in fact, the exilarch of the latter one at all. The story recalls that cited above, 'demonstrating' how uninformed *a* Mar 'Ukba was in Ginzak (Gazaca). It can have no relationship to those about a learned judge who studied with, but supervised, Rav and Samuel.

Hyman[1] cites the tradition of R. Sherira, which holds that after Rav Huna, Mar 'Ukba was appointed exilarch, but notes, as we have, that R. Sherira's evidence is highly ambiguous. He also cites the *SOZ*, and quite reasonably identifies 'Akov with Mar 'Ukba. He holds that the same Mar 'Ukba was the student of Samuel, and interprets the letters noted above as correspondence *to* the exilarch. As to the letter *from* Mar Ukba *to* the Exilarch (y. Meg. 3.2) Hyman holds that this letter was sent from Palestine by 'another Mar 'Ukba.' There can be no doubt that there was a Palestinian by the name of Rav 'Ukba, or Rabbi Mar 'Ukba. Hyman holds that it was because R. Hisda lived in Kafri that he cited Mar 'Ukba's sayings with unusual frequency, but since he regards all the Mar 'Ukba sayings as having been said by a single man, his explanation, while self-consistent, explains nothing. It poses chronological problems, the least of which is how a man lived so long as Mar 'Ukba would have to cite both Samuel's Father and to correspond with R. Eleazar b. Pedat in Palestine at the end of the third century. There is no evidence of unusual longevity concerning any of the Mar 'Ukba's. In any event, Hyman holds that the Mar 'Ukba who died in Samuel's lifetime (b. B.M. 70a) was *not* the exilarch of the same name. In discussing Nathan of Zuzita, Hyman[2] holds that he and Mar 'Ukba were one and the same. He cites She'iltot traditions on Nathan of Zuzita, explaining the strange name and providing other Ge'onic traditions on the man. He offers a number of emendations of the *SOZ*, to support his viewpoint, none of which is convincing. Yavetz[3]

---

[1] II 975f.

[2] II 956.

[3] VII, appendix B.

holds likewise that Mar 'Ukba was exilarch, and regards the Yer, datum on a letter *from* him *to* the exilarch as an unsatisfactory reading, which he 'corrects' by comparison to b. Git. 7a (sic!). He asks, (in his criticism of Graetz, who came to the conclusion that Mar 'Ukba was not exilarch, on the basis of a small part of the evidence we have considered) why Samuel submitted to Mar'Ukba's will, if he was not exilarch?

My view[1] is that there were, in fact, two Mar'Ukba's who held the office of exilarch in the third century, the first, in Rav and Samuel's day, and the second, at the end of the century. Mar 'Ukba (I), who concerns us here, was a scion of David, and got on very well indeed with Samuel, with whom he studied the Law. Samuel submitted to the judicial authority of the exilarch, whom he honored because of his Davidic origins. Mar 'Ukba I received information from Palestine concerning the regulation of the Jewish calendar, as had the exilarchs before his day, served as appellate judge in the Jewish administration, and won a good name for himself for his generosity toward the poor, his learning, and his meticulous honesty. His relationships with the scholars of his day were, nonetheless, by no means smooth, for, as we shall see below, he did not hesitate to resort to force in imposing his judgment on Rav, requiring the latter to conduct his administration of the markets according to his own, and not the Palestinian, standard. But, as we have noted (b. M.Q. 16b), he remained on excellent terms

---

[1] On Nathan of Zuzita and Mar 'Ukba, see especially J. Perles, *Etymologische Studien* 87; Kohut, *Arukh*, V, 397, and M. Gaster, *Exempla of the Rabbis* (London, 1924), No. 35, 192, and compare Shab. 56b, Sanh. 31b, Men. 44a, Git. 56a, and Sifre Num. 115. On the imprisonment of Rav by the exilarchate, see below, section iv. Weiss, *op. cit.*, III, 143, holds that Rav was not imprisoned by Mar 'Ukba, but by an exilarch whose name we do not know, because Mar 'Ukba was a kindly person (etc.), and therefore Mar 'Ukba was not exilarch. Graetz holds (II, 512) that Mar 'Ukba was chief judge in Kafri, nothing more. Compare the remarks of David Hoffmann, *op. cit.*, 27-30, 74-7. He points out that Graetz' reliance on the *SOZ*, which omits mention of Mar 'Ukba, is dubious, and that the tradition reported by R. Sherira to the contrary is a strong one, supported by much Talmudic evidence. He notes that R. Joshua b. Levi had a student by the name of Mar 'Ukba (b. Ber. 10a), which would provide at least one Palestinian instance of the name 'Ukba, to explain the letter cited in y. Meg. See also Lazarus, *op. cit.*, 74f., on Mar 'Ukba as Nathan Ukban I, whom he dates at 210-240, followed by Huna II, 240-260. On Mar 'Ukba and the calendar, see M. Beer, "Exilarchs'', 24. On the power of the exilarchate to appoint judges, 14; on the relationship of Rav and the exilarch, 19, and on Mar 'Ukba as *Av Bet Din*, 9 n. 16. Funk, *Juden*, appendix, pp. X-XIV surveys the 3rd century exilarchate as well. Following Lazarus, he proposes the following order: Huna I, in the time of R. Judah the Prince; Mar 'Ukba I; R. Huna II; and finally, Mar 'Ukba II. On the father of Mar 'Ukba, see Zuri, *Rav*, 11. See also Halevi, *Dorot*, II, 246-52.

throughout his life with Samuel, whom he honored, both as his student, and by making him executor of his estate (a function Samuel's father served faithfully before him). Although no explicit source calls this Mar 'Ukba the exilarch, the Ge'onic traditions, combined with the Talmudic evidences, leave no doubt whatever that he was *more* than an important judge. Merely as 'chief judge of the Jews,' moreover, the exilarch performed the *functions* of the leading religious-political figure in the Jewish community, by analogy to the *Herpatan Herpat* of the Mazdean church, for judicial functions were never divorced from communal, religious ones in the Sasanian Empire. To be chief judge *was* to head the community of the faithful and as nothing more (if that is all he was) than *Av Bet Din*, Mar 'Ukba was in fact serving as head of the Jewish community. We have, moreover, explicit evidence that there *was* an exilarch in the period of Rav and Samuel, which we shall examine below (section v), and I see no reason whatever to deny that it was Mar 'Ukba, who performed the *functions* of the exilarch and therefore must have held the *office*, to whom these sources refer, Graetz's demurrer notwithstanding.[1]

I cannot explain why the sources on 'the exilarch' and Rav and Samuel do not specify that that particular exilarch was Mar 'Ukba. Perhaps, for a time, the title was forbidden by the Persians. It may be that deeper knowledge of how the Talmudic traditions were formed will indicate that some motive, now unclear to us, precluded such a specification.[2] Even our brief examination of one small matter has shown the varying tendencies which colored the treatment of the exilarchate in general and Mar 'Ukba in particular. On the one hand, Mar 'Ukba was ignorant of very simple matters. On the other, Mar 'Ukba was a student of sages, and famous for his piety and generosity. Nor is there any consistency in the sources, so far as we can understand them, relating to a specific Mar 'Ukba, for the traditions on the contemporary of Rav and Samuel tell us (below) that he imprisoned Rav, forced Karna to declare the law contrary to Samuel's and Rav's view, and otherwise exercised high-handed power over the sages,

---

[1] Even though Geniva was a student of Rav, I share the view of Funk, Halevi, Beer, and others that the quarrel between him and Mar 'Ukba in fact involved Mar 'Ukba II, and hence I shall consider it in vol. III. See Funk, *op. cit.* Appendix p. XIII, and esp. M. Beer, "The Quarrel of Geniva with Mar 'Ukba", (in Hebrew) *Tarbiz* 31, 1962, 281-6. It seems reasonable to suppose that Rav was an old man when Geniva was associated with him, but that it was only ca. 270-280 C.E. that he quarreled with Mar 'Ukba (II) and was put to death by the Sasanian Government.

[2] See vol. III chap. II.

while honoring them in the school house. Those on the contemporary of R. Ḥisda will be seen to be just as ambiguous. I have no doubt whatever that the Mar ʿUkba known to us as Rav's and Samuel's contemporary was in fact the exilarch, a judgment in part based on Mar ʿUkba's functions, as I said above. Furthermore, to conclude the contrary would force us to postulate the existence of one high judicial court, under Mar ʿUkba, and yet *another* contemporary, unnamed Jewish authority, supposedly doing exactly the same things as Mar ʿUkba. An alternative view, which I find less satisfactory, would postulate that while Mar ʿUkba (I) was a chief judge, the exilarch, unknown by name, supervised *his* affairs. I cannot think of a good explanation for either state of affairs, and it is simplest and most reasonable to regard Mar ʿUkba as exilarch, an hypothesis which economically accounts for all evidence at hand.

IV. OTHER TRADITIONS ON THE EXILARCHATE

If we had no references whatever to an exilarchic office called *Resh Galuta* dating from this period, we might have concluded that there was no such office in early Sasanian times, and that Mar ʿUkba, who was, as we have seen, never designated as exilarch, was merely a chief-judge. A number of sayings, which do not specify *who* held the office, indicate without any question that there *was* an exilarch in the time of Rav and Samuel:

> Rav said, He who wishes to decide monetary cases by himself and to be free of liability in case of error should obtain sanction from the Resh Galuta, and so said Samuel.[1]
>
> (b. Sanh. 5a)

> There came before the Resh Galuta a young deer whose hind legs were broken. Rav examined it in the region of the juncture of the tendons and permitted it. He was about to eat a portion of it grilled when Samuel said to him, Master, have you no fear lest it was bitten by a snake? Then what is the remedy? Let it be put into an oven and it will expose itself. It was forthwith put into an oven, and fell into pieces. Samuel said to Rav, 'There shall no mischief befall the righteous' (Prov. 12.21). Rav replied, 'No secret troubleth thee' (Daniel 4.6).
>
> (b. Ḥul. 58b)

> Rav was appointed *agoranamos* by the exilarch . . .
>
> (y. B.B. 5.5)

---

[1] See below, section v, p. 108-111.

Levi gave a practical decision at the house of the Resh Galuta in the case of a goat and something else [= pig] roasted together ...

(b. Pes. 76b)

Samuel said, In all my life I said the Additional Prayer (Musaf) only once, when the son of the exilarch died, and the community did not pray, so I said [the prayer myself].

(y. Ber. 4.6)[1]

There are, in addition, many sayings on the exilarchate which cannot be dated with certainty, but which seem to apply to this period.[2]

From these sayings, one must conclude that there was, in fact, an exilarch in the time of Rav and Samuel. He exerted great authority, appointing arbitrators or judges who could not be held liable for judicial errors. He employed Karna, Levi, Rav, and Samuel in his administration, and consulted them on the law. When his son died, the community paid him the highest honors. There is no evidence whatever of tension between the exilarch and the rabbinical authorities *as a group*, as there was in later times, but both he and they seem to have respected one another. The specific difficulties he had with Rav, which we shall consider below, do not indicate that the exilarch was an ignorant figurehead, but rather that he disagreed with Rav about the functions of a particular administrative office, and had the power to do something about it.

v. SHILA AND KARNA

If Mar 'Ukba was exilarch, then one cannot conceive of tension between him and the sages, for the evidence at hand suggests, quite to the contrary, that the sages were *agents* of his administration over the Jews, and preserved in their academies stories about his exemplary qualities as a scholar and man of piety. I think it quite reasonable to suppose that all those rabbis who exercised political and judicial offices, as did Rav, Samuel, Shila, and Karna, did so as part of a *single* institution of Jewish selfgovernment. To assume the contrary is unrealistic, as I said, for it would require us to postulate the existence of two systems of Jewish government in the troubled times of early

---

[1] See above, p. 103 n. 3, and pp. 32-34.

[2] See for instance b. B.Q. 102b, b. Shab. 58a, on Samuel to R. Ḥinena b. Shila, "No scholars of the house of the exilarch may go out with a cloak bearing a seal [on the Sabbath] excepting you, because the house of the exilarch is not particular about you." Samuel regarded him as a slave.

Sasanian Babylonia, one run by the rabbis, the other by the exilarchate. The later tensions between the former and the latter were not in evidence in this period at all; and to read the sources otherwise is quite anachronistic.

If I am correct in my supposition[1] that Rav was in fact related to the exilarch, then it is most striking that still another major figure exerting judicial-political authority, Shila, was designated a brother of R. Hiyya, and hence a relative of Rav, according to the famous *beraita* on the sons of Aibu.[2] The exilarch thus used his own relatives in his administration. R. Shila was a civil authority in Babylonian Jewry; we have already considered the case of his administering lashes to a man who had intercourse with a gentile woman, and the difficulties he faced in consequence of that action. As an agent of the exilarch, acting by his authority, R. Shila confronted without success the problem of finding a way of adjusting to the Sasanian regime. He was certainly a man of great learning, possessing Tannaitic traditions, and associating with Rav, Samuel, and other leading rabbinic authorities.[3] He taught a version of the Mishnah.[4] It may well be that by his time, the Palestinian traditions were studied in the Babylonian academies,[5] such as that established at Huzal by the students of R. Ishmael eighty years earlier, in an up-to-date form. There can be no question that Shila was as much a part of the rabbinic movement in Babylonia as were Rav and Samuel, and it is equally certain that he was a judge by appointment of the exilarch. According to R. Sherira, he was "Resh Sidra in Babylonia, called Resha' derabbanan," or the chief of the rabbis. Halevi interprets this to mean, correctly in my view,[6] that he conducted an academy in which he taught the law, a function that was normally combined with the *administration* of law for the Jews, as it was for the Iranians. The law he taught, of which we have record, concerns quite practical matters, such as the rules of testimony,[7] a negligent bailiff,[8] and other laws pertaining directly to the administration of justice. When Rav returned to Baby-

---

[1] Vol. I 101-112.

[2] b. Sanh. 5b—*if* this is the same Shila.

[3] Compare b. Ber. 15b, Yoma' 20b, y. Ta'anit 4.2, b. Shab. 4a, Pes. 39b, 80b, M.Q. 17b, Yev. 121a, where Rav and Samuel oppose his decision; and b. A.Z. 23a.

[4] b. Yev. 24a. Compare Y. N. Epstein, *Mavo LeNusaḥ HaMishnah* (Jer. 1954) I, 171.

[5] Halevi, *op. cit.* II 223-5, compare Yavetz, *Toldot*, VII, 21.

[6] See Mantel *op. cit.* 186, 223, on "rabbanan'.

[7] b. Qid. 43b.

[8] b. Git. 52b.

lonia, he served under R. Shila, who treated him without the respect
due to his learning, as the two disputed the meaning of the Mishnah.
After R. Shila's death, however, Rav inherited his title as "chief of
the rabbis."[1]

Another Jewish judge of this period was Karna. We have already
noted that Samuel referred him to the court of Mar 'Ukba in Kafri.[2]
Along with Samuel, he was called a "judge of the exilic community,"
and like Rav, he served as a market officer.[3] He received his fees from
the parties at judgment:

> Karna used to take one istira from the innocent party, and one from
> the guilty party, and then he informed them of his decision.[4]

Like Samuel, he compiled a collection of laws of torts (Nezikin),
which would have been important for a civil judge:

> Did not Rava say in R. Huna's name in that of Rav: The sages agree
> with R. Joshua b. Korha in respect to testimony concerning real
> estate? Moreover R. Idi b. Abin learned in Karna's compilation on
> torts (Nezikin), The sages agree with R. Joshua b. Korha in respect
> to [evidence regarding] first-born [animals], real estate, hazakah
> [possession by force majeure], and [the symptoms of puberty] in males
> and females likewise.
>
> > (b. Sanh. 30b)[5]

This collection, cited occasionally in the Talmud, included beraitot
compiled by Karna and his court, and referred to by them in judging
cases. Its existence, and the form it took, reveal substantial knowledge
of contemporary and past Palestinian discussions.[6]

It is significant that the chief areas of law mastered by Karna and
Shila were those relating to rules of testimony and to torts (a negligent
bailiff, the Mishnah on Nezikin). As we shall see below (chapter VIII),
it was precisely in such practical laws that rabbinical authority was
most effective, for whatever the state of the religious life, the rabbis
most certainly exerted great authority in civil litigations, as lawyers
and judges, here exemplified by Shila and Karna. As agents of the

---

[1] b. Hul. 137b. See Epstein, *loc. cit.* Hoffmann (p. 28) holds that Samuel inherited
his post in Nehardea about 219.

[2] Above p. 101.

[3] b. Sanh. 17b, b. B.B. 89a. See below, section vi. Compare b. B.B. 70a, 100b,
107b.

[4] b. Ket. 105a.

[5] Compare Yavetz, VII, 27, Weiss, *Dor* III 164.

[6] Another minor figure in the Jewish administration was Jacob, father of R.
Nahman (b. B.M. 16b) who served as a scribe.

exilarchate and therefore administrators of Jewish community affairs, the rabbis were able to carry out their view of how the law should apply to day-to-day commerce, and hence, as in the case of Shila and Karna, the laws receiving greatest attention were those which, in fact, they enforced in their courts, or which were important to court procedures.

VI. THE ADMINISTRATIVE AND JUDICIAL FUNCTIONS OF RAV AND SAMUEL

We have already noted Samuel's importance as representative of the Jews, and leader of Jewish opinion, in the early Sasanian regime. If there were a shred of evidence to support it, one might easily conjecture that he himself was, in fact, the exilarch, for the Jews could have found no more effective agent in achieving a *modus vivendi* with the new government than one who so sagaciously adapted his opinions to the change in political circumstance, and was both learned and rich. Samuel held office as a judge and only that. Whatever other functions he performed, he carried out as agent of the exilarch, over whom he possessed considerable influence as a major legal authority, but to whom he remained subservient. Like Karna, he was a 'judge of the exile,'[1] and he was officially recognized as such, as evidenced not only by his numerous legal sayings, but also by his penetrating comments on the organization of courts and their proper administration. He was a chief judge. (Since by "exile" Pumbedita was frequently meant, it may be that he was chief in that region, though since he himself lived in Nehardea and conducted his academy there, I think it more likely that in his case "exile" means the whole of Jewish settlement in central Babylonia.[2]) The decisions we have in the name of the "judges of the exile," who were appointed by the exilarch,[3] concerned property law, in one instance the transfer of that of a married woman, in the second the residual property rights, where specified, of a vendor. While these two categories of law certainly do not exhaust the areas of adjudication of Jewish courts, they indicate that Samuel did exert substantial *civil* authority, and not

---

[1] b. Sanh. 17b, following *Dik. Sof.* References to "judges of the exile" will be found in b. B.B. 50b, where Rav refers to, and supports the view of, the judges of the exile. See b. B.B. 69b. Compare Lieberman, *Hellenism* 63.

[2] Compare b. R.H. 22b, Sanh. 32b. We shall discuss the location of Jewish settlement below, chapter VII.

[3] Following Beer, *op. cit.*, 14-15, see b. Sanh. 52a.

merely spiritual influence (see below, chapter VIII). To administer the laws concerning property, the Jewish judges had to have an official place in the Sasanian legal system, for if they did not, their decisions could have had no force, and the people could not depend upon the Jewish courts for actions in such areas. Whatever the imperial government may have decided concerning broader political issues, it seems to me quite clear that at the very outset, it did *not* upset the civil functioning of the Jewish courts, for if it had, then the kinds of decisions, reported, without the slightest doubt about their practical effectiveness, in sources relating to this period, simply could not have been issued. Nor is there the slightest ground to assume that these decisions were of a theoretical nature, for the case-reports indicate quite the contrary.

When Rav returned to Babylonia, he was appointed by the exilarch as a market supervisor:

> The Exilarch appointed Rav *agoranomos* [market-supervisor], and he supervised weights but not measures. The Exilarch imprisoned him. Rav Karna came to visit him. He [Rav] said to him, The *agoranomos* of which they spoke supervised weights but not measures.
>
> (y. B.B. 5.5)[1]

Samuel supported Rav's view:

> Our rabbis taught, 'Thou shalt have a full and just weight, a full and just measure you shall have, that your days may be prolonged in the land which the Lord your God gives you' (Deut. 25.15). This teaches that market officers are appointed to superintend measures [as specified in the verse] but no such officers are appointed for prices. Those of the Nasi's house[2] appointed market officers for both measures and prices. Samuel thereupon said to Karna, Go forth and teach them, Market officers are appointed for measures but no such officers are appointed for prices. But he went forth and exposited: Market officers are appointed for both measures and prices. He said to him, Is your name Karna? Let a horn (Qeren) grow out of your eye. A horn [= sty] grew out of his eye.
>
> (b. B.B. 89a)[3]

Samuel's instruction to Karna does not mean that he sent the latter to Palestine with a message to the patriarch, but rather that he told

---

[1] Compare Baron, *Jewish Community*, I, 130-1.

[2] *Nasi* means Exilarch here, see S. Lieberman, *HaYerushalmi Kifshuto* (Jerusalem 1934) 175-6. As in y. Ta'anit 4.2, Samuel and the "members of the house of Shila" would greet the *Nasi* every day.

[3] Samuel taught that measures must not be increased, nor coins debased, even by common agreement, more than one sixth, see b. B.B. 90a.

him to issue a public instruction contrary to the view of the exilarchate. Rav's position, following the view of the *Tosefta* on the market-supervisors of Jerusalem before 70, reflects the Palestinian tradition on the matter. The exilarchate, however, expected that he would follow its policy, and, whatever the familial relationship between Rav and the exilarch, used force to impose its will. Spicehandler comments,[1] "It would indeed be strange that the *dayyanim* [judges] appointed by the Exilarch would take a stand in opposition to that of their patron." It does indeed, yet it seems perfectly reasonable to suppose that Rav, early in his Babylonian career, should exercise his own judgment, following Palestinian opinion, contrary to that of the exilarchate, since he had been given permission to judge civil cases in Babylonia when he left Palestine. On this account, he was made to feel the weight of the exilarch's authority. The office itself, Spicehandler points out, is not mentioned elsewhere as a Babylonian Jewish one, (though it is mentioned in Dura, Seleucia, and in Sasanian sources.[2]) In Egypt, the market-supervisor surveyed lands, kept records of property sales, and was in charge of water canals. Likewise, Spicehandler cites a Parthian bronze weight bearing the inscription '*agoranomos*,' who was police chief, in charge of weights and measures in Parthian Seleucia. The title was held by minor officials in Dura. In Greece, the *agoranomos* provided food for the city during a shortage, as did Samuel in Nehardea.[3] There can be no question that Rav did eventually accept the authority of the exilarch, who used this first occasion of a difference of opinion with the Palestine-educated judge in order to demonstrate his superior authority in no uncertain terms, whatever permission the latter may have acquired elsewhere. Rav had more difficulty, in the long run, with the merchants whom he supervised, than with the exilarch whom he served. He tried to keep the markets open for strangers, following the teaching, ascribed to Ezra, that itinerant merchants might carry on business without permission from the local guilds:[4]

> R. Nathan b. Abba in the name of Rav said: The rich men of Babylonia will go down to Gehenna, for once Shabbetai b. Marinus came to Babylonia and entreated them to provide him with facilities for trading [= 'ska', business], and they refused this to him, neither

---

[1] The Local Community in Babylonia, unpublished diss., Hebrew Union College-Jewish Institute of Religion, Cincinnati, Library, 170f.
[2] And it was a Sasanian office, see Sprengling, *op. cit.* 34, ἀγορανόμος=vačarpat.
[3] b. B.B. 90b.
[4] b. B.B. 22a.

did they give him any food. He said, These are the descendants of the
'mixed multitude' (Ex. 12.28), for it is written, 'And he will show thee
mercy and have compassion upon thee' (Deut. 13.18), meaning,
Whoever is merciful to his fellow-men is certainly of the children of
our father Abraham, but whoever is not merciful to his fellow-men
is certainly not of the children of our father Abraham.

(b. Beẓah 32b)

One recalls Rav's view that people prosper because of the merits
of their forebears, accumulated in a given place. Here he holds,
consistently, that cruel people exhibit the stigma of inferior parentage,
a matter of grave concern in Babylonia. The involvement of Rav in
commercial law recalls the advice he gave to his son, to concentrate
his efforts in commerce and not in agriculture. Rav's knowledge of
business derived not only from his administrative tasks, but also
from his own family's experience in international trade, which doubtless was one of the reasons for his appointment to the market supervisor's post in the first place.[1] Both Samuel and Rav regarded making

---

[1] On the position of the *agoranomos*, see also Mantel, *op. cit.*, 202-3 who explains
(202 n. 201) that since the *agoranomos* in Greek cities controlled prices in time of
famine, it may be that Rav and the exilarch disputed whether the situation was
grave enough to be considered a famine. However, the sources explicitly indicate
that the dispute concerned what the market-supervisor must do under any
circumstances, and there is no hint that a famine prevailed. See also S. Klein,
Ma'amarim Shonim (Vienna 1924), 38-40, cited by Mantel. Spicehandler (243 n. 31)
points out that the office is frequently mentioned in Palestinian sources, and was
a very important one there. The agoranomos tested the quality of wine, supervised weights and measures, and could *influence* prices, as Samuel did, though
whether he could in fact set them or not is not clear. See also Beer, *op. cit.*, 21f,
on supervision of the markets; S. Krauss, *Talmudische Archaeologie*, II, 373, on
collection of taxes, 374; Y. S. Zuri, *Shilton HaNesi'ut veHaVa'ad* (Paris, 1911),
I, 336-8, who holds that in keeping prices down (as b. B.B. 90b), Samuel was in
fact reflecting an opinion contrary to Rav's. But this is not correct, as we have
seen. Whatever he thought, he did not do so as market-supervisor. See his *Rav*
147-8; Newman, *Commercial Life*, 36-8; Beer, *Ma'amadam*, 79, 89-90; Epstein,
Mishnah, 174. Both Rav and Samuel were in frequent contact with traders and
merchants from distant lands, attempting, for example, to clarify the meanings
of difficult words by consulting the men around the docks. Rav described the
coral industry's technology:

'Neither shall the gallant ship pass thereby' (Is. 33.21). Rav said, This refers
to the great ship. How it is carried out? They bring there six thousand men
for twelve months (or, twelve thousand for six months), and load the boat
with sand until it rests on the seabottom. Then a diver goes down and ties a
rope of flax to the coral, while the other end is tied to the ship, and the sand
is then taken and thrown overboard, so that the boat rises and pulls up the
coral with it. The coral is worth twice its weight in silver. There were three
ports, two belonging to the Romans. [See Obermeyer, 74=Suristan, land of
Syrians] and one to the Persians. From the Roman [Aramaean] side they

satisfactory provision for commercial life as of the greatest religious importance:

> 'And Jacob came whole' (Gen. 33.18). Rav interpreted, Bodily whole, financially whole, and whole in his learning. "And he was gracious [RSV: encamped against) to the city". Rav said, He instituted coinage for them [in place of barter]. Samuel said, He instituted markets for them . . . .
>
> (b. Shab. 33b)

In any event, Rav's early run-in with the exilarch did not diminish his importance, for, in later times, he was teacher and judge, becoming the chief judge of a region in southern Babylonia. Further, his daughter married the son of the exilarch, further strengthening the ties between the two families, which, to begin with, probably thought they had a common ancestor.[1]

Rav acted as an official judge of the exilarch, not merely as a person who expressed an opinion on the law without in fact exercising practical authority. He had scribes, to whom he gave very careful instructions about the preparation of legal documents,[2] and conducted a court:

> Rav, whenever he was to sit in court, used to say, Of his own free will the judge goes forth to meet death. He makes no provision for the needs of his household, and empty-handed does he return home. Would only that he returned as he came [clean of hands]. When he saw a crowd escorting him, he said, 'Though his excellence mount up to the heavens and his head reach into the clouds, yet he shall perish forever like his own dung' (Job. 20.6-7).
>
> (b. Sanh. 7b)

Both Rav and Samuel acted not only as judges, but as supervisory, though not appellate, authorities. This is indicated not only by Samuel's instructions, which Karna ignored in favor of the view of Samuel's chief, the exilarch himself, but also by the following:

> Once a man drowned in the swamp of Samki, and R. Shila permitted his wife to marry again. Said Rav to Samuel, Come, let us place him under ban [for he has acted against the law of the Mishnah]. Let us first, Samuel replied, send to ask for an explanation. On sending to him

---

brought up coral, from the Persian, pearls. The Persian was called the port of MŠMHYG [=Mashmahig. See Levy, *Wörterbuch* III 283, s.v., "der Hafen der Regierung"] (b. R.H. 23a).
See Krauss, *Paras*, 19-20.

[1] b. Ḥul. 92a.

[2] b. Yev. 116a See also b. Shab. 154a, Rav appointed R. Mari b. Rachel as "collector of Babylonia".

their inquiry, 'If a man has fallen into limitless waters, is his wife forbidden or permitted [to remarry],' he replied, 'Forbidden.' And they asked, 'Is the swamp of Samki regarded as water that has an end or not?' It is such as water that has no limit.' 'Why then did the master act in such a manner?' 'I was really mistaken', he replied, 'I was of the opinion that as the water was gathered and stationary it was to be regarded as water which has a limit, but the law is in fact not so, for owing to the prevailing waves it might well be assumed that the waves carried the body away. Samuel thereupon applied to Rav the text, 'There shall no mischief befall the righteous' (Prov. 12.21), for Rav was spared guilt for the injustice of placing R. Shila under the ban, while Rav replied to Samuel, 'But in the multitude of counsellors there is safety.' (Prov. 11.14).   (b. Yev. 121a)

This story indicates that Rav and Samuel were prepared to enforce conformity to Mishnaic law by means of the ban of excommunication. I doubt that the needs of the exilarchate compelled them to do so, for if they were acting as the agents of Mar 'Ukba, they could well have used force, as did the exilarch against Rav himself. What was at issue seems rather to be *which* body of laws and precedents would be enforced in the Jewish courts. Rav, who had come from Palestine, and was deeply committed to the enforcement of R. Judah the Prince's Mishnah, here appeared to be quite eager to demonstrate the authority of that law, even before the case was adequately clarified; but Samuel was no less eager to enforce the same principle. The failure to resort to an appeal to the exilarch would suggest that the exilarch would not have supported the rabbis' position, against one of their number who differed, but would prefer to allow the judges themselves to decide, when not immediately relevant to his political or administrative purposes, what the law should be. In a case of family law, which Rav was specifically permitted to adjudicate by his authorization from R. Judah the Prince, the exilarch was apparently prepared to stand aside, while, by contrast, in cases involving economic policy, he was not. Enjoying great prestige, Rav and Samuel could denounce a dissident judge, who declined to enforce the law as they saw it, and thus apparently possessed a certain freedom of action in some areas of the law, but not in others, with moral and religious sanctions to enforce their views, but not political ones, in such areas as the exilarch neglected.

For his part, Samuel had announced, in conformity with the exilarch, that Persian law had to be obeyed, and though he regretted that riparian wharfage rights were governed by Persian law, he enforced that law:

Samuel said, He who takes possession of the wharfage of a river is an impudent person but he cannot be legally removed. [Under Iranian law, the person who paid the land tax could take possession of the land. A large space on the river bank was originally left open for unloading. No one had claim to it, and revenue suffered. The Persians apparently accepted payment of taxes in exchange for title of formerly common land.] But nowadays that the Persian authorities write [in a title], 'Possess it [the field on a river bank] as far as the depth of the water reaching up to the horses neck, he is removed [though the owners fence off their field at some distance from the water's edge, the land belongs to them and none can legally seize it.]

(b. B.M. 108a)

Thus the Persians determined the form of Jewish legal documents. Likewise, he accepted the possibility that 'heathen courts,' which can only mean Persian ones, might interfere even in Jewish divorce proceedings, with the compliance of the Jewish courts.[1] In the period following Samuel's death, the exilarchate enforced Persian law among the Jews even in *preference* to Jewish law, a position Samuel never took:

A certain person cut down a date tree belonging to his neighbor. When he appeared before the exilarch the latter said to him, I myself saw the place. Three date trees stood close together and they were worth a hundred zuz. Go pay thirty-three and one-third zuz. Said the defendant, What have I to do with an exilarch who judges in accord with Persian law? He therefore appeared before R. Nahman [Samuel's student and heir] who said that the valuation should be made in conjunction with sixty.

(b. B.Q. 58b)

When Samuel said that the government's law is law, he did not mean to say that, therefore, it must take precedence in Jewish courts. The exilarch, after Samuel's death, must have gone much further than the rabbis approved, by bringing into Jewish justice the precedents of Persian law, something the earliest *entente* could not have included.

One may, therefore, discern three areas of law in which the exilarch and the rabbis were involved. The first was law which concerned only the Jewish religion and the inner arrangements of the Jewish community, as the case, cited above, of when a woman might remarry. Here the rabbis from the very beginning probably had a completely free hand, for the exilarchate, using them as judges and

---

[1] b. **Git.** 88b.

agents for other purposes, may well have been quite content to rely upon their traditional learning to decide cases with no practical bearing upon public policy. The second was law which involved the economic, social, and political welfare of the community. The exilarch here proved to be quite willing to intervene as he saw fit, and to impose his judgment, perhaps based on practical necessities, rather than on traditional precedents. Such a case is represented by the imprisonment of Rav for refusing to supervise the pricing of goods in the market, a refusal which, as we have seen, was based upon ample precedent in Palestine. The third area of law concerned the relationship between the Jews and the government. Such cases included the collection of taxes, as in the case of R. Kahana and Rav cited above (p. 31), the regulation of land ownership, and the like. Here both the rabbis and the exilarchate had to submit to Persian overlordship. Clearly, many compromises had to be reached, many issues had to be clarified, many relationships had to be worked out over a long period of years. The final case, cited above, concerning a man who, displeased with the *kind* of law he found before the exilarch's court, repaired to a rabbinical authority, represents a tension we find only in incipient form, if at all, in the lifetimes of Rav and Samuel, between the rabbinical view of justice, and that of the more practically-oriented exilarch. In the period at hand, however, there was no significant tension between the rabbis and the exilarchate, except in the very specific issues we have noted above.

Rav and Samuel laid great stress upon the honor due to authority. Rav held that even the superintendent of a well is appointed from heaven,[1] and at the same time he emphasized the need for restraint by community leaders, warning:

> Any community leader who makes himself unduly feared by the community for other than religious purposes will never have a scholar for a son as it says, 'Therefore if men fear him he shall not see any wise of heart' (Job 37.24).

(b. R.H. 17a)

For his part, Samuel held that once a man is appointed head of a community he should not publicly do manual labor.[2] Quite consistently, Rav taught that Saul was punished because he forewent the honor which was due to him. Both teachers insisted likewise on the honor due to sages.[3]

---

[1] b. B.B. 91a.
[2] b. Qid. 70a.
[3] b. Shab. 119b, compare 105b and y. Bik. 3.3.

These sayings presuppose the fact that 'community officials' and 'sages' were one and the same. If, later on, that was not the case, we ought not anachronistically to view this period as one marked by tensions between political authority, on the one hand, and religious-intellectual leadership, on the other. Rav, Samuel, Karna, Shila, and others were in fact acting under the suzerainty of the exilarchate, and whatever practical authority they possessed depended upon that fact.

VII. THE EXILARCHATE UNDER ARDASHIR AND SHAPUR

There can be no doubt whatever that the exilarchate survived the early years of Ardashir, and in time, achieved a *modus vivendi* with the Sasanian government. The evidence we have examined informs us that in the earliest period, when the new regime had taken power but before it had achieved a significant awareness of the realities of its new empire, the activities of Jewish judges were severely supervised, being regarded with considerable suspicion. At the same time, the story about R. Shila and the *frestak* indicates that the Persian official *was* in fact prepared to accept the activity of the Jewish judge, *if* this conformed to Persian law. There was no question that the Jewish courts would continue to exist, or that the Jewish judges would continue to apply their community's law to the Jewish people under their power. I do not, therefore, believe that the Sasanians ever *actually* attempted direct administration of the inner affairs of the Jews. The issue before them was exactly how they would supervise the autonomous regimes which from Arsacid times interposed between the central government, or the local satrapy, and the several *millets* in Babylonia. On the one hand, as we have seen, the Persians had no great need to accommodate local groups, none of which had contributed to their rise to power, and some of which, including the Jews, were deeply involved in the politics of Arsacid times. Perhaps on that account the Persians were especially concerned with the Jewish courts. On the other, if they did not intend to make radical changes in the ethnic structure of Babylonia, then they would have to achieve a rapprochement with the existing local communities. It was one thing to attempt to win over individuals to the Mazdean faith; it was quite another to force the conversion of whole groups, and this the Persians never attempted to do with the Jews. The boast of Kartir was that he 'opposed' the several religious minorities of the empire; he could not accurately boast that he had destroyed them or that he had forcibly wiped out the vestiges of their cults.

We have seen, moreover, that the Jewish courts throughout this period actually did make decisions affecting important legal concerns, for example, the transfer of property, and they did administer law *with* the assent of the Persian regime. Moreover, a central Jewish authority in Babylonia, who must be regarded as the exilarch, did regulate the Jewish calendar, did appoint Karna, Shila, Rav, and Samuel to their judicial-administrative posts, and did supervise their activities; and such appointment did render his appointees free of the need of having to make restitution in case of an erroneous decision. This evidence proves, as we said at the outset, that Jewish self-government continued, restricted but without interruption, under the early Sasanians. When Rav came home, he found the exilarchate impaired but intact. If this is the case, then we must assume that some kind of *entente* was reached. We do not know when or how, nor can we be certain that the Persians actually confronted the issue of self-governing minority groups in any articulated, conscious fashion. It may have been that, whatever unrest and upheaval accompanied their advent to power, they allowed daily life to continue its routine without interruption, as would have suited the needs of a new regime anxious to restore order and establish its permanent rule of a new empire. Within the routine of daily life there flourished among the Jews an ancient institution, which, the Sasanians decided, would be supervised but not destroyed. That in fact seems to have happened, perhaps not by choice or by a decision at a given hour, but on account of the inertia of former practices among the Jews, and of the convenience of the new government.

In time, the Jewish government must have proved its usefulness to the Persians. Though, as we have seen, they never elaborately exploited Jewish support in their foreign affairs, as had the Parthians, they did pay attention to local public opinion, and the existence of a Jewish regime, dependent upon the sovereign for its authority and therefore amenable to its policies, would have been a good means to assure the maintenance of Jewish subservience, as Samuel proved in Shapur's time. Indeed, Samuel's negotiations with Shapur, if that is what they were, could have taken place only with the knowledge and approval of the exilarchate. We may well regard Samuel as the Jewish official who was designated to represent the Jewish community at the court of the tolerant emperor, just as his student R. Judah[1] on

---

[1] If *Mar* and *Rav* Judah were the same man.

at least one occasion had an audience with the emperor. If this was the case it is curious that Mar 'Ukba himself did not enter negotiations with the emperor. Perhaps, assuming that Lazarus correctly dates Mar 'Ukba's death at ca. 240 (and we know that he died before Samuel, ca. 260), Mar 'Ukba himself was dead, and his successor lacked the prestige and know-how of Samuel, who, in the years from 240 to his death, must have enjoyed a very substantial reputation among both Jews and Persians in Babylonia. It may well be that Samuel, known to the chancellery at Ctesiphon as a major Jewish official long before Shapur's time, was called into court as the means for seeking a rapprochement with the Jews, partly because of his own reputation, and partly because Mar 'Ukba was no longer available and his successor was an unknown quantity. In any event, Mar 'Ukba could never have negotiated anything with Ardashir, who in the period from 226 to his retirement in 240 showed no disposition toward·such negotiations, and under whom the best that could be hoped for was maintenance of the *status quo*. We may therefore regard the exilarchate under Ardashir as a tolerated institution, whose existence depended on nothing more than precedent. Under Shapur, a new status would have been negotiated, the terms of which are abundantly clear: in exchange for the recognition of Persian law as valid in Jewish courts ("the law of the land is law") the exilarchate might operate without day-to-day supervision by the Sasanian administration over the conduct of its affairs. In exchange for a remission of the harsh and repressive measures of Ardashir's time, the Jewish authorities would, additionally, seek to preserve the loyalty of the Jews toward the home government.[1] In retrospect, it is difficult to see how either side could have found any genuine alternative to such an agreement. The Jews could not effectively rebel against the Sasanians, who were masters of every frontier, and effectively ruled their empire through a very elaborate bureaucracy, nor is there any evidence that they wanted to. The Persians, for their part, found that they could make very few long-term innovations in the lives of the non-Iranian peoples. After discovering that neither proselytism nor persecution would bring non-Mazdeans into the imperial faith, but would pointlessly create unrest in prosperous but threatened satrapies, they had to seek a new policy, which was, as we have seen, to legitimize the *ad hoc* arrangements of Ardashir's reign, and to make

---

[1] See above, pp. 64-72.

the best of them. For both sides, the maintenance of domestic peace and prosperity was the chief goal, and each moved toward a compromise to achieve it. (Indeed such an arrangement with the Jews would obviously constitute a parallel to the encouragement given to Mani.)

One very practical motive encouraged the Persians to seek an accommodation. They collected taxes not from individuals, but from regions, communities, and the like. As Beer points out,[1] the Jews, including the rabbis, paid the poll tax to the authority of their own town or village. The state would assess the census of a given region, and, in Jewish areas, a Jewish agent would collect it.[2] The Jewish agents could intervene with the authorities to free a pauper from the head-tax, at least in a later period. Lazarus[3] held that the exilarch was responsible to collect these taxes and transmit them to the royal treasury, just as did the Christian *catholicus*. Beer points out, correctly, that there is no evidence (applying to this period in any case) that such was his responsibility. Nonetheless, he also notes that the sages had to collect the poll-tax in their own towns, and supposes that this must have been done 'with the permission' of the exilarch. I think it quite likely that the sages were, in fact, doing so as *agents* of the Jewish autonomous government, at the very least in this period, and that this was one of the responsibilities they assumed as exilarchic agents. If so, it certainly would have well served the Sasanians to strengthen an institution which they were using, and intended to continue to use, for fiscal purposes.

Moreover, the Persians had, like the Romans in Palestine, to take account of the fact that the Jews lived by their own laws, and would continue to do so, no matter what the imperial regime decided. The very nature of their religious culture demanded that they conduct their lives according to the revealed law of Moses, and by the traditions that had developed around it. Without a very keen interest in many internal matters, as we have noted above (section vi), the Persians in time must have determined that if there were to be Jewish courts, *they* would supervise the chief of such a system of internal administration, and, as we have seen, would make use of his services as they found it convenient. If they had not, they would have been faced,

---

[1] "On the Question of Tax Exemption of Babylonian Amoraim", *Tarbiz* 33, 1964, 247-58. Beer cites fully the relevant scholarly literature on Sasanian tax-collections.

[2] *Ibid.* 249.

[3] *Op. cit.* 132; see Beer, *Zion* 28, 1963, 22-3.

as they were early in their regime because of Rav's and R. Shila's actions, with the illegal enforcement of Jewish law by subterfuge, a very difficult matter to control. It must have seemed best in the long run to take the Jewish government in hand, rather than to attempt to destroy in one form what would surely develop in another, perhaps subversive, one.

The exilarchate eventually developed into a most elaborate institution, and the limited evidence applying to this period, considered above, adumbrates its later greatness. Here we have seen that the exilarch appointed administrator-judges; his agents (Karna, Samuel, Rav) supervised the education of Jewish lawyer-teachers; he himself judged cases as well, and did so according to Jewish law. Nor was his only an appellate court, for he was expected to deal with very humble matters, as in the case Samuel assured his student the exilarch would handle. His own bureaucrats, called 'rabbis of the exilarchate' must therefore have served elsewhere, as did he in his own town, as Jewish judges for matters great and small. Later on, he may have established a hierarchy for judicial procedures. In any event, the only Jewish judges in Babylonia who were officially recognized as such were his appointees, which gave him substantial power over the Jews. Doubtless part of any agreement with the Sasanians would have been their agreement to support his monopoly of the administration of justice over Jews against any other claimant. Nor was the economic life of the Jews exempt from his supervision. It seems reasonable to suppose that his authority applied exclusively to towns which had Jewish majorities. (In later times the exilarch was given special privileges in addressing the people on festival days, though in this period I find no evidence of it.) He assumed the power to regulate the calendar for Babylonia, a right fiercely contested when first exercised there by R. Ḥananiah, nephew of R. Joshua a century or more earlier, but he did so (despite Samuel's great knowledge of astronomy) only as the representative of the Palestinian consistory, from which instructions were sent to Babylonia as to elsewhere in the Jewish diaspora. The Palestinians addressed him with the highest respect. While later generations of rabbis found reason to criticize the behavior of the exilarch and his servants, in *this* generation, as I said, one can find neither criticism, nor grounds for it, apart from the singular show of force toward Rav shortly after his return from Palestine.[1] For his part, the exilarch found good use for the rabbis.

---

[1] On the exilarchate in this period, see also Funk, *Juden*, 31-41.

Their knowledge of law was superior to his, and he did not hesitate to acknowledge it in his studies with Samuel. In the day-by-day development of case law, the rabbis could provide answers to new dilemmas, which would enjoy the prestige of tradition, and they could, when necessary, legislate, upon the foundation of old principles, to meet new problems.

The change in regime, therefore, did not in the end destroy the continuity between the old Jewish government and the new one. What had changed was, at first, the circumstances in which the Jewish officials exerted their authority, for as we have seen their freedom of action was considerably limited. Second, the exilarch was no longer privy to the highest circles of the Persian government, as he had been under the Arsacids, and only slowly was he able, through Samuel's mediation, to begin to restore the substantial position in the state, such as he had formerly held.

The important fact, however, is that during a period in which Judaism faced serious difficulties, with Jews meeting persecution in the conduct of their religion, the Jewish autonomous government did in fact survive, and after the early repressions, it was able to regain a measure of its former status. Even in the hardest times it was able to retain its control of Jewish affairs, and to prevent the Persian government from directly ruling the Jews, or, through its officials, enforcing its own law among them. This was no mean achievement under the circumstances, and it could most certainly *not* have been attained had not the vast majority of the Jews supported their own autonomous government, and refrained, even when sorely tempted, from acting as did the man who complained against R. Shila. That fact points to a very widespread acceptance, not only of the exilarch's claim to be descended from David, but of the exilarch's functionally more significant claim to govern the Jews no matter what might happen. Only if the Jews wanted to be ruled by him, could he have, through his agents, continued to administer their affairs under a hostile government. Indeed the very hostility of the government doubtless contributed to the willingness of most of the Jews to support their own ruler and to submit to his authority even when he was not ruling by force, as he had been able to earlier, but only by persuasion. One may conjecture further that it was only the removal of outside pressure, during Shapur's time and afterward, which permitted the rabbis to recognize substantial differences between themselves and the exilarch, who was their inferior in knowledge of 'the Torah,' and in time led to difficult relationships between the sages and their government. Then the terms of the agreement negotiated by Samuel, submitting Jewish law to the measure of that of the Persians, began to gall, as we have noted, and exilarchic power seemed paradoxical, by contrast to his inferior learning. In this period, however, rabbis, the exilarch, and the people drew together to face troubled and threatening times, and in so doing, they successfully negotiated a difficult passage.

CHAPTER FOUR

RABBINIC JUDAISM IN EARLY SASANIAN
BABYLONIA (I): PERSONNEL

i. RAV

The beginning of the so-called 'Amora'ic period is conventionally dated at Rav's return to Babylonia, which, according to Rav Sherira's letter, took place in the *Seleucid year* 530 = 219. (Of course R. Shila, Samuel, and other rabbis were already living in Babylonia.) R. Sherira's chronology has been much discussed.[1] His dates relating to Samuel's death and the destruction of Nehardea are unreliable. I can find no solid grounds for accepting it for Rav's "return." In fact, we know that Rav came and went several times, studying in Palestine, returning to Babylonia, and going back to Palestine, before he finally took up permanent residence in his homeland. If his final settlement was connected with some great event in either Palestine or Babylonia, we have no knowledge of it. We do not know how R. Sherira calculated his chronology or what sources he used. In saying Rav died in 247 (=Seleucid year 558) R. Sherira cites only the Talmudic sources quite available to us, which indicate that Rav predeceased Samuel. His traditions on both 219 and 247 are interesting but of limited value.

Rav was unusually handsome, and the sources comment on it:

> The beauty of R. Kahana was a reflection of the beauty of Rav, and that of Rav, of R. Abbahu, and that of R. Abbahu, of our father Jacob, and of Jacob, of Adam.
>
> (b. B.B. 58a)[2]

Born in Kafri, Rav was educated in Huẓal,[3] site of an academy

---

[1] See ed. B. Levin, 78 1. 5. Compare Spicehandler, *op. cit.*, 177 n. 2, who provides a full bibliography of discussions on this point. The correct reading of R. Sherira's letter has been much debated. Graetz and Funk accept the date 500 (=189), but the majority of MSS and editions read 530, see Funk, *Juden* I, Appendix p. VI, n. III to p. 1, and D. Hoffmann, *op. cit.*, 62-8; Zuri, *Rav*, 114-5. Zuri dates Rav's original migration to Palestine in 175. Compare H. Graetz, "Zur Chronologie der Talmudischen Zeit", *MGWJ* 34, 1885, 433-53, and Halevi, *Dorot*, II, 210-222. I cannot regard the matter as a very fruitful inquiry, given the lateness of R. Sherira's letter.

[2] Compare Num. R. 9.24, "Rav was the tallest man in his generation".

[3] b. Shab. 92a, see vol. I. 150-2. See also Zuri, *Rav*, 51f.

organized originally by the students of R. Ishmael in the time of the Bar Kokhba war, and he studied for a number of years in Palestine as well. Eventually, Rav was accepted as a member of R. Judah's consistory, and was one of the youngest:

> Rav said, I was once one of the voters in the school of Rabbi and it was with me that the voting began.
>
> (b. Sanh. 36a)[1]

But in time, he progressed, and in the end, held a distinguished position in the academy:

> When Isi b. Hini went up to Palestine, R. Yoḥanan found him teaching his son [etc.] ... R. Yoḥanan asked, Who is head of the academy in Babylonia? Abba Arika [he replied]. And you simply call him Abba Arika! I remember when I was sitting before Rabbi seventeen rows behind Rav, and seeing sparks of fire leaping from the mouth of Rabbi into the mouth of Rav, and from the mouth of Rav into the mouth of Rabbi, and I could not understand what they were saying, and you call him simply 'Abba Arika'!
>
> (b. Hul. 137b)[2]

There can be no doubt, moreover, that Rav taught authoritatively in Palestine before his final migration to Babylonia, as this is stated explicitly within the dialectic of a discussion.[3] Before that time, Rav made a number of trips to his homeland. One such is reported as follows:

> Rav once came to Babylonia and noticed that they recited the Hallel on the New Moon. At first he thought of stopping them, but when he saw that they omitted parts of it, he remarked, It is clearly evidence that it is an old ancestral custom with them.
>
> (b. Taʿanit 28b)[4]

The reports of Rav's final settlement invariably use the word 'ata,' while here the word 'ikla' ('YQL') is used, the normal meaning of which is 'happened by.' When Rav finally migrated, he received the permission of the patriarchate to decide ritual and monetary cases, but not cases involving the permanent unacceptability of first-born animals, even though he had allegedly devoted considerable time (eighteen months, according to the source) to learning which ble-

---

[1] Compare b. Git. 59a.

[2] On 'resh sidra', see Zuri *Shilton HaNesiʾot*, I, 247f.; on Abba Arika, b. Nid. 24b.

[3] b. Ber. 45b.

[4] See also b. M.Q. 20a-b, Yev. 63a, Pes. 4a.

mishes were permanent and which were not.[1] His return was recognized, in his lifetime, and even more so after his death, as a
turning point in Babylonian Jewish history. We shall discuss its
legal importance below (chapter VIII). The actual event is described
as follows:

> Samuel and Karna were sitting by the bank of the Royal Canal and
> saw the water rising and becoming discolored. Said Samuel to Karna,
> A great man is arriving from the west who suffers from stomach
> trouble, and the water is rising to give him welcome. Go and smell
> his bottle [= examine his knowledge[2]]. So he went and met Rav. He
> asked him, How do we know that the tefillin may be written only on
> the skin of a clean animal? Because it is written, 'That the law of the
> Lord may be in thy mouth' (Ex. 13.9), meaning, of that which is
> permitted in thy mouth, he replied. How do we know that blood is
> red, he asked. Because it is said, 'And the Moabites saw the water over
> against them as red as blood' (II Kings 3.22).[3] How do we know that
> circumcision must be performed in that particular place? 'His 'orlah'
> (Gen. 17.14) is stated here, and 'its 'orlah' (Lev. 19.23) is stated
> elsewhere: Just as there something that produces fruit [is meant] so
> here, something that produces fruit [is meant]. Perhaps it means the
> heart, for it is written, 'Circumcise therefore the foreskin of your
> heart' (Deut. 10.15)? Perhaps it means the ear, for it is written,
> 'Behold their ear is uncircumcized' (Jer. 6.10)? We learn the complete
> "'orlato' from the complete "'orlato' but we do not learn the complete
> "'orlato' from "'orlat' [which is incomplete.] What is your name, he
> (Rav) asked. Karna. May it be his will that a horn shall sprout out
> from between his eyes,[4] he retorted. Subsequently Samuel took him
> into his house, gave him barley bread and a fish pie to eat, and strong
> liquor to drink, but he did not show him the privy that he might be
> eased. Rav cursed him, saying, He who causes me pain, may no sons
> arise from, him, and thus it was.
>
> (b. Shab. 108b)

Rav's resettlement was accompanied by a dramatic gesture to
demonstrate not mere competence in legal exegesis of scripture, by
which Babylonian law characteristically had been developed, but
mastery over the whole of the law, for he announced that he was
the 'Ben Azzai of this place,' meaning that, like Ben Azzai in the

---

[1] b. Sanh. 5a. He later requested the additional right, perhaps in preparation
for founding his own academy, according to Weiss, *op. cit.* III 135. On Rav's
ordination, see Weiss, III, 132; Halevi, *Dorot.*, II, 216, Epstein in *REJ* 44, 1902.

[2] See b. Ket. 105a, and Obermeyer, *Landschaft*, 247.

[3] The question is, How can we prove it *from Scripture*. One recalls Rav's
saying that judges are only admitted to court if they can prove that reptiles are
not impure *according to Scripture*.

[4] Samuel issued the same curse. Compare Lev. R. 25:6.

marketplace of Tiberias, he would take on the theoretical questions of all comers.[1] Rav retained contact with the Palestinian academies, and was well informed about the politics of the court there:

> Rav was told, A great, tall, and lame man has come to Nehardea, and has lectured, A coronet is permitted [to be worn on the Sabbath]. He said, Who is a great and tall man who is lame? Levi. This proves that R. ʾAfes is dead and R. Ḥanina now sits at the head of the academy, so that Levi has none for a companion and therefore he has come hither.
>
> (b. Shab. 59b)[2]

He likewise used to correspond with R. Yoḥanan.[3]

Rav's family included a cousin, Rabbah bar Ḥana, with whom he remained in touch,[4] his uncles, R. Ḥiyya and R. Shila, Ḥezekiah and Judah, R. Ḥiyya's sons, in Palestine; and at least one daughter and two sons, though he may have had other children, for like some of the other rabbis, he married more than once and, if the following source is accurate, many times:

> Rav, whenever he happened to visit Dardeshir [= Veh-Ardashir, formerly Seleucia-on-the-Tigris], used to announce, Who would be mine for the day.
>
> (b. Yev. 37b = Yomaʾ 18a)[5]

This was contrary to the saying of R. Eliezer b. Jacob, that a man should not marry in more than one place, lest his children marry one another unawares, but it was felt that the rabbis come under a special category since they are well known. Rav's wife, like his aunt, R. Ḥiyya's wife, was a termagant:

> When Rav was once taking leave of R. Ḥiyya, the latter said to him, May the All-merciful deliver you from anything which is worse than death. When he went out and considered the matter, he found (Koh.

---

[1] y. Peʾah 6.3, Sotah 9.2. Compare b. Ber. 62a, where a saying of Rav is identical with one of Ben Azzai. See Zuri, *Rav*, 65.

[2] Compare b. Ket. 103b for a briefer, probably older version.

[3] b. Ḥul. 95b.

[4] b. B.B. 52a.

[5] On "Who will be my wife for a day", see R. Margoliot and S. Krauss, "Who Will be My Wife?" (In Hebrew), *Sinai*, XI, 176-9, XII, 299-302, and Baron, *Social and Religious History*, II, 410 n. 11. Margoliot points out that Rav was in fact eager to propagate the custom of an engagement before marriage among the Jews, and this passage is not consistent with his general viewpoint. Nonetheless the embarrassed "explanations" of Margoliot and Krauss do not help much, as Baron says.

7.26): 'And I find more bitter than death the woman . . .' Rav was constantly tormented by his wife. If he told her, Prepare me lentils, she would prepare him small peas; if, small peas, she made lentils. When his son Hiyya grew up, he gave her [his father's] instructions in reverse order. Your mother, Rav once remarked, has improved. It was I, Hiyya replied, who reversed the order to her. This is what people say, Rav replied, Thine own offspring teaches thee reason. You must not, however, continue to do so, for it is said, 'They have taught their tongue to speak lies' (Jer. 9.4).

R. Hiyya was constantly tormented by his wife. Nevertheless whenever he obtained anything suitable, he wrapped it up in his scarf and brought it to her. Said Rav to him, But surely she is tormenting the master? It is sufficient for us, R. Hiyya replied, that they rear our children and deliver us from sin.

(b. Yev. 63a)

One may well understand why Rav's wife behaved like a shrew, considering her husband's habit of adding to her rivals. Rav said:

One should always be heedful of wronging his wife; for since her tears are frequent, she is quickly hurt. He also said, He who follows his wife's counsel will descend into Gehenna, for it is written, 'But there was none like unto Ahab which did sell himself to work wickedness in the sight of the Lord, whom Jezebel his wife stirred up' (I Kings 21.25).

(b. B.M. 59a)

Any evil but not an evil wife.

(b. Shab. 11a)[1]

While Rav's son, Hiyya, became a distinguished teacher,[2] his son Aibu did not, and, as we have seen, Rav advised him to go into business. For his part, Rav had at least one house-servant, and was certainly not a poor man, but probably well-to-do.[3] Rav also had a daughter, who married R. Hanan:

Rav was once going to his son-in-law, R. Hanan, when he saw a ferry boat coming towards him. He said to himself, When the ferry boat comes to meet one it is a good omen. He came to the door and looked through the crack of the door and saw the meat of an animal hanging up. He then knocked at the door and everybody came out to meet him including the butchers. Rav did not take his eyes off the meat, and said, If that is how you look after things you are giving my

---

[1] Compare y. Git., 4.3, Rav told his daughter-in-law that theoretically, all her property belonged to him.

[2] y. Shab. 1.2, Rav taught him the laws of saying Grace, and compare b. Ber. 53b, B.B. 23b.

[3] b. Shab. 152a.

daughter's children forbidden meat to eat, and Rav did not eat of
that meat.

(b. Ḥul. 95b)

The children of this marriage were regarded as of special excellence,
Rabbana Ukba and Rabban Neḥemiah.[1]

The wisdom of the rabbis, like that of other religious-cultural
leaders, included magical knowledge, how to bless and curse, how
to heal and ensure one's entry into heaven, how to read signs and
omens and other aspects of the occult. As we have seen, Rav regarded
a ferry boat as an omen, and he, like the other rabbis, had a rich store
of information about both good and evil omens. He taught his sons
and students many kinds of 'good advice,' similar to that cited above:

> Rav said to Rav Assi, Do not dwell in a town in which no horses
> neigh, nor dogs bark, or in which the leader of the community is a
> physician. And do not marry two women, but if you do, marry a third.
> Rav said to Rav Kahana, Deal in carcasses but not in words (gossip).
> Flay carcasses in the market place and earn wages but do not say, I
> am a priest and a great man, and it is beneath my dignity. Even if you
> merely ascend to the roof, take food with you. Even if a hundred
> pumpkins cost but a zuz in town, let them be under your skirts
> [stock up].
>
> Rav said to Ḥiyya his son, Do not take drugs [for medicine], and do
> not leap in great jumps, and do not have a tooth extracted, and do not
> provoke an Aramean woman.

(b. Pes. 113a)

Much of his wise advice concerned medical matters. Like Samuel,
Rav mastered medical lore, one of the subjects in which Babylonian
culture was particularly rich, and in which the Jews, among other
Babylonians, took considerable interest. These traditions contained
both general medical aphorisms, such as instruction to relieve oneself
early in the morning and in the evening,[2] sage observations about
the course of illness, and how to maintain good health:

> Fever sustains for not less than six days nor more than thirteen.

(b. Sanh. 108b)

> One should always sell [even] the beams of his house and buy shoes
> for his feet. If one has let blood and has nothing to eat, let him sell his
> shoes and provide the requirements of a meal, which are, according
> to Rav, meat; according to Samuel, wine. Rav said, Meat, life for life.

---

[1] b. Ḥul. 92a.
[2] b. Ber. 62a.

Samuel, Wine, red to replace red ... Both Rav and Samuel say, He who is bled should not sit where a wind can enfold him, for the cupper drained him of blood and reduced it to just a bit, and the wind will come and drain him still further and endanger him. Rav and Samuel both say, He who is bled must partake of something, and then go out. If he does not eat anything, and meets a corpse, his face will turn green; a homicide, he will die; a pig, it is harmful in respect of something else [sex]. Rav and Samuel both say, One who is bled should tarry a while and then rise ... Rav said, A hundred gourds for one zuz a hundred heads for one zuz, a hundred lips for nothing ...

(b. Shab. 129b)

This phrase means that these are of slight benefit and worth having for very little; or, alternately, 'a hundred surgeon's horns' mean bleedings, 'a hundred heads,' haircuts, 'a hundred lips,' trimming of the moustache. These were free if done at the same time as bleeding or haircutting. Likewise Rav warned of the dangers of the various winds, the south being most violent, the north, the most common.[1] The administration of law required the widest possible scope of knowledge; for instance the Sabbath law, permitting the saving of life, but not the treatment of illness except *in extremis*, required knowledge of the relative value of various medicines, and the relative gravity of various illnesses.[2] This accounts in part for the sages' medical training. Beyond this, Rav knew many folk remedies:

R. Judah in the name of Rav stated, Of all that the Holy One blessed be He created in his world, he did not create a single thing without a purpose. Thus he created the snail as a remedy for a scab, the fly as an antidote to the hornet's sting, the mosquito crushed for a serpent's bite, a serpent as a remedy for an eruption, and spider as a remedy for a scorpion's bite ...

(b. Shab. 77b)[3]

The source of this folk-wisdom was frequently a chance acquaintance. Rav cited the culinary advice of Adda the Fisherman of Bar Shappir (=Firuz Shabur)[4], on how to eat fish, how to prepare it, and what to drink with it.[5] Likewise, Rav took an interest in astrological matters, regarded as irrelevant to Israel, but which engaged broad popular interest.

The wisdom of the rabbis included the knowledge of how to make an effective curse. Rav, for example,

---

[1] b. Git. 21b.
[2] b. Shab. 129b, 134b, y. Shab. 14.4, b. Sanh. 87b, ʿEruv. 56a.
[3] Perhaps a comment on the way in which Mazdeans execrated insects.
[4] Obermeyer, *op. cit.*, 226.
[5] b. M.Q. 11a, See b. Ber. 40a, small fish are good for the bowels.

saw a man sowing flax on Purim, and cursed him so that the flax did
not grow.   (b. Meg. 5b)

Likewise he, like other rabbis, believed that merits could determine
one's fate, stop plagues, cause rain, and bring about, or prevent, a
fatal accident:[1]

> In Nehardea there was a dilapidated wall and neither Rav nor
> Samuel would go past it although it had remained standing in the
> same position for thirteen years. One day R. Adda b. Ahava happened
> to come there, and Samuel said to Rav, Come, sir, let us walk around
> it. The latter replied, this precaution is not necessary now because
> R. Adda b. Avaha is with us. His merit is great, and therefore I do
> not fear.
>
> (b. Taᶜanit 20b)

Like Magi, rabbis were believed capable of 'putting the evil eye'
on a person who displeased them:

> And Rav also ruled that the child is legitimate . . . . for once a man
> came and appeared before Rav and asked him, What is [the legal
> status of a child] where an idolater or a slave had intercourse with the
> daughter of an Israelite? The child is legitimate, the master replied.
> Give me then your daughter, said the man. I will not give her to you.
> Said Shimi b. Ḥiyya to Rav, People say that in Media, a camel can
> dance on a *kav*. Here is the *kav*, Here is the camel. Here is Media. But
> there is no dancing! [Why not put ruling into practice?] Had he been
> equal to Joshua ben Nun, I would not have given him my daughter,
> he replied. Had he been like Joshua b. Nun, the other retorted,
> others would have given him their daughters, if the master had not
> given his! With *this* man, if the master will not give him, others also
> will not give him. As the man refused to go away, he fixed his eye
> upon him and he died.
>
> (b. Yev. 45a)

Rav knew a smattering of Greek and Pahlavi.[2]
The students of Rav eulogized and buried him:

> Rav said to R. Samuel b. Shilat, Be fervent in my funeral eulogy
> for I shall be standing right there.
>
> (b. Shab. 153b)

---

[1] b. Taᶜanit 20b, 21b, 24a, Yomaᵓ 87a, b. Ned. 7b, Mak. 11a, "The curse of a
sage, though causeless, takes effect".

[2] As to his knowledge of Greek, Professor Lieberman writes (in a personal
communication, May 14, 1965), "He could not read Greek written documents.
Whoever is familiar with the Greek script of that time knows that you had to be
experienced at it in order to read legal documents. Rav was not able to do so,
but being a sojourner of Palestine for many years he most probably picked up a
number of Greek phrases." Compare W. Bacher, *Agada.* 32 n. 206, and Lieberman,
Hellenism, 26-7.

When Rav died, his disciples followed his bier. When they returned they said, Let us go and eat a meal by the river Danak. After they had eaten, they sat discussing the question, 'When we learned "Reclining" is it to be taken strictly, as excluding sitting, or perhaps when they say, Let us go and eat bread in such and such a place, it is as good as reclining.' R. Adda b. Ahava rose and turned the rent in his garment from front to back and made another rent, saying, Rav is dead, and we have not learned the rules of grace after meals.

(b. Ber. 42b-43a)[1]

II. SAMUEL

Since Samuel died sometime after 260, he was probably born between 180 and 200 C.E. I have already discussed[2] the story concerning the prediction of his birth by R. Judah b. Bathyra in Nisibis. Since, however, R. Judah b. Bathyra probably died well before 200, and perhaps before 180, there is no reason to believe that that story is historically reliable, though details given *en passant* are. In any event, Samuel's father, Abba bar Abba, was not only a leading figure in Babylonian Jewry, but also a man of considerable wealth and public prestige. He educated his son at home in Nehardea, and also probably in Nisibis.[3] While he was at home, the following took place:

The father of Samuel once found Samuel crying, and asked him, Why are you crying? Because my teacher beat me, he replied. But why? Because he said to me, You are feeding my son, and you did not wash your hands before doing so. And why did you not wash? *He* was eating, why should *I* wash? Said the father, It is not enough that he is ignorant of the law, but he must also beat you!

(b. Ḥul. 107b)[4]

Samuel is the only rabbi of whom we have a detailed physical description. He was allegedly short, with a big stomach, swarthy and had large teeth.[5] (Whatever the explanation of his nickname, Arioch, it therefore certainly did not refer to his height)[6] Samuel had

---

[1] On the name 'Abba Arika', see Baron, *Social and Religious History* II, 190. See also Zuri, *Rav*, 61. It may have meant tall, b. Shab. 59a, compare Taıg. Gen. 14.1, and see below, n. 6.

[2] Vol. I, 88-9. If he had unmarried daughters ca. 260, however, he may have been born as late as 210-220, and his daughters ca. 240. Compare Hoffmann, *op. cit.*, 8, n. 1 and appendices A, III, VII.

[3] Epstein, *Mishnah*, 211-2.

[4] Compare y. Peʾah 8.8.

[5] b. Ned. 50b.

[6] The name appears in b. Shab. 53a, Qid. 39a, Men. 38b, Ḥul. 76b. Fessler, *op. cit.*, 9, provides a good summary of earlier views of the nickname. Graetz, II, 520, says, 'Arioch' means 'the Aryan, partisan of Persia' following Fürst, *Litte-*

at least one brother, Phinehas, and he and his brother married sisters.[1]
He had several daughters, as we have already seen, and possibly a
son.[2] His grandsons were among the rabbis of the third generation
in Babylonia.[3] Like his father, Samuel was a man of considerable
wealth. He had fields, which others worked,[4] held slaves,[5] and
engaged in commerce, as did his son.[6]

Mar Samuel is conventionally identified with the Samuel of the
following story:

> Samuel Yarhina'ah was the physician of Rabbi [Judah the Prince].
> Now Rabbi Judah contracted an eye ailment, and Samuel offered to
> treat it with a lotion, but he said, I cannot bear it. Then I will apply
> an ointment to it, he said. This too I cannot bear, he objected. So he

---

raturblatt d. Orient, 1847. This is obviously impossible however. Compare Lam.
R. V, 4.1, "R. Joshua b. Levi said, Nebuzaradan is identical with Arioch (Dan.
2.14). Why was his name called 'Arioch'? Because he roared at the captives like
a lion [ari] until they reached the Euphrates.' Hoffmann, *op. cit.*, 7, n. 2, comments
"Die berühmten Gesetzlehrer führen öfters den Ehrennamen *ari.*" Compare
J. Levy, *Wörterbuch*, I, 165, s.v., who compares the word to *arxos*, king, "d.h.
Samuel ist könig, gewöhnlich, namentlich im Civilrecht." It seems to me that the
occurrence of the name in a biblical setting precludes either Persian or Greek
comparisons. Jastrow calls it 'probably a Persian word for judge'. I am not sure
what word he refers to. We do have the Armenian *arjak*, unbound, free, which
Hübschmann traces (425) to the Pahlavi *andarz*, meaning injunction, but I do not
think Jastrow is referring to such an etymology, which in any case is far-fetched.
See also S. Krauss, *Arukh Supplement* IX 67, who cites Moses Xorenazi's reference
to the country of the *Arik* (see my "Jews in Pagan Armenia", *JAOS* 84, 1964,
239, on the Amaduni in Armenia), that is, Khorassan. Krauss says that it is 'not
impossible' that Rav was born there. I think it is quite impossible, as we have
seen above. If his family came originally from Khorassan, he is the only one whose
name 'reveals' it, along with Samuel, who came from an old family in Nehardea!
The other explanations cited here are equally impossible. The simplest is that
suggested by the context, as given by Hoffmann, and I see no reason to go beyond
Hoffmann's explanation. See also Funk, *Juden*, I, 42 n. 2., and E. S. Rosenthal,
in *H. Yalon Memorial Volume*, (in Hebrew, Jerusalem, 1963), ed. S. Lieberman,
pp. 332-6, who concludes that Arika clearly does not refer to a place.

[1] b. Sanh. 28b. Compare b. Bekh. 39a, Phinehas asked Samuel a question
about the blemishes of firstlings; b. M.Q. 18a, he was instructed by Samuel in the
laws of mourning.

[2] See above, p. 43-4, and compare b. Ket. 23a, Nedarim 55a.

[3] R. Mari son of Samuel's Daughter, quoted by Abaye, b. B.M. 110a, R. Jacob
son of Samuel's Daughter, b. Ber. 25b. There is a reference to Rav, son of Samuel,
in the name of Samuel in Midrash on Psalms 9.1, ed. Braude I, 131, but Braude
notes (II, 424 n. 3) that Theodor, in the parallel passage in Gen. R., suggests
that it is R. Nahman.

[4] b. B.Q. 92a.

[5] b. Git. 38a, Bezah 14b, etc. See S. Zeitlin, "Mar Samuel and Manumission
of Slaves", *JQR* n.s. 55, 1965, 267-9.

[6] b. Ned. 55a.

placed a vial of chemicals under his pillow, and he was healed. Rabbi was very anxious to ordain him but the opportunity was lacking. Let it not grieve thee, he said, I have seen in the Book of The First Man [Adam HaRishon] in which it is written, Samuel Yarḥinaʾah shall be called sage, but not rabbi, but Rabbi's healing shall come through him.

(b. B.M. 85b)

There is no doubt whatever that Samuel was a physician, and that he used eye-lotions is attested elsewhere. But this is the only place where he is called "Yarḥinaʾah," normally interpreted to mean ʾastronomer.' He did not study in Palestine; he had no other contact with R. Judah, and that R. Judah did not ordain him meant absolutely nothing at all for his later career, nor is it ever again referred to. It is not out of the question that Samuel went to Palestine; he may have gone on business, and if so, would certainly have attended R. Judah's consistory. But the evidence that he did is based on this one story, which speaks of him—if it is he—by a nickname never again used, and in a curious context. I suspect the story was invented, with Samuel in mind, to explain why he never received ordination in Palestine, perhaps by a disciple eager to defend his master's reputation.[1] But I do not think it is historically reliable.

---

[1] Compare L. Ginzberg, *Legends*, VI 82; Funk, *Monumenta*, I, 324. On Samuel in Palestine, see also Halevi *Dorot*, II, 167-8. Compare Frankel, *Mevo Ha Yerushalmi*, 124, who holds Samuel was never in Palestine. He notes that quotations by Babylonian rabbis of Palestinian authorities, as in b. Git. 66b, Samuel citing R. Judah, do not *prove* that the Babylonians actually went to Palestine, but in fact heard such opinions from others, or received written reports of them. (In this connection, we note Samuel's enforcing the decree of Palestine permitting the use of pagans's olive oil.) Compare Weiss, *Dor*, III, 146-7, and n. 9. The reference to the "Book of Adam" recalls Gen. R. 24.2:

> R. Judah b. R. Simon said, While Adam lay a shapeless mass (Golem) before Him at whose decree the world came into existence, He showed him every generation and its sages, every generation and its judges, scribes, interpreters, and leaders. Said He to him, 'Thine eyes did see unformed substance' (Ps. 139.16): the unformed substance which thine eyes did see has already been written in the Book of Adam', that is 'This is the Book of the Generations of Adam' (Gen. 5.1).

Compare b. Sanh. 38b, Ex. R. 40.2.3, Lev. R. 26.7. There is a large Adam literature, in both Jewish and Christian sources, and he played a great role in gnostic, Manichean, and other speculation. In this instance, however, the reference is clearly to a Jewish belief that Adam knew about the future. It seems reasonable to suppose that some such 'book of Adam' was compiled in the consistory of R. Judah's court. But Samuel was not the physician of R. Judah the Prince, nor was the question of his ordination in Palestine ever discussed again. Samuel specifically said that it was the permission of the exilarchate which made official the office of a Jewish judge in Babylonia. On the other hand, there is no serious chronological problem, since R. Judah the Prince was alive when Samuel was a young man;

Samuel was not well-known in Palestine, nor was he highly regarded there, according to the following:

> During the lifetime of Rav, R. Yoḥanan used to address him thus in letters: 'Greetings to our *Master* in Babylonia'. After Rav's death, R. Yoḥanan wrote to Samuel, 'Greetings to our *colleague* in Babylonia'. Said Samuel to himself, Is there nothing in which I am his *master?* He thereupon sent to R. Yoḥanan the calculations for the intercalation of months for the coming sixty years. Said R. Yoḥanan, He only knows mere arithmetic. So he [Samuel] wrote out and sent thirteen camel-loads of questions concerning doubtful cases of *terefah*. Said R. Yoḥanan, It is clear that I have a master in Babylonia. I must go and see him. He said to a child, Tell me the last verse you learned. 'Now Samuel was dead' (I Samuel 28.3). Said R. Yoḥanan, This means that Samuel has died. (But it was not the case, Samuel was not dead then, and this only occurred so that R. Yoḥanan should not trouble himself.)
>
> (b. Ḥul. 95b)

While the Palestinians, who had known Rav and respected him, could not in his case follow their usual habit of denigrating the leaders, and achievements, of the diaspora, it is clear that they neither respected Samuel, nor admired his achievements. For his part, as we shall see below, Samuel did not take seriously the authority, or the qualifications, of the Palestinians.

Like the other leading rabbis, Samuel was a sage, physician, astronomer, and magician. He interpreted omens;[1] like Rav, was able to bring death upon those who made derogatory remarks about him, or angered him,[2] and he was believed to the able to communicate with the dead:

> The father of Samuel had some money belonging to orphans deposited with him. When he died, Samuel was not with him, and they called him 'The son who consumes the money of orphans.' So he went after his father to the cemetery, and said to them [the dead]: I am looking for Abba. They said to him, There are many Abba's here. I want Abba b. Abba, he said. They replied, There are also several Abba b. Abba's here. He then said to them, I want Abba b.

---

nor, as I said, is it impossible that Samuel actually did accompany his father to Palestine at one time or other. See also b. B. Q. 114b = Ket. 26a, which would suggest that he *was* in Palestine.

[1] b. Ḥul. 95b. The story, cited above, is told to indicate that R. Yoḥanan believed in the revelatory power of biblical verses cited at random, Samuel, of books, and Rav, of ferryboats.

[2] y. Ber. 2.6, Benjamin of Ginzak [=Gazaca] taught contrary to Samuel's opinion; b. Ber. 19a, a certain man made derogatory remarks about Mar Samuel, and a log fell on his head, so that he died.

Abba, the father of Samuel. Where is he? They replied, He has gone
up to the academy of the firmament. Meanwhile he saw Levi [who was
also deceased] sitting outside. He said to him, Why are you sitting
outside. He replied, Because they said to me, For as many years as
you did not go up to the academy of R. 'Afes and thus hurt his
feelings, we will not let you come up to the academy of the firmament. Meanwhile his father came. Samuel observed that he was both
weeping and langhing. He said to him, why are you weeping?
He replied, Because you are coming here soon. And why are you
laughing? Because you are highly esteemed in this world. He thereupon
said to him, If I am esteemed, let them take up Levi, and they did take
up Levi. He then said to him, Where is the money of the orphans.
He replied, Go and you will find it in the case of the millstones. The
money at the top and bottom is mine, and that in the middle is the
orphans. He said to him, Why did you do that? He replied, So that if
thieves come they should take mine, and if the earth destroy any of it,
it should destroy mine.   (b. Ber. 18b)

One of Samuel's chief interests was in medicine, a field in which he
achieved wide renown. It was, as we have noted, necessary to master
aspects of anatomy and medicine because of the nature of Jewish law,
and Samuel, like Rav, did so.[1] But Samuel knew far more than was
required for legal decisions. He concerned himself with all aspects
of life, from conception, labor, and the needs of the woman in travail,
to the causes of sterility and death. Thus Samuel taught:

A spermatic emission that does not shoot forth like an arrow cannot
fructify.   (b. Hag. 15a)[2]

He emphasized the dangers of catching a chill after blood-letting:

If one lets blood and catches a chill, a fire is made for him even on
the Tammuz [summer] solstice. A teak chair was broken up for
Samuel, a table of juniper wood was broken up for R. Judah.
                              (b. Shab. 129a = y. Shab. 18.3)

Likewise he ordained that the Sabbath may be desecrated to ensure
that a woman in confinement was kept warm and comfortable.[3]
He not only treated ailments, but also studied medical phenomena:

R. Berekiah and R. Bibi in Samuel's name said: A woman can give
birth only at the 271st, 272nd, or 273rd days, which is at nine months
plus the days of conception.   (Gen. R. 20.6)

He prescribed specific remedies for eye diseases,[4] and after a

---

[1] For example, b. Hul. 76b, Shab. 77b.
[2] Compare b. Yev. 75a-b.
[3] b. Shab. 129a.
[4] b. Shab. 78a, Ned. 55a.

trauma, insisted that eye inflamation must be treated on the Sabbath where necessary:

> It once happened to a maidservant in Mar Samuel's house that her eye became inflamed on a Sabbath. She cried, but no one attended her, and her eye dropped. On the morrow, Mar Samuel went forth, and propounded that if one's eye gets out of order, it is permissible to paint it on the Sabbath, because the eyesight is connected with the mental faculties.
>
> (b. A.Z. 28b)

Likewise he taught that circumcision must be delayed if the child is ill, and required a full period of convalescence.[1] We have already noted that he exchanged medical traditions with Ablat, the Iranian sage, in particular on bloodletting. On the same subject he taught:

> The correct interval for bloodletting is every thirty days. In middle age one should decrease the frequency; at a more advanced age, he should again decrease. Samuel also said, The correct time for blood-letting is on a Sunday, Wednesday, or Friday, but not on a Monday or a Thursday, because, a Master said, He who possesses ancestral merit may let blood on Monday and Thursday because the Heavenly Court and the earthly one are alike then. Why not on Tuesday? Because the planet Mars rules at the even numbered hours of the day. But on Friday, too, it rules at even numbered hours? Since the multitude are accustomed to it, 'The Lord preserves the simple' (Psalm 116.6). Samuel said, A Wednesday which is the fourth of the month, the fourteenth, and the twenty-fourth, a Wednesday which is not followed by four days (in the same month), all are dangerous. The first day of the month and the second cause weakness, the third is dangerous, the eve of the festival causes weakness, the eve of Pentecost is dangerous, and the rabbis laid an interdict upon the eve of every festival on account of the festival of Pentecost, when there issues a wind called Taboah (slaughter), and had not the Israelites accepted the Torah it would absolutely have killed them.
>
> Samuel said, If one eats a grain of wheat and then lets blood, he has bled in respect of that grain only [it lightens that meal, but has no wider affects]. Yet that is only as a remedy, but if it is to ease one, it does ease. When one is bled, drinking is permissible immediately, eating until half a mile [the time it takes to walk that distance].
>
> (b. Shab. 129b)

The striking mixture of medicine, astrology, and theology in the above saying provides a good glimpse into the mental processes of the sages, and of the people who looked to them for wisdom about every aspect of life. They observed as keenly as they knew how,

---

[1] b. Yev. 71a, compare Shab. 136a.

transmitted all the information they possessed, which must have come largely from ancient Babylonian sources, and added to the matter the outlook of Jewish theology, which held, first, that all things that happen, happen on account of Heaven—and for the best; second, that the specific merits of a person, achieved both through his own actions and through his ancestry, affect his health, both moral and physical; and third, that through prayer, fasting, and atonement, one may avert evil. Thus he responded to word of a pestilence in Khuzistan:

> Once Samuel was informed that pestilence was raging among the inhabitants of Be Hozae (Khuzistan), and he ordained a fast. The people said, Surely it is a long distance away from here. He replied, Would then a crossing prevent it from spreading?
>
> (b. Ta'anit 21b)

Nothing was accidental, but all things carry out the will of God:

> Samuel saw a scorpion borne by a frog across the river which then stung a man so that he died. He quoted, 'They stand forth this day to receive thy judgements for all are thy servants' (Ps. 119.91).
>
> (b. Ned. 41a)

He and Rav debated on the medical causes of death. Rav took the view that the 'evil eye' or some other supernatural force contributed fatality, while Samuel took a far more naturalistic viewpoint, as in to the following case:

> And the Lord shall take away from thee all sickness" (Deut. 7.15). Rav said, By this the evil eye is meant. This is in accordance with his opinion, for Rav went up to a cemetery, performed certain charms, and then said, Ninety-nine have died through an evil eye, and one through natural causes. Samuel said, This refers to the wind. Samuel is self-consistent, for he said, All [illness] is caused by the wind. But according to Samuel, what of those executed by the State? Those too—but for the wind [which enters the wound] an ointment could be compounded for them [which would cause the severed parts to grow together] and they would recover.
>
> (b. B.M. 107a)

Like Rav, Samuel also commented on how to maintain general good health, and on the bodily functions in their normal operation:

> Samuel said, Urinating at dawn is like a steel edge to iron, evacuation at dawn is like a steel edge to iron.
>
> (b. Ber. 62b)

> All potions taken between Passover and Pentecost are beneficial.
>
> (b. Shab. 147b)

Until the age of forty, food is more beneficial (to the body). Thenceforth, drink is more beneficial.

(*ibid.* 152a)[1]

In his day, Samuel was regarded as the greatest Jewish astronomer, and this probably meant, astrologer as well. We have noted how he linked blood-letting with the position of Mars. In a late source, he allegedly treated his astrological knowledge with a measure of embarrassment:

'It is not in heaven' (Deut. 30.11). Samuel said, The Torah is not to be found among astrologers whose work is to gaze at the heavens. People said to Samuel, Lo, you are an astrologer, and yet you are also great in the Torah. He replied, I only engage in astrology when I am free from studying the Torah. When is that? When I am in the bath.

(Deut. R. 8.6)

It is clear, however, from earlier sources, that Samuel studied astrology with considerable energy, and that he took the subject seriously.[2] His reputation as astronomer was known in Palestine, for he had written to R. Yoḥanan to ensure that it would be, as we noted above. Likewise, he boasted,

I am quite able to make a calendar for the whole of the diaspora. Said Abba, Father of R. Simlai, to Samuel, Does the master know [the meaning] of that which is taught in 'The Secret of Intercalation': 'If the new moon is born before midday or after midday'? He replied, I do not. He then said to him, Since the master does not know this there must be other things which the master also does not know.

(b. R.H. 20b)

Since the Palestinians had jealously guarded their right to determine the Jewish calendar, and especially feared, from the time of R. Ḥananiah the nephew of R. Joshua b. Ḥananiah[3], that the Babylonians, with their access to superior astronomical traditions, would arrogate that right to themselves, Samuel's boast, accompanied by flaunting of his knowledge to R. Yoḥanan, must have represented a considerable

---

[1] On Samuel's medical traditions, see Hoffmann, *op. cit.*, 13-14; Funk, *Juden*, 59-60, and especially, Julius Preuss, *Biblisch-Talmudische Medizin* (Berlin, 1923), *passim*. For our purposes, it is sufficient to note that the great Amoraim were also renowned physicians. Preuss provides a full analysis of their medical information, and its place in the history of medicine. Other medical sayings are in b. A.Z. 28a; b. Sanh. 101a, 'Change of diet is the first step to indigestion'; b. Yoma' 83b=y. Yoma' 8.5, Where does a mad dog come from; b. Nid. 38a, etc.
[2] y. Ber. 9.2, b. Ber. 58b.
[3] Vol. I, 113-120.

challenge. His astronomical knowledge is illustrated in the following sayings:[1]

> The lunar year consists of no less than 352 nor more than 356 days. If two (months) are full, there are six, if two (months) are incomplete, there are two, and if one is complete and one incomplete, four.
>
> (b. ʿArakhin 9b)

> Samuel said, The vernal equinox occurs only at the beginning of one of the four quarters of the day, that is, either at the beginning of the day, or at the beginning of the night, or at midday, or at midnight. [That is, the vernal equinox begins at a different quarter of the solar day in the course of every four years.] The summer solstice only occurs either at the end of one and a half or at the end of seven and a half hours of the day or night. The autumnal equinox only occurs at the end of three, or nine hours of the day or night, and the winter solstice only occurs at the end of four and a half or ten and a half hours of the day or night. The duration of a season of the year is no longer than 91 days and seven and a half hours, and the beginning of one season is removed from that of the other by no more than one half of a planetary hour. Samuel further stated, The vernal equinox never begins under Jupiter but it breaks the trees, nor does the winter solstice begin under Jupiter but it dries up the seed. This however is the case only when the new moon occurred in the moon hour or in the Jupiter hour.
>
> (b. ʿEruv. 56a)

> What are 'zikin'? Samuel said, A comet. Samuel also said, I am as familiar with the paths of the heaven as with the streets of Nehardea, with the exception of the comet, about which I am ignorant. There is a tradition that it never passes through the constellation of Orion, for if it did, the world would be destroyed. Samuel contrasted two texts. It is written, 'Who maketh the Bear, Orion, and the Pleiades' (Job 9.9), and it is written elsewhere, 'That maketh Pleiades and Orion' (Amos 5.8). How do we reconcile these? Were it not for the heat of Orion the world could not endure the cold of Pleiades, and

---

[1] See also b. Sanh. 12b, on intercalating the calendar; *Midrash Samuel*, ed. S. Buber (Vilna 1925), 3.1, on the length of a *regaʿ* (second). Compare b. Ber. 59a, Rav explains the meaning of *berakim* (lightning):
> A single flash, white lightning, blue lightning, clouds that rise in the west and come from the south, and two clouds that rise facing each other are all signs of trouble. What is the practical need? [To teach that] prayer is needed [to avert the omen].
On Samuel's definition of the length of a *regaʿ*, see Ginzberg, *Perushim* I, 59. See especially W. M. Feldman, *Rabbinical Mathematics and Astronomy* (repr. N.Y. 1965), 12, 17, 74, on the 'seasons' of Samuel, 199. He points out that Rav's saying that Saturnalia fell before the winter solstice represents acceptance of Samuel's system of calculation. See also F. Cumont, *Oriental Religions in Roman Paganism* (N.Y. 1956) 162-95 on astrology and magic.

were it not for the cold of Pleiades, the world could not endure the heat of Orion. There is a tradition that were it not for the tail of the scorpion placed in the stream of fire [Dan. 7.10] no one who has ever been stung by a scorpion could live. This is what is referred to in the words of the All-Merciful to Job, 'Canst thou bind the chains of the Pleiades or loose the bands of Orion' (Job. 38.31). What is meant by 'Kimah' [= Pleiades]? Samuel said, About a hundred [kʿmeʾah] stars.

(b. Ber. 58b)

Nonetheless, Samuel held that Israel is not subject to astrology (planetary influence), and insisted that the merit of man determined his fate, and that 'Charity delivers from death' (Prov. 10.2) meant not only an unnatural death, but from death itself.

Samuel outlived Rav by a number of years:

When they said to Samuel, Rav's soul has gone to rest, he rented on account of him, thirteen garments, and said, Gone is the man before whom I trembled.

(b. M.Q. 24a)

and comforted Rav's son, R. Ḥiyya, by telling him his father's 'pearls,'[1] that is, Rav's wise sayings. He took a lenient view of the veneration of Rav's grave:

It was the practice of the people to take earth from Rav's grave, and to apply it on the first day of an attack of fever. When Samuel was told of it, [that people were using an object belonging to the dead, which is forbidden, see A.Z. 29b], he said, They do well, for it is natural soil, and natural soil does not become forbidden, for it is written, 'And he cast the dust thereof upon the graves of the common people' (II Kings 23.6a), thus comparing the graves of the common people to idols: just as idols are not forbidden when they are attached to the earth, for it written, 'You shall utterly destroy all the places *upon* the mountains' (Deut. 12.2), that is, their *Gods*, which are upon the high mountains, but not the *mountains* which themselves are their gods—so too here what is attached is not forbidden.

(b. Sanh. 47b)

Samuel's exegesis thus permitted a practice which the people must have regarded as meritorious, but which the rabbis could not, if asked *ab initio* for permission, have approved. That the graves of the sages were venerated suggests that they were believed to possess power, or mana, not ordinarily found in other men. They were not merely teachers and judges, therefore, but 'holy men,' who talked to

---

[1] b. Ber. 12a, Hag. 14a.

the dead, cursed or blessed effectually, mastered occult sciences, healed, and read the secrets of the stars.

III. OTHER CONTEMPORARIES OF RAV AND SAMUEL

We have already discussed Karna, Shila, and Mar 'Ukba above (ch. Two, sections iii and v). Here we shall briefly consider other contemporaries of Rav and Samuel.

Rabbah bar Hanah, Rav's cousin, was born in Babylonia, and went with his uncle, R. Hiyya, to Palestine, from which he returned apparently about the same time as Rav.[1] He exercised judicial powers, and erred in his decision, and when he returned to Palestine, asked R. Hiyya whether he was required to make restitution. He spent most of his life in Palestine, where he taught and judged, but he probably ended his days in Babylonia,[2] where he was treated with respect by Rav and others. He made his living as a wine merchant.[3]

R. Simlai, a Palestinian from Lud, whose father, Abba, asked a difficult question of Samuel,[4] was educated in Palestine, with R. Judah Nesi'ah, in the first third of the third century.[5] When R. Judah's court permitted gentile oil to be consumed by Jews he was sent to Babylonia, via Nisibis, to announce it.[6] The decree was reported in Babylonia by R. Yizhak b. Samuel b. Marta before he reached Babylonia.[7] He settled in Babylonia, at Nehardea, but returned at least once to Palestine:

> R. Simlai came before R. Yohanan and asked him, Let the Master teach me the Book of Genealogies. He said to you, Where do you come from? He replied, From Lud. And where do you dwell? In Nehardea. He said to him, We do not discuss it either with the Ludians or with the Nehardeans, and how much the more so with you who are from Lud, and live in Nehardea!   (b. Pes. 62b)

Samuel b. Shilat was allegedly descended from Haman.[8] He was a teacher of young children in Babylonia,[9] and was also a funeral orator in Sura, and preached, as we noted, at Rav's funeral.[10]

---

[1] b. Sanh. 5a. At least one trip was made together with Rav, according to this source.

[2] b. Hul. 44b.

[3] b. B.M. 83a.

[4] b. R.H. 20a.

[5] b. Bekh. 36b.

[6] b. A.Z. 37b.

[7] y. Shab. 1.4.

[8] b. Sanh. 9b.

[9] b. Ket. 50a, 62a, B.B. 8a, 21a.   [10] b. Shab. 153a.

Rav Hamnuna, a priest and student of Rav in Sura, will be discussed along with Rav Huna, Rav Ḥisda, and other students of Rav, in vol. III. Rav Kahana was a student of Rav and colleague of Rav ʾAssi.[1] When Rav returned to Babylonia, Rav Kahana (I) joined him at Sura, and he is described as wanting to learn about Rav's traditions, but not needing to learn how to reason about them.[2] He was an eager student.[3] We have already noted some of the advice Rav gave to him. He migrated to Palestine long before Rav's death.[4] He probably never returned to Babylonia, according to Hyman. His uncle was a distinguished rabbi[5] but otherwise we know nothing at all about his family.

Another Babylonian, associated with Rav, who migrated to Palestine, was Rav Zeʿiri, a student of R. Ḥiyya and colleague of Rav[6] who remained in Palestine after Rav returned home.[7] He himself returned to Babylonia later on,[8] and taught many of the leading disciples of both Rav and Samuel. Like other rabbis he was believed to have conversation with the dead:

> Zeʿiri deposited some money with his landlady while he was away visiting Rav [or, at the school house], and she died. So he went after her to the cemetery and said to her, Where is my money? She replied, Go and take it from under the ground in the hole of the doorpost . . . and tell my mother to send me my comb and my tube of eye-paint by the hand of so-and-so who is coming here tomorrow.
>
> (b. Ber. 18b)

(There was a second Zeʿiri, who was a student of Rav, and who likewise migrated to Palestine, where he studied with R. Yoḥanan.)

Rav ʾAssi was a leading figure in Huẓal,[9] and decreed laws for the town. When Rav came to Nehardea, he found that Rav ʾAssi and Rav Kahana were already distinguished leaders. Rav ʾAssi was honored by Rav and Samuel:

> Rav, Samuel, and Rav ʾAssi once met at a circumcision, (or, some say, at the party for the redemption of the first-born.) Rav would not

---

[1] Hyman, *op. cit.*, III 841, distinguishes among *five* Rav Kahanas, of which the first is so designated, and the second was a student of Rav.

[2] b. Sanh. 36b, compare b. Nazir 19a, b. Ber. 62a.

[3] b. Pes. 113a.

[4] b. Zev. 59a, Men. 23a, and see above, p. 131.

[5] y. Yev. 11.1.

[6] b. B.Q. 30b, Git. 24b.

[7] b. Ḥul. 110a.

[8] b. Ber. 22a.

[9] b. Meg. 5b, Ḥul. 26b.

enter before Samuel, nor Samuel before R. ʾAssi, nor R. ʾAssi before Rav, and they therefore argued who should go in last, and it was decided that Samuel should go in last, and that Rav and R. ʾAssi should go in together . . . .

(b. B.Q. 80b)

We have noted above that like Rav Kahana, he was well trained in dialectics before Rav's coming, but required knowledge of his traditions.[1] He would accompany Rav on his judicial circuit,[2] and probably studied with Levi b. Sisi, whom Rav ʾAssi called 'master',[3] and with Samuel. He taught many of the distinguished students of the next generation, particularly in Rav's school, including R. Huna, R. Judah and others. He outlived Rav by a very few years. He was, like other rabbis, a rich man:

> R. ʾAssi used to inspect his property daily. He exclaimed, Where are all those *istiras* of Mar Samuel. One day he saw that an irrigation-pipe had burst on his land. He took off his coat, rolled it up, and stuffed it in the hole. He then called, and people came and stopped it up. He exclaimed, Now I have found all those *istiras* of Mar Samuel. [For Samuel had said, He who inspects his property daily will find an *istira*].

(b. Ḥul. 105a)

A second R. ʾAssi, colleague of R. ʾAmi, lived as a youth in Babylonia in the time of Samuel and R. Judah, that is to say, ca. 250 after the death of Rav.[4]

R. ʾAdda b. ʾAhava was born in Babylonia, in ʾAkra dʿAgma, near Pumbedita, about 210[5] and his birth was allegedly known to R. Judah the Prince, or at least, coincided with R. Judah's death.[6] He was Rav's student, and precept at his academy. He also studied with Samuel, probably after Rav's death. He was regarded as possessing considerable merit,[7] more than Rav and Samuel, and was remembered for his piety and his unusually long life. His colleagues were R. Huna, R. Ḥisda, R. Naḥman, and others of the next generation. We shall consider other aspects of his career in vol. III.[8]

---

[1] Such traditions as Rav brought back would have been prized by the Babylonians, who did not have easy access to the Palestinian *beraitot*.

[2] b. A.Z. 57a, Ḥul. 95b.

[3] b. A.Z. 38b.

[4] y. Sheqalim 2.4.

[5] b. Qid. 72b, when Rabbi Judah the Prince died. But the date is merely conjectural.

[6] Compare Gen. R. 58.2.

[7] b. Taʿanit 20b.

[8] On Rav ʾAmi's studies with Rav in Babylonia, see Zuri, *Rav*, 75; on Rav

IV. RABBI AND MAGUS

From the stories cited above, the rabbi emerges as a wonder-working sage, master of ancient wisdom both of Israel and of Babylonia, and privy to the occult. He was believed able to cast an evil eye, to consort with the dead, and to interpret the signs and omens not only of the stars but also of the animal and natural world. His advent was marked even by the rivers. He was clairvoyant. He was well-known, and his doings were widely noted wherever he went. He could bless, and his blessing would bring prosperity; he could curse with evil consequence. His advice covered every aspect of human affairs: whom to marry, where to live, how to preserve health, whom to avoid, and whom to honor. He was learned in the medical traditions of his region, and achieved a wide reputation as an interpreter of physiological phenomena. He would gather wisdom wherever he went, from fishermen, shepherds, traders. He shared the popular conviction that he, or one of his colleagues, could preserve sufficient merit, not merely through learning, but on account of piety or genealogy, to preserve the safety of the city. He was, therefore, more than a judge and educator, involved in regional politics and law. He was, as I said, a holy man, whose sanctity far transcended his wisdom and piety. A man who could cause the death of one who angered, or made derogatory remarks about himself, who could raise the dead and cast a horoscope, and who also authoritatively interpreted the Torah—such a man would well find veneration among the people in his lifetime, and for the dust of his grave after death.

The rabbi was a new kind of religious leader for Babylonian Jewry, appearing from the first-century onward. We know that before and after that time, Babylonian Jews had political leaders, who held high rank in the imperial administration, and who were quite well informed about legal matters. We have no evidence that they were held to be miracle-workers as well. The priests, settled in Babylonia from earlier times, who were believed to possess special merit and power because of their lineage, must have retained considerable influence, as they did in Palestine, from the beginnings of Jewish settlement. No one doubted that their genealogy was unusually 'pure.' They and the Levites, received the agricultural tithes and offerings until

---

Kahana I, 136. On Ze'iri, Halevi *Dorot* II, 242-6; on Rav Kahana and Rav 'Assi, 228-242. Halevi points out that other Amoraim of this period bore the same names as men of subsequent generations, and it is very difficult to find out who was who.

the middle of the third century, and one may suppose that, in exchange, the people expected them to bless and teach. In this period, however, the tithes were annulled, and transcending the historical-political explanation for that fact, given by R. Yoḥanan, the *fact* itself suggests that other kinds of leaders had taken the priests' place in the popular mind. It may well be that the people themselves had gradually ceased to patronize the local priests, and with the natural decline of the practice of tithing, an adequate explanation was sought, and found, in the depredations of the Palmyrene army; if so, it is a *post facto* explanation. For their part, the rabbis enjoyed considerable economic benefit, being allowed to sell their merchandise first in the market place, and claiming (but not getting) special tax exemptions.[1] It seems reasonable, therefore, to suppose that the rabbis gradually replaced the priests as the Jewish religious authorities in Babylonia, just as they did in Palestine from the first century onward, and that they therefore gained economic benefits, as the priests lost them.

If, from the rabbis' perspective, the Magus was a sorcerer, or blasphemer, the Iranians probably understood the rabbi to be some kind of Magus. I can discern only one significant difference between the functions of the rabbi, on the one hand, and of the Magus, on the other. The Magus performed sacerdotal rites, while the rabbi did not. The Magus, like the Israelite priest, originated in a tribe consecrated to the service of God. By Sasanian times, however, he had assumed important social and cultural functions. Enjoying great ancestral merit, he possessed powerful influence among the people. He was a teacher, and custodian of cultural traditions. Agathias, the Armenian Christian historian, observed that the Magi were, as we noted above, widely revered, even venerated. Public affairs were guided by their counsel and their predictions, and "Nothing among the Persians is regarded as legitimate or just, if not affirmed by a Magus." The Magus, as a state official, legalized marriages, performed priestly rites, spread the faith, and served the state, just as the rabbi in this period acted as a functionary of the Jewish government. The rabbi exerted considerable liturgical influence, though without sacrifices and purification rites, Judaism could not provide him with a fully equivalent sacerdotal function. Zaehner describes the Magi as "a hereditary caste entrusted with the supervision of the national religion, whatever form it might take and in whatever part

---

[1] See M. Beer, in *Tarbiẓ* 33, 1964, 247-58.

of the Empire it might be practiced." In this, they differed, however, from the rabbis, who were not part of a *caste* but successors of one.

Otherwise the resemblance is striking. The Magi were philosophers, men who possessed *maga*. (From the first century onward, Pythagoreans looked at the Magi as masters of astronomy and exponents of elevated ethical teachings, theurges and theologians.) They were were regarded as masters, par excellence, of astrology, necromancy, magic, and medicine.[1]

It is difficult, therefore, to find substantial *functional* differences between the rabbi and the Magus, at least so far as the western part of the empire was concerned. Both fulfilled political, judicial, cultural, and educational roles. Both were regarded as holding unusual powers and knowledge. Both could predict the future, read omens, consult the dead, heal the sick. Both enjoyed great intellectual influence, and shaped their respective religious traditions. While the rabbi was not a priest, he was held in the eyes of the Jews to have those peculiar powers and merits associated by the Mazdeans with their priests. From the perspective of the Babylonian pagan, therefore, the rabbi's style would have made him appear as a Jewish Magus.[2]

These parallels do not suggest that the rabbis were Iranized, for some Palestinian rabbis were similarly endowed, it was widely believed, with extraordinary powers and exercised far more than merely legal and pedagogical authority. At the same time, one should stress how different Rav and Samuel and their contemporaries appear by contrast to Rabban Yohanan ben Zakkai and those of his first-century colleagues who shared his view that healing was *not* the task of the rabbi, but rather of another kind of theurge. Indeed, it would be valuable to restudy the lives of the Tannaim and early Amoraim and to develop categories to isolate and organize the particular functions performed by each man. We know that some Tannaim specialized in learning particular sections of the law. It may

---

[1] See especially Joseph Bidez and Franz Cumont, *Les Mages Héllenisés* (Paris, 1938) I, *passim*; R. C. Zaehner, *Dawn*, 161-7; Christensen, *L'Iran*, 110-17; Widengren, *Religionen*, 259-65; Duchesne-Guillemin, *La Religion*, 157f., 245f. The important fact is not what the Magi were at the beginning, but how they functioned in this period. See also Alessandro Bausani, *Persia Religiosa* (Milan, 1959), 81-3; Zaehner, *Zurvan*, 19-20; and F. Cumont, *Oriental Religions in Roman Paganism* (repr. N.Y. 1956), 138f., 144f., 188f., and his *Astrology and Religion among the Greeks and Romans* (N.Y. 1960), 16, 61.

[2] See also Klima, *Manis Zeit*, 145, who notes the similarity in functions of Mani and Samuel. Both were, he says, theologians, astronomers, physicians; both were friendly with Shapur.

well have been that to others were ascribed particular theurgical functions. In any event, it is clear that the third-century Babylonian rabbis were regarded as especially competent physicians when, as in the case of Samuel, they visited Palestine. If the rabbis were not Iranized, however, it is quite obvious that the Magi were scarcely Judaized. Both are examples of Hellenization, a process well advanced by the third-century A.D. Each represents a *modality* of Hellenization, however, in which inherited culture determined the specific forms that Hellenization would take. We do not therefore profitably contrast Judaized Magi with Hellenized Magi. The rabbi and the Magus were similar because both represented responses to conditions common to their respective cultures. It remains for scholars competent to study these matters to explain what was Hellenistic and what was not in the qualities and functions ascribed to both Jewish and Iranian religious-political leaders.

I think it clear, finally, that the combination of magical and political functions common to both rabbi and Magus and rendering them parallel figures is uncommon elsewhere. Some have supposed that any such "holy man" would do the things ascribed to the rabbi and the Magus, and hence the parallels are so extensive as to be meaningless. The rabbi, however, represents a very different type of leader in the history of Israelite culture from, e.g., the *kohen* or the *nabi*. The *kohen* was, as we have noted, primarily a sacerdotal figure, and yet in other ways bears no significant comparison to the Magus. The *nabi* held no such central position in politics and culture as did the rabbi. Neither the Magus nor the rabbi is remotely similar to the *shaman*. Nor, as I have said, is the combination of political and theurgic functions commonplace within the rabbinic movement before the third century, for theurgy and medicine were regarded in the first-century as distinctly unrabbinical functions by Rabban Yohanan ben Zakkai. There are many kinds of "holy men", but among them, it seems to me that the rabbi and the Magus have much in common with one another, and much to distinguish them from others.

CHAPTER FIVE

RABBINIC JUDAISM IN
EARLY SASANIAN BABYLONIA (II):
THEOLOGY AND LITURGY

If the rabbi and the Magus exhibited certain functional similarities, the faith exposited by the rabbi bore no significant parallels to that of the Mazdean religious tradition. At points of contact, we have discerned, on the contrary, a determined effort on the part of the rabbi to underline the many ways in which Judaism condemned the theological ideas of the surrounding people, even though the cultural traditions of Babylonia made a striking impact. For the most part, the rabbis determined to remain absolutely true to the biblical imperatives of both law and theology, and one should not be surprised to find little innovation, but rather the continuing development of themes and ideas already familiar in Tannaitic Judaism.

i. Ideas about God

While rabbinic ideas about God were expressed in concrete and generally folkloristic forms, rather than in abstract, creedal, and dogmatic ones, an insight into theological motifs may be gained through a consideration of the more general sayings of Rav and Samuel about the nature and activities of God. What is most striking about these sayings is that they are so strictly biblical, unspeculative, and exegetical. I do not believe that there is a single new idea in early Amoraic traditions; all are, as I said, developments of biblical or Tannaitic themes. The most general and abstract statement of Rav is as follows:

> R. Simon taught, In the Torah are mentioned thirteen attributes of God, through every one of which the Holy One, blessed be He, may grant mercy to the children of Israel, for it is said, 'The Lord, the Lord, God, merciful, and gracious, long-suffering, and abundant in goodness and truth, keeping mercy unto the thousandth generation, forgiving iniquity, and transgression, and sin' (Ex. 34: 6-7). Rav said, There are eleven such attributes. The rabbis said that there are ten. Which one of these attributes was Moses thinking of when he prostrated himself in prayer? Rav said, The attribute of being 'abundant

in goodness' for it is said, 'And Moses made haste, and bowed his head toward the earth, and worshipped.' (Ex. 34. 8).[1]

(Midrash on Psalms 93.8, ed. Braude II, 129)

Likewise, R. Huna in the name of Rav said:

'Touching the Almighty, we cannot find him out' (Job. 37.23), That is, we shall never find a limit to the power of the Holy One blessed be He.

(*Ibid.* 19.2, Braude I, 273)

For the rest, we have, as I said, folkloristic sayings about how God spends his day, how he prays, and the like:

R. Judah said in the name of Rav: The day consists of twelve hours, during the first three of which the Holy One, blessed be he, occupies himself with [study of] Torah; during the second, he sits in judgment on the whole world, and when he sees that the world is so guilty as to deserve destruction, he transfers himself from the seat of justice to the seat of mercy; and during the third he feeds the whole world from the horned buffalo to the brood of vermin; and during the fourth he sports with Leviathan, as it is said (Ps. 104.26) 'There is Leviathan . . .'

(b. A.Z. 3b)

Likewise, he prays to himself:

R. Zutra b. Tobi in the name of Rav said, 'May it be my will that my mercy may suppress my anger, and that my mercy may prevail over my [other] attributes so that I may deal with my children in the attribute of mercy, and on their behalf stop short of the limit of strict justice.'

(b. Ber. 7a)

For the rest, he engages in acts of lovingkindness, supporting the invalid, and doing other deeds of mercy.[1] That Rav's viewpoint contains little, if anything, new is indicated by the fact that a Tannaitic beraita holds exactly the same view, that God's presence abides at the head of the sick person.

The duty of man is to accept submissively and gratefully the artifacts of divine judgment. R. Huna in the name of Rav quoted R. Meir's citation of R. Akiba, that a man should always accustom himself to say, Whatever the All-Merciful does is for the good.[2] Rabbinic Judaism retained a strong sense for the sovereignty of God not only over the affairs of nations, but especially over those of individuals, and both

---

[1] b. Shab. 12b.
[2] b. Ber. 60b.

Rav and Samuel stated, as quoted by R. Judah, that by a just measure is meted out whatever a man receives. Similarly Rav said,

> Forty days before an embryo is formed, a bat-kol issues forth on high, announcing, The daughter of so-and-so is to be wife to so-and-so, such-and-such a field is to belong to so-and-so . . .
>
> (b. Sotah 2a)[1]

Here too, Rav was stating an idea that antedated him.[2] He likewise held that not only men, but the ministering angels exist for the glory of God, and cease to be at his will,[3] and had a vivid belief in Satan.[4] These ideas were very ancient; their persistence in the old forms and without significant modification provides a good insight into the stability and inner consistency of rabbinic theology.

Likewise, the sages of this period, as those before and afterwards, believed that Israel received the particular care of the divinity. They held, along with the prophets, that Israel's history formed a vehicle for the revelation of the divine will, and that God participated empathetically in it:

> R. Isaac b. Samuel says in the name of Rav: The night has three watches, and at each watch, the Holy One blessed be He sits, roars like a lion, and says, 'Woe to the children on account of whose sins I have destroyed my House and burned my temple and exiled them among the nations of world.'
>
> (b. Ber. 3a)

Moreover, God mourned the destruction of the Temple.[5] The Divine Presence dwells in Israel, and was attested, while the Temple stood, by the western lamp of the Temple candelabrum, into which the same quantity of oil was poured as into the others, and yet from which the others were kindled; when the priest came to clean them out, it was still burning.[6]

Rav pursued the mystical speculations of rabbinic tradition centering on the creation of the world (Ma'aseh Bere'shit) and on Ezekiel's Chariot (Ma'aseh Merkavah), and made a great impact on

---

[1] In the name of Rav, b. Sanh. 22a, daughter, house, and field; in the name of Samuel, see b. M.Q. 18b.

[2] b. M.Q. 18b, Rav in the name of R. Reuven b. Iztrobili.

[3] b. Hag. 14a, Samuel to R. Ḥiyya b. Rav in Rav's name: 'Every day ministering angels are created from the fiery stream, and utter song, and cease to be'.

[4] b. Shab. 32a.

[5] Lam. R. 1.1, R. Naḥman in the name of Samuel citing R. Joshua b. Levi.

[6] b. Shab. 22b, Men. 86b.

Jewish mystical theology. (Uninterested in mysticism, Samuel prepared a kind of bread as described in Ezek. 4.9 but instead of eating it, he threw it to his dog.[1]) Rav commented on a Merkavah passage:

> 'And I looked, and behold a stormy wind came out of the north' (Ez. 1.4), Where did it go? R. Judah in the name of Rav said, It went to subdue the whole world under the wicked Nebuchadnezzar. The wings of the ḥayot were diminished [Comparing Isaiah 6.2 and Ezek. 1.6]. R. Hananel in the name of Rav said, Those with which they utter song [were taken away] for here it is written 'And with two he did fly, and one called to the other and said . . .' and elsewhere it is written, 'Wilt thou set thine eyes upon it? It is gone' (Prov. 23.5). A fiery stream issued and came forth before him' (Dan 7.10). Whence does it come forth? From the sweat of the ḥayot. And whither does it pour forth? R. Zutra b. Tobiah said in the name of Rav, Upon the head of the wicked in Gehenna, for it is said, 'Behold the storm of the Lord . . . . it will burst upon the head of the wicked.' (Jer. 23.19).
>
> (b. Ḥag. 13b)[2]

That God was conceived of essentially in the terms of the visions of Daniel, Isaiah, and Ezekiel,[3] cannot be doubted. God, or the Shekhinah, glows with blinding brightness:

> Rav said, When the globe of the sun and moon go in to ask leave to depart from the Holy One, blessed be He, their eyes grow dim with the brilliance of the Shekhinah. They seek to go forth to give light to the world and cannot see anything. What does the Holy One . . . do with them? He shoots arrows before them and they move by their light. Hence it is written, 'The sun and the moon stand still in their habitation; at the light of Thine arrows they go, at the shining of thy glittering spear' (Hab. 3.11), and it is written, 'The sun and the moon are become black, and the stars withdraw their shining' (Joel 2.10).
>
> (Lev. R. 31.9)

Rav's greater interest was, however, in the magical mysteries of creation. The world was created by a word; the word consisted of letters, and he who knew the proper combination of letters might likewise participate in the wonder of creation. That that combination was known cannot be doubted. God had numerous names and nick-

---

[1] b. 'Eruv. 81a.

[2] The 'sweat' issuing forth is cited as an example of Jewish anthropomorphism by the author of the Škand Gumanik Vičar, see XIV, 34-5, and my translation, "A Zoroastrian Critique of Judaism" *JAOS* 83, 1963, and my "Škand Miscellanies", *IAOS*. Note above, b. Ḥag. 14a as well. These sayings are all a part of the Merkavah speculations. See also Hans Lewy, *Chaldaean Oracles and Theurgy* (Cairo, 1956), 14-5, on the 'bearers of the throne' in Chaldaean hymns and oaths.

[3] See b. Shab. 80b. on a Merkavah preacher from Galilee in Babylonia.

names, and the proper one, in the proper hands, contained great potency. Rav must have known a number of such mysterious names:

> R. Judah in the name of Rav said, The forty-two-lettered name is entrusted only to him who is pious, meek, middle-aged, free of bad temper, sober, not insistent on his rights. And who knows it is heedful thereof, and observes it in purity, is beloved above and below, feared by man, and inherits both worlds.
>
> (b. Qid. 71a)[1]

One who knew the secret of creation was Beẓalel:

> R. Judah in the name of Rav said, Beẓalel knew how to combine the letters by which heavens and earth were created. It is written here, 'And he hath filled him with the spirit of God, in wisdom, understanding, and knowledge' (Ex. 35.31) and it is written elsewhere (Prov. 3.19-20) 'The Lord by wisdom founded the earth, by understanding he established the heavens, by his knowledge the depths were broken up.'
>
> (b. Pes. 55a)

Rav himself offered many comments and speculations on the biblical passages dealing with creation and with Adam. Some of these comments were exegetical.[2] Others exhibit considerable development, along mythological and cosmogonic lines, of the biblical text,[3] such as the following:

> R. Judah in the name of Rav said: When the Holy One . . . wished to create man, he created a company of ministering angels and said to them, Is it your desire that we make man in our image? They

---

[1] See Bacher, *Agada*, 17-18, esp. n. 114 who relates the "ten things through which the world was created" with the forty-two lettered name of God, and cites both Talmudic and Geʾonic traditions on it. Bacher says, "Wenn man aber die Buchstaben der zehn hebräischen Worte summirt, welche die eben erwähnten schöpferischen Potenzen bezeichnen, und noch die vier Buchstaben des Tetragrammaton hinzunimmt, so erhält man gerade die Zahl von zweiundvierzig Buchstaben. Der 42buchstabige Name Gottes ist also nichts Anderes als der Ausdruck für das Wesen Gottes und seine Attribute. . ." These are חכמה, תבונה דעת, כח, גבורה, גערה, צדק, משפט, חסד and רחמים containing 38 letters in all, plus the four of the Ineffable Name.

[2] E.g. y. Ḥag. 2.1, on Ps. 31; y. Ber. 1.1. See also b. ʿEruv. 18a, 'The Lord God builded the side' (Gen. 2.22), Rav and Samuel, one held it was a full face, the other, a tail. Compare b. Ber. 61a. On the name of heaven (shamayim), Gen. 1.8, see Gen. R. 4.7, 'Rav said, Shamayim is a compound of ʾesh (fire) and *mayim* (water). R. Abba b. Kahanʾ in the name of Rav said, The Holy One, blessed be He, took fire and water and beat them up together, and from them the heaven was made.' Compare Gen. R. 4.2.

[3] Other comments on Genesis will be treated below, pp. 187ff.

replied, Lord of the Universe, what will be his deeds? Such-and-such will be his deeds. Thereupon they exclaimed, Lord of the Universe, 'What is man that thou art mindful of him and the son of man that thou thinkest of him' (Ps. 8.5). Thereupon he stretched out his little finger among them and consumed them with fire. [The same happened a second time, and finally the third company said] Lord of the Universe, what did it avail the former when they spoke to thee? The world is thine and whatsoever thou wishest to do therein, do it. When he came to the men of the age of the flood and of the division (of tongues) whose deeds were corrupt, they said to him, Lord of the Universe, did not the first company speak right? He retorted (Is. 46.4), 'Even to old age I am the same, and even to hoary hairs will I forebear.'

R. Judah in the name of Rav said: The first man reached from one end of the world to the other, as it is written (Deut. 4.32), 'Since the day that God created man upon the earth even from one end of heaven unto the other.' But when he sinned, The Holy One . . . laid his hand upon him and diminished him, As it is written (Ps. 139.5), 'Thou hast hemmed me in behind and before . . .'

R. Judah in the name of Rav said, The first man was a *Min*, for that is what is written, (Gen. 3.9) 'And the Lord God called unto Adam and said unto him, where art thou?'

(b. Sanh. 38b)[1]

Adam's trunk came from Babylonia, his head from Palestine, his limbs from elsewhere.[2] Rav likewise speculated on the order and means of creation:

R. Zutra b. Tobiah in the name of Rav said, By ten things was the world created: By wisdom, understanding, reason, strength, rebuke, might, righteousness, judgment, lovingkindness, and compassion.

(b. Hag. 12a)[3]

Rav articulated the ancient creation legends, or, seizing upon their Scriptural elements, did not hesitate to reconstruct them, along the lines of ancient Babylonian myths, which he must have learned in Babylonia, as in the following remarkable instance:

R. Judah in the name of Rav said: All that the Holy One . . . created in his world he created male and female. Leviathan the slant serpent and Leviathan the tortuous serpent he created male and female, and had they mated with one another they would have destroyed the whole world. What did he do? He castrated the male and killed the female, preserving it in salt for the righteous in the world to come, for it is written, 'And he will slay the dragon that is in the sea' (Is. 27.1). And

---

[1] On the cosmic man, compare b. Hag. 12a.
[2] b. Sanh. 37b.
[3] Proof texts are cited for each quality. See above, p. 155 n. 1.

also 'Behemoth' on a thousand hills were created male and female, and had they mated with one another they would have destroyed the world. What did the Holy One ... do? He castrated the male and cooled the female and preserved it for the righteous for the world to come, for it is written, 'Lo now his strength is in his loins' (Job 40.16) —this refers to the male; 'And his force is in the stays of his body' This refers to the female ...

R. Judah in the name of Rav further said, At the time when the Holy One blessed be He desired to create the world, he said to the Angel of the Sea, Open thy mouth and swallow all the waters of the world. He said to him, Lord of the Universe, It is enough that I remain with my own. Thereupon he struck him with his foot and killed him, for it is written, 'He stirreth up the sea with his power and by his understanding he smiteth through Rahab' (Job 26.12).

(b. B.B. 74b)

These sayings quite obviously signify the recovery of ancient, pre-Mosaic Israelite cosmogonic mythology, which was based mainly upon Babylonian themes. Ginzberg points out that the story of a Leviathan pair may be compared to the Babylonian myth concerning Tiamat and Kingu, according to which the latter was vanquished and the former slain by Marduk. Similar parallels are self-evident. I cannot say whether Rav produced these legends by means of exegetical traditions relating to Isaiah 27, Job 26, and other Scriptures, which would have been preserved in the Babylonian Jewish community from very ancient times, or whether Rav himself learned Babylonian legends, available in his times among descendants of the ancient Babylonians, and Judaized them. I think it far more likely that such traditions were preserved among the Jews themselves, since Rav is not the first, or only tradent to refer to these themes. What is most significant here is that at just this time he found it important to produce a Jewish cosmogonic legend, resurrecting ancient mythology. There can only be one explanation, namely that the Jews found it necessary because of the prevalence and attractiveness of gnostic, Iranian, and other pagan cosmogonies, to reclaim or to develop their very own mythological traditions. These traditions emphasized that God, and not the angels, created man; that the Most High God did so, and not a lesser figure; that he did so despite opposition; and that he intended only good. In the face of competing traditions, which told mythologies about the grand error of the demiurge when he made the world, which denigrated this world and material creation, which saw the world as the product of forces in competition, or hostile to the 'Most High God,' Rav's mythologies represent a polemic of great force. Moreover, in gnosticism, including its very much present Mandean form, Adam played a great role. Rav's saying that he was a heretic, whom God treated harshly (see above, p. 156) doubtless based simply on the biblical text itself, represented, similarly, a judgment on the central place Adam held in competing doctrines.[1]

(Adam was discussed, again by Rav, in more historical terms as well. A vegetarian,[2] he was warned by God, "I am God, do not curse me, I am God, do not exchange me for another, I am God, let my fear be upon you . . ."[3])

As to man's moral obligations to God, these were two: to keep the commandments, and to study the Torah. The purpose of keeping the commandments was to purify man, or Israel:

> Rav said, The commandments were given only as a means to purify Israel.
>
> (Midrash Samuel, ed. Buber 4.1)[4]

The Torah and commandments keep man alive:

> R. Judah in the name of Samuel said: Why is it written, 'And thou makest man as the fish of the sea and as the creeping things that have no ruler over them' (Hab. 1.14). Why is man here compared to the fishes of the sea? To tell you, just as the fishes of the sea, as soon as they come on to dry land die, so also man, as soon as he abandons (study of) the Torah and commandments [dies].
>
> (b. A.Z. 3b)[5]

Ideally, Rav said, they should be done 'for their own sake,' but in any case, they should be done, for from doing them not for their own sake, man may come eventually to do them from the right, disinterested motive.[6] This was one of his favored, and most often cited, teachings. Likewise, one should keep the law privately as

---

[1] See Alexander Altmann, "The Gnostic Background of the Rabbinic Adam Legends", *JQR* n.s. 35, 371-91.

[2] b. Sanh. 59b.

[3] b. Sanh. 56b.

[4] Here this appears as a Midrash on Prov. 17.3, while in Gen. R. 44.1, it is based on II Sam. 22.31, 'The way of God is perfect, the word of the Lord is tried.'

[5] This is based on R. Akiba's similar saying. Most of Samuel's exegeses are in the manner of R. Ishmael.

[6] The most complete form is b. Sotah 47a, where Rav's saying appears as a midrash on Num. 32.1, and 14.29. See also b. 'Arakhin 16b, Horayot 10b, Sanh. 105b, Sotah 22b, Nazir 23b, Pes. 50b.

publicly, even where a prohibition of an action is based merely on appearances' sake.[1]

We shall postpone the interpretation of these sayings until we have considered the liturgical compositions of Rav and Samuel, which contain important elaborations of theological ideas, and their legal dicta on synagogue worship.

II. Contributions to Liturgy

Rav and Samuel contributed to the liturgy for daily worship and for the Days of Awe. We shall first consider the texts which preserve their liturgical discussions, and determine whether they themselves wrote these prayers or not, and finally consider their relevance to contemporary events.

Each was credited with composing an abbreviated prayer in place of the full Eighteen Benedictions, to which reference is made by R. Joshua b. Hananiah in the Mishnah, as follows:

> What is meant by 'an abbreviated Eighteen?' Rav said, An abbreviated form of each blessing. Samuel said, 'Give us discernment, O Lord, to know thy ways , and circumcise our heart to fear thee, and forgive us so that we may be redeemed, and keep us far from sufferings, and fatten us in the pastures of thy land, and let them who err from thy commandments be punished, and lift up thy hand against the wicked, and let the righteous rejoice in the building of thy city, and the establishment of thy temple, and in the exalting of the horn of David thy servant, and in the preparation of a light for the son of Jesse thy messiah. Before we call may you answer. Praised are you, O Lord, who hearkens to prayer.'

> (b. Ber. 29a)

Samuel's version of the abbreviated prayer was criticized. Abaye, for instance, seventy-five years later 'cursed anyone who said it.' Samuel, for his part, said that his version might replace the full text of the Eighteen Benedictions throughout the year, except in the evening prayers after the Sabbath and festivals, when special prayers are inserted in a paragraph of the full Eighteen. What is striking here is Samuel's contribution. He did not, obviously, set the text of the original prayer, but here rather composed a summary of it, which laid greatest emphasis on the messianic images of the old liturgy, including the return to Zion, rebuilding the temple, and the coming of the Messiah. Thus Samuel reinterpreted the prayer, in the

---

[1] b. A.Z. 12a, Bezah 9a, y. ʿEruv. 8.9, Kilaʾim 9.1. In the Kilaʾim version, the saying is challenged. Compare S. Lieberman, *HaYerushalmi Kifshuto* 349.

act of composing a précis, placing greatest stress on the messianic and eschatological aspects of the Eighteen Benedictions, to the neglect of themes which are more central in the original. In a parallel text Samuel required 'the beginning of each blessing' of the Eighteen, which suggests that his revised version did not reach Palestine immediately, and an alternate text, in the Palestinian Talmud, confirms this.[1]

Additionally, Rav composed a prayer to be recited at the end of the Eighteen Benedictions:

> May it be thy will O Lord our God to grant us long life, a life of peace, a life of good, a life of blessing, a life of sustenance, a life of bodily vigor, a life in which there is fear of sin, a life free from shame and confusion, a life of riches and honor, a life in which we may be filled with love of Torah and fear of heaven, a life in which thou shalt fulfil all the desires of our heart for good.
>
> (b. Ber. 16b)

(This prayer is now said on the Sabbath on which the New Moon is proclaimed in the synagogue.) An additional lacuna in the Daily Prayerbook concerned what the congregation says when the precentor repeats the paragraph, 'We give thanks':

> Rav declared, 'We give thanks unto thee O Lord our God because we are able to give thee thanks.' Samuel declared, 'God of all Flesh, seeing that we give thee thanks.' R. Simai declared, 'Our creator and creator of all things in the beginning seeing that we give thee thanks'. The men of Nehardea say in the name of R. Simai, 'Blessings and thanksgiving to thy great name because thou hast kept us alive and preserved us, seeing that we give thee thanks' .... R. Papa said, Consequently, let us recite them all.
>
> (b. Sotah 40a)[2]

It is not clear that these sayings refer to original prayers composed by the several Amoraim, since the meaning of the above passage may be that the several men were merely referring to known, alternate prayers. However we have, in fact, compositions clearly prepared by Rav for this purpose, and hence may conclude that the early

---

[1] y. Taʿanit 2.2, compare y. Ber. 4.3. On the abbreviated Eighteen Benedictions, see Y. Heinemann, *Prayer in the Period of the Tannaim and Amoraim* (Jerusalem 1964), 37, 46, and 151.

[2] Compare y. Ber. 1.5, Rav said, 'We thank you that we are obligated to praise your name. My lips shall rejoice for I sing to thee, and my soul which thou hast redeemed. Blessed art thou, God of praises.'

Amora' im were composing new prayers for the need which they discerned.[1]

Rav and Samuel likewise discussed the blessing to be said after the Havdalah prayer, Rav holding that it is to be concluded 'who sanctifies Israel,' and Samuel, 'who makes a distinction between holy and profane.'[2] The two men composed, or instituted, a prayer to be inserted in the fourth benediction of the '*Amida* for festivals:

> R. Joseph said, I only know that Rav and Samuel instituted for us a precious pearl in Babylonia: 'And thou didst make known unto us O Lord our God thy righteous judgments and didst teach us to do the statutes of thy will, and thou hast caused us to inherit times of gladness and festivals of rejoicing, and has given us as an inheritance the sanctity of the Sabbath and the glory of the season and the rejoicing of the festival. Thou hast distinguished between the sanctity of the Sabbath and the sanctity of the Festival, and has sanctified the seventh day from the seven days of work. Thou hast set appart and sanctified thy people Israel in thy holiness and hast given us . . .'
>
> (b. Ber. 33b)

This form of the Havdalah prayer is used with slight variants on a festival that follows the Sabbath.[3]

Rav's and Samuel's contributions to the liturgy for the Days of Awe are substantial. The texts include the following:

> R. Hinena the Elder in the name of Rav said, Throughout the year one says in the Tefillah 'the holy God' and 'King who loves righteousness and judgment' except during the ten days between the New Year and the Day of Atonement when he says, 'The Holy King' and 'the King of Judgment'.
>
> (b. Ber. 12a)

(Rav likewise held that if one cannot eat his secular food in a state

---

[1] As above, y. Ber. 1.5, y. Ber. 1.6, R. Ba, R. Judah, in the name of Rav said, We thank you that thou hast brought us forth from Egypt and redeemed us from the house of slaves to praise your name'. But compare y. Ber. 9.3, Samuel *refers* to a prayer, but did not write it.

[2] b. Pes. 104b.

[3] On this prayer, see A. Z. Idelsohn, *Jewish Liturgy* (N.Y. 1932) 29. See especially I. Elbogen, "Die Tefilla für die Festtage", *MGWJ* 55, 1911, 426-46, 586-599; and his, *Der Jüdische Gottesdienst* (Hildesheim, 1962), 260-71; Y. Zunz-H. Albeck, *op. cit.*, 181-2. On the abbreviated forms of the Eighteen Benedictions, see especially L. Ginzberg, *Perushim* III, 315, 321. He emphasizes that Rav required a blessing to be said at the end of each paragraph. He points out (III, 321) the many differences between the readings of the Bab. and Yer. Talmuds concerning Samuel's prayer. He holds that Samuel did not write this prayer, but that it was already in existence, which accounts for the many readings in current versions. But compare the penetrating view of Y. Heinemann cited above, p. 140 n. 1.

of ritual purity throughout the year, he ought still to do so during those ten days.[1]) He allegedly prepared the following prayer, now included in the Additional Service on Rosh Hashanah:

> This day, on which was the beginning of the works [of creation], is a memorial for the first day, for it is a statute for Israel, a decree of the God of Jacob. Then also sentence is pronounced upon countries, which of them is destined to the sword, and which to peace, which to famine and which to plenty; and each separate creature is visited thereon and recorded for life or for death.
>
> (Lev. R. 29.1)[2]

Both men composed confessions for the Day of Atonement:

> What is [the confession]? Rav said, Thou knowest the secrets of eternity. Samuel said, From the depths of the heart . . . Levi said, And in thy Torah it is said . . . R. Yoḥanan said, Lord of the Universe . . . R. Hamnuna said, 'My God, Before I was formed I was of no worth, and now that I have been formed, it is as if I had not been formed. I am dust in my life, how much more in my death. Behold I am before Thee like a vessel full of shame and reproach. May it be thy will that I sin no more, and what I have sinned wipe away in thy mercy, but not through suffering.' That was the confession used by Rav all the year round, and by R. Hamnuna the younger on the Day of Atonement. Mar Zutra said, All that [is necessary only] when he did not say: 'Truly we have sinned', but if he said, 'Truly we have sinned', no more is necessary, for Bar Hamdudi said, Once I stood before Samuel, who was sitting, and when the public reader came up and said, 'Truly we have sinned', he rose. Hence he inferred that this was the main confession.
>
> (b. Yoma' 87b)

The prayer of Rav is as follows:

> 'You know the secrets of eternity, and the most hidden mysteries of all living. You search the innermost recesses, and test the feelings and the heart. Nothing is concealed from you, or hidden from your eyes. May it be your will, O Lord our God and God of our fathers, to forgive us for all our sins, to pardon us for all our iniquities, and to grant us remission for all our transgressions.'
>
> (Current printed texts)

Samuel's confession, discovered in a Geniza fragment by Israel Abrahams, and translated by him, is as follows:

---

[1] Lieberman, *Yerushalmi*, 34-5.

[2] See also Pesikta de Rav Kahana, ed. B. Mandelbaum, II, 333, and y. R. H. 1.3. See also Yavetz, *Toldot.* VII, app. IC, p. 5.

Thou knowest the depths of the heart and art cognisant of the mysteries of the reins. The imaginations of all creatures are revealed before thee and our devices are not hidden from thee. Forgiver of iniquity and transgression wast thou called, thou art he O Lord our God who knowest that our end is the worm. Our iniquities we confess before thee, O Lord our God, incline thine ear to our entreaty.[1]

Abrahams comments that Samuel's confession, independent of Rav's, is too similar to the latter for both to have been incorporated [in the spirit of Rav Papa, above, 'let us say them all'] in the early days of liturgical development. Samuel's 'abbreviated Eighteen Benedictions' survived Rav's, but Rav's Confession drove out Samuel's.

Conventional interpretations of the 'teki'ata deve Rav,' (cited in y. R.H. 1.5, A.Z. 1.2, and as above[2]) hold that that prayer is identical with the following, in the current New Year Additional Service:

It is our duty to praise the Lord of all, to ascribe greatness to him who formed the world in the beginning, since he hath not made us like the nations of other lands, nor placed our lot like that of other families of the earth, since he hath not assigned unto us a portion as unto them, nor a lot as unto all their multitude. For we bend the knee and offer worship and thanks before the King of the King of Kings, the Holy One, blessed be he, who stretched forth the heavens and laid the foundations of the earth, the seat of whose glory is in the heavens above, and the place of whose might is in the loftiest heights. He is our God. There is none else. In truth he is our king. There is none besides him, as it is written in his Torah (Deut. 4.39), 'And thou shalt know this day, and lay it to thine heart, that the Lord he is God in heaven above and upon the earth beneath. There is none else.' We therefore hope in thee, O Lord our God that we may speedily behold the glory of thy might, when thou wilt remove the abominations from the earth, and the idols will be utterly cut off, when the world will be perfected under the kingdom of the Almighty, and all the children of flesh will call upon thy name, when thou wilt turn unto thyself all the wicked of the earth. Let all the inhabitants of the world perceive and know that unto thee every knee must bow, every tongue must swear. Before thee O Lord our God let them bow and fall, and unto thy glorious Name let them give honor. Let them all accept the yoke of thy kingdom, and do thou reign over them speedily and

---

[1] Israel Abrahams, "The Lost 'Confession' of Samuel", *HUCA* I, 1924, 377-85. Text is on 380-3.

[2] See also Tanḥuma, Ha'azinu 4, Pesikta Rabbati 46, b. R. H. 27a. For discussion of such interpretations see especially Zunz-Albeck, *op.cit.*, 181-2, and below.

forever and ever. For thine is the kingdom, and to all eternity thou wilt reign in glory, as it is written in thy Torah, 'the Lord shall reign for ever and ever.' (Ex. 15.18)

This entire prayer has been ascribed to Rav by Zunz and his followers. However, the passages which refer to the 'teki'ata of the school of Rav' cite only the words (as above):

'This is the day of the beginning of your works, a memorial to the first day . . . . .'

(y. A.Z. 1.2)

Elbogen states[1] that the "introduction to the *Zikhronot* [as cited above] is called in the sources...teki'ata deve Rav." Elsewhere, he cites the passages given above, and says, "There they [the New Year Additional Prayers] are attributed to the 'teki'ata deve Rav,' and according to the style of all three introductions [not only that cited above] they are all similar [sic!], and the work of Rav in arranging prayers is well known. Therefore it is possible that all the introductions to the Sovereignty, Remembrance, and Shofar [verses] are Rav's."[2] In fact, the passage "This is the day" etc. occurs in the *Zikhronot* passage, which is as follows:

Thou rememberest what was wrought from eternity, and art mindful of all that hath been formed from of old. Before thee all secrets are revealed, and the multitude of hidden things since the creation. For there is no forgetfulness before the throne of thy glory, nor is there ought hidden from thine eyes. Thou rememberest every deed that hath been done: not a creature is concealed from thee. All things are manifest and known unto thee, O Lord our God, who lookest and seest to the end of all the ages. For thou wilt bring on the appointed time of remembrance, for the judgment of every spirit and soul, and the memory of many actions, and the multitude of hidden things without number. From the beginning thou didst make this thy purpose known, and from aforetime thou didst disclose it. *This day, on which was the beginning of thy work, is a remembrance of the first day, for it is a statute for Israel, a decree of the God of Jacob. Thereon also sentence is pronounced upon countries, which of them is destined to the sword, and which to peace, which to famine, and which to plenty, and each separate creature is judged thereon, and recorded for life or for death.* Who is not judged on this day? For the remembrance of every creature cometh before thee, each man's deeds and destiny, his works and ways, his thoughts and schemes, his imaginings and achievements. Happy is the man who

---

[1] p. 264.
[2] *Toldot HaTefilah veHa'Avodah beYisra'el*, I, Jerusalem-Berlin 1924, 101.

forgetteth thee not, and the son of man who strengtheneth himself in thee, for they that seek thee shall never stumble, neither shall any be put to shame who trust in thee. Yea the remembrance of all works cometh before thee, and thou enquirest into all the doings of them all.

(Cited according to the usual printed texts)

It is true that the sentence taught by Rav's Tanna is here included. However, it is by no means obvious that to Rav, or his academy, ought to be attributed this entire prayer, and with it the *whole* of the New Year Additional liturgy, as many have assumed. Furthermore, the Tosefta refers to the structure of the New Year Additional Service, as follows:

They said before him the Sovereignty, Remembrance, and Shofar [passages]. Sovereignty, in order that they would accept his rule over them. Remembrance, So that there should come before him your memory for good. Shofar, so that your prayer should go up with the sound of the Shofar before him.

(Tosefta R.H. 1.12)

This passage, which certainly long antedates the founding of a 'school of Rav' in Babylonia, adumbrates the structure of the Additional Service as we now have it, and the language echoes that in the current liturgy. There is no sign whatever that the ideas or language of these passages ought to be attributed to Rav. In fact, the entire New Year liturgy under study is far, far older than this period. My view is that Rav did not compose the *Alenu* ("It is our duty...") prayer, since there is absolutely no evidence that indicates he did.[1] The passages cited to 'prove' the contrary in fact prove

---

[1] See S. Lieberman, *Tosefta Kifshuta* (N.Y. 1962) V, 104-5, and Y. Heinemann, *op.cit.* 61-2, 81. In fact, Heinemann argues, quite plausibly, that it is substantially earlier, see pp. 173-5.

Heinemann points out that the *'Alenu* part of the Sovereignty Prayer almost certainly did *not* originate in the schoolhouse. Heinemann cites the passages considered here, and says, "One rightly assumes that the name 'Teki'ata' relates to the Sovereignty, Memory, and Shofar verses in general, and that all were written by Rav or his students." But Heinemann shows convincingly that the opening paragraph is quite different from the others, and was written before them, as we now have the texts, but was taken over without change for synagogue liturgical use. See also K. Kohler, "Alenu", *JE* I, 336-8, "The Alenu prayer had already been in use when there were attached to it the three portions of the liturgy of the New Year ... Zunz and his followers, who ascribe the prayer to Rab simply because in his school the Jewish liturgy received its permanent form—disregarded the fact that it stands in no organic connection with the rest of the New Year's prayer."

See also Leon J. Liebreich, 'Aspects of the New Year Liturgy" *HUCA* 34, 1963, 159-163, and 168 n. 117 Liebreich likewise holds that Rav did not write

nothing of the sort. I share the view of Kohler, reaffirmed with great force by Y. Heinemann, as well as of S. Lieberman and L. J. Liebreich, that the prayer in question was very old indeed, and was probably read in the Temple before its destruction. Heinemann's arguments in favor of this view are, to my mind, decisive. The sources which describe the prayer of Rav's Tanna specify only the sentences given above (p. 162), and I see no reason to attribute to him or to the Tanna of his school more than that. In any event the exaggerated attribution to him, or his students, of the whole Additional Service on the New Year and other liturgies in addition is groundless.[1]

'*Alenu* but that the prayer is substantially older, and maintains the same position, as do I, for the following paragraph. On the words added by Rav for the Ten Days between New Year and the Day of Atonement, see Liebreich's "The Insertions in the Third Benediction of the Holy Day 'Amidoth'," *HUCA* 35, 1964, 79-101, particularly 94-101, where a very full survey of the *Malkhuyot* problem will be found.

   I am glad, finally, to report the opinion, in a letter (July 8, 1965) of Professor Saul Lieberman. Professor Lieberman holds that the nine blessings of the New Year liturgy are based on an ancient tradition, concerning which the schools of Hillel and Shamai debated. In their time, these blessings were said in the Morning, and not in the Additional, Service. See his *Tosefta Kifshuta* for Berakhot III, 13, p. 41. In the Morning, not Additional, Service, the Sovereignty, Remembrance, and Shofar verses were recited, at that time (first century). In each blessing was a central theme, to which afterward other expressions were added, at different times and places. The expression "Teki'ata de ve Rav" means, "The *Teki'ot* of the Tanna of Rav, of the beraita which was taught in Rav's academy". The y. R.H. passage therefore means that this was the view of the *Tanna* of Rav's academy. Rav was believed to hold that the world was created on the New Year, because it was taught by the Tanna of his academy "This is the day" etc. The discussion thus assumes that that was Rav's opinion. It is reasonable to suppose that the Tanna of Rav's academy normally did not teach in opposition to Rav's view, though this is *not* invariably the case. In any event, Rav did not create the prayer in question, but the Tanna of his academy taught an older version, which was under discussion. For example, R. Joshua b. Hananiah held that in Nisan the world was created, and certainly according to his view, the prayer "This is the day" was not said on the New Year. Note also the text of b. R.H. 27a "R. Samuel b. Isaac said, According to whom do we pray *at this time* 'This is the day'? According to R. Eliezer, who said that the world was created in Tishri." From the language "at this time" it may be understood that the text is not older than that period, but it certainly antedates Rav.

   In all, I think it is beyond question that Rav did not write the prayers ascribed to him by Zunz and his followers, but that these prayers are substantially older. Both the meaning of the texts on the 'teki'ata deve Rav' and other sources abundantly support this contention.

   [1] See also the discussion on when is Ne'ilah, y. Ber. 4.1. See Ginzberg, *Perushim*, III, 67, 104. I am unable to find any support for the frequently-made attribution of "On account of our sins" to Rav, see Zunz-Albeck, *op. cit.*, 181. See also Z. Yavetz, *Toldot* VII, 5, who argues that the Rosh Hashanah prayers discussed here are not old prayers referred to by Rav, but in fact written by Rav

One ought not to ignore the particular relevance to their own day of the prayers composed by Rav and Samuel. It is noteworthy, first of all, that Samuel, who, as we saw, sought to diminish messianic fervor, nonetheless wrote an abbreviation of the Eighteen Benedictions which stressed the messianic hope. The advent of the new, and astonishingly repressive regime, must have deeply dismayed Babylonian Jewry, and led some to doubt the messianic promise, just as others exaggerated its imminence. Here Samuel reaffirmed the often-postponed hope, which must have brought strength to the discouraged people. Rav's simple prayer for a long and prosperous life similarly expressed the most basic aspirations of the humble folk. At the same time, his majestic prayer for the Additional Service on Rosh Hashanah reaffirmed that the wonders of creation themselves testify to the sovereignty and concern of Israel's God, who passes sentence on all nations, and decides which, in those troubled times, were destined to the sword and which to peace. His alteration of the liturgy for the Days of Awe similarly emphasized the sovereignty of the God of Jacob. His 'Confession' likewise recalled the belief that God knows every detail of a person's actions. So for both the nations and the individual, God's rule was reaffirmed, in a time when some, witnessing the rise of a new pagan monarchy, and, in the vicissitudes of war, seeing the fortunes of men change without respect to their merits, might have come to doubt it. In their liturgical compositions, the rabbis showed themselves aware of the deepest perplexities of both their times and their people, who looked to them for guidance. Their prayers brought reassurance that the Messiah would come, that God continued to reign sovereign, that He knew what was happening, and that the great empires would in time know it as well, as surely as the heavens and earth endured. His time would come, and his people would be vindicated: it was for this that Rav and Samuel taught the people to wait and pray.

I can think of no more remarkable parallel to the teaching of

---

himself. He holds that Rav wrote the *entire* Additional Service of Rosh Hashanah! This is also the view of W. Bacher, "Abba Arika", *JE* I 29-30. Nor can it be concluded that it was Rav who resolved earlier disputes on the nature of Rosh Hashanah by calling it the 'day of Judgment', following the view of R. Judah b. Ilai, and therefore wrote the prayer cited in the text. Zuri, *Rav*, 258-304, likewise takes an extreme view of Rav's liturgical contributions, holding that the *whole* of the New Year Additional Service is to be attributed to him. His "proofs" of Rav's authorship of various prayers are completely unconvincing, consisting mainly of showing alleged parallels in language or sentiment, which could be multiplied manyfold for other rabbis. See esp. 296-304.

Rabban Yoḥanan ben Zakkai at the time of the Temple's destruction. While he had said that one should remain skeptical of messianic claims, he nonetheless reaffirmed, as his eyes closed for the last time, that the Messiah would surely come.[1] As in many other ways, Rav and Samuel here reveal how deeply rooted they were in such ideas, just as the political theory of Rabban Yoḥanan shaped theirs, as we saw above.[2] His interpretation of the theological implication of, and proper religious response to, great events offered a powerful paradigm for another age. In the end, skepticism and quietism were not sufficient. They were at best shrewd and practical ways of coping with current events. Beyond, however, lay the real issue, that of faith, to be resolved by the power of prayer. If the Temple lay in ruins, if, as now, the benevolent Arsacids fell before the Persians, whose Magi seemed like destroying angels, then what was to become of Israel and its frail, outwardly faulty hope? In the prayers of Rav and Samuel, as in the homily of R. Shila, we find the answer, here phrased in unmistakable terms through the language, and puissance, of public devotion. Political quietism did not, therefore, exhaust their counsel at all. They believed in prayer, and in God who hears and answers it, and so it was through prayer that they would effectually act.[3] Political passivity, even renunciation, was therefore merely a mask for extraordinary theurgic activity.

III. PRAYER AND FASTING

Prayer was regarded as a direct communication between man and God. It not only promised specific blessings, if hearkened, but also helped man to acquire merit before God. Thus a Palestinian contemporary, R. Yoḥanan taught:

> When they told R. Yoḥanan that there were old men in Babylonia, he was astonished, and said, But it is written, 'That your days may be multiplied, and the days of your children, upon the land.' (Deut. 11.21). Upon the land, but not outside the land [of Israel]. When they told him that they came early to the synagogue and left late, he said, That is what helps them.
>
> (b. Ber. 8a)

One must pray not only the prescribed liturgy, but also, and

---

[1] See my *Life*, 172-3.

[2] Above, p. 66-67.

[3] Compare the view of R. Yoḥanan, that prayer keeps the Babylonian Jews alive to old age.

especially, for the needs of one's self, for a good king, a good year, a good dream,[1] and for the needs of one's fellow.[2] A particular time in the service, at the end of the Eighteen Benedictions, was set aside for such private prayer:

> R. Ḥiyya b. Ashi in the name of Rav said, Although it was laid down that a man asks for his requirements in 'that hearkens unto prayer', if he wants to say something after his prayer, even something like the Order of Confession on the Day of Atonement, he may do so.
>
> (b. Ber. 31a)

Of greatest importance was the requirement to pray first thing in the morning:

> Rav said, If one gives greeting to his fellow before he has said his prayers, it is as if he made him a high place, as it says, 'Cease ye from man in whose nostril is a breath, for how little is he to be accounted' (Is. 2.22). Read not 'how little' (bammeh) but 'high place' (*Bammah*). Samuel interpreted, How come (*bammeh*) you esteem this man and not God?
>
> (b. Ber. 14a)

One must greet God, through prayer, before his fellow man.

One means of peculiarly private devotion to God was through fasting. In former times, fasting on the part of the community was a commonplace response to drought or other catastrophe, and carefully regulated by the rabbis. Rav held, however, that "There is no fast in this time"[3] by which he meant, public fasts, for there were many kinds of private fasts which continued to be observed. In such a private fast, the person was required to make mention in his prayers of the specific incident with which he was concerned, according to Rav[4] who regarded private fasting as an excellent way to counteract a bad dream.[5] Nonetheless, he reported with approval R. Yosi's warning that a person should not afflict himself by fasting, lest he come to need the help of his fellow men, and it may be that they will not have mercy on him.[6]

---

[1] b. Ber. 55a, based on verses to prove that such prayers were valid, for the king, Prov. 21.1, year, Song 11.12, and dream, Is. 38.16.

[2] b. Ber. 12b.

[3] y. Taʿanit 2.1.

[4] y. Taʿanit 2.2, Ber. 4.3, and see Ginzberg, *Perushim* III, 297.

[5] b. Shab. 100a, Gen. R. 44.12.

[6] b. Taʿanit 22b.

IV. BLESSINGS

Rav and Samuel both contributed to the definition of various blessings. These blessings took two forms, first, the so-called 'blessings of enjoyment,' to be said, according to Samuel, in gratitude for worldly gifts:

> R. Judah in the name of Samuel said: To enjoy anything of this world without a benediction is like making personal [worldly, sacrilegious] use of things consecrated to heaven, since it says (Ps. 24.1), 'The earth is the Lord's and the fulness thereof.'
>
> (b. Ber. 35a)

The second type of blessing, which we shall consider below, was said before the performance of a *mizvah*. In both cases, Rav and Samuel made substantial contributions mainly not to the formulation but to the elaboration of the legal requirements of prayer. The prayer of blessing was intended to express in words the meaning of an action, or the grateful response of the recipient of a blessing. The form of a blessing could be quite simple:

> Benjamin the shepherd made a sandwich and said, Blessed be the master of this bread, and Rav said that he had performed his obligation.
>
> (b. Ber. 40b)[1]

On the whole, however, Rav laid down that the form of a blessing should be constant, and should include reference to the sovereignty of heaven.[2]

A blessing represented a confession of thanksgiving, and biblical precepts or precedents were cited, as always in Talmudic Judaism, to demonstrate that such blessings were imperative. Thus Rav cited Ps. 107: 4-8 to prove that one who successfully traversed the desert must offer thanksgiving; Ps. 107: 10-15, for one who was set free from prison; Ps. 107: 12-21, for one who recovered from an illness; and Ps. 107: 23-32, for one who crossed the sea and reached a safe harbor.[3] The chief interest of the early Amoraim was, however, not so much to *justify* the saying of blessings, but rather to *define* precisely when and what blessings needed to be recited. The question was

---

[1] Compare y. Ber. 6.2, a certain Persian came before Rav, and asked, When I eat my crust, and I am not a sage, I bless it and say, Blessed is he that created this crust'—do I thereby fullfill my obligation? He said to him, Yes.' See also Heinemann, *op.cit.*, 100-1.

[2] See y. Ber. 9.1 See Heinemann, *op. cit.*, 26, 38, 54, 61, etc.

[3] b. Ber. 54b.

raised, for instance, how much rain must fall for one to recite a blessing:

> R. Yosi in R. Judah's name, and R. Jonah and R. Judah in Samuel's name: At the beginning, as much as will fructify, at the end (of prolonged drought), even just a little.
>
> (Gen. R. 13.15)

The actual blessing required was by no means firmly established by this time, but rather elicited considerable discussion. The blessing over rain should, according to Rav, be "We give thanks to thee O Lord our God for every single drop which thou hast caused to fall upon us."[1] On the other hand, a contemporary, Ezekiel, the father of R. Judah (student of Rav and Samuel) said, "One should say, 'Thy name be blessed, exalted, and magnified for every single drop which thou bringest down to us and keepest apart one from the other.'" Thus the form of the kaddish was regarded as paradigmatic by Ezekiel, but not by Rav, who preferred a more direct, simple form. In other instances, a blessing was inherited from Tannaitic times, but a concluding sentence, felt to be necessary, was not unequivocally included in earlier tradition:

> On leaving a privy, one says, Blessed be he who has formed man in wisdom . . . . How does the blessing conclude? Rav said, Blessed art thou that healest the sick. Samuel said, Abba has turned the whole world into invalids! No, what he says is, 'That healest all flesh.'
>
> (b. Ber. 60b)

Another area of blessings which required definition concerned precisely what blessing, of a given number of existing ones, was to be recited over specific substances, including spices and perfume,[2] and the like:

> R. Hiyya b. Abba b. Nahmani in name of R. Hisda in name of Rav said, Over all incense-perfumes the blessing is, Who createst fragrant woods. R. Giddal in the name of Rav said, Over jasmine the blessing is, 'who createst fragrant woods.' R. Hananel in the name of Rav said, Over sea-rush, the blessing is, 'Who createst fragrant woods'. R. Zutra b. Tobia in the name of Rav said, Whence do we learn that a blessing should be said over sweet odors? Because it says, 'Let the whole [lit.: every] soul praise the Lord' (Ps. 150.6). What is that which gives enjoyment to the soul and not to the body? Fragrant odors. Mar Zutra b. Tobia in the name of Rav said, The young men of

---

[1] b. Ta'anit 6b.

[2] y. Ber. 6.6.

Israel [MS Var: Who have not tasted sin] are destined to emit sweet fragrance like Lebanon as it says, 'His branches shall spread and his beauty shall be as the olive tree and his fragrance as Lebanon' (Hosea 14.7).

(b. Ber. 43a)

Likewise, over foods, Rav and Samuel reasoned from the known to the unknown:

Over the whiteheart of the palm, R. Judah said, [one should say] 'Who created the fruit of the ground. Samuel said, 'By whose word all things were made.' R. Judah argued, Because it is a foodstuff. Samuel said, since it will eventually be hardened, you cannot say 'fruit of the ground.' Said Samuel of R. Judah: Shinena, Logical reasoning is on your side, for there is the case of the radish, which is eventually hardened, and yet 'fruit of the ground' is said over it. Yet this argument is not conclusive, since people plant radish to eat it while it is soft, but no palm tree is planted with the intention of eating its white heart.
(b. 'Eruv. 28b)[1]

A similar debate concerned *shatita* (flour-beer made of dried barley mixed with honey) in which Samuel held that the proper blessing should be determined by the flour-ingredient, hence it should be 'who createst various kinds of foods' and Rav held that, as a liquid, the blessing should be 'by whose word all things come into being.'[2] Rav and Samuel had, in fact, laid down the general principle that anything containing an ingredient of 'the five species'[3] requires the blessing 'who createst various kinds of foods"[4] However, they held that that blessing is said *only* over such species.[5] These discussions concerned the following: olive oil,[6] boiled vegetables,[7] as well as the marginal foods, foods made of two kinds of substances each of which, when separate, requires its own blessing, and the like. While the necessity to bless fragrant odors may have been instituted by Rav, one finds little evidence that the requirements of blessing most foods required extensive definition. The limited number of foods for which the early Amoraim devised blessings indicates that for the

---

[1] See also b. Ber. 25b.

[2] b. Ber. 38b.

[3] Mentioned in the blessing of the land, honey, pomegranates, olives, wheat, barley, figs, and wine, see Deut. 8.8.

[4] b. Ber. 36b, 37b.

[5] b. Ber. 25b.

[6] *Ibid.*

[7] y. Ber. 6.1.

basic foods, blessings were clearly spelled out earlier, and Rav and Samuel did not need to do so.

Samuel instituted a major principle, that all *miẓvot* require the recitation of an antecedent blessing except for the blowing of the Shofar on Rosh Hashanah and ritual bath, which exceptions were accepted by the school of Rav as well.[1] For his part, Rav declared both the requirement to say a blessing over the Hanukah candles, and the actual words which must be said, "who has sanctified us by his commandments and commanded us concerning the commandment of lighting the Ḥanukah light."[2] Samuel decreed that a blessing must be recited over the *lulav* all seven days of *Sukkot*, but over the *Sukkah* only on the first. It is not likely that he in fact first instituted the requirement to *say* such blessing; rather he was determining a minor detail, namely, *when* they should be said.[3]

Another important blessing was the grace after meals. There is, again, no doubt that it existed in substantially its present form from Tannaitic times. The contribution of the early Amoraim was to fill in lacunae, to define situations not covered by the existing law, and otherwise to complete the Tannaitic formulation. A good example of the work of Rav in this connection is as follows:

> R. Giddal said to R. Zera, If one forgot and did not mention the Sabbath in the Grace, he says, 'Blessed be he who gave Sabbaths for rest to his people, Israel, in love, for a sign and a covenant. Blessed is he who sanctifies the Sabbath.' Said R. Huna to him, Who made this statement? He replied, Rav. He then continued, If one forgot and did not mention the festival, he says, 'Blessed is he who gave holy days to his people Israel for joy and for remembrance. Blessed is he who sanctifies Israel and the Sabbaths.' Who made this statement? Rav .... When once R. Giddal b. Manyumi was in the presence of R. Naḥman, the latter made a mistake in the grace, and went back to the beginning. He said to him, What is the reason that your honor does this? He replied, Because R. Shila said in the name of Rav, If one makes a mistake he goes back to the beginning. But R. Huna has said in the name of Rav, If he goes wrong, he says, 'Blessed be he who gave' [etc.]. He replied, Has it not been stated by R. Menashia b. Taḥalifa in the name of Rav, This is the case only where he has not commenced the paragraph 'Who is good and does good', but if he has, then he goes back to the beginning. R. Idi b. Abin in the name

---

[1] y. Ber. 9.3, b. Pes. 7b, 119b, Suk. 39a, Meg. 21b.

[2] b. Suk. 46a, that a benediction is required; y. Suk. 3.4 the text of the blessing. Note above, his discussion of the daily miracle of the candelabrum, perhaps an echo of the Hanukah miracle-story, a miracle for which Rav decreed a blessing.

[3] b. Suk. 45b.

of R. Ramram in the name of R. Naḥman in the name of Samuel
stated, If one by mistake omitted to mention the New Moon in the
Tefillah [Eighteen Benedictions] he is made to begin again. If in the
grace, he is not made to begin again.

(b. Ber. 49a)

Other such definitions of how to act if one has forgotten a relevant
part of the grace are offered elsewhere.[1] If one forgot to say grace
at all, Samuel held that he must fulfill his obligation until the food
is digested.[2] Rav laid great stress on washing one's hands after the
meal as a preliminary to saying grace:

R. Judah in the name of Rav said, 'Sanctify yourself' (Lev. 11.44)—
this refers to washing hands before the meal. 'And be ye holy'—refers
to washing hands after the meal. 'For holy'—this refers to the oil. 'Am
I the Lord your God'—this refers to grace.

(b. Ber. 53b)[3]

He also held that he who does so first has the privilege of saying
grace.[4] The beginning of a meal was likewise signified by washing
one's hands, according to Rav.[5] The blessing said over wine at the
end of the meal, in the Grace, constituted the conclusion of the meal,
and afterward according to Rav, one must not drink wine any more.[6]
Another law requiring further definition concerned how one might
join a company at a meal so as to participate in the grace following
it, and might one leave a company, in the midst of the grace,[7]
which was at the end of the first paragraph according to Rav.[8]
Both Rav and Samuel taught many of these laws while eating with
their students, and at the death of Rav, as we noted, his disciples
lamented the fact that they did not fully master the rules of grace
after meals as he had taught them.[9]

Similarly, the requirement to recite Qiddush, sanctifying Sabbaths
and festivals, was well established, and the legal issues pertaining to
the prayer were both secondary and tangential, for instance whether

---

[1] b. Ber. 49a, y. Ber. 7.4.

[2] y. Ber. 8.7.

[3] See Lieberman, *Yerushalmi*, 23-4.

[4] b. Ber. 43a, 46b, see also 42a, it must be followed immediately, without
interruption, by the recital of the grace.

[5] y. Shab. 9b.

[6] b. Pes. 103a-b, Ber. 40a, 42b, 53b, Nazir 66b, Ḥul. 86b, etc.

[7] b. Ber. 47a, 48a.

[8] y. Ber. 7.1, compare b. Ber. 49b-50a.

[9] b. Ber. 42b-43a. But it may therefore be the case that the students stated as
abstract dicta descriptions of what they saw the masters do.

one may say the prayer over a substance other than wine, such as bread[1] or beer. Rav held as follows:

> R. Zutra b. Tobia in the name of Rav said, The Qiddush of the Day [Sabbath] must be proclaimed on such wine as is fit to be brought as a drink offering upon the altar.
>
> (b. B.B. 97a)

The quantity of wine that must be consumed was defined by Rav as a mouthful.[2] It was regarded as highly meritorious to say the prayer over wine, even if it meant considerable sacrifice:

> R. Huna once came before Rav girded with a string. He said to him, What is the meaning of this? He replied, I had no wine for Qiddush, and I pledged by girdle so as to get some. He said, May it be the will of heaven that you be smothered in robes of silk. One day when Rabbah his son was to be married, R. Huna, who was short, was lying on a bed and his daughters and daughters-in-law stripped clothes from themselves and threw them on him, until he was smothered in silks. When Rav heard this he was chagrined, and said, When I blessed you why did you not say, The same to you sir!
>
> (b. Meg. 27a)[3]

Rav and Samuel debated whether Qiddush must be said at home if it has been heard in the synagogue. Rav maintained that people who had sanctified in the synagogue need not do so at home, and Samuel maintained that they must. In any event, Rav recognized that children and the household would make it necessary to repeat the Qiddush at home, and Samuel admitted that the travellers who eat drink, and sleep in the synagogue necessitated repeating the prayer there.[4]

They likewise laid down rules about reciting the Havdalah prayer. If it is recited in the course of the evening *Tefillah*, it must also be recited over a cup of wine, according to Samuel.[5] One must recite a blessing over light at the termination of the Sabbath, since it was then created for the first time, again according to Samuel, and Rav held likewise.[6] One does not actually make use of the light which he blesses, but must stand near enough to it to use it if he should want

---

[1] b. Pes. 106b-107a.

[2] b. Pes. 107a.

[3] But compare b. Pes. 107a.

[4] b. Pes. 101, compare y. Ber. 6.6. Note that in the Dura synagogue a hostel was provided for visiting coreligionists.

[5] b. Shab. 150b.

[6] b. Pes. 53b, Gen. R. 11.2, Rav's version of the creation of fire.

to.[1] If a festival fell after the Sabbath, then the order of blessings had to be defined:

> Samuel's Father sent to Rabbi: Let our master teach us what is the order of *havdalot*? He sent back to him, Thus did R. Ishmael the son of R. Yosi say in the name of his father in the name of R. Joshua b. Hananiah: Light, Havdalah, Wine, Qiddush. When a festival falls after the Sabbath, Rav said, the order is Wine, Qiddush, Light, Havdalah, and Samuel said, Wine, light, Havdalah, and Qiddush.
>
> (b. Pes. 102b)[2]

Thus the original question, raised in the preceding generation, was answered, but only yielded a new problem, relating to the proper order for prayers on a special occasion. It seems inconceivable that the prayers were not in fact said before Samuel's Father's day. More likely, before his time, the order was probably not fixed, which led him, in due time, to inquire what the Palestinian court decreed on the subject. The question raised by Rav and Samuel naturally followed. Similarly one finds the existence of ancient customs, as we noted above:

> Rav once came to Babylonia and noticed that they recited the Hallel on the New Moon. At first he thought of stopping them, but when he saw that they omitted parts of it, he remarked, It is clearly evident that it is an old ancestral custom with them.
>
> (b. Ta'anit 28b)

Nonetheless, he defined the Hallel prayer which must be recited on Passover.[3]

For whom were the rabbis actually laying down these liturgical definitions? The account above suggests that it was not for the masses of the people, who had ancient traditions and followed them. The meticulous recitation of blessings over every kind of food, the careful specification of which blessings were said over what item, the details of reciting grace after meals, and the like were effected first of all in the school house, where the laws were originally taught. The simple prayer, approved by Rav, of Benjamin the shepherd, on the other hand, would probably have been characteristic for the masses of the people, who would have found the complicated innovations of the rabbis difficult at the outset to conform to. The practices of centuries' antiquity could not be modified by a decree, or even within one

---

[1] b. Ber. 53a, 59b, y. Ber. 8.6.

[2] Compare y. Ber. 8.1, 8.5.

[3] y. Pes. 10.5.

generation. It was only with the growing knowledge of the tradition as the rabbis exposited it, and as their students fulfilled and exemplified it, that the masses were brought under the influence of the rabbinic laws.

v. Laws Pertaining to Synagogue Worship

The blessing said before reading the Torah in the synagogue was widely neglected:

> R. Judah in the name of Rav said, What is meant by (Jer. 9.11) 'Who is the wise man that may understand this, and who is he to whom the mouth of the Lord hath spoken that he may declare it why the land perishes?' The question was put by the sages, but they could not answer it, by the prophets but they too could not answer it, until the Holy One blessed be He himself resolved it, as it is written, 'And the Lord said, Because they have forsaken my Torah which I set before them' (Jer. 9.12). R. Judah in the name of Rav said, This means that they did not first utter a benediction over the Torah.
> (b. B.M. 85a-b)[1]

The need to lay such extraordinarily strong emphasis on a blessing implies that many omitted it. Whether this concerned Torah reading in the synagogue, or in the school house, is not clear. I think it was the former, as the rabbis directed the practices of their Schools. Samuel defined the benediction to be said before study of the Torah as "Blessed art thou...who has sanctified us by thy commandments and commanded us to study the Torah."[2] This would suggest that saying a blessing over study of the Torah represented an innovation, or otherwise the necessary blessing would not have required Samuel's formulation. Samuel also decreed at what age a minor is allowed to read in the Torah in the synagogue, when he could understand the nature of a blessing, namely, *Whom* he is blessing.[3] Likewise, Rav defined the benediction over the prophetic lesson in special circumstances:

> R. Giddal in the name of Rav said: If the New Moon falls on the Sabbath he who reads the haftarah need not mention the New Moon since but for the Sabbath there is no prophetic lesson on the New Moon. Said R. Ahadebui in the name of R. Mattenah in the name of Rav: When a festival falls on the Sabbath he who reads the haftarah at the Sabbath afternoon service need not mention the festival since but

---

[1] Compare b. Ned. 81a.
[2] b. Ber. 11b, see Ginzberg, *Perushim* I 168-71.
[3] y. Ber. 7.2, Gen. R. 91.3.

for the Sabbath there is no prophetic lesson at the afternoon service on festivals.

> (b. Shab. 24a)

On the other hand, he did not require a blessing after reading in the Torah on a public fast.[1] He and Samuel also defined the biblical passages to be read in the synagogue on specific occasions, including the 9th of Av, on which, Rav said, the passage should be Isaiah 1.21;[2] when the portion of Remembrance should be read;[3] and what is the portion of Shegalim:

> Rav said, 'Command the children . . .' (Num. 28.2), and Samuel said, 'When thou takest' (Ex. 30.12).
>
> (b. Meg. 29b)

These are secondary issues, and one must assume that the primary questions had long been solved.[4]

Rav held that certain portions of the service which required a quorum could not be said if the tenth man was standing outside the door.[5] Of a more general nature were comments on when and how one should pray. Samuel's Father required absolute serenity of mind, and would not pray for three days after returning from a journey; for his part, Samuel would not pray where alcoholic drink was present.[6] It was taught:

> Rava b. Hinena the Elder in the name of Rav said: In saying the Tefillah, when one bows, one should bow at the word 'Blessed' and when returning to an upright position, one should return at the mention of the Divine Name. Samuel said, What is Rav's reason for this? Because it is written, 'The Lord raises up them that are bowed down' (Ps. 146.8).
>
> (b. Ber. 12a)[7]

Likewise he held that one should pray facing a wall:

> R. Judah in the name of Rav said, How do you know that when one prays there should be nothing interposing between him and the wall?

---

[1] b. Meg. 22a.

[2] b. Meg. 31b.

[3] Ibid. 30a.

[4] Compare b. Taʿanit 27b.

[5] b. Pes. 85b.

[6] b. ʿEruv. 65a.

[7] The same requirement was cited by Samuel, with approval, to R. Ḥiyya b. Rav, "Come and I will tell you a fine saying enunciated by your father. Thus said your father, When one bows, one should bow at 'blessed' and when returning to the upright position, one should return at the mention of the Divine name".

Because it says, 'Then Hezekiah turned his face to the wall and prayed' (Is. 38.2).

(b. Ber. 5b)

Samuel and Rav likewise discussed the rules regarding saying the Shemaʿ and the use of *tefillin*. Samuel permitted the placing of *tefillin* under one's pillow.[1] Since the Shemaʿ might be repeated anywhere, the question was raised whether one may say the Shemaʿ in a place where urine was to be found. Samuel held that one might not, so long as it moistens the ground, while Rav held that so long as the mark was discernible, it was prohibited.[2] Again in regard to relatively secondary matters, Rav held that one did not have to recite the third section of the Shema 'in the evening, and that if one recited only the sentence 'Hear O Israel' and then fell asleep, he had performed his obligation.[3] Samuel held that the proper blessing after the Shemaʿ in the morning was "with abounding love" though he said this in the context of Mishnah commentary, and that law was known long before his time.[4] Rav laid great emphasis, as did others in his time, on 'joining redemption with the prayer,' which means reciting the Eighteen Benedictions immediately upon the conclusion of the final blessing over the Shemaʿ.[5]

With reference to the public repetition of the prayers, the main question was, What is the law if a person forgot and omitted a prayer,[6] or if he remembered suddenly that he had already recited it?[7] Rav held that he interrupts himself, and Samuel, that he does not.

> R. Ḥelbo in the name of R. Huna in the name of Rav: If he erred in saying the first three blessings, he goes back to the beginning; in the last three blessings, he goes back to the ʿAvodah; if he erred and does not know where he erred, he goes back to the place which is clear to him (that it has already been said).

(y. Ber. 5.3)

The laws pertaining to prayer, like those of the grace, were frequently derived by the students from observations of the masters' behavior:

---

[1] b. Ber. 23b.

[2] b. Ber. 25a, compare 25b, 26a.

[3] b. Ber. 13b, 14b.

[4] b. Ber. 11b, see 12a.

[5] b. Ber. 10b. See Ginzberg, *Perushim*, I, 229f., 253f.

[6] b. Ber. 29b, 30b.

[7] b. Ber. 21a, y. Ber. 4.4, see Ginzberg, *Perushim* III, 339.

Rav was once at the house of Genivah and he said the Sabbath Prayer on the eve of the Sabbath, and R. Jeremiah b. Abba was praying behind Rav, but Rav finished and did not interrupt the prayer of R. Jeremiah. Three things are to be learned from this, First, a man may say the Sabbath Prayer on the eve of the Sabbath; second, a disciple may pray behind his master, and third, it is forbidden to pass in front of one who is praying. But . . . how could R. Jeremiah act thus, seeing that R. Judah in the name of Rav said, A man should never pray either next to his master nor behind him [because he seems to be bowing down to him] . . . .

(b. Ber. 27a-b)

They likewise discussed whether an individual was required to say the Additional Prayer on the Sabbath. Samuel held that one did not, in a place where the congregation, meeting elsewhere, would recite it.[1]

VI. RAV'S THEOLOGY

A generation ago, the various sayings of Rav would have been interpreted according to an opaque, ethically-centered hermeneutic, which held that mysticism made no impact upon rabbinic Judaism. His several sayings, moreover, could not easily have been seen as related to one another, for no unifying principle had yet been discovered to show that they were, in fact, parts of a single, unified theological pattern. Because of Gershom G. Scholem's researches into the history of Jewish mysticism, we are able to discern the context of Rav's sayings, and to relate his discrete theological dicta to one another.

As we shall see below, Rav continued the exegetical traditions of the school of R. Akiba, by whose students he was educated in Palestine, and Samuel those of the school of R. Ishmael, at the academy of whose disciples in Babylonia he had been trained. Similarly, Samuel's few theological sayings reveal the traditional, non-mystical emphases of R. Ishmael's disciples.[2] These sayings reflect ancient and well-established convictions, that God, and not the stars, determines the

---

[1] y. Ber. 4.6, b. Ber. 30a-b, see above, p. 41. On Rav's view of what one should do if he has prayed and then found a proper quorum, see Ginzberg, *Perushim*, III, 436.

[2] See the penetrating analysis of the theologies of R. Ishmael and R. Akiba by A. J. Heschel, in *Torah Min Hashshamayim* (London, 1962). Heschel points out that R. Akiba's theology was based on a highly immanental view of the divinity, holding that God inheres in the world and its artifacts, while R. Ishmael's normally stresses God as 'wholly other', outside of the world and transcendent over it. See below, p. 232-236.

fate of each person down to the smallest detail; and that man should
seek life by study of the Torah and performance of the commandments. His prayers repeat the old themes, and fill lacunae in the
already-available liturgical corpus. Moreover, apart from his précis
of the Eighteen Benedictions, his contributions to the liturgy were
practically indistinguishable from those of Rav, which were oriented
partly toward the needs of the devout, partly toward theological
motifs. His confession consisted of a reaffirmation of the belief that
God knows everything that happens and is done on earth, a belief
expressed in well-known biblical images. Samuel's contribution to
the legal literature on the liturgy is more substantial, as one might
expect, but reveals no very original perspective. His single very
important innovation was the requirement to say a blessing before
the performance of a *miẓvah*, but I cannot see how it revealed a fully
articulated theological attitude. (One may conjecture that this requirement was intended to underline the *real* meaning of doing the commandment, directing the heart of the worshipper toward God who
commanded him to do such-and-such, and thus preventing the action
from appearing to be mere hocus-pocus, or a gesture *ex opere operato*
capable of bearing inherent religious significance, or coercing the
divinity. But I cannot find support for such a conjecture either in
other sayings of Samuel, or in the sources relevant to this period.
We are left with a legal requirement, and no clear idea of what it
meant or why it was instituted.)

Rav is quite another matter. His was the greatest theological mind
in rabbinic Judaism in third-century Babylonia. To understand the
various sayings noted earlier (section i), we must review Scholem's
discussion of Jewish mysticism in this period, by the light of which
we may discern connections between Rav's discrete sayings and
rabbinic mysticism. Scholem points out[1] that from the first century,
mystical doctrines were taught as exegeses of the Creation story
and the first chapter of Ezekiel, *Ma'aseh Bere'shit* and *Ma'aseh Merkavah*, Works of Creation, and of the Chariot, respectively. These
exegeses soon developed themes separated from the Biblical texts.
For instance, the 'living creatures' of Ezekiel became angels at the
celestial court. Organized schools existed, moreover, to develop
and transmit specific mystical traditions. Those admitted to the
schools were taught the gnosis permitting ascent of the soul from

---

[1] *Major Trends in Jewish Mysticism* (repr. N.Y. 1954) 40-79.

earth and return to the heavens. The emphasis of the Merkavah mystic was upon the kingship of God, a "Judaized form of cosmocratorial mysticism concerning the divine king," Scholem notes. The *Ma'aseh Bere'shit* tradition lays stress on cosmology. Scholem points to the saying of Rav, that the world was created through ten qualities, wisdom, insight, knowledge, force, appeal, power, justice, right, love, and compassion, as an example of the semi-mythological speculation on creation. These *middot* are hypostatized attributes of God; Scholem compares them to the aeons and archons of the Gnostics. In his work dealing with second and third century mystical materials,[1] Scholem points out that the Merkavah texts were in no way heretical, but adhered strictly to monotheistic concepts; this is a *rabbinic* gnosis, consisting of illuminations and revelations 'granted to the adepts...[in conformity with] the Jewish vision of the hierarchy of beings' (10). Accepting the attribution to Rav of the New Year Malkhuyot prayer, "It is our duty to praise the Lord of all, to enhance the greatness of the Yoẓer Bere'shit." Scholem comments that this hymn is in the same rhythm as many of the Merkavah ones (p. 27). He points out that Rav's saying on Beẓalel, who could combine the letters, reflects belief in the occult power, acquired by the Merkavah mystic, to combine letters and uncover secret names of God (p. 79), as illustrated by the following, cited by Scholem, from the Hebrew Book of Enoch ch. 41:

> Come and behold the letters by which the heaven and the earth were created ...
> The letters by which the throne of glory and the wheels of the Merkavah were created ...
> The letters by which wisdom, understanding, knowledge, prudence, meekness, and righteousness were created, and by which the whole world is sustained.

In his essay "The Meaning of the Torah in Jewish Mysticism"[2] Scholem explains this conception of God's name, as "the highest concentration of divine power." The view, shared by Rav (below Ch. six), that the various sections of the Torah do not exhibit a proper order, is based upon the concept that the correct order and arrangement *must* be hidden, lest knowledge of their secrets would permit the gnostic to upset the mundane order. Scholem emphasizes that

---

[1] *Jewish Gnosticism, Merkabah Mysticism, and Talmudic Tradition* (N.Y. 1960), *passim.*

[2] *On the Kabbalah and its Symbolism* (N.Y. 1965), 32-86.

this view reflects considerable interest in magic, for magical names could be put to theurgic uses. Thus Bezalel was able to imitate the Creation on a small scale, the Tabernacle being viewed as a microcosm of heaven and earth.[1] Finally, in his essay on "Kabbalah and Myth,"[2] Scholem points out that while rabbinic Judaism stood in opposition to myth, Kabbalah preserved in its various forms a vividly mythological idiom. Similarly Ginzberg[3] interprets Rav's enumeration of the ten objects created on the first day as an effort to 'Judaize the un-Jewish conception of primal substances by representing them also as having been created.' At the same time, Rav preserved, as we noted above, numerous details of a pre-Mosaic Israelite cosmogonic myth, which he discerned in Scripture and articulated. Bacher[4] likewise sees Rav's sayings on cosmology as highly mythological, despite their exegetical foundation; the forty-two lettered name of God is "nothing other than the expression for the gnosis [Wesen] of God and his attributes." Reconsidering Rav's several theological sayings in the light of Scholem's discussion, we cannot escape the conclusion that Rav was, in fact, a Jewish 'gnostic,' and that his sayings are all part of a fully articulated, Jewish 'gnostic' system.

It is important, however, to distinguish gnosticism, as a *style* characteristic of a number of pagan and Christian thinkers, from a substantially different Jewish formulation, congruent only to such a *style*, but not to the content, of pagan or Christian gnosticism. There was no Jewish gnosticism in the classical sense, for within the framework of Judaism could be located no place whatever for such concepts as the *evil* demiurge ("Yozer Bere'shit"); for the Hebrew Scriptures as collections of lies; for the God of Israel as a being of inferior status in the heavenly hierarchy; for the Redeemer as other than a historical-eschatological figure. Nonetheless, I follow Scholem's view that the term 'gnostic' remains a convenient one, even in studying Jewish theology, to apply to a religious movement "that proclaimed a mystical esotericism for the elect based on illumination and the

---

[1] *Ibid.* 165f.

[2] *Ibid.* 87-117.

[3] *Jewish Law and Lore* (Phila. 1955) 188.

[4] W. Bacher, *Agada* 16-21. See also Zuri, *Rav*, 374-9, who sees Rav's interest in the Works of Creation as a continuation of the 'school of the South', for, Zuri holds, the Galileans pursued the Merkavah tradition. There is no evidence to support this view; Rav himself shared in both traditions. Zuri's continuing explanation of all phenomena by the hypothesis that the Galileans preserved culture mostly in isolation from the Southerners, is one of the least convincing parts of his work.

acquisition of a higher knowledge of things heavenly and divine. It is to this knowledge that the very term 'Gnosis,' meaning 'knowledge,' that is to say, knowledge of an esoteric and at the same time soteric (redeeming) character, alludes."[1] If Rav's sayings are superficially biblical, exegetical, and mostly unspeculative, they really represent his formulation of a traditional rabbinic gnostic doctrine phrased in mythological terms, with roots, at the very latest, in the first century academy of R. Yoḥanan ben Zakkai,[2] but probably much earlier than that.

Rav reaffirmed that God's power is without limit and characterized by goodness, against the gnostic view that the Creator-God was either a bumbling fool, who made a mess of creation, or malevolent. God spends his day in study of the Torah, judgment of the world, provision of food for the creatures from the greatest to the least, and playing with Leviathan. He mourns for the condition of Israel, and himself diminished the wings of the heavenly creatures in permitting Nebuchadnezzar to punish Israel. His saying that the fiery stream which issues from the sweat of the ḥayot pours out on the head of the wicked in Gehenna represents an allusion to the doctrine, enunciated by R. Ḥanina nephew of R. Joshua, a second century Babylonian teacher, cited by Scholem as follows:

> There are rivers of fire which pass before the Shekhinah like streams of water mingled with fire . . . .[3]

Scholem sees this saying as an elaboration of Daniel 7.10, to which Rav's dictum was likewise attached, and hence as part of a wider body of doctrine about rivers, and bridges spanning them, in Hekhalot texts, in III Enoch 33.4-5, and elsewhere. The vision of God as blindingly brilliant recalls the Hekhalot speculation, similarly, about the appearance of God (Shi'ur Qomah), and offers a parallel to the concept, in Pirke de R. Eliezer[4] that the heavens were created from the light of the garment in which God was clothed, which a contemporary of Rav, R. Simeon b. Yehoẓadak, derived from Psalms 104: 2, "He covers himself with light as with a garment."[5] Scholem points out, moreover, that the heavenly bearer of this garment is

---

[1] *Jewish Gnosticism*, 1.

[2] See my *Life* 96-102. Note Rav's reference to Nebuchadnezzar, similar to that of R. Yoḥanan ben Zakkai in the latter's mystical doctrine.

[3] *Jewish Gnosticism* 56.

[4] *Ibid.* 58.

[5] *Ibid.* 58 n. 8.

designated by one of the secret names, and adds, "These names, of which only a very few have a plausible etymology, may designate different aspects of the divine glory in its appearance upon the throne."[1] Rav's view that the secret name of God, of forty-two letters, must be entrusted only to him who exhibits the proper virtues, recalls the insistance of R. Judah the Prince, in the Mishnah (Ḥagigah ch. II) that esoteric lore must likewise be preserved only for him "who is capable of understanding 'of his own gnosis'." Thus it was not a public but a secret doctrine that was being transmitted. Such a man is especially beloved 'above' and likewise 'feared by man' as well he might be. One notes in this context the stories about pagans who used the name of the God of Israel for blessings and curses, and suffered on that account. Possession of such magical names endowed the gnostic with veritable power. Rav underlined his conviction that such creative power was used by God, and ought to be similarly used by man, for benevolent and not malevolent purposes. Thus God himself destroyed several companies of angels who hinted to the contrary.

The sayings about 'the First Man,' who was a Golem, reached from one end of the world to the other, and was made from the dirt of every country, are likewise best understood in the light of Scholem's discussion of "The Idea of the Golem."[2] Adam is a being who was taken from the earth and returns to it, on whom the breath of God conferred life and speech. Scholem cites Philo, who says, "It is conceivable that God wished to create his man-like form with the greatest care and that for this reason he did not take dust from the first piece of earth that came to hand, but that from the whole earth he separated the best." Likewise Rav believed that God gathered Adam's dust from everywhere. Adam's vast proportions, in Rav's mind, reveal, following Scholem on the Golem, two conceptions: first, that he was a vast primordial being of cosmogonic myth, and second, his size "would seem to signify in spatial terms that the power of the whole universe is concentrated in him."[3] In the context of Rav's cosmogonic myth about the szyzygous creation of the world, one can hardly doubt Scholem's view that we are, in fact, dealing with an Adam who is the center of such a mythology.

Rav's story about the creation and sterilization of Leviathan, about

---

[1] *Ibid.* 59.
[2] *On the Kabbalah,* 158f.
[3] *Ibid.* 162.

the assistance of the Angel of the Sea and his veiled hints about the opposition of Leviathan and Behemoth to the divine creation,[1] his citation of the Scriptures which modern scholars have interpreted as remnants of a pre-Mosaic Israelite creation mythology,—all indicate that his gnostic doctrine contained, in fact, a fully developed, wholly articulated cosmogonic myth, which took the place, in his mind, of the non-mythological creation story in the Bible itself, but which was elicited by it. Rav thus followed, as I said, the gnostic *style* of telling Creation myths, but resurrected monotheist-Jewish ones, based upon the Scriptures which preserved an ancient Israelite cosmogony, in which God, while facing opposition, plays a wholly decisive role, monopolizing the acts of creation quite without the direction, or accompaniment, of an 'unknown God' above him. It is further to be derived from ancient Babylonian myths, but, I think, based on biblical exegeses, as the text makes clear.

One may see in these sayings, therefore, the adumbration of a Jewish anti-gnostic gnosticism, in which the gnostic *style* characterized the rejection of gnostic *doctrine*.[2] Rav's prayers gave similar emphasis

---

[1] See Hans Jonas, *The Gnostic Religion* (Boston 1958), 117-8.

[2] I am unable to find a single parallel to Rav's view of Adam in the Gnostic systems cited by Jonas, in which Adam plays such an important part. See Jonas, 64, 69, 73f., 83f., 86-9, 92f., 154f., 203f., 226-31. Rav's ideas derive from ancient Near Eastern, and not contemporary Gnostic, mythology. Compare Louis Ginzberg, *The Legends of the Jews* trans. H. Szold (Phila. 1947), I, 47-101, V, 83-131. Ginzberg comments (V, 59, n. 12) with reference to the angels' opposition to making man, that this view opposes that of Philo and the Gnostics, that man was made by lower powers, not by God himself. "In opposition to this view, that man was . . . created by the evil or lower powers, the Jewish legend lays stress upon the fact that the angels had nothing to do with man's creation, which they tried rather to prevent." Similarly, on the Creation legend as Rav formulated it, the ten attributes etc. see V, 7, n. 15; on creation by "letters"; V, 5, n. 10; on heavens as fire and water, 7 n. 16; on the rebellion of the waters, I, 15 and V, 18 n. 52-3 etc. I, 18-19; on Leviathan, I, 27-8, and V 41, n. 115-117, "The Leviathan pair may be compared to the Babylonian myth concerning Tiamat and her only mate, Kingu, according to which the latter is vanquished by Marduk and made harmless, while the former is slain". On God's playing with Leviathan, V, 42 n. 124; on Behemoth, p. 44 n. 127.

Note especially p. 46, ". . . One must not look exclusively for Babylonian myths, and one is not warranted to identify, on the basis of Enoch, Behemoth and Leviathan with Tiamat and Kingu respectively of the Babylonian mythology, since not only the rabbinic sources but also Job 40 clearly describes Behemoth as a land monster. It may therefore be said that Behemoth belongs to quite another cycle of myths, but owing to learned combinations, the pseudepigraphic authors made it the consort of Leviathan, whereas the rabbinic sources retain the original conception of it as a land monster. The allegorical interpretation of the Leviathan-Behemoth legends originated at a very early date, and is found

to the view that God, the creator, was the supreme master of knowledge, who knows not only the 'secrets' of unethical behavior, but
the secrets of eternity, which suggests a far more than ethical dimen-
sion; and that the New Year represents the celebration of divine
knowledge and judgment.

One cannot ignore the fact that Rav's theology "in the gnostic
manner" produced not a rejection of law, or of the Law, but rather
a very detailed, legalistic contribution to the practical liturgy. As we
noted above, like Samuel, he paid attention to the lacunae in the
inherited liturgy, and through the composition of prayers which
would meet the day-to-day needs of the people, and through the
promulgation of laws about when prayers are said and the like, he
exerted lasting influence on the configuration of synagogue liturgy.
For him, as for almost every major figure in the history of Jewish
mysticism, no tension existed between mysticism and law.[2] As in
the cases of R. Yoḥanan b. Zakkai, R. Akiba, R. Ḥiyya (Rav's uncle),
and many others in this period, the lawyer *was* the mystic, and through
the law he was able to bring to bear upon the common life the practical
consequences of his mystic doctrine.

---

not only among the Gnostics . . . but also in rabbinic sources". (I find in Rav's
saying no *allegory* at all, but rather a retelling of pre-biblical mythology). On
Adam as a *min*, see V, 99, n. 78, "Adams wickedness and persistence in sinning
are frequently referred to in the Haggadah; comp. Sanh. 38b where he is declared
to have been a heretic (see also Tertullian, Adversus Marcionem, 2.2: Who will
hesitate to declare that Adam's great sin was heresy?)." But compare the critical
view of A. Altmann, cited above, p. 158 n. 1.

[1] *On the Kabbalah*, 1f., for a very subtle and rich explication of the relationship
between religious authority and mysticism.

CHAPTER SIX

RABBINIC JUDAISM IN
EARLY SASANIAN BABYLONIA (III):
BIBLICAL EXEGESIS AND HISTORY

The rabbis viewed biblical study for its own sake as religiously significant. Here we shall review their exegetical legacy, postponing comment to sections vi and vii.

I. THE PENTATEUCH

We have considered the comments on the Creation and Adam legends above (Chapter Five). Other comments on Genesis were mainly philological and historical. Commenting on the word *tardemah* (Gen. 2.21) Rav said, 'There are three kinds of torpor (*tardemah*), of sleep, of prophecy, and of unconsciousness (or trance).'[1] He explained the words "at the cool of the day" as follows:

> Rav said, He [God] judged him [Adam] in the east side of the universe, for 'le ruaḥ hayom' implies in the side ['ruaḥ'] which rises with the day [= sun]. Zabdi b. Levi said, He judged him in the west side, for 'le-ruaḥ ha-yom' implies, in the side which sinks with the day. In Rav's view, he was severe toward him, just as the more the sun ascends the hotter it becomes. In Zabdi's view, he was lenient toward him, just as the further the sun declines the cooler it grows.
>
> (Gen. R. 19.8)

On the other hand, Rav commented:

> At the east (mi-qedem). Rav said, In every case the east affords asylum. To Adam, 'So he drove out the man and causes him to dwell at the east of the Garden of Eden.' To Cain: 'And Cain went out from the presence of the Lord and dwelt in the land of Nob on the east of Eden' (Gen. 4.16). To a homicide: 'Then Moses separated three cities beyond the Jordan towards the sun-rising'—i.e. in the east (Deut. 4.41).
>
> (Gen. R. 21.9)

As to the sign of Cain, Rav said, He gave him a dog.[2] R. Judah, citing, Rav, citing R. Joshua b. Ḥananiah proved that the serpent

---

[1] Gen. R. 17.5, 44.17.
[2] Ibid. 22.12.

goes with its young for seven years, on the basis of Gen. 3.14, 'Cursed art thou from among all cattle.'[1] The coats of skin referred to in Gen. 3.21 were, according to Rav and Samuel, either material that grows from the skin, or material from which the skin derives pleasure.[2] With reference to Gen. 9: 20-24, the sons of Noah were accused by Rav and Samuel, either of castrating, or of sexually abusing, their father.[3] These comments on the early chapters of Genesis reveal that apart from the mystical interpretations of the Creation story, the interest of the early 'Amora'im lay simply in spelling out exegetical details, without a specific line of inquiry or interest, for the sake of 'study of the Torah.'

The tendency of the 'Amora' im of this period was to magnify the achievements and influence of Abraham. Thus we find:

> Rav said, Our Father Abraham kept the whole Torah, as it is said, Because Abraham hearkened to my voice, kept my charge and my commandments (Gen. 26.5). R. Shimi b. Ḥiyya said to Rav, Perhaps this refers to the seven laws (applying to the sons of Noah)? If it were so, he replied, there was also that of circumcision. Then say, he answered, that it refers to the seven laws and circumcision? If that were so, why does Scripture say, My commandments *and* my laws?
> (b. Yoma' 28b)

He served superior meals to those of Solomon:

> 'And Abraham ran into the herd and fetched a calf tender and good' (Gen. 18.7), Whereon Rav observed, a calf, one, tender, two, and good, three, means, three calves for the three men . . .
> R. Judah in the name of Rav said: Everything which Abraham personally did for the ministering angels, the Holy One, blessed be he, did in person for his sons, and whatever Abraham did through a messenger, the Holy One did for his sons through a messenger, thus, 'And Abraham ran unto the herd' and 'Behold I will rain bread from the heavens' (Exodus 16.4). "He stood by them under the tree' and 'Behold I will stand before thee there upon the rock.' (Exodus 17.6)
> (b. B.M. 86b)

From Abraham, one learns that hospitality to wayfarers is greater than receiving the divine presence.[4] Abraham's relations with God were described in detail, and applied to contemporary religious questions, as we noted with reference to astrology (b. Ned. 32a)

---

[1] b. Bekh. 8a.
[2] b. Sotah 14a.
[3] b. Sanh. 70a.
[4] b. Shev. 35b, with reference to Gen. 18.3.

above. Since astrology was such a major concern of Babylonian culture, Abraham provided a good proof that Israel need not look to the stars. On the other hand, Abraham, according to Samuel, provides a good example of how *not* to behave as well:

> Samuel said, [Abraham was punished and his children were doomed to 210 years in Egypt] because he went too far in testing the qualities of the Lord, as it is written (Gen. 15.8), 'And he said, Lord God, whereby shall I know that I shall inherit it?'
>
> (b. Ned. 32a)

The behavior of the angels likewise teaches good conduct:

> 'And they said to him, where is Sarah thy wife, and he said, behold she is in the tent' (Gen. 18.9). R. Judah in the name of Rav said, The Ministering angels knew that our Mother Sarah was in the tent, but why [bring out the fact that she was] in her tent? In order to make her beloved of her husband [to impress him with her modesty.]
>
> (b. B.M. 87a)

When he died, Abraham was mourned by the whole world:

> R. Ḥanan b. Rava in the name of Rav said, On the day when Abraham our father passed away from the world, all the great ones of the nations of the world stood in line and said, Woe to the world that has lost its leader, and woe to the ship that has lost its pilot.
>
> (b. B.B. 91a)

There can be little doubt that some of the above sayings were part of a single commentary on Gen. 18,[1] while others, in particular the story of Abraham's death and his keeping the whole Torah, were created for other than merely exegetical purposes. The commentary on Gen. 18 reveals the simple hermeneutical interest of the rabbis, to derive from the Scripture good lessons for their own time and at the same time to explain Scripture in its own terms.[2]

We may suppose that where a comment is mainly of the exegetical variety, there we are dealing with a fragment of a continuing commentary, while where it is mainly of homiletical or theological interest, there we are dealing with a fragment of a sermon. Of the first variety, with reference to Jacob, is the following, (cited above as well):

> 'And Jacob came whole' (Gen. 33.18). Rav interpreted, Bodily whole, financially whole, and whole in his learning. 'And he was

---

[1] Gen. 18.3,=b. Shev. 35b, b. Shab. 127a, etc.
[2] As in the Esther and birth of Moses stories, see above, p. 57-63.

gracious [lit. encamped] to the city'. Rav said, He instituted coinage
for them. Samuel said, He instituted markets for them. R. Yoḥanan
said, He instituted baths for them.

(b. Shab. 33b)

Of a theological interest are the following:

'And as he was about to destroy, the Lord beheld and he repented'
(I Chron. 21.15). [What did he see?]. Rav said, He beheld Jacob our
Father, as it is written, 'And Jacob said when he beheld them' (Gen.
32.3). Samuel said, He beheld the ashes of the ram of Isaac, as it says,
'God will see for himself the ramb' (Gen. 22.3).

(b. Ber. 62b)

'And thou shalt carry me out of Egypt and bury me in their burying
place' (Gen. 47.30). Karna remarked, Some inner meaning [must be
here]. Our father Jacob well knew that he was a righteous man in
every way, and since the dead outside of the land will also be resurrected, why did he trouble his sons? Because he might possibly be
unworthy to [roll through the cavities of the earth.]

(b. Ket. 111a)

The above passages are not part of a connected commentary on
a given chapter, but rather part of a homiletical, or theological
discourse.[1]

The tendency of the rabbis in dealing with Leah was to praise her
and defend her reputation, on the one hand, but also to win approval
for her husband's treatment of her on the other. Her eyes were weak,
but it was no disgrace:

She heard people talking at the crossroads and saying, Rebecca has
two sons and Laban has two daughters, the elder should be married
to the elder, and the younger to the younger. She sat at the crossroads
and asked, How does the elder one conduct himself? Along came the
answer, He was a wicked man, a highway robber. How does the
younger conduct himself? 'A quiet man, dwelling in tents' (Gen. 25.27).
And she wept until her eyelashes dropped. And this accounts for the
text, 'And the Lord saw that Leah was hated' (Gen. 29.31). Why
hated? Not actually hated, but he saw that Esau's conduct was hateful
to her, so he 'opened her womb' (Gen. 29.31).

(b. B.B. 123a)

'And afterwards she bore a daughter and called her name Dinah'
(Gen. 30.21). What is meant by 'afterwards'? Rav said, After Leah had
passed judgment on herself, saying, Twelve tribes are destined to

---

[1] The comment on the Jacob's merit obviously recalls the debates with Christians about whether Israel remained worthy of the covenant or not, but I cannot
see the point of Karna's saying about Jacob.

issue from Jacob. Six have issued from me, and four from the concubines, making ten. If this child will be male, my sister Rachel will
not be equal to one of the handmaids. Forthwith the child was turned
to a girl, as it says, 'And she called her name Dinah.'

(b. Ber. 60a)[1]

I cannot think of any reason pertaining to this particular period
to explain why Leah's reputation should have needed rabbinical
polishing. It is possible that these are fragments of a continuous
commentary on Gen. 29-30, though the evidence is slight. Rav
commented on the place name Timnah (Gen. 38.13), that there are
two places by this name, one in reference to Judah, the other with
Samson (Judges 14.1).[2]

While the comments are on unconnected passages, the following
are probably fragments of a connected commentary on the Joseph
story:

> 'And Potiphar, an officer of Pharoah, bought him' (Gen. 39.1). Rav
> said, He bought him for himself, but Gabriel came and castrated him
> and mutilated him for originally his name is written 'Potiphar' but
> afterwards, 'Potephera' (Gen. 41.45).
>
> (b. Sotah 13b)

> 'He went into the house to do his work' (Gen. 39.11). Rav and
> Samuel held that it really means, either, to do his work, or, to satisfy
> his desires.
>
> (b. Sotah 36b)

> R. Judah in the name of Samuel said, All the gold and silver of the
> world Joseph gathered in and brought to Egypt, for it is said, 'And
> Joseph gathered up all the money that was found' (Gen. 47.14).
>
> (b. Pes. 119a)

These comments are not homiletical, but merely expository.
The Joseph story yielded two homilies:

> 'To all of them he gave changes of raiment, to Benjamin, five'
> (Gen. 45.22). Is it possible that that righteous man should fall into
> the very mistake from which he himself suffered? For Rava b. Mehasia
> said in the name of R. Hama b. Guria in the name of Rav: Through
> two sela's weight of fine silk which Jacob gave to Joseph over what
> he gave to his brothers, a ball was set rolling and our ancestors
> eventually went down to Egypt.
>
> (b. Meg. 16b)[3]

---

[1] The word-play is on 'din' and 'Dinah'.
[2] Gen. R. 85.6, similarly on Gen. 23.9, the Cave of Machpelah, b. 'Eruv. 52b.
[3] Compare b. Shab. 10a for a more abstract version.

Why was Joseph called 'bones' during his lifetime (Gen. 50.25), asked R. Judah in the name of Rav? Because he did not interfere to safeguard his father's honor when his brothers said to him, 'Thy servant our father . . .' and he made no reply to them. R. Judah in the name of Rav (others say, R. Ḥama b. R. Ḥanina), Why did Joseph die before his brothers? Because he put on superior airs.

(b. Sotah 13b)

In both instances, the Joseph story provided the occasion for a comment on family relationships, which is quite natural given the substance of the story, but the story itself was not thereby elucidated, rather being used as the occasion for illumination of contemporary affairs.

We have already noted the evidences that Rav and Samuel took special care to exposit Exodus 1-3, and suggested why that narrative should especially interest them. Remarks of a strictly historical nature included Samuel's, cited by R. Judah, that the Song (Ex. 15) was uttered by Moses and Israel when they ascended from the Red Sea.[1] Exegesis of the construction of the tent of meeting was mainly, likewise, of historical interest, though it provided some information also on the construction of the Temple, in particular its dimensions.[2] The same texts yield the fact that Moses, who spread the tent, was therefore ten cubits high;[3] Moses was also high priest,[4] who established the priestly courses for Israel,[5] in the view of Rav. Samuel held, by a play on the word 'besought' (veyeḥal, Exodus 32.11) that Moses risked his life for Israel, with Exodus 32.32 as a proof text.[6] He was given the secrets of creation:

Rav and Samuel, One said, Fifty gates of understanding were created in the world, and all were given to Moses save one, as it is said, 'Yet thou hast made him but little lower than a god' (Ps. 8.6). 'Now Kohelet sought to find out words of delight' (Eccles. 12.10), that is, Kohelet sought to be like Moses, but a bat kol went forth and said to him, It is written 'uprightly even words of truth' (Koh. 12.10), 'There arose not a prophet again in Israel like Moses' (Deut. 34.10). The other said, Among the prophets there arose not, but among the kings there did arise. How then do I interpret the words, Kohelet sought to find out words of delight? Kohelet sought to pronounce

---

[1] b. Pes. 117a.
[2] The future Temple will conform to the model of the one in the wilderness, according to Rav, b. Shab. 127a, y. Sanh. 1.3. See also b. 'Eruv. 21-32, b. Suk. 4b.
[3] b. Bekh. 44a, Shab. 92a.
[4] b. Zev. 101b.
[5] b. Ta'anit 27a.
[6] b. Ber. 32a.

verdicts from his own insight, without witnesses, without warning, [thus unjustly] whereupon a *bat kol* went forth and said, It is written uprightly, even words of truth, 'At the mouth of two witnesses (Deut. 19.15).

(b. R.H. 21b)[1]

Elsewhere the first view is ascribed to both Rav and Samuel, that fifty gates of understanding were created and all but one were given to Moses.[2] Since Rav held that the future Temple would be like the one in the wilderness, these exegeses doubtless bear a messianic and eschatological implication. Yet the peculiarly exegetical form of Jewish eschatological expectations is striking. Whatever the rabbis thought about the Temple and its reconstruction 'in time to come,' they said by means of descriptions of that of Moses. It should be noted, moreover, that the tendency to denigrate Moses, discerned elsewhere in rabbinic thought[3] is quite absent here, where Moses is treated as the arch-priest and master, like Bezallel, of the secrets of creation. The Dura Fresco shows a similar view of Moses.

The origin of the Sabbath, instituted in the wilderness, was given:

'Observe the Sabbath day . . . as the Lord thy God commanded thee' (Deut. 5.12), whereon R. Judah in the name of Rav said, 'As he commanded thee at Marah (Exodus 15.25).

(b. Shab. 87b)

and a theological homily was based on the same passage:

R. Judah in the name of Rav said, Had Israel kept the first Sabbath no nation or tongue would have had dominion over them, for it is said, 'And it came to pass on the seventh day there went out some of the people . . .' which is followed by, 'Then came Amalek' (Exodus 16.27, 17.8).

(b. Shab. 118b)[4]

In the book of Numbers, four passages attracted the attention of Rav and Samuel, the story of the Mana, Korah, Balaam, and the Gatherer of Wood on the Sabbath (Daughters of Zelophehad). In addition, in examining the early chapters of Numbers, Rav noticed,

---

[1] b. Ned. 38a.

[2] *Ibid.* 38a.

[3] See Wayne Meeks, *op. cit., pass.*

[4] Again an echo of the language of R. Yoḥanan b. Zakkai, "Happy are you O Israel! When you do the will of your father in heaven, no nation nor tongue has dominion over you", Mekhilta Baḥodesh 1, ed. Friedman 61, Lauterbach II, 193-4. See my *Life,* 139-40. See above, p. 66-67. The connection is clearly via R. Eliʿezer b. Hyrcanus.

and enunciated, one of the primary hermeneutical principles of rabbinic literature. Since Numbers 1.1 is chronologically a month later than Numbers 9.1, Rav, cited by R. Menasiah b. Taḥilifa, stated, 'This proves that there is no chronological order in the Torah.'[1] As we have seen above,[2] this hermeneutical principle emerges from Rav's mysticism, for, as Scholem points out, the mystic exegete regarded the 'order' of the Torah as we now have it as intended to obscure the secrets of the process of creation. Scholem cites the exegesis of R. Eleazar, contemporary of Rav, as follows:

> 'No man knoweth its order' (Job 28.13). Rabbi Eleazar [b. Pedat] declared, The various sections of the Torah were not given in their correct order. For if they had been given in their correct order, anyone who read them would be able to awaken the dead and perform miracles. For this reason the correct order and arrangement of the Torah were hidden, and are known only to the Holy One, blessed be He, of whom it is said (Is. 44.7), 'And who, as I, shall call, and declare it, and set it in order for me.'
>
> (Midrash Psalms ed. Buber p. 33)[3]

Scholem underlines that this statement 'implies a magical view of the Torah.' In the light of his view of the theurgic use of divine names by Jews and non-Jews alike, it is quite clear that here Rav's mysticism led him to a major hermeneutical insight. At the same time, it should be noted that Rav did not invariably ignore the actual historical order of Scripture. Most of the sayings cited here reflect his conviction that Scripture does exhibit a chronological order of events. Hence the view that 'there is no chronological order in the Torah,' derived from the comparison of Numbers 1.1 and 9.1, should not be regarded as a predominating exegetical attitude, but rather one which came to bear only at specific points. On Numbers 11, we have another connected commentary:

> 'We remember the fish which we were wont to eat in Egypt for nought' (Num. 11.5). Rav and Samuel, one said, Fish means real fish, the other, Fish is a euphemism for illicit intercourse.

---

[1] b. Pes. 6b.

[2] See above, p. 182-183.

[3] *On the Kabbalah*, 37-8. See also W. Bacher, *op. cit.*, 31. Bacher found this statement "an early anticipation of the later so-called 'practical Kabbalah'," and therefore doubted its authenticity. However, in the light of the many 'practical' magical sayings we have noted, there is no reason whatever to doubt that Rav had exactly this attitude, and that he found convenient proof-texts in Numbers to authenticate it.

'Or beat it in mortars' (Numbers 11.8). R. Judah in the name of Rav, or, some say, R. Ḥama b. Ḥanina, stated, That teaches that there came down to Israel, with the manna, cosmetics for women.

(b. Yoma' 75a)

Rav's comment on the Koraḥ story was probably intended to influence affairs in his own day:

Rav said, Koraḥ was an Epicurean. What did he do? He went and made a talith which was entirely of blue. He came to Moses, and said, Moses our Master, A Talith which is entirely blue, is it required to have fringes? He said, It is required, as it is written (Deut. 22.12) 'You shall make yourself fringes'. A House which is full of books, does it require a mezuzah? He said to him, It requires a mezuzah, as it is written (Deut. 6.9), 'And you shall write them upon the mezuzot of your house' He said to him, A white spot as big as a bean, what is the law? He replied, Unclean [of leprosy]. If it spreads throughout? It is clean. At that hour, Koraḥ said, The Torah is not from heaven, and Moses is not a prophet, nor Aaron a high priest. In that hour, Moses said, Lord of all Worlds, If the earth was created with a mouth from the six days of creation, it is well, and if not, let it be given a mouth now. [See Numbers 16.30, 'And if the Lord creates something new, and the ground opens its mouth . . .'].

(y. Sanh. 10.1)

This Koraḥ was regarded as the prototype of the man who raised logical questions against Scriptural injunctions, pointing up paradoxes in them, a skill required of judges, in Rav's view, but easily perverted. Rav held that "He who is unyielding in a dispute violates a negative command, as it is written (Num. 17.5), 'And let him not be as Koraḥ and as his company'."[1] One of the original followers of Koraḥ became the occasion for a sermon on the guile of wise wives:

'And 'On, the son of Pelet' (Num. 16.1). Why was he called 'On [the pun is on 'Onen, a mourner]. Because he spent all the rest of his days in mourning. Why the 'son of Pelet'? Because he was a son for whom miracles [pela'ot] were wrought. Rav said, 'On the son of Pelet was saved by his wife. She said to him, What has this dispute to do with you? If Aaron be High Priest you are but a disciple, and if Koraḥ be high priest, you are still but a disciple. I know, she said to him, that the whole assembly is holy, for it is written of them 'All the congregation are holy' (Num. 16.3). What did she do? She gave him wine to drink, made him drunk, and put him to bed. Then she sat down at the entrance along with her daughter, and dishevelled her hair, so that anyone who came for 'On, her husband, on seeing her, turned back. Meanwhile the others were swallowed up. Thus the

---

[1] b. Sanh. 110a.

text 'Every wise woman buildeth her house' (Prov. 14.1) applies to the wife of 'On, 'but the foolish plucketh it down with her own hands' applies to the wife of Korah.

(b. Sanh. 109b)[1]

Numbers 25 was subjected to a verse by verse exegesis, of which we have the following remnants:

'Did the children of Israel slay with the sword' (Num. 25.1-9). Rav said, They subjected him (Balaam) to four deaths . . .

(b. Sanh. 106b)

R. Naḥman in the name of Rav said, What is meant by a greyhound [*zarzir matnaim* = energetic of loins], and a hegoat also, and 'a king against whom there is no rising up' (Numbers 25.12)? That wicked man (Zimri) cohabited four hundred twenty four times that day, and Phinehas waited for his strength to weaken, not knowing that [God is] a king against whom there is no rising up.

(b. Sanh. 82b)

There are a number of sayings also on the daughters of Zelophehad (Numbers 36.6). Regarding the same verse, Samuel said that on the 15th of Av, it was permitted for the tribes to intermarry with one another.[2]

On the book of Deuteronomy, we have isolated exegeses, which indicate only the specific verses that most interested Rav and Samuel. These include the following anti-astrological saying:

Rav said, What means the following 'Which the Lord thy God hath divided (ḥalak) to all the peoples under the whole heaven' (Deut. 4.19) This teaches that he made smooth their words, to banish idolaters from the world.

(b. A.Z. 55a)

R. Judah citing Samuel said, "The days of the Messiah shall endure as long as from the Creation until now," citing Deut. 11.21.[3] That one's own poor take precedence over those of other places is proved from Deut. 15.4.[4] Rav Judah in the name of Rav exposited the verse on the false prophet (Deut. 28.20), applying its several clauses to different kinds of deceivers, probably for exegetical reasons alone:

'The prophet which shall presume to speak a word by my name' (Deut. 28.20)—this applies to one who prophesies what he has not

---

[1] See also Num. R. 18.20.

[2] b. B.B. 119a, 120a; on Samuel's saying, b. B.B. 121a, Taʿanit 30b. See below, p. 233.

[3] b. Sanh. 99a.

[4] b. B.M. 30a, 33a.

heard. 'Which I have not commanded him to speak'—implying that which I did command his neighbor, hence, one who prophesies what has not been told to him personally. 'Or that shall speak in the name of other gods'—connoting one who prophesies in the name of idols. And then it is written, 'Even that prophet shall die' and every unspecified death sentence in the Torah requires strangulation.

(b. Sanh. 89a)

The curses of Deut. 28 were interpreted not in eschatological, but in familial terms by Rav:

Thy sons and thy daughters shall be given unto another people (Deut. 28.32)—R. Ḥanan b. Rava in the name of Rav said, This refers to one's stepmother.

'I will provoke them with a vile nation' (Deut. 32.21)—R. Hanan b. Rava in the name of Rav said, This refers to a bad wife, the amount of whose *ketuvah* is large.

(b. Yev. 63b)

The same interpretation of Deut. 28.32 is given in Rav's name by R. Jeremiah b. Abba.[1] On Deut. 28.59, Rav's comment was as follows:

The Torah is destined to be forgotten in Israel, because it is said: 'Then the Lord will make plagues wonderful' (Deut. 28.59). Now I do not know what this wonder is, but when it is said, 'Therefore behold I will proceed to do a wonderful work among these people, even a wonderful work and a wonder, and the wisdom of their wise men shall perish' (Is. 29.14), it follows that this wonder refers to the Torah.

(b. Shab. 138b)

The tendency of Rav to interpret the curses in this-worldly terms, applying them to family affairs and to study of the Torah, is seen in the following as well:

'And it shall come to pass when many evils and troubles are come upon them' (Deut. 31.21)—What means 'evils and troubles'? Rav said, Evils which become antagonists of one another, as the wasp and the scorpion, and Samuel said, This refers to one who furnishes money to the poor only in the hour of his extremity. 'Then my anger shall be kindled against them in that day, and I will forsake them and hide my face from them' (Deut. 31.17). R. Bardela b. Tavyumi in the name of Rav said, To whomever 'hiding of the face' does not apply is not one of them [Israel] and to whomever 'and they shall be devoured' does not apply, is not one of them.

(b. Hag. 5a)

---

[1] b. Ber. 56a.

Here Rav interpreted the verse to mean that sharing in the suffering of Israel is the requirement for participation in its eventual redemption. On Deut. 29.18, we find still another sermon on family affairs:

> R. Judah in the name of Rav said, One who marries his daughter to an old man, or takes a wife for his infant son, or returns a lost article to a Kuti, concerning him Scripture says, 'That he may bless himself in his heart saying I shall have peace though I talk in the imagination of mine heart to add drunkness to thirst, the Lord will not spare him' (Deut. 29.18).
>
> (b. Sanh. 76b)

Since these sayings quite manifestly refer to phenomena observed and condemned by Rav and Samuel, it stands to reason that many of their exegeses were prompted by contemporary problems. At the same time, we recall that Rav and Samuel interpreted Lev. 26 and Deut. 28 with reference to the suffering of Israel in the time of Ahasueros and Haman. Rav's interpretation of the curses of Deut. 28 in terms of family relationships is consistent with the view, suggested above (p. 59-60) that he read these chapters from the perspective of contemporary affairs. Thus, just as "thy life shall hang in doubt" applied to the time of Ahasueros/Ardashir, so bad stepmothers, unworthy wives with large marriage-settlements, and other commonplace punishments would follow the violation of the commandments, but the sins were similarly mundane, such as niggardliness, inhumane marriage-arrangements, and the like. The apocalyptic force of the Deuteronomic curses was thus vitiated, neither the sins nor the punishments fitting the cosmic dimensions of the original.

II. THE PROPHETIC BOOKS

Rav explained the requirement, stated to Joshua, to circumcize Israel a second time, holding that the commandment given to Abraham was not completely explicated according to all its requirements.[1] Apart from this saying, we have a connected comment on Joshua 7, the story of 'Achan:

> 'And the Lord said to Joshua, get thee up' (Joshua 7.10). R. Shila explained this, 'the Holy One said to him, Thine is greater than theirs is, for I commanded, 'And it shall be' ... (Deut. 27.4) .... But when he had gone out Rav set up his interpreter to speak for him, and expounded, 'As the Lord commanded Moses his servant, so did Moses command Joshua, and so did Joshua, he left nothing undone

---

[1] b. Yev. 71b.

of all that the Lord commanded Moses' (Joshua 11.15). What then do the words, 'Get thee up' teach? The Lord said to him, Thou hast brought upon them, and for that reason, he said to him with reference to Ai, 'And thou shalt do to Ai and her king as thou didst to Jericho and her king' (Joshua 8.2).

'The sons of Zeraḥ, Zimri' (Joshua 7.24). Rav and Samuel, One said, the real name was ʿAchan, and he was called Zimri because he acted like Zimri [Joshua 7.24, compare Numbers 25.14] and the other, His real name was Zimri, and he was called ʿAkhan because he wound the sins of Israel about him like a serpent. 'And they burned them with fire, and I saw among them spoil a goodly mantle of *shinar* and 200 shekels of silver' (Joshua 7.21). Rav said, a silk mantle, and Samuel said it was a cloak dyed with alum.

(b. Sanh. 44a-b)

Rav described Samson as follows:

And the child grew and the Lord blessed him (Judges 13.24)— Wherewith? R. Judah in the name of Rav said, Not with his physique, which was like that of other men, but with his manly strength which was like a fastflowing stream. 'And Samson called unto the Lord and said, O Lord remember me I pray thee and strengthen me I pray thee that I may be at once avenged of the Philistines for my two eyes' (Judges 16.28). Rav said, Samson spoke before the Holy One blessed be He, Sovereign of the World, Remember on my behalf the twenty years that I judged Israel, and never did I order anyone to carry my staff from one place to another.

(b. Sotah 10a)[1]

In the exposition of texts, Samuel and Rav disagreed from time to time on the basis of Rav's Palestinian interpretations. One such instance is clearly as follows:

'But wilt thou give unto thy handmaid a man-child' (I Sam. 1.25). What is meant by man-child? Rav said, A man among men. Samuel said, Seed that will anoint two men, namely, Saul and David. (R. Yoḥanan said, Seed that will be equal to two men, namely, Moses and Aaron).

(b. Ber. 31b)

At first appearance, this passage yields nothing particularly "Palestinian." However, the passage continues that Rav Dimi, in a later period, brought a Palestinian version to Babylonia which explained the passage meaning, not too tall, or too short, or lame, or too wise, or too foolish, thus the equivalent to Rav's "man among men," rather than to Samuel's messianic interpretation.

---

[1] This saying recalls Rav's comments on the proper attitude of a judge.

Rav explained 'And the kine took the straight way' (I Sam. 6.12) [vayishsharnah] to mean, 'they directed their faces toward the ark and rendered song,'[1] as in the Dura painting.

In the 'Chapter of a King' (I Samuel 8), Samuel held that all which is set out therein is permitted to a king, while Rav held that it was intended only to inspire the people with awe, for it is written 'Thou shalt not in any wise set him king over thee" (Deut. 17.15), meaning, 'His awe should be over thee.'[2]

Saul was not highly regarded by Samuel:

> R. Huna said in the name of Samuel, The real famine ought to have come in the days of Saul, and not in the days of David, but since Saul was but the stump of a sycamore tree, and would have been unable to withstand it, the Holy One blessed be He deferred it, and brought it in the time of David, who, since he was a scion of an olive tree, was able to withstand it.
>
> (Ruth R. 1.4)

Saul was punished, according to Rav, because he was too weak to secure his own honor:

> R. Judah in the name of Rav said, Why was Saul punished? Because he forewent the honor due to himself, as it is said, 'But certain base fellows said, How shall this man save us, and they despised him and brought him no present, but he was as one that held his peace' (I Sam. 10.27). And it is written immediately following, 'Then Nahash the Ammonite came up and encamped against Jabesh Gilead' (I Sam. 11.1).
>
> (b. Yoma' 22b)

Those who committed unjust deeds under Saul were eventually punished:

> R. Judah in the name of Rav said, Why was Abner punished? Because he should have protested to Saul [regarding the slaughter of the priests of Nob, I Sam. 22.18] and did not [see II Samuel 3.33].
>
> (b. Sanh. 20a)

Those who were, on the contrary, kind to David were rewarded:

> 'And it came to pass after the ten days that the Lord smote Nabal' (I Sam. 25.38). How come these ten days here? R. Judah in the name

---

[1] b. A.Z. 24b. Compare Scholem, *Jewish Gnosticism*, 20-31, "The Merkabah Hymns and the Song of the Kine in a Talmudic Passage", in which Scholem shows that the song of the kine cited by R. Isaac b. Napha is reminiscent of the Hekhalot hymns. Note also the important pictorial representation of the incident in the Dura synagogue.

[2] b. Sanh. 20b. Note also b. Shab. 55b, Rav said, neither Phinehas nor Ḥophni sinned.

of Rav said, They correspond to the ten dishes which Nabal gave to the servants of David.

(b. R.H. 18a)

David's life was exposited by the early 'Amora'im in several dimensions. First of all, the actual texts were expounded, as we shall see. Second, many of the Psalms, believed to have been composed by David, were studied as sources revealing the relationship between God and David. Finally, David was regarded as the prototype of the Talmudic sage (see below, Section iv). In the first category is the following:

> 'And there went out a champion (*benayim*) out of the camp of the Philistines' (I Sam. 17.4). What does *benayim* mean? Rav said, That he was built up [*mebunneh*] without blemish. Samuel said, That he was the middle [*benoni*] of his brothers. The School of R. Shila said, He was made like a building.

(b. Sotah 42b)

A similar kind of philological inquiry relates to the earlier story of the Ammonites and Shovah. The name appears as Sho*b*ah (II Sam. 10.16) and Sho*f*ah (I Chron. 16.16). On this disparity, we have the following:

> Rav and Samuel, one held that he name was Shofah, but he was called Shovah because he was made like a dove cot. The other said, he name was Shovah, and was called Shofah because who ever beheld him was [through terror] poured out [nishpakh] before him like an ewer.

(b. Sotah 42b)

Other comments were more homiletical:

> R. Judah in the name of Rav said: All the curses with which David cursed Joab were fulfilled in David's own descendents . . . .

(b. Sanh. 48b)

This saying is spelled out in full with appropriate citations. Still other remarks were biographical:

> R. Judah in the name of Rav said, David had four hundred children, all born of 'yefot to'ar' (Deut. 21.10-14), and all with their hair trimmed in front and locks growing long, and all sat in golden chariots and went at the head of armies, and they were the 'strong men of the house of David.'

(b. Qid. 7b)[1]

---

[1] See also b. Sanh. 48b, 21a, Tamar was the daughter of a 'yefat to'ar'.

On the occasion of the sin against Tamar (II Sam. 13.19), the decree was issued against permitting a man to be alone with a woman, whether unmarried or married.[1]

Most frequently, however, Rav created full speeches appropriate to scenes from David's life, in the manner of classical historians. For example, as to the meaning of (II Sam. 15.14) 'Arise and let us flee, for else none of us shall escape from Absalom, make speed to depart, lest he overtake us suddenly, and bring down evil upon us and smite the city with the edge of the sword,' Rav said:

> David meant, 'Absalom will bring down the evil of death upon us. We are like the inhabitants of a city condemned to be smitten with the edge of the sword.'
>
> (Midrash on Psalms 3.3, ed. Braude 1.51)

The story of David's adulterous relationship with Bath Sheba was embellished with the following theological details:

> R. Judah in the name of Rav said: One should never bring himself to the test, since David king of Israel did so and fell. He said to Him: Lord of the Universe, Why do we say [in prayer], 'God of Abraham, God of Isaac, and God of Jacob' but not, the God of David? He replied, They were tried by me, but you were not. Then he replied, Lord of the Universe examine and try me, as it is written 'Examine me O Lord and try me' (Ps. 26.1). He answered, I will test you and yet grant you a special privilege, for I did not inform them [about their trial] yet I inform you that I will try you in a matter of adultery. Straightway 'And it came to pass in an eventide that David arose from off his bed . . .' (II Sam. 11.2).
>
> (b. Sanh. 107a)

Likewise David was ordered by God to avenge the priests of Nob:

> 'And Ishbi-Benob, which was of the sons of the giant . . . thought to have slain David' (II Sam. 21.16). What is meant by 'And Ishbi-be-Nob'? R. Judah in the name of Rav said, A man who came on account of Nob. For the Holy One, blessed be He, had said to David, How long will this crime be hidden in thy hand [unpunished]. Through you, Nob, the city of priests, was massacred; through you, Doeg the Edomite was banished. Through you, Saul and his three sons were slain. Would you rather your line to end, or be delivered to the enemy's hand? He replied, Lord of the World, I would rather be delivered into the enemy's hand than that my line should end. One day, when he (David) ventured forth to Sekhor Bizzae, Satan appeared before him in the guise of a deer. He shot arrows at him, but did not reach him, and was thus inveigled into the land of the Philistines. When Ishbi-

---

[1] Thus ascribing a more recent law to biblical times.

Benob spied him, he exclaimed, It is he who slew my brother Goliath. So he bound him, doubled him up, and cast him under an olive press, but a miracle was wrought, and the ground softened under him, and hence it is written, 'Thou hast enlarged my steps under me, that my feet did not slip.' (Ps. 18.37).

(b. Sanh. 95a)[1]

Rav's story goes on to tell how David was saved by Abishai son of Zeruah, who did so by pronouncing the divine name. Likewise David was smitten with leprosy for six months:

R. Judah in the name of Rav said: Six months was David smitten with leprosy [in punishment for the sin of Bath Sheba]. The Shekhinah deserted him and the Sanhedrin held aloof from him. 'He was smitten with leprosy' as it is written, 'Purge me with hyssop and I shall be clean, wash me and I shall be whiter than snow' (Ps. 51.9). The Shekhinah deserted him, as it is written, 'Restore unto me the joy of thy salvation and uphold me with thy free spirit' (Ps. 51.14). And the Sanhedrin kept aloof from him, as it is written, 'Let those that fear thee turn unto me and those that have known thy testimonies' (Ps. 119.79). [How do we know that it was for six months? Because it is written, 'And the days that David reigned over Israel were forty years: seven years he reigned in Hebron, thirty three years he reigned in Jerusalem' (I Kings 2.11) while elsewhere it is written, 'In Hebron reigned he over Judah seven years and six months' (II Sam. 5.5). Thus these six months are not counted, proving that he was smitten with leprosy.] He prayed to him, Lord of the Universe, Forgive me that sin. 'It is forgiven thee'. Then show me a token for good, that they which hate me may see it and be ashamed, 'because thou Lord hast helped me and comforted me' (Ps. 86.17). He replied, In thy lifetime I will not make it known, but in the lifetime of thy son Solomon. When Solomon built the Temple, he wished to take the ark into the Holy of Holies, but the gates cleaved to each other. He uttered twenty-four psalms but was not answered. He further prayed, 'Lift up your head o Ye gates and be ye lifted up ye everlasting doors.' (Ps. 24.7 f). And it is said, 'Lift up your heads.' Still he was not answered. But on praying, 'O Lord God, turn not away the face of thine anointed, remember the mercies of David thy servant' (II Chron. 6.42) he was immediately answered. In that hour the faces of David's enemies turned [black] as the bottom of a pot, and all Israel knew that the Holy One blessed be He had forgiven him that sin.

(b. Sanh. 107a)[2]

David's physical prowess was frequently remarked upon. Even during his illness, he fulfilled the conjugal rights [of his eighteen wives],[3] and in his old age he cohabited with Bath Sheba thirteen

---

[1] See also b. Sanh. 104a, Midrash on Psalms 18, ed. Braude I, 263.
[2] Also b. Yoma' 22b, b. Shab. 30a, b. M.Q. 9a.
[3] b. Sanh. 107a.

times in one night.[1] As the progenitor of the Messiah, David's life was examined carefully, and he was defended in every instance, except in the matter of Uriah the Hittite.[2] Rav and Samuel debated on whether he paid heed to slander or not.[3] On this account, according to Rav, great tragedies happened:

> R. Judah in Rav's name said, When David said to Mephiboshet, Thou and Ziba divide the land, a heavenly echo came forth and declared to him, Rehoboam and Jeroboam shall divide the kingdom. R. Judah in the name of Rav said, Had not David paid heed to slander, the kingdom of the house of David would not have been divided, Israel would not have engaged in idolatry, and we should not have been exiled from our country.
>
> (b. Shab. 56b)

Further, Rav interpreted many psalms in terms of David's life:

> R. Judah in Rav's name said, What is meant by the verse, 'Lord make me to know my end and the measure of my days what it is, let me know how frail I am' (Ps. 39.5). David said before the Holy One, blessed be he, Lord of the Universe, 'Lord make me know mine end'. It is a decree before Me, he replied, that the end of a mortal is not made known. 'And the measure of my days, what it is'—It is a decree before me that a person's span of life is not made known. 'Let me know how frail I am.' Said he, You will die on the Sabbath. Let me die on the first day of the week, he replied. The reign of your son Solomon shall already have become due, and one reign may not overlap another even by a hairbreadth. Then let me die on the eve of the Sabbath, 'For a day in thy courts is better than a thousand'. He replied, Better to Me is the one day that you sit and study Torah than the thousand burnt-offerings which your son Solomon is destined to sacrifice before me on the altar. Now every Sabbath day he would sit and study all day. On the day that his soul was to be at rest, the angel of death stood before him, but could not prevail because Torah did not cease from his mouth. What shall I do to him, he said. Now there was a garden before his house, so the angel of death went, ascended, and sat in the trees. David went out to see. As he was ascending the ladder, it broke under him. Thereupon he became silent and his soul had repose. Then Solomon sent to the school house. My father is dead and lying in the sun and the dogs of my father's house are hungry, what shall I do? They sent back, Cut up a carcass and place it before the dogs [to feed them, on the Sabbath] and as for thy father, put a loaf of bread or a child upon him and carry him away. Then did Solomon well say, 'For a living dog is better than a dead lion'.
>
> (b. Shab. 30a)[4]

---

[1] b. Sanh. 22a, re I Kings 1.5.
[2] b. Shab. 56a.
[3] *Ibid.*
[4] See also Koh. R. 5.20.2.

(Other such treatments of Psalms are found.[1]) David was permitted to see the destruction of both Temples:

> R. Judah in the name of Rav said: What is meant by the verse, 'By the rivers of Babylonia there we sat down, yes we wept when we remembered Zion' (Ps. 137.1). This indicated that the Holy One blessed be He showed David the destruction of both the first and second temples. Of the first it is written, 'By the rivers of Babylonia there we sat', and of the second it is written, 'Remember o Lord against the children of Edom the day of Jerusalem.'
>
> (b. Git. 57b)[2]

The flight of Joab to the Temple was explained by Rav. He erred in thinking that the tent would afford protection (I Kings 2.2) but only the roof of the altar affords asylum, and he took hold of the horns, while only the altar of the Temple in Jerusalem does, and he had caught hold of the altar at Shiloh.[3]

The life of Solomon provided the Amoraim with numerous sermons. Like David, he was regarded as a source of legal enactments, a fully rabbinic figure:

> R. Judah in the name of Samuel said, When Solomon ordained the laws of *'eruv* and the washing of the hands, a *bat kol* issued forth and problaimed: 'My son, if thy heart be wise, my heart will be glad, even mine' (Prov. 23.15), and furthermore it is said in Scripture, 'My son, be wise and make my heart glad that I may answer him that taunteth me.'
>
> (b. 'Eruv. 21b)

The two events in Solomon's life which attracted most comment were, first, his building of the Temple, and, second, his marriage of foreign wives. The building of the Temple entailed numerous miracles, as we have already noted in connection with David. The cherubim stood, though there was no room for their bodies.[4] Further, the Temple on earth was modeled after one in heaven:

> 'And Solomon sent to Hyram king of Tyre saying, Behold I am about to build a house for the name of the Lord my God to dedicate it to him, and to burn before him incense of sweet spices . . . This is an ordinance forever to Israel' (II Chron. 2.2-3). R. Giddal in the name of Rav said, The words 'This is an ordinance for ever' allude to the

---

[1] See b. Hag. 12b for Ps. 148. 7-8.
[2] b. Git. 57b, Midrash on Psalms 137.1, ed. Braude II, 330. On Ps. 23.3, see Braude I, 333. Also Midrash on Psalms 65.3, Braude I, 531.
[3] b. Mak. 12a, y. Mak. 2.6.
[4] b. B.B. 99a.

altar built in heaven, beside which Michael the great guardian angel
stands and brings an offering . . .

(b. Men. 110a)[1]

Hyram was execrated by Rav:

R. Judah in the name of Rav said, The Holy One said to Hyram
king of Tyre, At the creation I looked upon thee [observing your
future arrogance] and created therefore the excretory organs of man.

(b. B.B. 75a)

Solomon himself was regarded as the archetype of the misguided
ruler. He was permitted to act contrary to the law, but was severely
punished:

'I said of laughter, it is mad' (Koh. 2.2). How mixed is laughter!
For R. Aḥa said in the name of Samuel: For three acts [of Solomon]
the attribute of Justice allowed to succeed for a time, but in the end
was confounded and confused. It is written, 'Neither shall he multiply
wives to himself' (Deut. 17.17), and yet 'He had seven hundred wives,
princesses, and three hundred concubines' (I Kings 11.3). It is written
'He shall not multiply horses to himself' (Deut. 17.16), and yet
'Solomon had forty stalls of horses' (I Kings 5.6). It is written 'Neither
shall he greatly multiply to himself silver and gold' (Deut. 17.17) yet
'The king made silver to be in Jerusalem as stones' (I Kings 10.27).

(Koh. R. 2.2,3)

As a result, it was believed that Solomon was deposed, and Rav
and Samuel debated on whether he recovered the throne or not,
for the tone of Kohelet would indicate that all he had left at the end
of his life were bitter memories.[2] Rav and Samuel interpreted I Kings
5.4 to emphasize how Solomon, who had formerly reigned over the
whole world, in the end reigned over himself alone:

'For he had dominion over all the region on this side of the river
from Tifsah even to Gaza' (I Kings 5.4). Rav and Samuel, One says
that Tifsah was on one end of the world, and Gaza on the other, and
the other said, They were beside one another, and just as he reigned
over these, so did he reign over the whole world.

(b. Sanh. 20b)[3]

Samuel reported that in the list of those who have no portion in
the world to come, it was desired to include Solomon, but David
appeared and prevented it:

---

[1] Midrash on Psalms 134.1, ed. Braude II, p. 321.
[2] Midrash on Psalms 78, ed. Braude II, 35-6. b. Git. 68b, on Koh. 2.10. See
also b. Sanh. 20b.
[3] Compare Num. R. 13.14, and see p. 61, above.

Who drew up this list? Rav said, It was the men of the Great Assembly who drew it up. R. Judah in the name of Samuel said, They wanted to include Solomon among these. A figure with the features of David came, and prostrated itself beseechingly before them, but they paid no attention to it. A fire came out from the interior of the Holy of Holies and flared up all around them, but they paid no attention to it. A heavenly voice went forth, and said to them, 'Seest thou a man diligent in his business? He shall stand before kings' (Prov. 22.29). The man who gave priority to my house over his own, and moreover built my house in seven years while his own took thirteen, shall such a man 'stand before mean men?' No, he shall stand before kings. But they gave no heed to it, and so it came and said to them, 'Shall his recompense be as thou wilt? That thou shouldst reject, or that thou shouldst choose, and not I. What knowest thou to speak?' (Job 34.33). Forthwith they refrained from including him among them.

(b. Sanh. 104b)[1]

The comments of Rav and Samuel on the kings to 586 B.C.E. were brief and sporadic. They did not produce coherent commentaries, except possibly on II Kings 2-4, if the following are merely fragments of a longer commentary:

'And he looked behind him and saw them and cursed them in the name of the Lord' (II Kings 2.24). Rav said, He actually looked upon them, [as it has been taught. R. Simeon b. Gamaliel says, Wherever the sages set their eyes, there is either death or calamity.] Samuel said, He saw that their mothers had all conceived them on the Day of Atonement [!].

(b. Sotah 40b)

'And there came forth two she-bears out of the wood and tore forty-two children of them' (II Kings 2.24). Rav and Samuel, One said, It was a miracle, and the other, it was a miracle within a miracle.

(b. Sotah 46b)

'He took his eldest son that should have reigned' (II Kings 3.27). Rav and Samuel, one said, he offered him to God, the other, to a heathen deity.

(b. Sanh. 39b)

'Let us make I pray thee a little chamber on the roof' (II Kings 4.10). Rav and Samuel, one says It was an open upper chamber and they put a roof in it, the other, it was a verandah and they divided it into two.

(b. Ber. 10b)

'A Holy man' (II Kings 4.9). How did she know this? Rav and Samuel, one said, Because she never saw a fly pass by his table. The

---

[1] Compare Num. R. 14.1.

other said, she spread a sheet of linen over his bed and never saw a nocturnal pollution on it.

(b. Ber. 10b)

One held there was actually a forest, but no bears, and the other says that both the forest and the bears were created on the spot.

The above passages have in common a recurrent form: a verse, a question [or, an implied question], and answers in the name of Rav and Samuel. Since in the earlier instances of a connected commentary, it is quite clear that the process of transmission and the form were both unchanging (mostly, R. Judah reported the several sayings), it seems reasonable to suppose that here, on fairly continguous verses, we have an unchanging form, and therefore, a continuous commentary. For the rest, we have elucidations of specific verses:

> 'Then he brought out the king's son and put upon him the *nezer* and the testimony' (II Kings 11.12). *Nezer*, that is crown. What is testimony? R. Judah in the name of Rav, It was a testimony to the house of David that whoever was eligible for the throne fitted into the crown, but it would not fit anyone who was ineligible.
>
> (b. A.Z. 44a)

This comment is partly philological, and partly homiletical, as is indicated by Rav's comment that the meaning of 'exalted himself' in the boast of Adonijah the son of Haggit was that he thought the crown would fit him, while it did not.[1]

Ahab son of Omri enjoyed all the good things of this world, for, Rav said:

> The world was only created for Ahab, son of Omri, and for R. Hanina b. Dosa, for Ahab in this world, and for R. Hanina in the world to come.
>
> (b. Ber. 61b)

Elijah was fed by ravens, who brought him meat from the slaughter-house of Ahab,[2] according to Rav, which proves, according to Samuel, that an Israelite apostate in respect of idolatry may slaughter meat for Israelites.[3] On Hosea b. Elah, Rav said:

> R. Kahana and R. Assi said to Rav, It is written of Hosea son of Elah 'And he did that which was evil in the sight of the Lord yet not as the kings of Israel' (II Kings 17.2). And it is also written, 'Against him came up Shalmaneser, king of Assyria' (II Kings 17.4). [How so?]

---

[1] b. A.Z. 44a.

[2] b. Sanh. 113a, Hul. 5a. Note Rav's concern for strict observance of these laws, p. 130-131.

[3] With reference to Jehoshaphat, II Chron. 18.2.

He replied to them, Jeroboam had stationed guards on the roads to prevent the Israelites from going up [to Jerusalem] for the festivals, and Hosea disbanded them, but for all that the Israelites did not go up for the festivals. Thereupon God decreed that for those years during which the Israelites had not gone up for the festival, they should go a corresponding number into captivity.

(b. Git. 88a)[1]

The siege of Sennacherib was overwhelming. Rav said:

The wicked Sennacherib advanced against them with a force consisting of 45,000 princes, each enthroned in a golden chariot and accompanied by his ladies and harlots, 80,000 warriors in a coat of mail, 60,000 swordsmen of the front line, and the rest calvalrymen. A similar host attacked Abraham and a like force will accompany Gog and Magog.

(b. Sanh. 95b)

Whether he was wise in saying (II Kings 18.32) 'until I come and take you away to a land like your own land' was debated by Rav and Samuel; one held that he was wise, because, had he said, a land better than yours, they would have replied, you lie. The other held he was foolish, because if the land of exile would be no better than their own, what inducement did he offer?[2]

Hezekiah figured in two passages, first, because he was reputed to have intercalated Nisan in Nisan,[3] second, because of his display of his treasuries:

'And Hezekiah was glad of them' (Isaiah 39.2). Rav said, What is meant by 'the house of his precious things'? His wife, who mixed drinks for them. Samuel said, He showed them his treasury. R. Yohanan said, He showed them weapons which could destroy other weapons.

(b. Sanh. 104a)

Josiah's saying, 'Bear me away, for I am sore wounded' (II Chron. 35.21) was exposited as follows:

What is meant by 'for I am sore wounded'? R. Judah in the name of Rav said, This teaches that his whole body was perforated like a sieve.

(b. Ta'anit 22b)[4]

As to Zedekiah, Rav gave the following sermon:

---

1 See also Lam. R. Proem 23.
2 b. Sanh. 94b.
3 b. Ber. 10b.
4 Tanhuma, ed. Buber II, 84, and b. Sanh. 48b.

'Woe unto him that giveth his neighbors drink, that puttest thy venom thereto, and makest him drunken also, that thou mayest look on their nakedness' (Hab. 2.15). Woe to him that giveth drink—this is Nebuchadnezzar. 'His neighbor'—This is Zedekiah. Said the Holy One, blessed be He to him, Ah wretch, is he not a king like thee, is he not a shepherd like thee? That puttest thy venom (*hamateka*) thereto— why doest thou level charges against him in thy wrath (hamateka)? For Nebuchadnezzar said to him, Had you rebelled against me but not against your God, it would have been for your God to stand by you. Had you rebelled against your God and not rebelled against me, it would have been for me to stand by you. But you rebelled against both your God and me, and so it is written, 'And he [Zedekiah] also rebelled against King Nebuchadnezzar, who had made him swear by God.' (II Chron. 36.13).

(Esther R. 3.1)

Nebuchadnezzar, for his part, wished to engage in sex relations with Zedekiah, but was shamed into not doing so. He went to Gehenna.[1]

As to the Book of Chronicles, Rav held that it was given only for midrashic exposition,[2] and we have noted above some of the uses to which he put it.[3]

The comments of Rav and Samuel on the literature of classical prophecy took two forms, first of all, expositions of the meaning of a given verse, and second the development of homilies making use of, but not directly expositing, Scriptures. Of the former type are the following:

'And the Lord will lay bare (*ye-'areh*) their secret parts.' (Isaiah 3.17) Rav and Samuel, one said, This means that they were poured out like a cruse, and the other, their openings became like a forest. R. Judah in the name of Rav said, The men of Jerusalem were vulgar. One would say to his neighbor On what did you dine today, on well-kneaded bread or on bread that is not well-kneaded, on white wine or on dark, on a broad couch or on a narrow couch, with a good companion or with a poor one [the whole metaphor being sexual].

(b. Shab. 62b)

R. Hananel in the name of Rav said, Three divisions of ministering angels sing praises daily, one proclaims, 'Holy,' the other proclaims, 'Holy,' and the third proclaims, 'Holy is the Lord of Hosts' (Is. 6.3).

(b. Hul. 91b)

---

[1] b. Shab. 149b.
[2] Lev. R. 1.3.
[3] See b. Git. 62a, Men. 110a, B.B. 91b for examples.

How many were left [of the Assyrians]? Rav said, Ten, as it is written, And the rest of the trees of his forest that a child may write them. (Is. 10.10). What figure can a child write? Ten. Samuel said, Nine, as it is written, 'Yet gleaning the grapes shall be left in it' (Is. 17.6).

(b. Sanh. 95b)[1]

'And Elam bore the quiver' (Is. 22.6)—Rav said, A receptacle for arrows. 'With troops of men, even horsemen, and Kir uncovered the shield'—this indicates that they demolished the walls of their houses and made them into barricades. 'And it came to pass, when thy choicest valleys were full of chariots' (Is. 22.7). Rav said, They were filled to the same extent as the depth of the ocean . . .

(Lam. R. Proem 24)

The second kind of treatment, of Isaiah as of other prophets, provided development of various scriptures, at the outset expository, but in fact homiletical:

'Then shall lambs feed as in their pasture (KDVRM)' (Is. 5.17). Menassia b. Jeremiah in the name of Rav interpreted, 'As was spoken about them'. What does, 'As was spoken about them' mean? R. Hananel in the name of Rav said, The righteous are destined to resurrect the dead, for here it is written, 'Then shall the lambs feed', while elsewhere it is written (Micah 7.14), 'Then shall Bashan and Gilead feed as in days of old.' Now Bashan means Elisha, who came from Bashan, as it is said, 'And Janai Shaphat in Bashan (I Chron. 5.12), while it is written 'Elisha the son of Shaphat is here' (II Kings 3.11). Again, Gilead refers to Elijah, as it is said, 'And Elijah the Tishbite who was of the settlers of Gilead said' (I Kings 17.1).

(b. Pes. 68a)

This elaborate *midrash* is intended to point out that just as Elijah and Elisha resurrected the dead, so *feeding* alludes metaphorically to resurrection of the dead, the lambs being the righteous people. In other instances, Rav interpreted such lessons as these: 'Exile is a greater hardship on men than on women,' (based on Isaiah 22.16[2]) and 'A woman is a shapeless lump who concludes a covenant only with him who transforms her into a vessel,' (based on Isaiah 54.5).[3] Likewise, the teaching of Isaiah (58.7), 'When thou seest the naked, that thou cover him' was debated:

R. Adda b. Ahava in the name of Rav and R. Yoḥanan differ on the interpretation of this Scripture. One says that careful inquiry

---

[1] See also y. Sotah 9.3.
[2] b. Sanh. 26b, Ket. 28a.
[3] b. Sanh. 22b.

should be made with regard to beggars who ask for clothing, but no inquiries should be made in regard to food. The other says that in regard to clothing no inquiries should be made, on account of the Covenant of Abraham.   (Lev. R. 34.14)

A proof text was provided by Rav to show that God is infinitely merciful:

> R. Samuel b. Unia in the name of Rav said: Whence is it deduced that a divine dispensation against a congregation is not sealed? Is not sealed! Surely it is written, 'For though thou wash thee with nitre . . . thine iniquity is marked before me' (Jer. 2.22, marked = sealed). But this is the question, Whence is it deduced that even if it has been sealed, it is torn up? From the text (Deut. 4.7) 'As the Lord our God is whensoever we call upon him.' But surely it is written 'Seek ye the Lord while he may be found' (Is. 55.6)? No contradiction is here, for the latter applies to an individual, while the former to a congregation.
> (b. Yev. 105a)[1]

The rabbis wondered why the Book of Deuteronomy was not submitted to Jeremiah, but rather to Ḥulda, for authentication (II Kings 22.14):

> If Jeremiah was there, how could she prophesy? The school of Rav in the name of Rav said, Ḥulda was a near relative of Jeremiah and he did not object to her doing so.
> (b. Meg. 14b)

Rav interpreted Jeremiah's bitter words in a lenient manner:

> 'For I am married unto you and I will take you one of a city and two of a family.' R. Kahana before Rav said, This is meant literally. Rav said to him, Their Master [God] is not pleased that you should say so of them, but say, One of a city shall benefit the entire city, and two of a family will benefit the entire family . . .
> (b. Sanh. 111a)

In a number of instances, he and Samuel interpreted Jeremiah's words to apply to contemporary situations. Thus he said:

> R. Isaac b. Samuel b. Marta in the name of Rav: 'I will punish all that oppress them' (Jer. 30.20)—Even the collectors of charity.
> (b. B.B. 8b)

> 'My heritage is become unto me as a lion in the forest, she has uttered her voice against me' (Jer. 12.8). Mar Zutra b. Tobiah in the name of Rav said, This refers to an unfit person who steps down before the ark as reader.   (b. Taʿanit 16b)[2]

---

[1] Compare b. R.H. 18a.
[2] See also b. Ned. 81a, cited above p. 177 n. 3.

In another case, Samuel derived a moral teaching, that even the voice of a woman may be source of lewdness, from of Jeremiah 3.9, 'From the *sound* of her harlotry.'[1]

Further expositions of the teachings of Jeremiah include the following:

> 'Their quiver (aspah) is an open sepulchre, they are all mighty men' (Jer. 5.16). Rav and Samuel (some say, R. ʾAmmi and R. ʾAssi), One said, at the time when they shot an arrow they made heaps upon heaps of corpses. The other said, At the time when they relieved themselves they made heaps upon heaps of excrement.
>
> (b. Sotah 42b)
>
> 'Weep sore for him that goeth away' (Jer. 22.10)—R. Judah in the name of Rav said, Weep for him who goes childless.
>
> (b. M.Q. 27b = b. B.B. 116a)
>
> 'To give you a future and a hope' (Jer. 29.11). R. Judah son of R. Samuel b. Shilat in the name of Rav said, By this is meant palm trees and flaxen garments.
>
> (b. Taʿanit 29a-b)
>
> 'And there was a fire burning in the ʾaḥ (brazier) burning before him' (Jer. 36.22). Rav said, A willow fire (aḥwana), and Samuel said, Logs kindled by a willow fire.
>
> (b. Shab. 20a)

Likewise with reference to Ezekiel, apart from the exposition of the Merkavah vision, the comments of the rabbis were mainly concerned with the exposition of isolated, generally ethically-oriented, verses. For example, what was the meaning of the *tav* which was to be written on the foreheads of the people (Ezek. 9.6)?

> Said Rav, *Taw* stands for *tiḥyeh* (thou shalt live) and *tamut*, (thou shalt die), and Samuel said, The *tav* denotes that the merit of the patriarchs is exhausted (*tamah*).   (b. Shab. 55a)[2]

Likewise, the dead whom Ezekiel revived were identified:

> Rav said, They were Ephraimites who counted (the years) to the end but erred therein, as it is written, 'And the sons of Ephraim.' (I Chron. 7.20), and it is written, 'And Ephraim their father mourned' (I Chron. 7.22). Samuel said, They were those who denied the resurrection, as it is written, 'Then he said unto me, Son of man' (Ezek. 37.11).   (b. Sanh. 92b)[3]

---

[1] Compare Rav on Jer. 17.27, An outbreak of fire occurs only in a place where there is desecration of the Sabbath.

[2] See also Lam. R. 2.1.3. See S. Lieberman, *Greek in Jewish Palestine*, 185-7.

[3] A veiled warning, according to Rav, not to calculate the time of the Messiah's arrival.

Several strange words were defined:

> 'They shall *poll* their heads' (Ezek. 44.9), R. Judah in the name of
> Samuel said, A unique manner of hairdressing.
>
> (b. Sanh. 22b)

> 'And the leaf thereof for healing' (Ezek. 47.12). Rav and Samuel
> differed on the meaning of *letrufah*, One said, it means 'to heal,' as
> 'to open the mouth of the dumb,' and the other said, it means 'to heal'
> as 'to open the womb of a barren woman.'
>
> (Midrash on Psalms 23.7)[1]

Further, a few legal dicta were derived from Ezekiel's teaching in
particular regarding mourning procedures, and proper sandals for
ḥaliẓah.[2] Likewise the following:

> And he did that which is not good among his people (Ezek. 18.18)
> Rav said, One who comes with power of attorney. Samuel said: One
> who buys a field about which there are disputes.
>
> (b. Shev. 31a)

Finally, we have the following homiletical observations:

> R. Judah in the name of Rav: Whosoever departs from the words of
> Torah is consumed by fire, for it is said, 'But I will set my face against
> thee.' (Ezek. 15.7).
>
> (b. B.B. 79a)

> Rav said, A sigh breaks down half of the human body, for it is
> said (Ezek. 21.11). 'Sigh therefore thou son of man with the breaking
> of thy loins and with bitterness shalt thou sigh' . . .
>
> (b. Ket. 61b)

The minor prophets likewise elicited comments which were mainly
of an homiletical or historical character. On Amos, for example, we
have the following:

> 'For lo, he that formeth the mountains . . . and declareth unto a
> man what his conversation was' (Amos 4.13). Rav said, Even the
> superfluous conversation between man and wife is declared to a
> person at the hour of his death . . .
>
> (b. Hag. 5b)[3]

> 'And annoint themselves with the chief ornaments' (Amos 6.6)
> R. Judah in the name of Samuel said, This refers to spikenard oil.
>
> (b. Shab. 62b)

---

[1] Ed. Braude I, 334. Compare Song R. 4.12.4.
[2] b. Yev. 102b.
[3] Compare b. Ber. 62a.

'So he went and took Gomer daughter of Diblaim' (Hosea 1.3). Rav said, That all satisfied upon her their lust. Daughter of Diblaim means, daughter of ill fame and daughter of a woman of ill fame. Samuel said, It means that she was a sweet in everyone's mouth as a cake of figs.

(b. Pes. 87b)

Rabbah b. R. Adda in the name of Rav said, He who takes a wife for the sake of money will have unworthy children, as it is said (Hosea 5.7), 'They have dealt treacherously . . .'

(b. Qid. 70a)

Finally, a historical question was answered by Rav on the basis of Hosea:

Since when has the merit of the patriarchs been exhausted? Rav said, Since the days of Hosea son of Beeri, for it written, 'And now will I discover her lewdness . . . and none shall deliver her' (Hosea 2.12: 'None' meaning, merit no longer has power to save). Samuel said, Since the days of Hazael, for it is said, 'And Hazael king of Syria opposed Israel all the days of Jehoahaz' (II Kings 13.22), and it is written, 'But the Lord was gracious unto them and had compassion upon them and would not destroy them neither cast he them from his presence' (II Kings 13.22-23)—until now.

(b. Shab. 55a)

Similarly, Micah's accusation (2.2) 'And they oppress a man and his house, even a man and his heritage,' was the basis of the following homiletical illustration by Rav:

A certain man once conceived a desire for the wife of his master, he being a carpenter's apprentice. Once his master wanted to borrow some money from him. He said to him, Send me your wife and I will lend her the money. So he sent his wife and she stayed three days with him. He then went to him for her. Where is my wife whom I sent to you, he asked. He replied, I sent her away at once but I heard that the youngsters played with her on the road. What shall I do, he said. If you listen to my advice, he replied, divorce her. But she has a large marriage settlement. Said the other, I will lend you money to give her for her *ketuvah*, so he went and divorced her, and the other went and married her. When the time for payment arrived and he was unable to pay him, the other said, Come and work off your debt with me. So they used to sit and eat and drink while he waited on them, and tears used to fall from his eyes and drop into their cups. From that hour the doom was sealed.

(b. Git. 58a)

Zechariah's saying, "Dreams speak falsely" (10.2) was cited by Samuel when he had a bad dream; when he had a good one, he would say, "Do dreams speak falsely, seeing that it is written (Num. 12.6), 'I do speak with him in a dream'."[1] The reference to thirty pieces of silver (Zech. 11.12) alludes according to Rav, to thirty mighty men, and to R. Yoḥanan, to thirty precepts [which gentiles will observe when the Messiah comes].[2] Rav likewise sought to justify the separation of women from men in the Temple, on the basis of Zech. 12.12:

> 'And the land shall mourn, every family apart, the family of the house of David apart, and their wives apart.' Is it not a *kal veḥomer*? In the future, when they shall be engaged in mourning and the Evil Inclination will have no power over them, nonetheless the Torah says, men separately and women separately, how much more so now when they are engaged in rejoicing and the Evil Inclination has sway over them.
>
> (b. Suk. 51b)

A few unrelated verses in Haggai and Malachi were also exposited:

> 'Greater shall be the glory of the latter house than the former' (Haggai 2.9). Rav and Samuel (or, R. Yoḥanan and R. Eleazar), one says it refers to size, the other to duration, and both are correct.
>
> (b. B.B. 3a)

> 'Judah hath dealt treacherously' (Malachi 2.11). Rav said, This refers to idolatry, 'and abomination is committed' refers to pederasty, 'and Judah hath profaned the holiness' refers to harlotry. 'And hath been intimate with the daughter of a strange god'—this refers to sexual relations with a heathen woman. Now this verse is followed by, 'The Lord will cut off men that doeth this' (Mal. 2.12). This means, if he is a scholar, he shall have none awakening among the sages, and none responding among the disciples, and if he is a priest, he shall have no son to offer an offering unto the Lord of Hosts.
>
> (b. Sanh. 82a)

Malachi's saying (3.10)—that there shall be more than enough means according to Rav, 'Until your lips grow weary from saying, It is enough.'[3]

III. The Writings

The Book of Psalms, which Rav used to call 'Hallelujah'[4] elicited both philological and homiletical comments. The authorship of the book interested Rav, who was drawn to historical questions:

---

[1] b. Ber. 55b.
[2] Gen. R. 98.9.
[3] b. Taʿanit 9a, y. Taʿanit 3.9.
[4] Midrash on Psalms 1.6, Braude I, 11.

Ten men composed the book of Psalms: Adam, Abraham, Moses, David, and Solomon—these are five. With regard to these five there is no difference of opinion. Who are the other five? Rav and R. Yoḥanan gave different answers. Rav said, Asaph, Heman, and Jeduthun, and the three sons of Koraḥ [counted as one] and Ezra. R. Yoḥanan said, Asaph, Heman, and Jedutuhun, are only one. Add to them the three sons of Koraḥ, and Ezra . . .

(Song of Songs R. 4.4.1)

Likewise, the authorship of Ps. 73 was debated:

Rav and Levi: One said it was by Asaph the son of Koraḥ, the other said it was Asaph . . . .

(Lev. R. 17.1)

The basis for the disagreement was verse 2, it being unclear whether it referred to a son of Koraḥ, who almost fell into Gehinnom with his father, or not. Likewise, the meaning of the word 'sela' was debated by Rav and Samuel.[1] Rav and R. Yosi differed on the meaning of Ps. 32.4, *leshaddi*;[2] Rav discussed the meaning of *gol* (Ps. 22.9);[3] and he offered a Greek etymology as well:

The sorrows of death encompassed me (afafuni) (Ps. 18.5): Rav said that it means 'I am seized (epiponos) by sorrows.'

(Midrash on Psalms 18.10, Braude I, 238)

For the rest, apart from the *midrashim* on David's conversations with God, cited above, the comments were mainly moralistic. There was no sustained commentary or a continuous discussion by the 'Amora'im of this period on a given psalm. Rather we find teachings such as the following:

R. Adda b. Mattena in the name of Rav said, In the place where there is rejoicing there should also be trembling. (based on Ps. 2.11).

(b. Ber. 30b)

When redemption comes to Israel, Jacob will rejoice in it more than any of the other patriarchs, hence it is said (Ps. 14.7), 'When the Lord bringeth back the fortunes of his people, then shall Jacob rejoice and Israel shall be glad.'

(Midrash on Psalms 14, Braude I, 188)

Rav said: The dead is not forgotten until after twelve months, as it says (Ps. 31.31). 'I am forgotten as a dead man out of mind, I am like a lost vessel' [a thing is not given up for lost until after twelve months].

(b. Ber. 58b)

---

[1] *Ibid.* 139.5, Braude II 344.
[2] *Ibid.* 32.3, Braude I, 404.
[3] *Ibid.* 22.22, Braude I, 317.

R. Amram in the name of Rav said, 'Happy is the man that feareth the Lord' (Ps. 112.1)—the man, but not the woman? It means, happy is he who repents while he is still a man.

(b. A.Z. 19a)

R. Zutra b. Tobiah in the name of Rav said, What is meant by the verse (Ps. 144.12), 'We whose sons are as plants grown up in their youth, whose daughters are as corner pillars carved after the fashion of the temple.' 'We whose sons are as plants'—alludes to the young men of Israel who have not tasted the taste of sin. 'Whose daughters' alludes to the virgins of Israel who reserve themselves [seal their openings] for their husbands, and thus it is said (Zech. 9.15), 'And they shall be filled like basins.'

(b. Pes. 87a)

Other passages were expounded in a similar manner.[1]

Another kind of *midrash* elucidated not words or the obvious meaning of verses, but rather either juxtaposed Scriptures, frequently chosen from Psalms, to harmonize apparent contradictions, or, similarly, explained Scriptural juxtapositions of seemingly unrelated things, as the following:

'Man and cattle thou preservest, Lord' (Ps. 36.7)—R. Judah in the name of Rav said, This verse refers to those who are wise in understanding and conduct themselves humbly like cattle.

(b. Ḥul. 5b)

R. Judah said, Rav pointed out the following contradictions: It is written (Ps. 32.1) 'Happy is he whose transgression is covered, whose sin is pardoned' and it is written (Prov. 28.13), 'He that covereth his transgression shall not prosper.' There is no difficulty, the one speaks of sins that have become known, the other of sins that have not become known.

(b. Yoma' 86b)

As elsewhere, Rav also elucidated one Scripture by means of another one:

Rav said, He who visits the sick shall be delivered from the punishments of Gehenna, as it is written, 'Blessed is he that considereth the poor, the Lord will deliver him in the day of evil' (Ps. 41.2). And the poor (*dal*) means none but the sick, as it is written, 'He will cut me off from pining sickness (*midalah*)' (Is. 38.12) . . .

(b. Ned. 40a)

The Book of Proverbs, particularly beloved of the rabbis, was cited frequently with reference to study of the Torah, but yielded also the following moralistic interpretation:

---

[1] y. Shab. 2.6, not to sit in an unstable building; Midrash on Psalms 122.4, Braude II, 301; *ibid*. 137.6, Braude II, 336, etc.

'Hand to hand he shall not escape punishment (Prov. 16.5). Rav said, Whoever has intercourse with a married woman, though he proclaimed the Holy One blessed be he to be possessor of heaven and earth as did our father Abraham, of whom it is written 'I have lifted up mine hand' (Gen. 14.22)—he will not escape the punishment of Gehenna.

(b. Sotah 4b)

Similarly, the book of Job, which provided many verses to be explained in terms of study of the Torah, yielded only a few other comments, mostly of an expository nature. Rav did not approve of Job:

'Oh that my vexation were but weighed and my calamity laid in the balances together' (Job 6.2)—Rav said, Dust should be put in the mouth of Job, because he makes himself the colleague of heaven. 'I made a covenant with mine eyes, how then should I look upon a maid' (Job 9.33)—Rav said, Dust should be placed in the mouth of Job, he refrained from looking at other men's wives, but Abraham did not even look at his own, as it is written, 'Behold now I know that thou are a fair woman to look upon' (Gen. 12.11).

(b. B.B. 16a)

Rav provided expositions of two verses, Job 2.11, to teach that all three friends entered together through one gate, though they lived far away from each other,[1] and Job 39.26 to prove that the south wind is most violent, but is kept in check by the Son of the Hawk.[2] Likewise one homily emerged:

R. Judah in the name of Rav said, He who starves himself in years of famine escapes unnatural death, as it is said (Job 5.20), 'In famine he will redeem thee from death.'

(b. Taʿanit 11b)

Ezra was credited by Rav with writing both the book in his name and the genealogies of Chronicles up to his own time.[3] The following verse in Nehemiah was exposited by Rav:

What is meant by the text 'And they read in the book, in the law of of God, with an interpretation, and they gave the sense and caused them to understand the reading' (Neh. 8.8). 'And they read in the book, in the law of God.' means the text. 'And an interpretation' means the Targum; 'and they gave the sense' refers to the division of the sentences; 'so that they understood the reading'—to the accentuation.

(b. Meg. 3a = Ned. 37b)

---

[1] b. B.B. 16b.
[2] b. Git. 31b.
[3] b. B.B. 15a.

Ḥananiah, Misha'el, and Azariah were not regarded with great respect by the rabbis. Rav held that had the Babylonians lashed them, they would have worshipped the golden image;[1] that Daniel was punished for giving advice to Nebuchadnezzar;[2] that the 'rabbis' (Ḥananiah, Mishael, and Azariah) died through an evil eye (or, Samuel held, they drowned in spittle).[3] Rav, additionally, provided an interpretation of the writing on the wall, as follows:

> Mene—God has numbered thy kingdom; Tekel—thou art weighed; Pres—thy kingdom is divided.
>
> (b. Sanh. 22a)

Comments on Jonah touched upon one text only:

> 'Let them turn every one from his evil way and from the violence that is in their hands' (Jonah 3.8)—What is the meaning of 'from violence'? Samuel said, Even if one had stolen a beam and built it onto his castle, he should raze the entire castle to the ground and return the beam to its owner.
>
> (b. Taʿanit 16a)

As to the story of Ruth, Rav held that Ibzan (Judges 12.8) was identical with Boaz.[4]

As we have seen, Scripture provided not only occasion for detached analysis, nor merely a source of proof-texts for current theological thinking, but also insight into the 'way of the world,' and proof that the rabbis' insights into worldly ways, good manners, and the like, were shared by the Divinity and were inspired by him. Numerous examples have been provided in other connections. Female cosmetics were derived from the Esther-scroll:

> R. Judah in the name of Rav said, When the maidens of Israel attain puberty before the proper age, poor maidens plaster it [hair] with lime, rich ones with fine flour, royal princesses with oil of myrhh, as it is said, 'six months with oil of myrrh' (Esther 2.12).
>
> (b. Shab. 80b = Pes. 43a)

Many verses could prove one point:

> R. Judah in the name of Rav said, A man should always enter a town by day and set out by day.
>
> (b. Pes. 2a)[5]

---

[1] b. Ket. 33b.

[2] b. B.B. 4a.

[3] b. Sanh. 93a.

[4] b. B.B. 91a. See further b. Sanh. 18b on Ruth 3.8, and the disagreements of Rav and Levi on Ruth 4.8 (Ruth R. 7.12).

[5] Compare b. Ḥul. 91b, a scholar should not go out at night.

Three different verses are quoted to 'prove' this proposition, Gen. 1.4,[1] Gen. 44.3[2] and Exodus 12.22.[3] All three instances are stated by R. Judah in the name of Rav, in exactly the same language.

From the story about Reuben (Gen. 36.28), Rav proved that righteous men do not take what is not theirs.[4] From I Sam. 15.4, Samuel proved that as soon as a man is appointed administrator of a community he becomes rich.[5] From Ps. 119.91, Rav proved that when a man's end has come, all things have dominion over him.[6]

Similarly, they looked for Scriptural foundations for popular proverbs:

> There was a man who used to say, Happy is he who hears abuse of himself and ignores it, for a hundred evils pass him by. Samuel said to R. Judah, This is alluded to in the verse, 'He who letteth out water (of strife) causeth the beginning of Madon, that is, the beginning of a hundred strifes' (Proverbs 17.14).
>
> Again, there was a man who used to say, Do not be surprised if a thief goes unhanged for two or three thefts. He will be caught in the end. Samuel said to R. Judah, This is alluded to in the verse, 'Thus saith the Lord, for three transgressions of Judah, yea for four, I will not reverse it' (Amos 2.6).
>
> Yet another used to say, Let him who comes from a court that has taken from him his cloak sing his song and go his way? Samuel said to R. Judah: This is alluded to in the verse, 'The righteous man falleth seven times and riseth again' (Prov. 24.16).
>
> There was yet another who used to say, When a woman slumbers the basket drops off her head. Samuel said to R. Judah: This is alluded to in the verse (Koh.10.18), By 'slothfulness the rafters sink in.' Another used to say, The man on whom I relied shook his fist at me. Samuel said to R. Judah, This is alluded to in the verse, (Psalm 41.10) 'Yea mine own familiar friend in whom I trusted and who did eat of my bread hath lifted up his hand against me.'
>
> (b. Sanh. 7a)

IV. HEROES OF TORAH IN BIBLICAL TIMES

The single most common source of hermeneutical themes for the rabbis, however, was found in the ideal of study of the Torah. The Scriptures became, in their hands, practically a handbook on the

---

[1] b. Pes. 2a.
[2] b. Taʿanit 10a.
[3] b. B.Q. 60b.
[4] b. Sanh. 90b.
[5] b. Yomaʾ 22b.
[6] b. Ned. 41a, compare Samuel's treatment of the same verse, *ad loc.*

proper behavior of the sage, on the importance of his activities, and on the manner in which he should carry them out. The rabbis, in their polemic against the central role in the faith formerly played by the priesthood, were forever looking for Scriptures to prove that study of the Torah was not only as good as Temple sacrifice, but far better than the cultus, and that he who studied the Torah contributed toward the redemption of Israel, which would lead to the reconstruction of the Temple. Such proofs include, in this period, the following:

> R. Samuel b. Unia in the name of Rav said, The study of Torah is more important than the Tamid offering . . .
>
> (b. Sanh. 44b)[1]

> Samuel said, 'And if they be ashamed . . . make known unto them . . .' (Ezek. 43.11)—Was the form of the house in existence at that time? But the Holy One blessed be He said, As long as you engaged in the study thereof, it is as if you were building it.
>
> (Lev. R. 7.3)[2]

> Study of Torah is superior to building the Temple, according to Rav (or some say, R. Samuel b. Marta) for as long as Baruch b. Neriah was alive, Ezra would not leave him to go up to the land of Israel.
>
> (b. Meg. 16b)

Further, Rav held that the only reason the Kohelet was included in the canon was the fact that it began and ended with 'words of Torah.'[3] Torah-study was the source of life:

> 'Desirest thou life' (Prov. 16.12)—According to Rav, the Holy One blessed be He replied thus (to David) Desirest thou life? Look as from a watch-tower to the Torah, since 'She is a tree of life to them that lay hold of her, and happy is every one that holdeth her fast' (Prov. 3.18).
>
> (Midrash on Psalms 16, Braude I, 202)

> 'Sustain yourselves with grain, lest He be angry, and ye lose the way' (Ps. 2.12). Rav and R. Ḥiyya differed as to the precise meaning of this verse. According to Rav, it means, Sustain yourselves with the bread of Torah, as is said 'As for him that wanteth understanding . . . come, eat of My bread' (Prov. 9: 4,5), or else the measure of God's just anger will be aroused against you, and you will lose the way of Torah. R. Ḥiyya, however, said that the verse means: Sustain yourselves with the bread of repentance, or else the measure of God's just anger will be aroused against you, and you will lose the way of

---

[1] On Joshua 5.13, see also b. ʿEruv. 63b.
[2] Compare R. Yoḥanan on II Chron. 2.2, in Midrash on Psalms 134.1.
[3] b. Shab. 30b.

repentance. [God says;] 'Do not think that I need camps full of soldiers or siege-engines: If I kindle but one spark, I can make the world, which I created, perish,' for, as the verse concludes, 'Ye perish from the way, when His wrath is kindled but a little' (Ps. 2: 12).

(Midrash on Psalms 2.17 Ed. Braude I, 47)

The rewards of study of the Torah were not only spiritual, but also quite material:

Rav once came to a certain place, and decreed a fast, but no rain fell. The reader then stepped down at his request before the ark, and recited, 'Who causeth rain to fall'. And it rained. Rav asked, What is your merit? I teach young children, and do so for the poor as well as for the rich, taking no fees from any who cannot afford to pay, and keep a fishpond and bribe the reluctant boys with fishes from it.

(b. Ta'anit 24a)

Similarly, Rav held that 'he who teaches Torah to his neighbor's son will be privileged to sit in the heavenly academy' (based on Jer. 15.19), and he who teaches Torah to the son of an *am haarez*, even if the Holy One blessed be He makes a decree, He annuls it for his sake (based on Jer. 15.19).[1] The reward is in eternity as well:

'And they that turn many to righteousness live like the stars forever and ever' (Daniel 12.3)—This applies to the teachers of young children. Such as who, for instance? Rav said, To such as R. Samuel b. Shilat, for Rav once found R. Samuel b. Shilat in a garden, whereupon he said to him, have you deserted your post? He replied, I have not seen this garden for thirteen years, and even now my thoughts are with the children.

(b. B.B. 6b)

Furthermore, all the great biblical heroes were regarded by the rabbis as rabbis and students of the Torah. Abraham, according to Rav, 'equipped his servants with Torah' (Gen. 14.14),[2] (Samuel held he made them bright with gold, as their reward for accompanying him). Moses, like the 3rd century student, stood when he learned, and sat while he went over what he studied (based on contradiction between Deut. 9.9, 'and I sat on the mount,' and Deut. 10.10, 'and I stood on the mount').[3] Just as Rav's students lamented the fact that after he died, they had not mastered the most basic lessons he had taught them, so Joshua made the same lament over Moses:

---

[1] b. B.M. 85a. Compare b. Qid. 30a, To what extent is a man obliged?

[2] b. Ned. 32a. Samuel said, like Zebulun son of Dan, whom his grandfather taught *Scripture, Mishnah, Talmud, Halakhot, and Aggadot.*

[3] b. Meg. 21a, see Sotah 49a.

R. Judah in the name of Samuel said, All the 'grapeclusters' ['eshkolot] who arose from the days of Moses until Joseph b. Jo'ezer learned Torah like Moses our rabbi [that is, were as scrupulous]. From that time onward, they did not learn Torah like Moses our rabbi. But did not R. Judah report in the name of Samuel, Three thousand laws were forgotten during the period of mourning for Moses?.....

R. Judah in the name of Rav said: When Moses departed for the Garden of Eden, he said to Joshua, Ask me concerning all the doubts you may have. He replied, Rabbi, have I ever left you for one hour and gone away? Did you not write concerning me in the Torah, 'But his servant Joshua the son of Nun departed not out of the tent' (Ex. 33.11). Forthwith the strength [of Moses, who was offended] weakened, and he [Joshua] forgot three hundred laws and there arose seven hundred doubts. Then all the Israelites rose up to kill him. The Holy One, blessed be He, then said to him, It is not possible to tell you. Go and occupy their attention in war, as it says, 'Now after the death of Moses the servant of the Lord it came to pass that the Lord spoke' (Joshua 1.1) and further it says, 'Prepare you food for within three days ...' (Joshua 1.11).

(b. Temurah 15b-16a)

Furthermore, Doeg aroused Saul's jealousy through Torah:

'Let our lord now command ... to seek out a man who is skilful in playing the lyre' (I Samuel 16.18). R. Judah in the name of Rav said, The whole verse was said by Doeg with nothing but evil intent. Thus, 'cunning in playing,' means skillful in asking questions; 'Mighty, valiant man', skillful in answering them; 'A man of war', means well versed in the battle of the Torah; 'understanding in matters', able to reason; 'and a comely person' means one who sustains his ruling by weighty reasons; 'and the Lord is with him'—everywhere the law is determined in accordance with his views.

(b. Sanh. 93b)

I can think of no more striking illustration of the rabbis' herme-neutic of 'Torah.' Here they take a verse which has absolutely nothing whatever to do with learning, and translate each of its clauses to reflect the conditions of their own studies, to 'prove' that Saul was jealous because David was a great student of the Torah, as Rav indeed said many times. Similarly, Doeg and Ahitophel were regarded as major rabbis:

Samuel found R. Judah leaning on a door post and weeping. He said Shinena, why do you weep? He replied, is it a small thing that is written concerning the *rabbis* (who went astray). 'Where is he that counted, where is he that weighed, where is he that counted the towers' (Is. 33.18) 'Where is he that counted'—for they counted all the letters in the Torah. 'Weighed,' for they weighed the light and the heavy matters in the Torah. 'Counted towers', for they taught three hundred laws concerning a 'tower that flies in the air'. And yet we have learned, Three kings and four commoners have no share in the world to come [including Doeg and Ahitophel, who were not saved by their learning]. What then shall become of us? said Samuel to him, Shinena, there was clay [impurity] in their hearts.

(b. Hag. 15b)[1]

Likewise David prayed that a traditional statement might be preserved in his name in this world.[2] The prophet Ahijah the Shilonite (I Kings 11.29) stood out alone:

'And they two were alone in the field' (I Kings 11.29)—R. Judah in the name of Rav said, All other scholars were as the herbs of the field before them.

(b. Sanh. 102a)[3]

It is quite natural, therefore, for the rabbis to have assigned to study of the Torah a central place in the fortunes of Israel. When Israel casts words of Torah to the ground, then the government can enact an oppressive measure and render it effective, as Samuel taught (based on Dan. 8.12).[4] Further, those who study the Torah must be respected:

R. Judah in the name of Rav said, He who despises a sage has no remedy for his wounds. What is meant by 'Touch not mine anointed' (I Chron. 16.22)? It refers to school children. 'And do my prophets no harm' refers to disciples of the sages.

(b. Shab. 119b)[5]

Similarly, he who is slothful to lament a sage deserves to be buried alive.[6] One who pretends to be a scholar and is not 'is not admitted within the circle of the Holy One.'[7] Further, those who know the Torah must share it:

R. Judah in the name of Rav: Whoever withholds a law from his disciple is as though he had robbed him of his ancestral heritage, as it is written (Deut. 33.4), 'Moses commanded us a law, even the inherit-

---

[1] Compare b. Ber. 61a, where Samuel says that the evil inclination is like a kind of wheat.
[2] b. Yev. 96b, Bekh. 31b, based on Ps. 61.5.
[3] Compare y. 'Eruv. 5.1.
[4] As above, p. 53-4, y. R.H. 3.8, Lam. R. Proem 2.
[5] Compare R. Ḥiyya's saying to R. Judah the Prince when he injured himself, y. Shab. 16.1, see vol. I, 106.
[6] b. Shab. 105b.
[7] b. B.B. 98a, based on Hab. 2.5, Ex. 15.13.

ance of the congregation of Jacob'—it is an inheritance destined for all Israel from the six days of creation.

(b. Sanh. 90b)

Rav likewise held that 'For she hath cast down many wounded' (Prov. 7.26) refers to the disciple who gives decisions before the age of ordination; and 'yea a mighty host are her slain' refers to one who has reached ordination age and does not give decisions (the proper age being 40). Further 'And whose leaf does not whither' (Ps. 1.3) proves that even the ordinary talk of scholars must be studied, for it is said, 'and whatsoever he doeth shall prosper.'[1] Moreover, those who misbehave may be punished by not having scholars among their progeny:

> R. Judah in the name of Rav said, Any communal leader who makes himself unduly feared by the community for purposes other than religious will never have a scholar for a son, as it says (Job 37.24), 'Therefore if men fear him he shall not see any wise of heart.'
>
> (b. R.H. 17a)

One must, on the other hand, be certain to teach worthy disciples:

> R. Judah in the name of Rav said, Whoever teaches a disciple that is unworthy will fall into Gehenna, as it is written (Job. 20.26), 'All darkness is laid up for his treasures, a fire not blown by man shall consume him that hath an unworthy remnant [*sarid*] in his tent' and *sarid* can refer only to the scholar as it is written, 'And among the remnant' (Joel 3.5).
>
> (b. Hul. 133b)

The Scriptures also provided hints as to how Torah should be studied. For example, one must learn by oral repetition:

> Samuel said to R. Judah: Shinena, Open your mouth and read the Scriptures, open your mouth and learn [Mishnah], that your studies may be retained and that you may live long, since it is said, 'For they are life unto those that find them and a healing to all their flesh' (Prov. 4.22). Read not, 'to those that find them,' but 'to him who utters them with his mouth.'
>
> (b. 'Eruv. 54a)

Rav corrected Rav Kahana, who dressed his hair as he came to sit before him, that the Torah shall not be found in one who attends to his own wants by studying it, with reference to Job. 38.13.[2] Study of Torah for some was not an easy enterprise:

---

[1] b. A.Z. 19b, b. Suk. 21b.
[2] b. Sanh. 111a.

R. Zera in the name of Rav said, 'What is meant by 'All the days of the afflicted are evil' (Prov. 15.15). This refers to the students of Talmud. 'But he that is of a merry heart hath a continuous feast'— This refers to students of the Mishnah.

(b. Sanh. 100b)[1]

'Neither was there any peace to him that went out or came in' (Zech. 8.10)—Rav said, As soon as man goes forth from halakhah to Scripture study, he no longer has peace, and Samuel said, It means, one who leaves Talmud for Mishnah.

(b. Hag. 10a)[2]

Nor was the master of the Torah always an easy one:

Rava b. Meḥasia in the name of R. Hama b. Goria in the name of Rav said, Let one be under an Ishmaelite, but not under a Roman, a Roman but not under a Magus, under a Magus but not under a scholar, a scholar but not under an orphan or widow.

(b. Shab. 11a)

R. Giddal in the name of Rav said, If any scholar sits before his teacher and his lips do not drip bitterness, they shall be burned, for it is said (Song 5.13), 'His lips are as lilies (shoshanim) dropping liquid myrrh.' Read not *more over*, but *mar over*, read not *shoshanim*, but *sheshanim*.

(b. Shab. 30b)[3]

On the other hand, greater respect is due to God than to the teacher:

R. Judah in the name of Rav said 'There is no wisdom nor under-standing nor counsel against the Lord' (Prov. 21.30). Wherever a profanation of God's name is involved, no respect is paid to a teacher.

(b. Ber. 19b)

This is apparently the key proof-text not to honor a dishonorable teacher, as it was cited without Rav's explanatory exegesis elsewhere, indicating that Rav's explanation seemed so obvious and acceptable as to require no further repetition.

Yet even in the world to come, the disciples of the sages have no repose:

R. Hiyya b. Ashi in the name of Rav stated, The disciples of the sages have no rest even in the world to come, as it is said 'They go from strength to strength, every one of them appeareth before God in Zion.' (Ps. 84.8).

(b. M.Q. 29a)

---

[1] b. B.B. 145b.
[2] On Zech. 8.10, compare also Sanh. 97b.
[3] See also Pes. 117a.

V. TANNAITIC HISTORY

Samuel and Rav, who lived at the beginning of a new era in the history of Judaism, and knew it, were the first and chief historians of the old. Rav, in particular, transmitted numerous teachings about earlier Tannaim, mainly of the Akiban school. Here we shall review the teachings of the two men about the preceding age. Rav transmitted a story about Salome Alexandra and how she was subjected to the rulings of the sages about the ritual purity of her dishes.[1] Samuel likewise preserved a teaching about the Hasmoneans:

> Whoever says, I am descended from the Hasmoneans is a slave[,] because there remained of them only one maiden who ascended a roof, lifted up her voice, and cried out, Whoever says I am descended from the House of the Hasmoneans is a slave, then she fell from the roof and died.
>
> (b. Qid. 70a)[2]

Samuel's interest in history was mainly due to his concern for correct genealogy, a particularly important subject in Babylonian Judaism. He cited Hillel, who taught that Ezra purified the Babylonian lineage when he migrated to Palestine,[3] which meant that those remaining in Babylonia were able to marry one another without hesitation, and thus opposed the genealogical pretensions of some families there. Samuel also interested himself in the *prosbul*, and hence in Hillelite decrees.[4] Likewise he taught that the Shamaites and the Hillelites agreed on laws regarding the uncleanness of hands, and he cited the eighteen decrees of the two schools.[5] He said:

> R. Abba in the name of Samuel said, For three years there was a dispute between Bet Shammai and Bet Hillel. One said, The law follows us, and the other, the law follows us. Then a Bat Kol issued forth and announced, both are the words of the living God, but the law follows Bet Hillel.
>
> (b. ʿEruv. 13b)

Rav was probably the most important student of Tannaitic history in the entire period of the ʾAmoraʾim.[6] Much of what we know about that period comes to us through him. As in his Bible study, he

---

[1] b. Shab. 16b.

[2] See also b. B.B. 2b.

[3] b. Yev. 37a, Qid. 75a.

[4] b. Git. 36b.

[5] b. Shab. 14b.

[6] On Rav as a historian, see Bacher, *op.cit.*, 14-15 and Zuri, *Rav*, 344-8.

followed some of the conventions of classical history, creating the kinds of conversations between historical figures, speeches, stories, and the like, which the imaginative historian regarded as his particular task. Regarding the first century Tanna, Ḥanina b. Dosa, he taught:

> R. Judah in the name of Rav said, Every day a heavenly voice goes forth and proclaims, The whole world is provided with food only on account of my son Ḥanina, while my son Ḥanina is satisfied with one basket of carob fruit from one Sabbath eve to the next.
>
> (b. Ḥul. 86a)[1]

Likewise he preserved a story about the great wealth of Nakdimon b. Gorion, before the destruction of Jerusalem in 70.[2] The devastation of Judea, after the Bar Kokhba war, interested both Rav and Samuel. Samuel passed on the saying of R. Simeon b. Gamaliel about the destruction of Betar,[3] and explained a law, that a man may not go out with a nailstudded sandal, by reference to a tragic accident after the fall of Betar.[4] Rav reported on the unhappy fate of the son and daughter of R. Ishmael b. Elisha.[5] He made a comment on the fate of R. Akiba:

> R. Judah in the name of Rav said, When Moses ascended on high, he found the Holy One, blessed be He, engaged in affixing coronets to the letters [of the Torah]. Said Moses, Lord of the Universe, Who stays thy hand [why these additions]? He answered, There will arise a man at the end of many generations, Akiba b. Joseph by name, who will expound upon each tittle heaps and heaps of laws. Lord of the Universe, let me see him. Turn around, he replied. Moses went and sat down behind eight rows and listened. Not being able to follow their arguments he was ill at ease, but when they came to a certain subject and the disciples said to the master, Whence do you know it, and the latter replied, It is a law given to Moses at Sinai, he was comforted. Thereupon he returned to the Holy One, blessed be He, and said, Lord of the Universe, thou hast such a man and thou givest the Torah by me? He replied, Be silent, for such is my decree. Then said Moses, Lord of the Universe, thou hast shown me his Torah, show me his reward. Turn around, he said, and Moses turned around, and saw them weighing out his flesh at the market stalls. Lord of the Universe, he said, Such Torah, and such a reward! Be silent, he replied, for such is my decree.
>
> (b. Men. 29b)

---

[1] See also b. Taʿanit 24b, Ber. 17b.
[2] b. Ket. 66b.
[3] b. B.Q. 83a, Git. 58a.
[4] b. Shab. 60a.
[5] b. Git. 58a.

Rav likewise preserved the story about Ḥananiah ben Ḥezekiah's effort to insure the canonicity of the book of Ezekiel:

> R. Judah in the name of Rav said, Verily may that man be remembered for good, and Ḥananiah the son of Ḥezekiah is his name, for if it were not for him, the book of Ezekiel would have been hidden away, for his words contradicted words of Torah. What did he do? He brought up three hundred kegs of oil and sat in a loft and exposited them.
>
> (b. Shab. 13b)

He preserved the story of the establishment of the Jewish school system in exactly the same form:

> R. Judah in the name of Rav said, Verily the name of that man is to be remembered for good, and Joshua b. Gamala is his name, for were it not for him, the Torah would have been forgotten in Israel. At first, if a child had a father, his father taught him, but if he did not, he did not learn at all [Deut. 11.19]. Then they ordained that teachers of children should be appointed in Jerusalem [Is. 2.3]. Even so, if a child had a father, the father would take him up to Jerusalem and have him taught there, and if not, he would not go up to learn there. They therefore ordained that teachers should be appointed in each eparchy, and that boys should enter school at age sixteen or seventeen. They did so, and if the teacher punished them, they would rebel and leave school. At length Joshua b. Gamala came and ordained that teachers of young children should be appointed in each eparchy and town, and that children should enter school at age six or seven.
>
> (b. B.B. 21a)

Similarly, he preserved the account of how the continuation of ordination was effected after the Bar Kokhba War:

> R. Judah in the name of Rav said, Verily, may this man indeed be remembered for good, and R. Judah b. Baba was his name, for were it not for him, the laws of fine would have been forgotten in Israel . . . For the wicked government decreed that whoever performed ordination should be put to death . . . .
>
> (b. Sanh. 13b-14a)[1]

That the expression 'verily, may this man' etc. was associated with Rav, and probably was a direct quotation of an expression he frequently used, is indicated by the following conversation between R. Yoḥanan and Resh Lakish, after Rav returned to Babylonia:

> R. Naḥman said, Rav used to rule that an examination must be made . . . R. Ḥiyya b. Joseph [said the same] before R. Yoḥanan and

---

[1] b. A.Z. 8b.

Resh Lakish. Resh Lakish retorted, Who is this Rav, who is this Rav, I know him not. Said R. Yoḥanan to him, Do you not remember that disciple who attended the lectures of the Great Rabbi and of R. Ḥiyya, and by God! All the years during which that disciple sat before his teachers I remained standing. And in what do you think he excelled? In everything! Immediately Resh Lakish exclaimed, *Verily that man is to be remembered for good*, for in his name the following dictum has been reported, If after slaughter . . .

(b. Ḥul. 54a)

The expression "Verily, May X be remembered for good" is clearly an expression Rav himself used quite frequently, and the form of these traditions therefore is his own, and not posthumous. This is at least one form, the purpose of which we can clearly isolate.[1]

VI. RAV AND SAMUEL AS HEIRS OF R. AKIBA AND R. ISHMAEL

Y. S. Zuri first pointed out[2] that substantial consistencies may be discovered in the methods of Scriptural and legal study in the several academies, and, at the same time, major hermeneutical differences distinguish one academy from another. In particular, Samuel's academy at Nehardea (and its successors in Maḥoza and Pumbedita), and Rav's at Sura, pursued legal and Scriptural exegesis in quite different ways. We shall review Zuri's findings, but I shall propose an explanation for the phenomena somewhat different from his. The Sura academy, following Rav, distinguished itself, Zuri demonstrates, in the inquiry after exegetical 'supports' for general principles, asking for example "how do we know [from Scripture] that such and such is the case?" Rav derived this approach from his masters, including R. Ḥiyya his uncle. Zuri traces the method to the southern Palestinians. Similarly Rav and his followers sought to provide a Scriptural foundation for *Tannaitic* attitudes and dicta. In Nehardea

---

[1] Other historical sayings relate to the marriage of Salome Alexandra's son (b. Shab. 16b); the details of the Jerusalem Temple (b. Men. 29a, Yomaʾ 54a, Suk. 51b, etc.); and so forth. We have cited numerous biblical-historical sayings above. Zuri points out three forms for the transmission of historical dicta, first, "If So-and-so had not done such and such, the matter would not have happened so and so", "One should never do such-and-such, since so-and-so did and transgressed", as well as that cited above, which served in particular for Tannaitic events. For the first form cited above, see b. Sanh. 104a, Shab. 56a; for the second, b. Sanh. 95b, ʿEruv. 44b. Both he and Samuel cited numerous stories of second-century masters, in particular as evidence for legal discussions.

[2] German Title: *Geschichte der Methodologie in den Hochschulen Judäas, Galäas, Suras, und Nehardäas*, I, Jerusalem, 1914, 1-32. On Rav's method, see also Bacher, *Agada*, 29-31.

and in Galilee, by contrast, the exegetical traditions were, to begin with, far smaller in quantity. Further, the Galileans learned from the Southerners' method and accepted their results. The Nehardeans likewise recognized that the Sura academicians were superior exegetes in finding Scriptural bases for current opinions, customs, and laws. Samuel, for example, asked a question of R. Huna, Rav's student, in seeking Scriptural support ("how do we know"). One recalls also the questions of Karna to Rav, all of which concerned the Scriptural basis for commonplace laws. Zuri holds that the chief exegetical interest of Sura was exactly in this area. Nonetheless, the Sura academicians pursued other approaches to Scripture-study; they were interested in the laws of writing a Torah-Scroll, unlike the Nehardeans; in textual criticism; in the meanings of words; and the like. Unlike the students of Samuel, they would seek to prove "from the Torah, Prophets, and Writings" that a given truth was biblically revealed. Indeed, Zuri cites the question posed to R. Akiba in Moses' presence, in the story cited above (p. 230) as particularly characteristic of Rav's method, "Rabbi, how do you know?" Zuri finds in the exegetical approach a means of liberalizing the law, for, he says, the Southerners would find a proof-text whenever they needed to liberalize the law. He further points out that the same approach characterized Rav's study of the Mishnah.[1] He would investigate it by source-criticism ("Our Mishnah follows whom?"), and by a search for logical consistencies in the opinions of Tannaitic authorities. The Nehardeans on the other hand emphasized strict exposition and explanation of the Mishnah, rather than source-criticism of its laws and opinions. Zuri sees the underlying difference between the two schools as fundamentally methodological: on the one side, one finds the willingness to compare, to find distinctions. The Galileans and the Nehardeans used such a method; the Southerners and the Surans did not. The former depended upon the powers of reason and dialectic, upon the discovery of distinctions, upon intellectual penetration and sharpness of mind, the latter upon exegesis and superior knowledge of traditions or of the traditional means of proving a new idea to be Scripturally founded. The distinction, recognized in the Talmud itself is between "Sinai," that is, one who holds traditional learning in abundance, and "Uprooter of Mountains," one whose reason penetrates to the heart of matters. Rav was the former, Samuel the latter.

[1] *Ibid.* 33-68.

While Zuri quite naturally tends to exaggerate the distinction he has uncovered, I think he has made a major discovery, and one which requires explanation. The explanation is, however, not to be found in geography alone. Zuri repeatedly says that it is mainly a matter of the Surans and the Southerners, on the one hand, and the Nehardeans and the Galileans, on the other. I do not find such a hard-and-fast distinction, for there are significant exceptions. For instance, Zuri notes that it was Rav who looked for the biblical beginnings of legal leniencies, citing the permission for the tribes to intermarry on the 15th of Av; yet as we saw above, it is at least possible, on the basis of alternate texts, to hold that Samuel, and not Rav, made the statement Zuri finds so very characteristic of Rav's method. Samuel was not half so indifferent to biblical exegesis as Zuri makes out. We have seen numerous instances to the contrary. He and Rav were matched over and over again in commenting on the meanings of words and the proper exegesis of sentences. Nonetheless, in the main, I think it is valid to follow Zuri in finding substantial differences between the two men.

The explanation for this phenomenon lies, I believe, not merely in the difference between one regional, or geographic, tradition and another. It is to be located rather in the fundamental training and orientation of the two men. The key is in Zuri's observation that Rav rarely cites R. Ishmael, while Samuel does so more frequently; Rav cites R. Akiba and his students far more frequently than does Samuel.[1] A simple historical fact explains this phenomenon: Samuel studied in Babylonia with the disciples (and their disciples) of Rabbi Ishmael, who had fled to Huzal following the onslaught of the Bar Kokhba War. Rav, for his part, studied in Palestine, with the disciples (and their disciples) of Rabbi Akiba. The two great masters of the earlier generation had devised, and pursued, very different methods of study, and the later generations continued to work in the manner of the early masters. As A. J. Heschel describes the opposing attitudes of R. Ishmael and R. Akiba[2] in theology and exegesis, it becomes clear that Samuel did, in fact, carry on the approach of the former, and Rav of the latter, as is quite reasonable to suppose, as I said, for strictly historical reasons. As Heschel sees it, R. Ishmael emphasized rational

---

[1] See his *Rabbi Akiva* (Jerusalem, 1924), 232-5, and his *Rav*, 128-9. On the students of R. Ishmael in Babylonia, see Bacher, *Agada*, 37, and vol. I, 128-35.

[2] *Torah Min Hashshamayim*, English title, *Theology of Ancient Judaism* (I, London & N.Y., 1962), XLI-LVI, 3-24.

explanation of details, R. Akiba sought visions of the whole; R. Ishmael stressed logical and straightforward analysis and simplicity of language, while R. Akiba stressed exegetical imaginativeness and daring. R. Ishmael emphasized the plain and simple meaning of Scripture; R. Akiba left behind the plain meaning in his search for mysteries; the former examined and criticized, the latter saw the Torah as a reflection of transcendental reality. R. Ishmael held that the language of the Torah was identical with that of commonplace, day-to-day speech, while R. Akiba held that it was of another order entirely, and that it could be interpreted by rules other than those pertaining to ordinary speech. Both attempted to relate laws to biblical teachings, but R. Akiba was willing, as Rav said, to interpret each apparently meaningless detail of Scripture.

R. Akiba's method would indeed call forth more sustained study of Scripture than R. Ishmael's, for it promised that whatever the exegete wanted could in the end be found in the text when it was properly searched, while R. Ishmael's did not. It stands to reason therefore that successive generations, following in the footsteps of R. Ishmael, would lay greater stress on rational, logical, dialectical studies than upon Scriptural exegesis, and so it was, as we have seen, with Rav and Samuel. Rav's principle, that temporal order does not exist in Scripture, was originally taught by R. Akiba. It is no accident, therefore, that Rav reported the stories (cited above) about R. Akiba and his exegetical prowess. Nor is it surprising that Samuel made a lesser contribution to wide-ranging exegesis for, as we noted, he possessed, to begin with, a hermeneutic capable of yielding far less *new* information than that of Rav.

As we review Samuel's exegetical remarks, we find far less interest in developing Scriptural lessons through his own imagination. Abraham was criticized because he tested the qualities of the Lord, just as Scripture made clear; God beheld the ashes of the ram of Isaac, just as Scripture said. For the most part, Samuel simply explained what required explanation, and extended biblical knowledge greatly in so doing. He differed with Rav on the plain meaning of texts. He made no comment about Rav's imaginative departures from that plain meaning. Rav, for his part, did not, so far as we can tell, make use of the technical hermeneutical devices of R. Akiba. I have found no instance where he produced an exegesis of such a word as "only" or "however" in the manner of R. Akiba. But he exposited Scripture very much in the *style* and spirit of R. Akiba, creating speeches between God and David; inventing legends about Solomon; expositing Abraham's feelings when he confronted God; underlining the hidden meanings of Scriptures in mystical, moral, as well as ethical dimensions. Following Zuri and Heschel, I find it quite clear that very substantial differences characterized the biblical exegeses of Rav and Samuel, and that these differences relate ultimately to the differing approaches to Scripture each had inherited from his teachers.

VII. EXEGESIS AND HISTORY

I find it striking to note the kinds of Scriptures on which we do *not* find exegeses, or the comments on which deliberately ignore the plain and obvious textual sense, in the legacy of this generation. Having considered in detail the biblical, particularly the prophetic, passages which interested the two leading rabbis, we notice that on the whole, they avoid eschatological Scriptures, or interpreted them in a mostly ethical and non-eschatological way. Their interest in the classical prophetic writings could not have been very great to begin with. While Rav provided many comments on the life of Moses and David, we have no similar exegetical expansion of the life of any literary prophet. The Elijah narrative elicited only one question. Where did the ravens find kosher meat? Scriptures in Habakkuk, Amos, and elsewhere were given a mainly one-dimensional and strictly ethical referent. David himself is a rabbi, rather than the prototype of the messiah. In the main, therefore, comments on prophetic writings were directed to a simple explication of problems of philology or meaning; or, for Rav, to a mystical, but non-historical interpretation in terms of the life of the heavenly court; or to an application to contemporary domestic life of prophetic dicta; or to study of the Torah. Just as the rabbis found their community ever more remote from power over the great events in contemporary history, so they looked back to Scriptures more for their application to the day-to-day affairs over which they did exercise considerable influence than for their meaning in a grand perspective. Their hermeneutical ideas were based upon the world as they saw it, and so the Torah yielded an account of how the rabbis of the Bible had lived life and encountered the divinity.

The only striking exception is the Book of Daniel, which, as we have seen, played a central role in the rabbis' sermons on the rise of

Ardashir. Daniel, believed to have been a contemporary of Nebuchadnezzar and Ahasueros, provided solace, for the promise of his
vision was that in the passing of empires, God's rule would in time
emerge. But what the rabbis looked for in Daniel was not a hint as
to *when* time would end, but rather reassurance *that* it would, that
events had meaning and Israel would be vindicated. In the end
Scriptures in Daniel and elsewhere were cited as examples of former
providential benevolence, rather than as texts which would speak of
an immediate and miraculous deliverance, to be expected shortly.
In seeking to comfort the people, the rabbis found these to be precious
Scriptures, but we have no hint that in them, they discovered more
than paradigms of remote redemption.

The rabbis' determined avoidance of apocalyptic, eschatological,
and messianic Scriptures (except for those treated above, p. 52-57),
stands in remarkable contrast to the highly charged events of their
day, in which still another pagan empire took its place at the center
of world history, and for a time, seemed to sweep all its enemies
before it. The capture of Valerian, for example, must in former times
have elicited extended comment from the apocalyptically-minded
seers who produced Daniel, and similar literature; indeed, as Olmstead
demonstrated, the Sybilline Oracles were greatly excited by that
and other great events. From the Babylonian rabbis, by contrast,
we have no explicit comment whatever. The fall of Caesarea Mazaca,
greatest city of Asia Minor, raised only one question, and that a most
unhistorical one: Should Jews mourn the massacre of the city's
Jewish community? The arrival of a great army posed a single problem
worthy of recording, Where shall we pray on the morrow? It is as
if the biblical genius at interpreting the theological substance of
historical forms had been lost, or abandoned, so long ago, that the
rabbis no longer cared about history at all. (Nor should it be thought
that earlier exegetes were concerned only for the meaning of Israel's
history, but not the nations', for events remote from Israel's immediate
circumstances had earlier elicited searching inquiries as well.) One
cannot, finally, suppose that the rabbis *did* make such exegetical
comments on contemporary history, beyond the few we have noted,
but that we no longer have them. The most abundant comments we
have cited above leave little doubt that we do, in fact, know much
about the kinds of Scriptures the rabbis chose to interpret, and the
tendency of their hermeneutics; they chose the Scriptures they found
congenial, and interpreted them from a highly tendentious perspective,

as one should expect. They also omitted verses that did not interest them.

We see here, as earlier, the coming to fruition of Tannaitic ideas. It was in response to the destruction of the Temple that Rabban Yohanan ben Zakkai had laid stress on an ethical, and anti-eschatological, focus for Judaism, saying, when Israel obeys God, then they will have political prosperity, and obedience to God meant conformity to the ethical and moral imperatives of Scripture. Similarly as we noted above, he had affirmed the messianic hope, but in very skeptical terms: if you are planting a sapling, and men come and tell you that the Messiah has come, finish planting the sapling, and then go forth to receive him. Rabban Yohanan's ideas did not take root at first, as the popular hope for the success of the holy war proclaimed by Rabbi Akiba and led by Simeon bar Koziba proves. In time, however, they did, and as we have seen, in Babylonia, the rabbis' response to political and historical events followed very closely the paradigms set forth originally at the end of the first century, whether these were immediately relevant and fruitful or not. We cannot, of course, know how widely the rabbis' views were accepted. The existence of the Sybilline Oracles suggests that in the Roman world, some Jews responded to grand happenings in a manner more like that of prophetic apocalypse than did the rabbis, and it stands to reason that in Babylonia, likewise, there were Jews who looked anxiously for signs and wonders, and, when they came, examined them carefully to know when the end would be at hand. As we saw, p. 214n.3) these were condemned by the rabbis. Such Jews would have found the eschatological passages of prophetic literature far more interesting than did the rabbis. But we do not know what they said about them.

In emphasizing the rabbis' continuities with Scripture, therefore, we must not ignore an extraordinarily radical discontinuity. In biblical times, people had a very serious interest in history, and therefore paid close attention to how it might reveal the will of God. In this period, by contrast, the rabbis whose comments we have considered were far less concerned with the actual history of their own age than with a mythical reconsideration of that of an earlier time. It is as if the rabbis, by projecting their values into an earlier time, deliberately chose to ignore their own day. If David and Doeg were rabbis, if Moses could visit the academy of Rabbi Akiba, then the boundaries between one generation and the next, so vivid in earlier days, were obscured, and time partook of a mythic, rather than a historical quality, in which all things happened under the aspect of eternity. I find this remarkable for two reasons. First, as we have seen, both Rav and Samuel took a keen interest in the history of the Tannaitic period, and were aware that a great age had ended, and its story was to be told. They were, therefore, historians of a sort. Second, as I said, grand and terrible events took place in this time; one empire tottered, another arose; great armies were on the move. So while in a narrow sense, Rav and Samuel showed historical interests, in a broad and classical one, they did not, but rather appear, in retrospect, to have turned their back on current affairs and declined to speculate, except in highly moralistic terms, implying no specific historical interpretation, upon their meaning. Their interest in the past is very different from that of ancient Israelite historians and theologians, and more like that of the Greeks, as described in M. I. Finley's study.[1] Indeed, I find it hard to characterize it as a *historical interest* in the commonplace meaning of these words. In elucidating Scripture, the rabbis were not seeking knowledge we can call historical, although they happened upon it with some frequency. They rather abstracted Scriptures from their setting, and shared with the biblical heroes one timeless universe, where Ardashir played no part, and Valerian counted not at all. It is clear to me as I said, that this came in consequence of Rabban Yoḥanan ben Zakkai's original skepticism of messianism, and his emphasis upon the necessity to transcend the catastrophes of his day. If one must look within, to the heart, to humble social realities, in order to find the raw material of redemption, then what happens outside, on the stage of history, no longer matters. Indeed, the dangers of messianic upheaval are best avoided when history and current affairs of grand weight are neutralized, and when, as it were, the eschatological fuse is detached from the historical 'bombshell.' If one must not calculate the time that the Messiah will finally appear, then what interest, given the perspective of earlier times, can historical events have had at all? Those of a homiletical fancy may say that thus the rabbis traded history for eternity. They did so, in the beginning, for very concrete, historical reasons, and continued to do so afterward because of the inertial force of the original exchange.

This is not to suggest that the messianic hope had died. As we saw

---

[1] M. I. Finley, "Myth, Memory, and History", *History and Theory* IV, 1965, 281-302.

above (p. 166-167), the rabbis gave expression to a very vivid expectation.But it was through prayer, not through politics, that they sought to realize it. Scriptures which might have encouraged the people to take very different action, and which, in other times, did lead to political upheavals, were sedulously ignored or drastically revised through exegesis. We see, therefore, a singular paradox: while on the one hand the rabbis led the people in prayer for eschatological fulfilment, on the other, they preached almost not at all on the Scriptures which promised it, or which might be used to ascertain when it was coming, or which aroused the hopes of men that it would be near at hand. One recalls, by contrast, the comment of Rabbi Nathan a century earlier:

> Rabbi Nathan said, This verse pierces and descends to the very abyss: 'For the vision is yet for an appointed time, but at the end it shall speak and not lie; though he tarry, wait for him, because he will surely come, he will not tarry.' (Hab. 2.3).

(b. Sanh. 97b)

I have conjectured[1] that Rabbi Nathan was engaged in undermining the stability of Jewish Palestine, possibly in preparation for a Parthian invasion. Emphasis on the inexorability of redemption would have suited his purpose. If so, de-emphasis of that same conviction is equally noteworthy. Treating verses such as this as relevant to everything but what they really referred to, namely, the coming of the Messiah, or, for the most part, ignoring them entirely, the rabbis spoke eloquently, though silently, about what they wanted. Through prayer, study of Torah, and compassionate action, Israel would achieve its reconciliation with God, a reconciliation which awaited not the fulness of time so much as the fervent penitence and prayer of the people.[2]

---

[1] Vol. I, 73-80.
[2] See below, Chapter VIII, p. 251 ff.

CHAPTER SEVEN

GEOGRAPHY AND POPULATION

I. Jewish Settlements in Babylonia

The evidence dating from Parthian times[1] indicated that large numbers of Jews lived in and around Nehardea, in Babylonia, including the towns of Nehar Pekod, Kafri, and Huẓal; in Seleucia-on-the-Tigris; Charax Spasinu; and Dura-Europos; as well as in the Mesopotamian towns of Nisibis and Edessa; in Adiabene; and in Armenia.[2] The sources for this period provide substantially more detailed information. The chief source is as follows:

> R. Papa the elder in the name of Rav said: Babylonia is healthy, Mesene is dead, Media is sick, Elam is dying. And what is the difference between the sick and the dying? Most sick are destined for life, most dying for death. How far does Babylonia extend [in respect to family purity]? Rav said, As far as the river Azak [east of the Tigris]. Samuel said, As far as the river Wani [Nahrewan, east of the Tigris and parallel to it. Thus the eastern boundaries are given.]How far on the upper Tigris? Rav said, As far as Bagdad and Awana [Var.: Okbara and Awana]. Samuel said, As far as Moxoene. How far on the lower reaches of the Tigris? Said R. Samuel: As far as lower Apamea. There were two Apameas, an upper and a lower; one was fit and the other unfit, and one parasang lies between them . . . . How far on the upper reaches of the Euphrates? Rav said, To Fort Tulbakene. Samuel said, to the bridge of Be-Pherat. R. Yoḥanan said, As far as the ford of Gizama.
>
> R. Ika b. Abin in the name of R. Ḥananel in the name of Rav said: Ḥalwan and Nehawand are as the Exile [Babylonia] in respect to genealogy . . .
>
> 'And the king of Assyria carried Israel away into Assyria and put them in Ḥalaḥ and in Ḥabor on the river of Gozan and in the cities of the Medes.' (II Kings 18.11).' Ḥalaḥ is Ḥulwan, Ḥabor is Adiabene, the river of Gozan is Ginzak, the cities of the Medes are Hamadan and its environs; others state, Nehawand and its environs. What are its environs? Said Samuel, Karag, Moschi, Hidki, and Rumki. Said R. Yoḥanan: And all these are unfit . . . . R. Ḥiyya b. Abin in the name of Samuel said: Moxoene is as the exile in respect to genealogy . . . .
>
> Rabbi [Judah the Prince], when he lay dying, said, There is Humania in Babylonia, which consists entirely of Ammonites; there is Misgaria in Babylonia, which consists entire of *mamẓerim*; there is Birka in

---

[1] See vol. I, 10, 13-15, for data from Arsacid times.
[2] See my "Jews in Pagan Armenia," *JAOS* 84, 1964, 230-40.

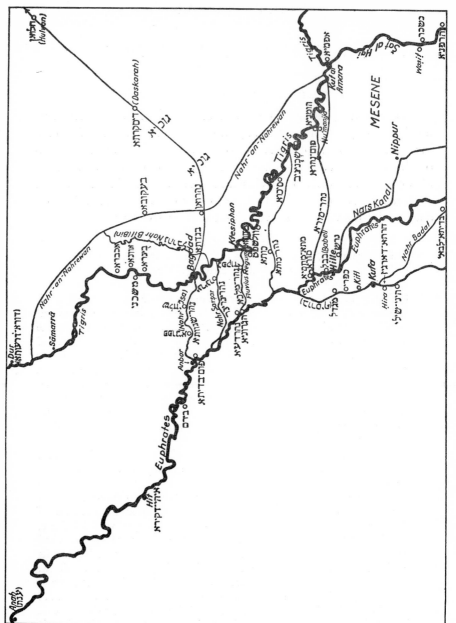

V. Jewish Sites in Babylonia (detailed map), by Jacob Obermeyer

Babylonia, which contains two brothers who interchange their wives; there is Birtha di-Satya in Babylonia ... there is Fort Agama in Babylonia ...

(b. Qid. 71b-72a, Compare b. Yev. 16b)[1]

That there were Jews at this time in Susa, Elam, and Shustar, is indicated by a further contemporary saying, which condemns the Israelites for having praised these places by comparison to Palestine.[2] Jews also lived in Bashkar.[3]

The extent of Jewish settlement was therefore considerable.[4] According to the evidences on this period, Jews continued to live in Adiabene[5] (though many had doubtless converted to Christianity); in Halwan, and Gazaca (Ginzak), on the shores of Lake Urmia; in Hamadan and in Nehawend. Northward, Rav gives a place on the Tigris, which Kohut and Berliner identify as Okbara and Awana, and Samuel names Moxoene as the farthest point. Southward, on the Tigris, Jews lived in Apamea and Mesene, as they had in former times. Northward on the Euphrates, Rav named the fortress Thulbakni, which, Krauss holds, is to be identified with Thilbencane, and Samuel names a bridge probably identical with Zeugma. By Babylonia itself was meant, strictly speaking, the section where the two rivers come most closely together. In general, Rav's view was that Babylonia extended further north on the Euphrates than Samuel thought. Obermeyer comments that the borders of Babylonia are set out by natural phenomena, from the Persian Gulf on the south, the Euphrates on the west, and the Tigris and Zagros mountains on the east.

The Iranians called Babylonia "Dile-Iran-Šahr," the heart of the Iranian empire, or Suristan, the land of the Syrians. The region was

---

[1] The meaning is that Jews in these localities have intermarried with pagans, and may therefore no longer intermarry with Jews. See b. Yev. 17a, for Samuel's view, based on Hosea 5.7, 'They have dealt treacherously, they have begotten strange children.' On Elam, see R. Yoḥanan's view, that 'We have a little sister and she hath no breasts' (Song 8.8) refers to Elam, who was privileged to study but not to teach, b. Pes. 87a. See also b. Git. 6a, and b. Qid. 49b; and Graetz, *Mesene*, 31, 'only with families of Central Babylonia may a learned Jew intermarry.'

[2] b. Sanh. 94a.

[3] b. Shab. 139a.

[4] See especially S. Krauss, "Babylonia", *JE* II 403-5; and the same author's *Paras* 19; H. Graetz, *Mesene*, 27-29; Adolf Berliner, *Beiträge zur Geographie und Ethnographie Babyloniens im Talmud und Midrasch* (Berlin 1884); Adolphe Neubauer, *La Géographie du Talmud* (Paris 1868) 320-368, for a very good, brief survey of place names and Talmudic citations on the several places cited here; and especially, Jacob Obermeyer, *Landschaft*, especially 71-128, where Obermeyer provides a detailed study of the sayings of Rav and Samuel cited above.

[5] See my "Conversion of Adiabene to Christianity", *Numen* XIII, 2.

divided into twelve districts; on the eastern bank of the Tigris, in the north, lay Sad-Hurmuz, with the chief town, Okbara; on the west bank was Maskin, and these two districts were the northern-most frontiers of Babylonia in this period. The Jewish settlements were not contiguous, but were separated by non-Jewish towns:

> 'The Lord hath commanded concerning Jacob that they that are round about him should be his adversaries' (Lam 1.17). Rav said, As for instance, Humania towards Pum Nahara.
>
> (b. Yev. 16b)

Since Humania was believed to be populated by 'Ammonites, Jews were not supposed to intermarry with its residents; Pum Nahara would, by inference, have had a large Jewish population.

The region between the Tigris and Euphrates from present-day Baghdad south east to present-day Shatt-al-Gharraf was proverbially fertile and productive.[1] A system of controlled irrigation insured a proper water supply, and at the same time, controlled the turbulence of the great rivers. In recent times, the land distant from the rivers has fallen into disuse, or returned to swamp, but the derelict embankments of ancient canals and the *tels* of forgotten settlements testify to the great prosperity and the region's capacity to support the large population characteristic of earlier periods. In Sasanian times, the alluvial plain between the two rivers, only twenty miles apart in the heartland of Babylonia, was very intensively cultivated.[2]

Of the two rivers, the Euphrates is the slower, and can be navigated further upstream. Both, however, flood annually. The sequence begins with autumn rains in the uplands, which cause a swelling of the water through winter and spring. The river crests in April and May, when the melting snow in the Armenian mountains adds to the flood, subsides in June, and sinks to its lowest level in September and October. The late flooding necessitated the erection of dikes and barrages to protect ripening crops from the water, and the preparation of water storage areas. Likewise, Oppenheim points out, it increased the tendency of the soil toward salinization due to rapid evaporation in the intense heat. Further, the mud, which could not be permitted to settle in the fields, clogged the canals that carried the water inland, and necessitated the improvement or periodical replacement of the canals.

---

[1] K. Mason, ed. *Iraq and the Persian Gulf, Naval Intelligence Division, Geographical Handbook Series B.R. 524*, London, 1944, pp. 71-3.

[2] Oppenheim, *op. cit.*, pp. 38-42.

The rabbis believed that the Euphrates was the mightiest and the highest of all rivers,[1] but it carries back water to the fountain of Etam, in the land of Israel, which was the highest eminence in Palestine.[2] Therefore, Rav held:

> If one vows to forbid himself the benefit of the waters of the Euphrates, he is forbidden to benefit from all the waters in the world.
>
> (b. Bekh. 55a)

They were familiar with the seasonal flow of the Euphrates:

> Rabin said in the name of Rav: The swelling of the Euphrates testifies abundantly to rain in the West. [Palestine was believed to he higher than Babylonia, so the water flows down and causes the swelling of the Euphrates. Thus the rise of a river is due to the Palestinian rains]. Samuel said, A river increases in volume from its bedrock. [It appears to swell through rains, but actually more water gushes upwards from river bed than is added by rain]. Now Samuel is self-contradictory, for Samuel said, Running water does not purify, except the Euphrates in Tishri. Samuel's Father made ritual baths for his daughters in Nisan and had mats set up for them in Tishri.
>
> (b. Ned. 40a)[3]

If a ritual bath is made of collected rain water, it is valid only if the water is still, but not flowing. A well with gushing water is valid even if it flows. During the whole year the river may contain more rain water or melted snow than natural (subterranean) water, and therefore it was not valid. In Tishri (September), however, the river may contain more rain water or melted snow than spring water, and therefore would still not be a valid ritual bath. The view of Samuel, on the one hand, that the river is fed mainly from its own springs, contradicts his father's view. In Nisan (March-April) the river was was swollen by rain, and Samuel's father did not permit his daughters to take ritual baths in the river. In Tishri they washed in the river; the bed was muddy; should their feet sink in, the water would not cleanse them, and the immersion would be invalid, and therefore he placed mats for them to stand on.[4] Further, Samuel said,[5] No water purifies when flowing except the Euphrates in Tishri alone;

---

[1] b. Bekhorot 55a, Gen. R. 16.3.
[2] b. Shab. 145b, Comp. Zev. 54b.
[3] See also b. Shab. 65a, and compare Obermeyer, 45, Rains in Northern Mesopotamia precurse those of Palestine.
[4] Obermeyer, 278.
[5] b. Shab. 65a.

that is to say, rain normally constitutes the bulk of the flow, contrary to the view stated above. While the observations of the rabbis were correct, their geography does not reflect the best knowledge of their times. Strabo had correctly held that the Euphrates and Tigris both rise in Armenia, and Pliny likewise had accurate information on the river systems of Mesopotamia. Neither writer indicates that he thought that system to be higher than any other.[1] The rabbis' notion derived from biblical exegesis and not from observation.

II. An Estimate of the Jewish Population

No accurate estimate of population is possible, for the state of our knowledge does not permit it. Nonetheless, I shall propose a rough guess, which may be of interest.

J. Beloch holds that Babylonia and Susiana held from six to eight million people, basing his estimate on a population density of 46 to 60 per kilometer.[2] If the Jews constituted a tenth to an eighth of the local population, and that would be a conservative figure, then according to Beloch's figures, there should have been from 600,000 to a million Jews in Babylonia and the surrounding territories.

On the basis of the detailed studies of Robert McC. Adams,[3] however, we may attempt another kind of estimate entirely. Adams found that the lower Diyala basin, east of Baghdad, was occupied more densely in Sasanian times than ever before or since:

> In the number or occupied sites, in the breadth of settlement and cultivation, in the dispersion of urban construction, and above all, in the massiveness of state-initiated irrigation enterprises upon which those other features largely depended, maxima were reached far in excess of anything before or since.[4]

In the Diyala basin, two cities were founded, among the many established in Sasanian times, Buzurg-Shapur by Shapur I, and Weh-Antiokh-i-Khosrau, by Khosroes I Anosharwan. On the other hand, the Roman invasions of later times brought widespread destruction of both settlements and agricultural infrastructure. Nonetheless, in the Diyala region, settlement was thirty-five times

---

[1] E. H. Bunbury, *A History of Ancient Geography* (N.Y. 1959) II, 288, 408.

[2] J. Beloch, *Die Bevölkerung der griech.-rom. Welt* (Leipzig, 1886) 250f., See also F. M. Heichelheim, *Economic History*, 153, and O. Klima, *Manis Zeit*, 19-20, n. 10.

[3] Robert McC. Adams, *Land Behind Baghdad, A History of Settlement on the Diyala Plains* (Chicago, 1965).

[4] Adams, 69.

as dense and widespread as in Achemenid times. Adams lists 437 recorded sites, including nine cities, four smaller urban centes, thirty-five large towns, fifty-nine small towns, 308 villages. In which of these places were found Jewish settlements? Of the nine cities, four smaller urban centers, and thirty-five large towns, only two contained Jewish populations, Daskara (Adams, 137, site number 41, Obermeyer 146f.), and Ctesiphon (Maḥoza was a Jewish suburb). Since a large town is defined by Adams as having a population in excess of 6,000, and since we know that two rabbis, R. Judah and R. Huna of Diskarta, came from Daskara, it may be supposed that a fair-sized Jewish community was present there in Sasanian times. The town was a caravanserie on the road to the east, and its Jewish population may be compared to that of Edessa, Nisibis, and Dura, where Jewish merchants formed the core of Jewries. If this is a fair comparison, then one notes that Dura Jewry constituted a very small and unimportant segment of the population, capable of meeting in a large room for synagogue services. Kraeling calls the Dura conmunity "a modest ethnic and religious group...an insignificant minority in a thoroughly pagan environment."[1] An educated guess of five hundred souls in all would probably err on the high side. What is more striking is the apparent absence of Jewish settlement elsewhere in the entire Diyala region, apart from the center of Ctesiphon, at the height of its population-density. I am unable to isolate another place, among the forty-eight significant sites listed in Adams's catalogue for Sasanian times, which corresponds to any known in the literary evidence cited by Obermeyer. Assuming that no very substantial Jewish community existed eastward of the Tigris outside of Diskarta except those named in literary sources and reported by Obermeyer, one would have to conclude that the Jewish population in this region was very small indeed, and almost entirely concentrated westward of the Tigris. On the other hand, the *beraita* considered above specifies that "Babylonia" continued into the Diyala basin, as far as Nahrawan. Since we have place names for very few of the hundreds of sites recorded by Adams, it stands to reason that Jews did live in more places than Diskarta/Daskara. The unanswerable question is, in how many places?

Still a third, and more promising, way of estimating Jewish population is to review Obermeyer's data. Following the course of his

---

[1] *Synagogue*, 328.

peregrinations Obermeyer refers to the following Jewish settlements in Babylonia (not Mesopotamia) attested in Talmudic sources:[1] from Mosul to (present-day) Baghdad and southward, Karkha di Bet Slokh (Kirkuk) (141), Dura de Riʿuta (142), Be Ketil (143), Argiza, Daskara (see above), Maḥoza (161-177), Be Gobar (178), Kurtabah (183), Apamia (183), Sikara, Shekunsib (190), Humania (192) and Pum Nehara (194) on opposite sides of the Sura canal and Neharpania (197); along the Euphrates from north to south, Pumbadita (215) across the river from Anbar; Astunia (Piruzšabur), Be Kubi, Be Tarbu, Be Hirmak (229-31), Artibana (232), Nehardea (244f.), Hagrunia opposite Nehardea (265), Nehar Pekod (270), Kuta (278), Sura (283), Mata Maḥseyea (287), Kamhunia (296), Barnis, Tatlafus (298), Afsatia, Damharia, all in the neighborhood of Sura; Huzali, Hasalpuni, Nares (306), Kafri (315), Hira (318), Hini-Sili (319), Bedita-Lebai, Kufa (329). As noted in the map (p. 242), Obermeyer thus finds Jewish settlements along both rivers, and at a few points on the connecting canals. From Anah north on the Euphrates, he notes nine cities on the Euphrates, with seven on its effluents; from Dura de Riʿuta in the north, ten cities, and on the connecting canals, north to south, six other cities, thirty-two in all. These places had very large Jewish populations, in most were Jewish majorities. The Jews lived in fairly compact settlements along the canals as well, but the difficulty in isolating Jewish settlements in the Diyala basin, and the fact that there were numerous such settlements on the rivers and along certain canals, suggests that in Babylonia itself, and not in the surrounding territories, most Jews were concentrated. This is to be expected, for Adams emphasizes that settlements were found almost exclusively on the banks of canals and rivers; the lands in between or at a distance from water were barren.

If 20,000 Jews lived in each of the cities which were mostly Jewish (the population of Seleucia, a metropolis before 165, was approximately 80,000, so this may not be an excessive estimate for smaller centers), then approximately 640,000 would have been found in medium- and large towns. This was, as Adams points out, a period of most intensive farming in the Diyala basin, and it is certainly reasonable to suppose that population density in the central and southern Babylonian areas, along the canals and rivers, would have been as high, if not higher. If the Diyala proportions were carried

---

[1] Page numbers in text refer to his *Landschaft*.

over—and if anything, Babylonia was more intensively cultivated—then one should expect to find the following proportions (following Adams, p. 72):

Cities: 13
Large Towns: 35
Small Towns: 59
Villages: 308

Of the sites enumerated by Adams, approximately 74% are villages, and 22% are small and large towns. Assuming that none of the Jewish sites listed above was a major city, or contained a Jewish population equivalent to that in a major city, except possibly Mahoza, then we should have to postulate the existence of approximately thirty-two small and large Jewish towns, or towns with fairly substantial (10-20,000) Jewish populations. If the Diyala proportions pertained, then there may well have been an additional 104 sites, containing small Jewish populations and mainly agricultural in nature, using the equation $\frac{94}{308} = \frac{32}{X}$. This is of course a very approximate guess. We have no reason to assume that the proportions of small and large towns to village sites were consistent between the two regions. Nonetheless believing that an educated guess is better than none at all, I may proceed to speculate that approximately 300 to 1,000 people, at an average of 500, lived in a given village site, and hence one may estimate that approximately 520,000 Jews lived in villages, and that central and southern Babylonia may have held approximately one million, two hundred thousand Jews in all.

I believe such a result may again err on the high side, since Adams bases his 'fairly large-town' estimate on 6,000. If, therefore, in the thirty-two significant urban sites were Jewish populations ranging from 5,000 to 20,000, with the latter figure applicable to Mehuza and perhaps Nehardea, and with the average at 10,000, we should have 320,000 Jews in larger towns and cities, and a population of approximately 840,000. The range is therefore neither very much under 800,000 *nor* very much over 1,200,000.

This figure is to be compared to the original conjecture of 600,000 to 1,000,000, based on Beloch's figures and my estimate, on that basis, of the proportion of Jews to the total population.

Adding to that figure small communities outside of the Tigris and Euphrates valleys, and as I said, I doubt that these numbered more than 500-1,000 each, one might augment the above estimates by twenty to thirty thousand, but no more. Hence the Jewish population of Sasanian Babylonia may have been approximately 860,000, which should be regarded as a conservative estimate.

CHAPTER EIGHT

THE PEOPLE AND THE LAW

i. The Problem

Our knowledge of Babylonian Jewish history in this period comes to us from essentially legal sources. The data cited in the preceding chapters constitute a very small segment of these sources, and is itself mostly preserved in the context of legal discussions. These discussions focus upon the Mishnah, its interpretation and application. In general, we have three kinds of legal material: explications of the Mishnah itself, statements on theoretical problems elicited by Mishnaic law, but not directly connected to the Mishnah, and citations of cases in which the law was actually applied. For historical purposes, the first two bodies of legal data are of limited value. The historian wants to know *how things were*, not how some people wished they might be.

We have no way whatever of determining how much of Mishnaic law, and the legal doctrines arising from it, actually influenced the life of the people. The language of legal discourse does not vary, whether it is discussing matters which were obviously theoretical, or day-to-day issues of practical law. A few examples of the former will suffice:

> R. Huna, R. Judah, and all the disciples of Rav maintained, A heathen is executed for violation of the seven laws applying to the sons of Noah . . . . .
>
> (b. Sanh. 57a)

The Jewish courts did not, as we have seen, possess the right to inflict capital punishment except under strict Sasanian supervision, if then. It is not likely that they would have had sufficient jurisdiction over non-Jews to enforce the Noaḥide laws among them. Similarly, we have numerous legal dicta regarding the sacrificial cult, which had ceased to exist more than a century and a half earlier:

> R. Zera in the name of Rav stated, If a non-priest slaughtered the Red Heifer, it is invalid because . . .
>
> (b. Men. 6b)

> Samuel to R. Hana of Baghdad said, Bring me ten people and I will teach you in their presence, If drink offerings are defiled, one makes a separate fire for them and burns them.
>
> (b. Zev. 92a)

> R. Judah in the name of Samuel said, If a peace-offering is slaughter-
> ed before the doors of the *Heikhal* are opened, it is invalid, as it is said,
> 'And he shall kill it at the entrance of the tent of meeting' (Lev. 3.2)—
> when it is open, but not when it is closed.
>
> (b. Zev. 55b)

> Samuel asked R. Huna, How do we know that when one who is
> unaware engaged in sacrifices, it is invalid . . .
>
> (b. Zev. 46b)

Whether the Red Heifer was actually slaughtered before 70 is not
entirely clear, since the Tannaitic traditions on the matter are notori-
ously inexact,[1] but it is certain that neither the red-heifer, nor peace-
offerings had been prepared, and that the defilement of drink offerings
had not in fact posed a practical legal problem, for over a century and
a half. It is striking that Samuel wished to make a public announcement
of his legal view, so that it would be regarded as an official statement.
The sacrificial cult is not the only area of law which elicited legal
inquiries, but it is the obvious example of how the dedication to study
of the Torah, including its legal sections, brought about consideration
of matters which could not have practical consequences except when
the Messiah came; and of how the appropriate language and procedures differed *not at all* from those relevant to very immediate, commonplace legal problems.

Furthermore, we have legal dicta on matters of normally private
concern, for example:

> Rav said, A man who wilfully causes erection is to be placed under
> ban.
>
> (b. Nid. 13a)

> Samuel said, The domestic and wild goose are forbidden copulation.
> (b. Bekh. 8a)

> Rav said, It is forbidden to sleep by day more than a horse's sleep.
> (b. Suk. 20b)

Even though the values of the rabbis played a very substantial part
in the formation of social mores, a very elaborate police force would
have had to have been employed to enforce dicta such as these.
For their part, the rabbis tried to encourage obedience to the law
by both promises and threats; for example:

> Rav observed, A *mamzer* [illegitimate child] never lives longer than
> thirty days.
>
> (Lev. R. 33.6)

---

[1] See my *Life* 51-3, 60-1, 70.

This saying is explained to mean that if a *mamzer* is known as such, he will not survive. Similarly:

> R. Huna said, Once in seventy years, the Holy One blessed be He brings a great pestilence upon the world, and consumes the *mamzerim*, taking the legitimate ones with them . . .
>
> (Lev. R. 33.6)

The rabbis could not invariably enforce their views of what were, and were not, acceptable marriages, but they could, and did, encourage the people to share their view that these marriages could not produce healthy children. They did not find that everyone acted accordingly. In the following case, we see that some of the rabbis possessed greater prestige than others, and the people obeyed whomever they saw fit:

> Rabbah b. Bar Hana gave money to Rav, and instructed him, Buy this field for me, but he went and bought it for himself. Did we not learn, What he did is done, yet he has behaved toward him as a cheat? For Rav, they showed respect, but not for Rabbah b. Bar Hanah.
>
> (b. Qid. 59a)

Finally, the rabbis themselves acted at variance with the prevailing view of the law:

> Rav once had his harvest gathered for him in the intervening days of the festival. Samuel heard and was annoyed.
>
> (b. M.Q. 12b)

Similarly, the rabbis sought to discourage the people from swearing oaths, because of the possibility of profaning the Divine Name, but all they could do about it was point to the dire consequences, as in the following case:

> R. Judah in the name of Rav, or R. Kahana, said: In a year of scarcity a certain man deposited a dinar of gold with a widow who put it a jar of flour. She baked the flour and gave the loaf to a poor man. The owner came and said, Give me back my dinar, and she said, May death seize upon one of my sons if I have derived any benefit for myself from your dinar, and not many days passed before one of her sons died. When the sages heard, they remarked, if such is the fate of one who swears truly what must be the fate of one who swears falsely.
>
> (b. Git. 35a)

The legal sources cannot, therefore, be used indiscriminately to provide testimony about the conditions of daily life. As we have seen, Mishnaic law treated legal issues which were quite remote, because of historical or other circumstance, from reality. Other kinds of sayings, in a legal formula, concerned actions and attitudes which easily eluded legal enforcement under the best of circumstances. The rabbis themselves differed not only in theory, but in practice, and the famous saying that Nehardea and its environs followed the view of Samuel, and Sura, of Rav, indicates that conformity to a single legal criterion was most difficult to attain.

Even if the rabbis had been unanimous about the great issues of the law, and even if their unanimity concerned specifically those legal problems which most affected day-to-day affairs, however, it would have been very difficult to render the law invariably, or even mostly, effective in the common life. First, even the exilarch did not possess means of physical coercion such as he formerly possessed (and later recovered). Second, even if he had, he was not the sole legal authority in Babylonia. He ruled—at best—only the affairs of his Jewish subjects, while other groups and territories, including those with substantial Jewish populations, were not under his control. One recalls[1] that some Jews, when confronted with rabbinic authority for Sabbath-breaking and having been excommunicated, simply abandoned Judaism and thus placed themselves quite beyond the pale of Jewish law. It does not prove that the rabbis possessed *no* authority whatever; but it does suggest that circumstances limited its effectiveness. Without armies or police, supported only by the *willingness* of Jews to obey the law, because it had been revealed by God to Moses on Sinai, and transmitted faithfully to their own generation, the rabbis had to rely in some measure upon persuasion, in some, upon the inertial force of accepted authority, in some, upon the willingness of the Persian government to accept their decrees, but mostly upon the acquiescence of the people themselves. Because of the precariousness of any kind of government, in an age in which the execution of law was slow and inefficient, and might be impeded by factors out of the control of any Jewish authority the mere proclama-

---

[1] b. Qid. 72a:
    When Rabbi [Judah the Prince] lay dying, he said, There is Humania in Babylonia, which consists entirely of Ammonites. There is Misgaria in Babylonia, consisting entirely of *mamzerim*. There is Birka in Babylonia, which contains two brothers who trade wives. There is Birta diSatya in Babylonia. Today they have turned away from the Almighty. A fishpond overflowed on the Sabbath, and they went and caught fish on the Sabbath, whereupon R. Aḥai son of R. Josiah declared the ban against them, and they renounced Judaism.
    See vol. I 147-8.

tion of law meant little practically. The issue of rabbinic authority over the people's life is considerably more complex than has been recognized, and the usefulness of rabbinic laws in recovering a clear notion of how affairs were conducted is somewhat less substantial than is widely assumed.

The rabbinic sources do not, moreover, convey a true and complete picture of how the laws shaped daily affairs, because they mostly suppress, or report only by indirection, actions and conduct contrary to rabbinic dicta. The two great bodies of archaeological evidence provide the most striking examples. No rabbinic source would have permitted us to predict the existence of a synagogue wall such as was unearthed at Dura-Europos; nor is there very adequate assistance in rabbinic literature as presently understood in interpreting the art of that synagogue. The incantation texts from Nippur tell us considerably more about the attitudes of the common people than does the Talmud, and what they tell us is that the people had no hesitation whatever about making use of the best magical science of their day in achieving their life's purposes. We have considered above (p. 35) some of the rabbis' sermons. Even discounting the homiletician's natural hyperbole, one would have to suppose that there were people who did not obey the dietary laws, attend ritual baths, and otherwise comport themselves properly, and that the rabbis had to call down upon their heads the most severe calamities by way of exhortation. The following sayings suggest that the rabbis took a very realistic view of their contemporaries, preaching sermons to encourage the people to behave in a moral manner:

> Rav said, On account of four things is the property of householders confiscated by the state [fiscus]: On account of those who defer payment of laborer's wages, on account of those who withhold the hired laborer's wages, on account of those who remove the yoke from off their necks and place it on the necks of their follows, and on account of arrogance. And the sin of arrogance is equivalent to all the others, whereas of the humble it is written (Ps. 37.11), 'But the humble shall inherit the land and delight themselves in the abundance of peace.'
>
> (b. Suk. 29b)
>
> R. Amram in the name of Rav said: Three transgressions which no man escapes for a single day are sinful thought, calculation on prayer and slander.
>
> R. Judah in the name of Rav said: Most people are guilty of robbery, a minority of lewdness, and all of slander.
>
> (b. B.B. 164b).

The Master said, Bet Hillel say, he that abounds in grace inclines (the scales) towards grace. How can this be, seeing that it is written, 'And I shall bring the third part through fire' (Zech. 13.9). That refers to wrongdoers of Israel who sin with their body. What are 'wrongdoers of Israel who sin with their body?' Rav said, This refers to the cranium which does not put on the phylactery. Who are the wrongdoers of the Gentiles who sin with their body? Rav said, This refers to [sexual] sin.

(b. R.H. 17a)

Jews lived in Babylonia, therefore, who did not put on phylacteries, and who did not meet the rabbis' standards for ethical economic and social behavior[1]; who did not even respect the rabbis, for Rav defined an 'Apikoros,' who is destined to be denied the blessings of the world to come, as one who insults a scholar (b. Sanh. 99b). However ominous such a lapse may have been under ordinary circumstances, one must suppose that in this period, disrespect was sufficiently serious for the rabbis to set aside a particularly unhappy fate for such a person. If, furthermore, we took the following source as probative, we should have to conclude that the Jews did not fight on the Sabbath:

R. Judah in the name of Rav said, If foreigners besieged Israelite towns, it is not permitted to sally forth against them, or to desecrate the Sabbath in any other way on their account, and so a Tanna taught as well.

(b. 'Eruv. 45a)

In fact, the narrative about the Jewish state of Anileus and Asineus makes it quite clear that the Jews not only fought on the Sabbath, but did so not merely to overcome a siege, but to mount aggressive attacks on the enemy.

Similarly, the rabbis themselves preserved comments on the mores of their contemporaries which present a picture quite at variance from the one we should derive from strictly legal sources. For example:

R. Giddal in the name of Rav said, If an inhabitant of Naresh kisses you then count your teeth. If a man of Nehar Pekod accompanies you, then it is because of the fine garments he sees on you. If a Pumeditan accompanies you, change your lodging.

(b. Ḥul. 127a)

Some thieves came up to Pumbedita and opened many casks. Rava said, The wine is permitted. What was his reason? The majority of

---

[1] Even the rabbis had lax servants, see b. Beẓah 14b.

thieves [there] are Jews. The same thing happened in Nehardea, and
Samuel said, The wine is permitted.

(b. A.Z. 70a)

While the rabbis laid great stress upon proper genealogies, holding
the descendants of illegitimate unions might not marry Jews, as
we have seen, the people in whole provinces paid no attention
whatever to their views, and were declared heretics. On the one hand,
the Babylonian rabbis insisted that Babylonia was, from the genealogical viewpoint, the acme of purity:

> R. Judah in the name of Samuel said, All countries are as dough in
> comparison with Palestine, and Palestine is as dough in comparison to
> Babylonia.
>
> (b. Qid. 69b)

They moreover regarded ethical and social conduct as a suitable
measure of genealogical purity:

> Rav said, Peace in Babylonia is the mark of pure birth . . . . R. Judah
> in the name of Rav said, If you see two people continually quarreling
> there is a blemish of unfitness in one of them and they are [provident-
> ially] not allowed to cleave to each other.
>
> (b. Qid. 71b)

> Samuel said, He who claims, 'I am descended from the royal house
> of the Hasmoneans' is a slave, because there remained of them only one
> maiden who ascended a roof, lifted up her voice, and cried out,
> 'Whoever says I am descended from the Hasmoneans is a slave.' On
> that day, many *ketuvot* were torn up in Nehardea. When he went out,
> they came to stone him [R. Judah, who reported the saying], but he
> threatened them, If you will be silent, well and good, but if not, I will
> tell what Samuel said, There are two families in Nehardea, one the
> House of Jonah, the other, the House of Urbati, and the sign thereof
> is 'Unclean to unclean', 'Clean to clean'. Thereupon they threw away
> the stones and created a stoppage in the royal canal.
>
> (b. Qid. 70a)

It was believed that Ezra had taken up with him all of the unsuitable
families, leaving Babylonia genealogically uncontaminated. On the
other hand, we may reconsider the geographical sayings cited above:

> R. Papa in the name of Rav said, Babylonia is healthy, Mesene is
> dead, and Elam is dying. What is the difference between the sick and
> the dying? The sick are destined for life, the dying for death. How
> far does Babylonia extend . . . .
>
> (b. Qid. 71b)

These definitions were provided for genealogical purposes. For instance, Samuel held that Moxoene is genealogically as pure as 'the Exile,' meaning Babylonia; Rav held that Halwan and Nehawand are similarly pure. They clearly reveal, first of all, that the sickness or health of a region was determined by its genealogies; secondly, that large territories were placed beyond the pale; and third, that, even in Babylonia itself were substantial numbers of people whose ancestry concealed a dubious alliance. The rabbis' knowledge of genealogy was regarded as thorough and sound. Rav's visitation and examination of a family was interpreted to mean that he had studied their genealogy. Given the importance ascribed to inherited, as well as acquired, merits, moreover, one can easily understand how the theological importance of proper breeding played such a significant part in the people's choice of marriage-partners. And yet: Mesene is dead and Elam is dying. And in Nehardea itself were many families who had reason to fear rabbinic examination.

One recalls, moreover, that Elam was held to produce students, but not teachers of the law. While a very few rabbis came from Mesene, Adiabene, Armenia, and elsewhere, the bulk of the students in the academies came from, and went back to influence, Babylonia itself. Whatever conditions prevailed in the 'Exile', the outlying districts were probably quite remote from rabbinic law, simply because the institutions and instruments for the propagation and application of the law were unavailable. However useful we may find legal dicta for describing life in the central Babylonian communities, we cannot, therefore, claim to know anything about that in the outlying districts. That is not to say that Jews in Dura, Arbela, Tigranocerta, or Charax Spasinu were not observant. They doubtless kept the bulk of the law, as they understood it; in Dura, provision was made for an 'eruv, which suggests that the Sabbath laws were observed with considerable care. We have no grounds, however, to believe that they kept the law exactly as the rabbis taught it.

The problem of using legal sources in order to describe social life cannot therefore find a simple solution. Here I shall attempt only a very limited step toward a full sociological appreciation of the legal literature. Since the scope of this study is narrowly defined by the first four decades of Sasanian rule, the only material available for study is that in the names of Rav, Samuel, their adult contemporaries, or clearly identified with their times. On such a narrow basis, one cannot even attempt a full description of the life of the people, for no one could reasonably hold that only those laws which Rav and Samuel discussed were actually known in their day, or that only those dicta the observance of which we can demonstrate were actually enforced. Yet a study within narrow chronological limitations will reveal useful information. It can provide evidence on the *minimal* areas of law which were enforced in the daily life of the people, and provide the basis for sound conjecture on those laws, in addition to the obvious ones cited above, which were not enforced, or which were discussed for theoretical purposes only, or which applied to the life of the academy alone. Of the three kinds of legal data, moreover, only the third, the numerous reports about the application and enforcement of the law in popular affairs, is useful here. As we shall see, these reports are by no means scattered evenly through each tractate. This is not to suggest that all legal theory, interpretation of the Mishnah and speculation about hypothetical cases, instruction in the academy, and the like, represented merely exercises of legal fancy. I do not argue that they did. The only exact and concrete evidence we have however, that the law *was* enforced, which therefore helps to provide a picture of the life of the people, is the report of a case that such-and-such a litigation came before one of the rabbis, who decided in such-and-such a manner. This evidence is decisive, and ought to be isolated and examined by itself. I do not know to what extent other kinds of law were carried out by the people. I do know from the kinds of evidence to be studied here that *some* of the law yielded court cases, inquiries to the rabbis from ordinary people, and other kinds of circumstantial evidence that parts of the law in fact influenced the conduct of life.

As I emphasized in the preface, the following pages will by no means exhaust the vast legacy of legal dicta left by Rav, Samuel, and their contemporaries. I do not believe that we shall have touched, in all, more than one-half of all the sayings in the names of early third-century rabbis. Several tractates containing numbers of their Mishnaic interpretations yielded not a single shred of evidence of actual law-enforcement, and will not, therefore, be considered here, even though it is quite reasonable to suppose that parts of such Mishnaic law were actually under practical as well as theoretical consideration. I hope eventually to be able to offer a valid description of Babylonian Jewish social life in Talmudic times, but only after the evidence pertaining to each period has been isolated and examined, and the possibilities of social changes have been taken into account.

II. AGRICULTURAL OFFERINGS

The rabbis believed that Babylonia was subject to the agricultural taxes decreed in Scripture or by ordinance of the prophets.[1] Samuel held, moreover, that hybridization is forbidden, not only to Jews but also to gentiles,[2] and that stipulations on land use supposed to have been laid down by Joshua applied in Babylonia as well.[3] We have, in addition, several sayings of Rav, which indicate that he believed the rules on tithing should be enforced, including one which must be theoretical:

> R. Judah in the name of Rav said, If a heathen separated heave-offering from his pile, then we examine him. If he said, I have separated it with the same intention as an Israelite, it is to be handed to the priest . . .

(b. ʿArakhin 6a)

I doubt that many gentiles would have done so. We cannot, nonetheless, conclude that the great number of the people actually observed these laws, since there is only one example of rabbinical enforcement.[4] On the contrary, one recalls the saying of R. Yoḥanan that "Our *rabbis* in the Exile used to separate heave offerings and tithes until the archers came,"[5] which we suggested, following Halevi, referred to the time of the Palmyrene invasion. The language of R. Yoḥanan is significant, for he holds that it was the *rabbis* who were meticulous on the offerings. It is difficult not to suppose that the laymen were not so conscientious. The rabbis, holding both a tradition and an exegesis based upon Lev. 19.19, acted according to their lights, and their discussions on the laws may be based in part upon their own practice. That the average farmer accepted the burden of offerings, which he may well have regarded as required only in Palestine, above the taxes he paid to the Sasanian government, is not likely. I think the people observed the tabu against sowing with mixed seeds, because we have both a case in which Samuel fined a man for breaking it,[6] and an inquiry from an outlying town about whether

---

[1] Mishnah Yadayim 4.3, "The rule touching Babylonia is the work of the prophets". Compare b. Bekh. 27a, giving *terumah* was a 'rabbinical' enactment.

[2] b. Sanh. 60a, Qid. 39a, based on an exegesis of Lev. 19.19.

[3] b. B.Q. 81b.

[4] The case involving Rav in b. Ḥul. 131a, about a Levite who used to snatch the priestly dues, could well have taken place in Palestine. We have no clear evidence on Babylonia whatever, except for y. ʿOrlah 3.7, cited below.

[5] Above, p. 51-2.

[6] Note, however, the discussions of Rav and Samuel on whether the agricul-

certain plants constituted 'mixed seeds' in a vineyard. I do not know about the rest. Where the biblical law was explicit and well-known, the people obeyed it, and consulted the rabbis about how to do so.

On the other hand, the Palestinian rabbis forbade the breeding of 'small cattle' in Palestine, but permitted it in Syria and in unsettled areas, where if the depredations of goats, for example, damaged the basic agricultural economy by ruining the forests, Jewish Palestine would not be affected. When Rav came to Babylonia, he decreed the same rule:

> R. Judah in the name of Rav said, We put ourselves in Babylonia with reference to the law of breeding small cattle on the same footing as if we were in Palestine. (b. B.Q. 80a)

(We have a similar ruling with regard to bills of divorce). In this matter, however, we have no clear evidence that Rav's legal dictum was in fact widely accepted, and I do not think it likely that the rabbis' authority was sufficient to enforce it. It would have required a very extensive reform of agricultural practices, and evidences of such a reform, in the form of court cases, stories of law enforcement, and the like, are not available. What is more likely is that the rabbis and those who were influenced by them, through sermons, study in the academies, and personal contact, may have followed the decree in this matter, but the greater number of Jewish farmers would not, in this period, have accepted it.

On the other hand, several of the rabbis were very rich men. Samuel, for example, was able to influence the price of produce by his marketing practices, in order to keep it down, as did his father.[1] He owned many slaves.[2] Whatever moral influence he may have exerted was certainly strengthened by his economic power, and in the area around Nehardea, he may thereby have been able to convince others to follow his practice.

Though superficially, this is an argument from silence, actually the absence of cases reporting the enforcement of the various agricultural taxes and most of the tabus is practically probative, for we

---

tural offerings and tabus had to b e ob served, in y. ʿOrlah 3.7. Here we have a case in which Samuel fined a man for disobeying the laws on mixed seeds, "The matter came before Samuel and he fined him". The rabbis were therefore prepared to *enforce* the laws if they could, but this is the only instance we have in which they actually did. See also y. Ḥal. 4.4 on Ḥallah and heave-offerings outside of Palestine, and b. Hul. 134b re R. Sheshet.

[1] b. B.B. 90b.
[2] b. Nid. 47a.

have extensive evidences showing that other kinds of law *were* either
enforced or voluntarily carried out by the people, who therefore
consulted the rabbis about the proper manner of fulfilling them.
It stands to reason that where we have no similar evidence, the law
in fact was mainly theoretical.

III. Transfers of Property, Torts, and Damages

There can be no doubt whatever that the rabbis did effectively
enforce the law as they saw it in *all* matters of transfer of property,
including litigations. The evidence is abundant that they did so.
It is, moreover, quite natural to suppose that they did. What the
farmers did on their farms would not normally come under the
supervision of the rabbis. Disapproved practices would have been
easily concealed; the rabbis could not inspect every farm in Babylonia
to ensure that their interpretation of the law was followed; nor did
they have the right to come to the farmer and extract from him the
agricultural offerings due to the priests and others. To do so
systematically would have entailed the use of a considerable police
force, which the rabbis did not have at their disposal. Transfers of
property were quite another matter. They had to be regulated by
public authorities; documents had to be written properly; and the
rabbis and their scribes *were* the official registrars of such documents.
Orderly and permanent transfer of property required public authorization, recognition, and confirmation. It was the rabbis, acting for the
exilarchate, and empowered, or at least recognized, by the Sasanian
government, who supervised such matters. When the people came
to them, the rabbis had a splendid opportunity to act as they thought
proper. As judges, therefore they had no difficulty in enforcing the
law by their own lights.

It should not, however, be concluded that the rabbis had an
entirely free hand. Practices which the people accepted could not
easily be changed. For example, the people widely practiced the
writing of a *prosbul*, which would annul the affect of the Sabbatical
year upon the remission of debts. Samuel said:

> We do not make out a *prosbul* save either in the Court of Sura or in
> the Court of Nehardea . . . This *prosbul* is an assumption on the part
> of the judges. If I am ever able, I shall abolish it.
>
> (b. Git. 36b)

The practice, however, continued into the next generation.[1]

---

[1] b. Git. 37b. See Weiss, *Dor*, III 153.

Samuel tried to limit the need, by decreeing that orphans do not require a *prosbul*,[1] but his most effective limitation was the requirement to obtain the document in only two courts, which would have necessitated considerable travel from other parts of Babylonia if it was to be met. There is no evidence on the progress of Samuel's policy. Since cases would most certainly have arisen, and come for litigation, under Samuel's decree, and since we have no cases of suit to obtain funds claimed to have been remitted because a document was, from Samuel's viewpoint, invalid, we may suppose that his decree was not widely observed, and that people continued to accept documents written elsewhere, without too much rabbinical opposition.

The rabbis did, however, exert considerable authority on the proper form of deeds and documents of all kinds. Deeds of transfer were brought to court, verified, and confirmed for action, and the rabbis laid down rules which were observed widely, for example:

> Samuel said, If one finds a deed of transfer in the street he should return it to the owners .... R. Naḥman said, My father was among the scribes of Mar Samuel's court when I was about six or seven years old, and I remember that they used to proclaim, Deeds of transfer which are found in the street should be returned to their owners ...
>
> (b. B.M. 16b)[2]

The rabbis adjudicated conflicting claims based upon legal documents; they laid down many rules on how to do so. I have no doubt whatever that these rules were put into effect.[3]

Transfers of inheritance and the execution of wills posed numerous knotty problems to the rabbinical courts. Samuel warned his student, R. Judah, to avoid transferring inheritances, on moral grounds, from a bad to a good son,

> ... because one never knows what issue will come forth from him, and much more so from a son to a daughter.   (b. Ket. 53a)[4]

Questions were addressed to the rabbis from outlying parts:

> The people of 'Akra di'Agma asked Samuel, Will our master teach us? What is the law in the case where one was generally held to be the first-born son, but the father declared another to be first born?
>
> (b. B.B. 127b)

---

[1] b. Git. 37a.
[2] Another case is in b. Ket 21a.
[3] For example, b. B.B. 34b-35a, b. Sanh. 28b, B.B. 51b.
[4] Also b. B.B. 133b.

> R. Jeremiah b. Abba reported, The following inquiry was sent from the academy to Samuel: Will our master instruct us? What about a dying man who gave all his estate to strangers in writing, and an act of acquisition took place . . .
>
> (b. B.B. 152b)

Cases were brought to them for adjudication:

> A case in Nehardea arose [in which a man said to his wife, My estate will belong to you and your children] and Samuel allowed her to receive one-half of the estate.
>
> (b. B.B. 143a)

There is no reason to doubt that the rabbis possessed sufficient authority to carry out the law. Since they were judging cases which *had* to be brought to their courts, they quite naturally enforced the law of the Mishnah as they understood it, and the significant number of such cases prevents any doubt whatever about the practical effectiveness of their decisions and opinions.

The principles of adjudication were widely proclaimed, moreover, so that people would not need to be constantly repairing to the courts, but would act, in the first place, according to the law. For instance,

> Samuel said to R. Ḥanan of Bagdad, Go and bring me a group of ten men so that I may tell you in their presence that if title is conferred upon an embryo, [through the agency of a third party] it does acquire ownership.
>
> (b. Yev. 67a)[1]

It was particularly important for people to know the proper way of effecting acquisition of property. In Jewish law, money payment does not constitute acquisition, but a formal action is required. Rav lectured in Kimḥania, near Sura, on how to acquire large cattle,[2] and Samuel issued many dicta on the subject of acquiring fields, trees, and so forth.[3] Cases came to court in which ownership of a property was in dispute:

> A certain lady had the usufruct of a date-tree to the extent of lopping off its branches [for cattle-fodder] for thirteen years. A man came and hoed under it a little, and claimed ownership. He asked Levi [or, Mar ʿUkba] who confirmed title to the land. The woman complained

---

[1] See b. Ket. 7b, Qid. 42a, where Rav provides a Scriptural basis through exegesis of Num. 34.18, B.B. 142b, y. Yev. 4.1.

[2] b. Qid. 25b.

[3] b. B.B. 54a.

bitterly. He said, What can I do for you? For you did not establish
your title properly.

(b. B.B. 54a)

Since it was in the hands of the court to confirm or deny title to
the land, the judges were able to effect their view of the law, even
though it ran contrary to popular practice. In this case, the woman
had assumed she owned the tree, and until someone challenged her
in court, no one assumed to the contrary. Hence it stands to reason
that most people identified usufruct with possession. The rabbis did
not, and when they came to apply the Mishnaic law, they were able
only through *force majeure* to sustain their decisions. Doubtless in time,
the people became better acquainted with these laws, as indeed they
would have had to in order to avoid chaos in economic affairs.

The rabbis encouraged the people to avoid purchasing disputed
lands, but to seek a clear title. As we have seen, Samuel applied the
verse, 'And did that which is not good among his people' (Ezek. 18.18)
to one who buys a field about which are disputes. Such disputes could
easily arise, for example, when the Persians allocated title to whoever
paid the delinquent taxes on a piece of property. The Jewish owner
could keep alive his claim to the land by protesting to the Jewish
court.[1] The frequency of cases involving improvement of land is
seen in the following:

> R. Naḥman in the name of Samuel said, In three cases the improve-
> ments are assessed and payment made in money, [to settle the debt of]
> the first-born to the ordinary son, of the creditor or of the widow who
> collected her ketuvah to orphans, and of the creditors to the vendees
> . . . . Samuel said, A creditor collects the improvements . . . *Cases
> arose daily* where Samuel ordered distraint even of the improvement
> touching the carriers . . .

(b. B.B. 110b)

In the third case, if the debtor sold his land, the vendee may lose
it to the creditor, but must be compensated for his improvements. The
range of laws which were actually enforced quite obviously extends
far beyond the few cited here; what is significant in those noted
above is that cases *are* cited, in which the rabbis, speaking quite
without guile, refer to decisions and precedents.

Cases of claim for loss or damages came quite regularly to the
rabbinical courts, and these were discussed in legal study in the
academies. For example:

---

[1] b. B.B. 39b, for example.

A certain person borrowed an axe from his neighbor and broke it. He came before Rav, who said to him, Go and pay [the lender] for his sound axe . . .

(b. B.Q. 11a)[1]

Abbuha b. Iḥi . . . bought a garret from his sister, and a creditor came and took it away from him. He appeared before Mar Samuel, who said, Did she write you a guarantee? No. Then, if so, go in peace. So he said to him, Is it not you, Sir, who said that [omission of a clause] mortgaging the debtor's property is due to an error of the scribe [and therefore not actionable]? He replied, This applies only to notes of indebtedness but it does not apply to documents of buying or selling, for a man may buy land for a day.

(b. B.M. 13b)

Normally, the litigants were given a choice of arbitration or litigation.[2]

The rabbis' judgments were carefully studied, and abstract legal principles were derived, sometimes wrongly, from their decisions:

R. ʿAnan in the name of Samuel said, An orphan's money may be lent at interest. R. Naḥman objected, Because they are orphans are we to feed them with forbidden food? What happened [in the case you have in mind, that you issue such a dictum]? He replied, A cauldron belonging to the children of Mar ʿUkba [who were orphaned] was in Samuel's care, and he weighed it before hiring it out, and weighed it when receiving it back, charging for its hire and for its loss of weight. But if a fee for hiring existed, there should be no charge for depreciation, and if there was a charge for depreciation, there should be no fee for hiring. [Hence, interest is involved]. He replied, Such a transaction is permitted even to bearded men, since he [the owner] stands the loss of wear and tear, for the more the copper is burned, the greater the depreciation.

(b. B.M. 69b)[3]

Hence it is clear that R. ʿAnan had no tradition whatever about Samuel's opinion, but only a story from which he deduced a saying. Since he did not indicate, in his original formulation, that he was transmitting his own interpretation of Samuel's view, it stands to reason that other such sayings in Samuel's name in fact were derived from his actions or court decisions. It is significant, I think, that such instances emerge only in matters of civil and commercial law, rather than, for instance, cultic or agricultural law. The legal sayings of the

---

[1] See also b. B.M. 96b.
[2] b. Sanh. 6b.
[3] Compare b. Git. 52a.

rabbis on dormant matters, such as the cult, or on areas of law which were mostly matters of theoretical discussion, such as agricultural tithing, did not give rise to any such speculation on the basis of action, as indeed they could not. It was where the law actually governed daily affairs that the rabbis' actions were subjected to close scrutiny.[1] We have a similar example for Rav:

> It was stated, If one enters his neighbor's field and plants it without permission, Rav said, An assessment is made, and he is at a disadvantage, and Samuel said, We estimate what one would pay to have such a field planted. Rav Papa said, There is no conflict, Samuel refers to a field suitable for planting [trees] and Rav to a field not so suited. Now this ruling of Rav was not explicitly stated, but inferred from a general ruling, for a man came before Rav. Go and assess it for him, he said. He demurred, But I do not desire it. He said, Go and assess it for him and he shall be at a disadvantage. But I do not desire it, he repeated. Subsequently he saw that he had fenced the field and was guarding it, and Rav said to him, You have revealed your mind that you desire it, Go and assess it for him, and the planter shall be at an advantage.
>
> (b. B.M. 101a)

Similarly, in a case of damages:

> It was stated, If one bailee entrusted to another, Rav said, He (the latter) is not liable, and R. Yoḥanan said, He is liable. R. Ḥisda said, This ruling of Rav was not stated explicitly but by inference. For there were certain gardeners who used to deposit their spades daily with one particular old woman. But one day they deposited them with one of themselves. Hearing the sounds of a wedding, he went out and entrusted them to that old woman. Between his going and his return, the spades were stolen, and when he came before Rav, he declared him not liable. Now those who saw this thought that it was because if a bailee entrusts to another, he is free, but that is not so. This case was different, seeing that every day they themselves used to deposit with that old woman . . .
>
> (b. B.M. 36a)

If we did not have the testimony of R. Ḥisda, we should have assumed that Rav held such an opinion, transmitted by the 'Amora' in the academy; but, in fact, he never expressed, and probably did not hold it. Such a case signifies that the actions of the rabbis were closely observed and widely discussed, a situation explicable, as I said, only if they in fact judged cases publicly. I have not attempted to cite *every* case of damages which the rabbis adjudicated; those given above provide sufficient evidence that their authority was effective and mostly unchallenged.[2]

---

[1] As in blessings over food, among the academicians, see below p. 274f.
[2] See for example, on the return of lost property, b. B.M. 24b; on damages

By contrast to the substantial number of civil suits, I know of not a single criminal action reported as a precedent, or described as a case under adjudication, in the time of Rav and Samuel, except for those cited above[1], in which 'a man wanted to show another's straw,' and another 'had intercourse with a Gentile woman.' These cases provide no significant exception, for they involved political, rather than merely judicial, policy, and do not prove that the rabbis judged criminal cases or executed the death penalty. On the contrary, the former was a case, at best, involving civil damages, which political circumstances transformed into something more serious. The latter entailed only flogging for immorality. In Parthian times, Jewish courts probably had the right to inflict the death penalty. In this period, they did not. We do not have the record of other cases, involving less serious penalties, which the rabbis judged. We know that there were Jewish courts, and that these courts did govern substantial matters, including significant civil and commercial litigations. We also have many sayings on criminal law by Rav and Samuel, but have no cases showing that they enforced their opinions in court-actions. Since, in a vast population, criminal cases must have arisen, we can reasonably assume that in this period the Jewish courts did not try them, but that the Sasanians mostly did.

IV. LAWS OF PERSONAL STATUS

In matters of personal status, the view of the rabbis was enforced in courts, and therefore prevailed widely. The reason is the same: the public recognition of the legality of a marriage and the legitimacy of its offspring depended upon court action, not merely upon private acquiescence, and since the rabbis were in charge of the courts, their views gained ascendancy. We have seen above that in territories where people were indifferent to rabbinical laws, there was little the rabbis could do but prohibit marriage with the inhabitants, and where appropriate, declare the offspring illegitimate. In Babylonia however, the rabbis' power and authority were substantial, and their courts possessed great prestige. We have reports of many cases where they were consulted, or their laws put into effect, in matters of personal status, marriage, and divorce, and in the preparation of documents

---

ensuing from depreciation of the coinage, b. B.Q. 99b, B.Q. 103a, b. B.M. 44b (not a court case), unpaid debts, b. B.M. 77b, loss because of error in ritual slaughtering, b. B.Q. 99b, damages through negligence, b. B.Q. 48b, B.Q. 27b.
[1] See above, p. 30-35.

relevant to such affairs. Their dicta were widely discussed. I have no doubt, therefore, that the law on these subjects reflects practical, and not only theoretical, situations.

The rabbis issued public instructions in matters of marriage, though we do not know whether they were invariably obeyed. Benjamin (of Gazaca) publicly preached that intercourse with a virgin may be performed on the Sabbath, against the view of Samuel.[1] Similarly it was the view of Rav that a barren marriage must be annulled after two and one-half years, but we have not a single record of a case in which such a law applied.[2] The normal means of law enforcement in cases of personal status was flogging:

> Rav ordered the chastisement of any person who betrothed by cohabitation [rather than by a document or money-exchange], who betrothed in the open street, or who betrothed without previous negotiation: who annulled a letter of divorce; or who made a declaration against [the validity of] a letter of divorce; who was insolent towards the representative of the rabbis, or who allowed a rabbinical ban upon him to remain for thirty days and did not come to the court to request the removal of the ban; and of a son-in-law who lived in his father-in-law's house. The Nehardeans stated, Rav ordered the chastisement of none of these except him who betrothed by cohabitation without preliminary negotiation [because this was sheer licentiousness].
>
> (b. Yev. 52a, Qid. 12b)

It seems most reasonable to accept the view of the Nehardeans, because the other cases would have involved the flogging of people who probably acted in a way they thought right, without evil intent, except for those who did not heed the decree of a rabbinical court, and these may have been so numerous that floggings would have been required everywhere, bringing the law and the rabbis into disrepute.

The rabbis' medical knowledge brought respect for their judgments of the legitimacy of children:

> Is a man [whose stones are] punctured incapable of procreation? Surely a man once climbed up a palm tree and a thorn pierced his stones, so that his semen issued like a thread of pus, and he begat children. In that case, as matter of fact, Samuel sent word to Rav telling him, Institute inquires respecting the parentage of his children.
>
> (b. Yev. 75a-b)

Here we see a case in which the rabbis were able to deny, if they

---

[1] y. Ber. 2.6.
[2] b. Yev. 64b.

chose, the legitimacy of children, and the implication is clearly that such a declaration would have carried weight. Indeed, since such a child would have been unable to claim his inheritance in court, and since the rabbis would not recognize (for judicial purposes) his marriage to a legitimate Israelite, they had considerable power. Similarly, we cited above[1] the case in which a rabbi was consulted on whether the wife of a man believed to have drowned might remarry. These cases indicate without question that the rabbis exerted considerable power over marriage, divorce, and similar affairs.[2]

Their students, moreover, believed that their actions were worthy of emulation, even where the courts could not, or would not, require behavior in like manner. Thus we have the following account:

> Rav Kahana once went in and hid under Rav's bed. He heard him chatting with his wife, and joking, and doing what he required. He said to him, One would think that Abba's mouth had never sipped the dish before. He said to him, Kahana, are you here? Go out, because it is not proper. He replied, It is a matter of Torah, and I need to learn.
>
> (b. Ber. 62a)

The students' eagerness to learn and transmit the ways of their masters in time extended the influence of the rabbis to matters far beyond those which their courts adjudicated, so that their values, embodied in exemplary action among the masses, came to shape those of the entire community. But in this period, it was mainly through court action and the threat of court-inflicted punishment that they were able to affect public behavior.

They were concerned that people who did not know the law should not deal with matters of marriage and divorce, since the consequences could be quite serious:

> R. Judah in the name of Samuel said, He who does not know the particular nature of divorce and betrothal [laws] should have no business with them . . .
>
> (b. Qid. 6a, 13a)

For their part, they investigated the validity of betrothals:

> R. Jeremiah b. Abba said, The disciples of Rav sent to Samuel saying, Would our master instruct us? If a woman was *reported* to have been engaged to one man, and then another came and betrothed her

---

[1] P. 115-116, b. Yev. 121a.

[2] As y. Qid. 3.12, y. Yev. 4.15, may the child of an Israelite woman and an "Aramaean" man marry a Jew?

formally, what is to be done? He replied, She must leave him, but I want you to ascertain the facts and inform me . . .

(b. Git. 89b)[1]

A certain man betrothed a woman with a bundle of tow cotton. Now R. Shimi b. Ḥiyya sat before Rav and examined it. If it was worth a perutah, well, and if not, it was not a valid betrothal . . .

(b. Qid. 12a)

A certain man betrothed with a myrtle branch in the market place. R. Aḥa b. Huna asked R. Joseph, How is it in such a case? He replied, Have him flogged in accordance with Rav, and demand a divorce in accordance with Samuel . . .

(b. Qid. 12b)

These are three cases which indicate that the rabbis did look into the validity of betrothals, and executed the law. In a further case, we have a report which almost certainly reflected actual practice:

Samuel said, One is allowed to betrothe a woman during the [weekdays of] a festival, lest another anticipate him . . . . It means, the preliminary terms, as R. Giddal in the name of Rav stated, How much do you give to your son? So-much and so-much. How much do you give to your daughter? So-much and so-much. If they then stood up and pronounced the dedication they have acquired their legal rights. These are matters that are legally concluded by word of mouth.

(b. M.Q. 18b)

Samuel likewise decreed that one might betrothe even on the 9th of Av.[2] While no cases provide illustration of the enforcement of this decree, the language cited by Rav reflects actual daily speech, and Samuel's dictum certainly does not contradict what one would expect people to have done. On the other hand, the rabbis demanded considerably more reticent behavior with women than they could possibly have publicly required:[3]

R. Judah and Rav were walking on a road, and a woman was walking in front of them. Rav said to R. Judah, Lift your feet before Gehenna [Speed on]. But you yourself said, he replied, that with respectable people, it is well [for two men to be alone with one woman]. Who says that respectable people mean such as you and me, he replied? Then such as whom? Such as R. Ḥanina b. Pappai and his companions.

(b. Qid. 8a)[4]

---

[1] See below, p. 273, and Git. 81a.
[2] y. Beẓah 5.2.
[3] b. Qid. 80b, 81a, 81b.
[4] See b. Qid. 39a.

Similarly, Samuel said that even the voice of a woman constituted an invitation to license. Rav held

> We flog on account of *yiḥud* [being alone with a woman] but we do not excommunicate on its account.
>
> (b. Qid. 81a)

Since there was no actionable case likely to arise from such matters, unless they produced significant complications, we have no reason to believe that the rabbis actually did any such thing, because, as in former instances, their police power was inadequate to it.

The dissolution of a marriage tie, on the other hand, bore significant consequences. Property had to be transferred, and persons had to be designated as free to remarry. Hence court action was invariably required, for the preparation of a document of divorce, or for the provision of a ceremony of *ḥaliẓah*. Yet even in the latter case, the peoples' pattern of behavior took precedence over rabbinic opinion:

> Rabbah in the name of R. Kahana in the name of Rav said, If Elijah should come and declare that *ḥaliẓah* may be performed with a shoe that covers the foot, he would be obeyed. If he said that *ḥaliẓah* may not be performed with a sandal, he would not be obeyed, for the people have long ago adopted the practice of [performing it] with a sandal.
>
> (b. Yev. 102a)[1]

Furthermore, individual rabbis supervised the ceremony in accord with their own, and not the majority, view.[2] Divorces, on the other hand, were easier to regulate, since they required correct documents, and the rabbis were implacably meticulous in enforcing the law, as well they could be:

> There was a certain man who said, If I do not come back from now until thirty days, grant a divorce to my wife. He came back at the end of thirty days, but the ferry prevented his crossing the river. He called, See I have come back, see I have come back, but Samuel said, That was not regarded as having come back.
>
> (b. Ket. 2b, Git. 34a)

Similarly, they had to adjudicate unclear situations:

> R. Joseph the son of R. Manasseh of Dewil sent an inquiry to Samuel saying, Would our master instruct us: If a rumor spread that so-and-so, a priest, has written a *get* for his wife, but she still lives with

---

[1] Compare y. Yev. 12.1.

[2] b. Yev. 104a. Compare b. Ket. 54a, Rav's town followed his practice in marriage-contracts, and Samuel's his.

him and looks after him, what are we to do? He sent back, She must leave him, but the case must be examined. What are we to understand by this? Shall we say that we examine whether we can put a stop to the rumor or not? But Samuel lived in Nehardea, and in Nehardea it was not the rule [of the court] to put a stop to rumors . . .

(b. Git. 81a)

What is striking here is the ability of the rabbis to intervene in a matter which the people could manage for themselves. One did not *have* to have a bill of divorce written by a court-appointed scribe, for as we have seen in the above case, a man might write his own divorce and have it recognized. Nonetheless the rabbis were able in fact to regulate the matter, and the laws yielded cases which leave no doubt about their practical application.[1] They could compel a man to divorce his wife, if sufficient cause could be shown.[2] Their power did not rest merely upon popular acquiescence, but upon the coercive capacities of their courts, and the practical consequences of the decrees these courts might issue. The writing of such decrees by the court scribes was carefully supervised by the rabbinical judges:

R. Jeremiah b. Abba said, An inquiry was sent from the school of Rav to Samuel, Would our master teach us, If a man said to two persons, Write and deliver a bill of divorce to my wife, and they told a scribe and he wrote it and they themselves signed it, what is the law? [Are the words, THEY SHOULD WRITE in the Mishnah to be understood literally, or do they denote merely signatures?] He sent back word, She must leave [her second husband] but the matter requires further study . . .

(b. Git. 66b)

Rav said to his Scribes, and R. Huna to his, When at Shili, write at Shili, although information was given to you at Hini, and vice versa.
(b. B.B. 172a)[3]

There was a certain woman named Nafa'atha and the witness on the bill wrote it Tafa'atha. R. Isaac b. Samuel b. Martha in the name of Rav said, The witnesses have discharged their commission.

(b. Git. 63b)

They similarly supervised the writing of marriage-contracts:

The marriage-contract of R. Hiyya b. Rav was written by day and signed by night. Rav himself was present and made no objection.
(b. Git. 18a)

---

[1] Compare b. Qid. 44b, y. Git. 6.1 for such cases.
[2] b. Git. 88b, with a case in y. Git. 3.8.
[3] b. Git. 80a, b. Yev. 116a.

The presentation of documents and their proper verfication were likewise strictly regulated.[1]

The cases cited here do not, of course, nearly exhaust the great number of sayings relevant to personal status. My intention is not to present a profile of the law, but rather to suggest those areas of law, a profile of which would be congruent to social realities. As we saw at the outset, a legal saying by itself testifies quite inadequately, if at all, to the prevailing social conditions. Some sayings, however, are part of a corpus of enforced law, specifically those dealing with matters of commerce, transfer of property, marriage, divorce and the like, and that corpus of law did shape public life, and can provide a valuable resource for describing the life of the people. The sayings of Rav, Samuel, and their adult contemporaries, however, constitute only a small portion of that resource, which accumulated over a period of three hundred years, and it would be misleading to isolate their sayings for such a purpose. I hope in time to attempt a more comprehensive portrait than is possible within the narrow chronological limits set for this study.

v. Laws on Religious Life

The Bible shaped the religious life of the masses. The rabbis did not need to urge the people to keep fundamental, biblically-ordained laws. This they did because they believed it was what God wanted them to do. Popular practice required rabbinical supervision of the *ways* the commandments were to be carried out. On matters where biblical laws and rabbinical interpretations were perfectly clear, well known, and widely accepted, there the rabbis merely guided, without need of coercion of any kind, the affairs of the people, who brought them their queries. Where rabbinical injunctions were more severe, or in some way not widely known or accepted, the rabbis had to rely upon a measure of coercion, as best they could. For the most part, however, more than they coerced, they were *consulted* by the people, because they were believed to know precisely the way the law should be obeyed, and they did not have to resort to floggings, excommunication, and the like, in commonplace areas of the law. This is not to suggest that the masses were quite so meticulously observant as the rabbis would have liked, nor that in some even elementary matters the law was easily enforced. We have seen that

---

[1] See for example b. Git. 6a.

R. Aḥai b. R. Josiah had to excommunicate a whole village because of Sabbath violations, and many married contrary to the law. Tension between a class of religious virtuosi and the masses of their followers is certainly not an uncommon phenomenon in the history of religions. Because they knew the Bible, the Jewish masses, however, provide an example of a community which, on the whole, proved amenable to the guidance of their leaders, even when they modified long-established customs, if they could base such actions on exegeses of Scripture. It was, in the end, the school-house which guided, and the academy which defined, obedience to the law.

The three kinds of laws most rigorously obeyed were those of Kashrut, menstrual separation, and the Sabbath. In all three, we find that the rabbis were frequently consulted, but it was mainly in Sabbath observance that they resorted to flogging. The rabbis could not supervise every kitchen in Babylonia, and therefore had, mostly, to wait to be consulted about the law, or to enforce it out-of-hand in the butcher shops if they could. When they were consulted, they could, of course, issue decrees which the people, if they wanted to do the right thing, might carry out. The laws governing the cessation of intercourse during a woman's menstrual period likewise could not be enforced except by voluntary action, for if the rabbis could not inspect every farm and every kitchen, they most certainly could not supervise every bedroom. The cases we shall examine indicate, however, that the people did consult them with frequency, and thus conscientiously sought to obey the menstrual tabus. The Sabbath, on the other hand, was publicly observed, and if it was broken, that, too, took place in public. The rabbis did not have to wait to be consulted; they aggressively punished Sabbath breaking, and the people doubtless expected them to, because of well-known biblical precedents. The cases we have, likewise, indicate that the rabbis used physical coercion to ensure proper Sabbath observance in their communities. We do not know how the Sabbath law was observed in areas not under rabbinical supervision. We have, however, numerous inquiries on the part of students, whose Sabbath observance would have carried the rabbis' influence far beyond the limits of their supervision. By contrast, the synagogue liturgies were not invariably conducted according to rabbinical opinion. The rabbi had no special function in synagogue affairs. He did not preside over the service, nor was his presence necessary for its conduct. As we shall

see, accepted and ancient synagogue practices were sometimes far
beyond the supervision or contrary to the will of the rabbis.

As in many other matters, the fundamental laws of ritual slaughter
were widely observed, while details varied from place to place.
For example, two teachings of Rav contradict one another:

> R. Huna in the name of Rav said, If the femur of a bird was dislodged,
> it is permitted. Rabbah b. R. Huna said to R. Huna, But the rabbis
> who came from Pumbedita reported the statement of R. Judah in the
> name of Rav, If the femur was dislodged it is prohibited [terefah]. He
> replied, My son, every river has its own course.
>
> (b. Ḥul. 57a)

> Rav once happened to be at Tatlefush[1] and overheard a woman
> asking her neighbor, How much milk is required for cooking a rib of
> meat? Said Rav, do they not know that meat cooked with milk is
> forbidden? He therefore stayed there and declared the udder forbidden
> to them.
>
> (b. Ḥul. 110a)

Since Rav apparently found an obedient audience, it cannot be
concluded that the people were hostile to observance of these laws.
They simply did not know the rabbinic exegesis on Exodus 34.26.
The rabbis differed among themselves, moreover, on details of the
food laws, and these differences may have been based upon varying
local customs, traditions, or view of what the facts in the case required:

> It was stated, If [hot] fish was served on a [meat] plate, Rav says,
> It is forbidden to eat it with milk sauce. Samuel says, It is permitted to
> eat it with milk sauce. [The issue is whether it imparted a flavor].
> This ruling of Rav ... was not expressly stated by him, but was
> inferred from the following incident. Rav once visited the house of
> R. Shimi b. Ḥiyya, his grandson. He felt a pain in his eyes, so they
> prepared an ointment on a dish. Later on he was served with stew in
> this same dish, and he detected the taste of the ointment in it. He
> remarked, Does it impart such a strong flavor? [Thus even an indirect
> taste is of consequence.] ....
>
> (b. Ḥul. 111b)

On the other hand, Samuel served fish upon a meat plate with milk
sauce. Similarly, the proper manner of ritual-preparation of meat
was debated, and people acted according to the opinion of one or
another of the rabbis:

> Bar Piuli was standing in the presence of Samuel and porging
> [removing the sciatic nerve] a side of meat. He was only cutting away

---

[1] Obermeyer 298.

the surface. Samuel said to him, Go down deeper, Had I not seen you you might have given me forbidden meat to eat. He was alarmed, and the knife fell out of his hand. Samuel said, Do not be alarmed, for he who taught you this taught you according to the view of R. Judah . .

(b. Ḥul. 96a)

Numerous cases came before the rabbis for practical decision;[1] as we noted above, the exilarch expected that his rabbinical judges would deal with such cases.[2] If they were present, they would also give an opinion where it was not solicited:

> Rav said, Meat which has disappeared from sight is forbidden. This rule of Rav was not expressly stated, but was inferred from the following incident. Rav was once sitting by the ford of the Ishtatit[3], when he saw a man washing the head of an animal in the water. It fell out of his hand, so he went and fetched a basket, threw it into the water, and brought up two heads. Said Rav, Is this what usually happens? And he forbade him both heads. R. Kahana and R. ᵓAssi asked Rav, Are only forbidden heads found here, and not permitted ones? He replied, Forbidden ones are more frequent. [It was a jetty frequented by gentiles]. Rav was once going to his son-in-law R. Ḥanan, when he saw a ferry boat coming towards him. He said to himself, When the ferry boat comes to meet one, it is a good omen. He came to the door, and looked through the crack, and saw the meat of an animal hanging up. He then knocked at the door, and everybody came out to meet him, even the butchers. Rav did not take his eyes off the meat, and said, If that is how you look after things, you are giving my daughter's children forbidden meat to eat, and Rav did not eat of that meat.
>
> (b. Ḥul. 95b)[4]

The rabbis therefore held much higher standards than the people, but there can be very little question that the people obeyed the basic laws, because they learned them in the Bible.

While most laws of ritual purity were inapplicable in Babylonia,[5] the biblical prohibition of intercourse with a menstruant was certainly observed by the people. The rabbis were consulted on the meaning of vaginal stains and excretions:

> Shila b. Abina gave a practical decision following Rav [that a woman in labor during eleven days of zibah who discharged some blood is unclean]. When Rav's soul was about to depart to its eternal rest, he

[1] b. A.Z. 68b, b. Ḥul. 44a, 53b.
[2] b. Ḥul. 58b, Pes. 76b.
[3] Obermeyer 300.
[4] See y. Sheqalim 7.2.
[5] See Funk, op. cit., I, 70, Ginzberg, Law and Lore, 13.

said to R. ʾAssi, Go and restrain him, and if he does not listen to you
try to convince him . . . .

(b. Nid. 36b)[1]

Further, the rabbis aggressively enforced the law when evidence
reached them that it had been broken:

> . . . When a certain sac was submitted to Mar Samuel, he said, This
> is forty-one days old, but on calculating the time since the woman had
> gone to perform her ritual immersion until that day and finding that
> there were no more than forty days, he declared, This man must have
> had intercourse during her menstrual period, and having been arrested,
> he confessed.

(b. Nid. 25b)

As I said, the rabbis did not have to wait for consultations on
Sabbath observance, nor did they need to resort to calculations to
discover when it had been violated. Sabbath observance was public
and communal, and the rabbis vigorously enforced its laws. Their
own Sabbath observance was closely watched, and emulated by the
disciples.[2] Two kinds of violations were easily punished, first, those
involving publicly-observed work on the Sabbath:

> Certain gardeners once brought water [on the Sabbath, from the
> public to private domain] through human walls [the men forming
> them were aware of the purpose] and Samuel had them flogged. He
> said, If the rabbis permitted human walls where the men composing
> them were unaware of their purpose, would they also permit such
> walls where the men were aware of the purpose?

(b. ʿEruv. 44b)

Secondly, the setting up of Sabbath limits (ʿeruvin) to permit
carrying within a specified village or courtyard was a public action,
and easily supervised:

> [Come and hear of the case of a certain alley in which Eibu b. Ihi
> lived.] He furnished it with a sidepost (for an ʿeruv) and Samuel
> allowed him his unrestricted use. R. ʿAnan subsequently came and
> threw it down. He exclaimed, I have been living undisturbed in this
> alley on the authority of Samuel. Why should R. ʿAnan b. Rav now
> come and throw the sidepost down!

(b. ʿEruv. 74a)

> R. ʿAnan was asked, Is it necessary to lock [the door of an alley] or
> not? He replied, Come and see the alley gateways of Nehardea which

---

[1] For other practical decisions see y. Nid. 2.5, 2.7, b. Nid. 66a, 65a, 25a.

[2] As b. ʿEruv. 102a, b. Shab. 146b, y. ʿEruv. 6.8, a question asked by disciples
to Samuel; b. Beẓah 16b, Samuel permits another to rely upon his ʿeruv tavshilin.

are half-buried in the ground [and cannot be moved from their open positions and locked] and Mar Samuel continually passes through these gates and yet never raised any objection . . . When R. Naḥman came, he ordered the earth to be removed . . . There was a certain crooked alley in Nehardea upon which were imposed the restriction of Rav and the restriction of Samuel . . . .

(b. ʿEruv. 6b)

In these cases, the rabbis could easily order that the Sabbath-limit conform to the law, or simply construct the ʿeruv they approved of.[1] In their travels, likewise, they lectured on Sabbath law,[2] and outlying towns wrote and asked for advice:

> The citizens of Bashkar[3] sent a question to Levi: What about setting a canopy [on the Sabbath]? What about cuscuta in a vineyard [is it prohibited on account of 'mixed seeds']?[4] What about a dead man on a festival [can you hold a funeral]? By the time it arrived, Levi had died. Said Samuel to R. Menashia, If you are wise, send them (a reply). So he sent word, As for a canopy, we have examined it from all aspects and do not find any aspect by which it can be permitted . . . Cuscuta in a vineyard—Rav said, He who wishes to sow cuscuta in a vineyard, let him do so. As for a corpse, he sent word, Neither Jews nor Arameans may occupy themselves with a corpse, neither on the first, nor on the second day of a festival.

(b. Shab. 139a)

It is significant that most of the cases illustrating the enforcement of Sabbath law relate to the statutes of ʿeruvin, and not, for the most part, to those of Sabbath work itself, except the case cited here and the one, dating from Arsacid times, about the men excommunicated by R. Aḥai b. R. Josiah. Given the complexity of those laws, and the conditions of life, one cannot easily assume that no Sabbath-law violations required attention, nor that only the relatively complex laws of ʿeruvin produced questions. The simple inquiry from Bashkar reflects, quite to the contrary, that people did not know very basic laws, and doubtless they were unaware of other such laws, without being instructed by the rabbis unless they sent inquiry, or having received a pastoral visit from one of the rabbis. For the most part, except for public actions in which the law was unequivocal, the rabbis could not easily enforce their will. Rav, for example, "saw a man

---

[1] b. Beẓah 16b, Samuel's Father used to set the ʿeruv for all of Nehardea.
[2] y. ʿEruv. 1.4, Rav happened to come to a certain place; b. ʿEruv. 6a, Rav at Damharia, near Sura; 100b, Rav at Afsatia.
[3] Obermeyer, p. 91.
[4] See above, p. 260-262.

sowing flax on Purim, and he cursed him, so the flax would not grow."[1] The rabbis' prestige far outweighed their coercive power, for people believed in their curses. On the other hand, Samuel's father was asked whether, if a man is compelled by force to eat unleavened bread [on Passover] he has performed his religious obligation to do so,[2] and he replied, that he had, which suggests that force was used in religious matters, yet not by the rabbis in this instance. It stands to reason, therefore, that the people themselves enforced religious law as they understood it; everyone knew that one should eat unleavened bread on Passover, and it might easily happen that villagers might force one of their number to do so. As we have seen, the rabbis relied on flogging and on the ban to ensure proper observance:

> Rav and Samuel both said, We impose the ban [for violation of] the two festival days of the diaspora.
>
> (b. Pes. 52a)

Such means were effective only in a context of general obedience, in which the people for the most part wanted to do the right thing, and required supervision and encouragement, and in the case of minor recalcitrance, a limited measure of coercion.

While the rabbis laid down many laws about proper mourning customs, we have only the case of the inquiry from Bashkar, about festival law, to illustrate popular adherence to their views. On the other hand, the following teaching was probably not invariably obeyed:

> R. Judah in the name of Rav said, When a person dies in town, all the townspeople are forbidden from doing work.
>
> (b. M.Q. 27b)

We have no example of punishment meted out for failure to observe that law. The rabbis' views on proper mourning procedure were most easily enforced among their own students, and I believe that it was *only* among the disciples, in this period, that meticulous observance of rabbinical enactments on mourning was found. We have questions addressed to the rabbis only from their students,[3] and the single case of law enforcement deals with a student:

---

[1] b. Meg. 5b.

[2] b. R. H. 28b.

[3] b. M.Q. 21a, Rabba b. Bar Ḥana is instructed by Rav.

A certain student of Samuel had intercourse [during a bereavement].
Samuel heard about it and was angry with him, and he died ...

(y. M.Q. 3.5)

(Such a matter could easily become public at a ritual bathhouse.)
I have no doubt whatever that the people observed mourning rites,
but there is no ground to assume that these rites followed rabbinical
enactments:

> [Mishnah: A Person should not stir up wailing for his dead nor
> hold a lamentation for him thirty days before a feast]. Why just
> thirty days? R. Kahana in the name of R. Judah in the name of Rav
> said, It once happened that a man saved money to go up for a feast
> [to Jerusalem] when a [professional] lamenter came and stopped at his
> door and the wife took her husbands savings and gave them to him,
> so he was prevented from going . . . .

(b. M.Q. 8a)

This case, which happened in Palestine, suggests that popular
mourning practices were well-established, and the rabbis would
have had difficulty modifying them.

Synagogue liturgies were likewise very ancient, and the people
had long conducted synagogue affairs without rabbinical supervision.
Even though such matters were public, and therefore easy to regulate,
the tenacity of ancient customs was such as to prevent the rabbis,
who had no sacerdotal function, from effecting their will. For example,
we cited above the following story:

> Rav once came to Babylonia, and noticed that they recited the
> Hallel on the New Moon festival. At first he thought of stopping
> them, but when he saw that they omitted parts of it, he remarked, It
> is clear that it is an old ancestral custom with them.

(b. Ta'anit 28b)

We have, further, the following remarkable account:

> Rav happened to be at Babylonia during a public fast. He came
> forward and read in the scroll of the Law. Before commencing he made
> a blessing, but after finishing he made no blessing. The whole con-
> gregation [afterwards] prostrated themselves, but Rav did not . . . .
> Why did he not fall on his face? There was a stone pavement, and it
> has been taught (Lev. 26.1), 'Neither shall ye place any figured stone
> in your land to bow down to it,' meaning, upon it ye may not bow
> down in your land, but you may prostrate yourselves on the stones
> in the temple. If so, why did only Rav refrain from prostrating him-
> self? The entire congregation should not have done so? It was in
> front of Rav. But could he not have gone among the congregation and
> fallen on his face? He did not want to trouble the congregation ...

(b. Meg. 22a-b)

> Was there not a synagogue 'which moved and settled' in Nehardea, and in it was a statue [of a king] and Rav and Samuel and the father of Samuel used to go in there to pray . . .
>
> (b. R.H. 24b)

These three cases (in addition to Dura) offer striking evidence that the rabbis did *not* govern synagogue life, did not approve aspects of it, and yet participated in it, and contributed to the liturgy. Their influence in the synagogue depended upon their prestige; they had no effective legal authority to change practices they did not like. Since the masses of the people had accustomed themselves to their current ways, the rabbis could not resort to a decree of excommunication, nor could they flog an entire congregation. In the end, however, their reputation as holy men gave them considerable influence:

> When Rav died, R. Isaac b. Bisna decreed that none should bring myrtles and palm-branches to a wedding feast to the sound of a tavla [bell], yet he [a certain man] went and brought myrtle and palm-branches at a wedding to the sound of the tavla, so a snake bit him and he died.
>
> (b. Shab. 110a)

Under the circumstances, it is likely that many would obey the rabbi, rather than risk his curse or some worse result. On the other hand, no legal system could depend for enforcement upon the vagaries of curses, snakes, and barren flax-seeds. The many stories in which a rabbi's curse was sufficient to bring down punishment upon the head of a recalcitrant sinner reveal that in such cases, it was only the curse, and not flogging, or an act of excommunication acceptable among the masses, that was probably available for enforcing the law. The laws, the breaking of which was punished by rabbinical curses, were most likely those which rabbinical courts could not otherwise cope with, or which were not subject to popular inquiries addressed to the rabbis about proper observance. We have too much contrary evidence about very practical law-enforcement to conclude otherwise.

VI. The Rabbis' Influence

Talmudic law as we have it for this period must, therefore, be used with considerable caution to recover a picture of the conduct of daily affairs. Among the masses, ancient customs, dating in some instances without doubt to the very beginnings of the Babylonian Jewish settlement seven centuries earlier, exerted considerable influence, and the rabbis were able to effect their own policies only in limited matters. On the other hand, within their academies, their authority was unlimited, and as they trained the judges of the coming generation, and students went out to their villages throughout Jewish Babylonia and beyond, the legal doctrines of the rabbis radiated into the common life. This was not a process which was completed in one generation, nor was the transformation of the life of approximately 860,000 people effected by a few men alone. The laws on proper blessings, for example, were probably observed in this period mainly in the academies. The many dicta on the etiquette of saying grace, on the proper forms of benedictions over food, conditions for prayer, and the like, produced only one case reflecting conditions outside of the academy, but many within it:

> Once when R. Giddal b. Minyumi was in the presence of R. Naḥman, the latter made a mistake in the grace . . .
>
> (b. Ber. 49a)

> When Rav died, his disciples . . . sat discussing the question, When we learned 'reclining' is it to be taken strictly, as excluding sitting . . . R. Adda b. Ahava rose and turned the rent in his garment from front to back, and made another, saying, Rav is dead, and we have not learned the rules of grace after meals . . .
>
> (b. Ber. 42b-43a)

> Said Rav to his son Ḥiyya, My son, Snatch [the wine] and say grace . . .
>
> (b. Ber. 53b)

> Once Rav and Samuel were sitting at a meal, and R. Shimi b. Ḥiyya joined them and ate very hurriedly. Said Rav to him, What do you want, to join us? We have already finished . . . The disciples of Rav were once dining together, when R. Aḥa entered. They said, A great man has come to say grace for us . . .
>
> (b. Ber. 47a)

> R. Judah gave a wedding feast for his son. The guests said a *moẓi* (blessing over bread) before the dessert. He said, What is this *ẓiẓi* I hear! Are you saying '*moẓi*'? They said, Yes, because R. Muna in the name of R. Judah said, Over bread with dessert you say a *moẓi*, and Samuel said that the law follows R. Muna . . .
>
> (b. Ber. 42a)

These cases exemplify the practical reports on blessings. The rabbis similarly discussed how R. Judah the Prince recited the Shema,[1] how to behave during the Silent Prayer, and many other matters.

---

[1] b. Ber. 13b.

What is significant is that among the numerous cases, questions, and discussions of the actual behavior of individuals, we find only one instance in which a common person, not a student of the academy, was discussed, that of Benjamin the shepherd, cited above (b. Ber. 40b). Significantly, this incident with a common person reveals great leniency on the part of the rabbi, for the required form of the liturgy was not there prescribed. The difficulty Rav's students found with the elaborate laws of grace suggests that the common people would have found it quite impossible, without the elaborate education provided in the academies, to do precisely the right thing. If this is so for the commonplace act of blessing food, one may reasonably suppose that more difficult or unusual matters were quite remote from public comprehension, let alone observance. The kinds of cases which prove *beyond doubt* the efficacy of rabbinical authority were, as I have said, specifically those which came before them in their judicial capacity.

One cannot conceive that before the foundation of rabbinical academies, after the Bar Kokhba war, Babylonian Jewry possessed neither laws nor authoritative doctrines. During the six preceding centuries, as we have seen,[1] indigenous traditions were cultivated, both of law and exegesis, and of doctrine as well. It could not have been otherwise. Babylonian Jews married, bore children and educated them; divided their estates and litigated their affairs; celebrated the ordained festivals and the Sabbath; and pursued the many affairs which required legal adjudication and produced a rich corpus of precedents,[2] for many centuries before the appearance of the first rabbi in their midst. The process by which Babylonian Jewish life was modified to conform to the rabbinical doctrines based on the

---

[1] Vol. I, 148-63.

[2] I had earlier thought that it would prove useful to compare the legal traditions of Rav and Samuel, for it seemed to me that Samuel's traditions, being almost wholly indigenous, would produce a picture of the law as it existed before the third century, and hence of more ancient social realities. [See vol. I, 154]. Research for this chapter has shown me, however, that such a comparison would not yield the kind of information I had sought, since the 'Babylonian' interpretation of the law would not necessarily yield an adequate portrait of the common life of the people, which is the purpose of my inquiry. The Babylonian traditions are, of course, of interest for their own sake, and I have no doubt that legal historians will greatly facilitate our understanding of the Babylonian *Tannaitic* heritage through a systematic comparison of such teachings. But it is not possible invariably to conclude that Samuel's viewpoints reflect 'Babylonian' conditions, and Rav's, the 'Palestinian' ones, nor did such viewpoints automatically reveal how people actually lived.

Mishnah was a long and slow one. In this period, as we have seen, while very substantial areas of law came under rabbinical supervision, other important aspects of daily life remained outside it. At the very least, one may say that the contact between the people and the law did not yield a literature of inquiry, precedent, and law-enforcement pertaining equally to each type of law and every area of rabbinical concern, but only to specific limited ones. What is remarkable, on the contrary, is that anything changed at all in response to rabbinical influence, for the inertia of centuries made the process of social and legal change painful indeed. The cases we have examined suggest that it was mainly where the rabbis were able to apply very specific pressures, in the form of legal opinions which they could enforce through the courts, that matters changed. We do not know whose authority the rabbis replaced even in these matters. If, as I said, people required legal documents before the third century, we do not know who employed the scribes who issued them, for example, or who presided over litigations. There can be little doubt that a judiciary of some kind existed,[1] and the rabbis represented a continuation of the authority of earlier figures, even though they applied the Mishnah, a corpus of law originating not in Babylonia but in Palestine, in place of whatever ancient precedents and biblical exegeses had accumulated in Babylonia itself. I do not think, on the other hand, that the Babylonian antecedents could have been profoundly different, for they were very strictly based upon biblical exegesis, which permitted only a relatively narrow range of options on how to decide basic issues, though of course secondary questions would have proven complicated, and may have resulted in very different judgments in Babylonia from those in Palestine. The rabbis found it easiest to enforce those laws which the Bible itself laid down, most difficult to effect decrees which the Bible did not make explicit. One must therefore regard as limited the 'revolution' in Babylonian Jewish affairs, resulting from the development of the rabbinic academies. The academies produced judges, and men learned in traditions which in part must have been relatively new to Babylonia. They did not however bring 'the Torah' to Babylonia, nor was it

---

[1] But for Parthian times I am fairly certain these authorities were upper-class, assimilated Jewish grandees, who possessed both military power *and* a knowledge of law, as in the case cited in vol. I, 94, 98, 104, 131, 137, 153, from b. Git. 14a-b and y. Git. 1.5. They probably issued decisions based upon their indigenous legal traditions, formed through a legal exegesis of Scriptures.

necessary to win the loyalties of the people to a new doctrine, but rather, to a renewed interpretation of a very old one.

One cannot ignore, finally the eschatological significance of law-observance. We noted above that the rabbis emphasized the conditional quality of redemptive promises. If Israel had kept the first Sabbath, or would now obey the will of their father in heaven, then no nation or race can rule over them. Similarly, Samuel taught that because Israel casts words of Torah to the ground, the heathen are able to make, and carry out, their decrees, and Rav Papa said, later on, that if the haughty will cease in Israel, then the *hazarapats* will cease among the Iranians. These words were not idle homilies, but rather provide the key to understanding why it was that the rabbis laid such emphasis upon law and upon the legal and social reformation of Israel. They possessed the "oral Torah," which, they believed, contained the true and exhaustive interpretation of the written, revealed laws, and as we have seen, they went to great lengths to enforce that law wherever and whenever they could. In the light of their view of history, we can understand the reason: it was through the complete realization of the Torah in Israel's life that they intended to bring the redemption. If Israel keeps the law, then they will no longer be ruled by pagan nations: this is the converse of Samuel's saying, and one which must be understood against his view that the Messianic time would be like the present one, except that the heathen would have no sovereignty over Israel. How better to respond to Sasanian rule, therefore, than to fulfil the Torah? If Israel did, the decrees of the pagans would be nullified, and *that very nullification* would signify for Samuel the advent of the age to come. The achievement of justice and morality, the protection of the rights of the poor and weak, the establishment of a serene and decent public order—these were crucially significant, because through them, as much as through prayer, Israel would carry out its side of the messianic contract. Prayer, study, and fulfillment of the Torah as a whole therefore represented in the end a very vigorous response to the cataclysmic events of the age, and from the rabbis' viewpoint embodied more powerful instruments than any other for the achievement of the better age for which Jews longed. Prayer, study, deeds—these three, but of greatest weight and consequence was the legal and judicial enterprise.

This was, quite obviously, the faith of the rabbis, but if had been theirs alone, I do not think we should have the evidences of law-enforcement that have come down to us. As I said, the Jews in Babylonia were a numerous group, possessing ancient customs and traditions. No matter how effective the exilarch's courts may have been, in the end they relied far more upon the acquiescence and cooperation of the people than upon force, and this was attained, I think, because the people were convinced that the rabbis were leading them in the right direction. Although we do not know how profoundly ancient practices were affected, we do know that they *were* modified; customary patterns of acquisition through usufruct represent a most tenacious body of precedents, and as we saw, these were challenged and changed by the rabbis. One thinks, by contrast, to the reaction, a century earlier, of the Jews of R. Aḥai b. R. Josiah's day, who, when excommunicated for a Sabbath violation, simply left Judaism altogether. By contrast, I know of no similar story in the period under study. And yet the rabbis' decrees were more far-reaching than earlier. I can think of one explanation only. The great number of Jews must have been convinced of the correctness of the rabbis' view that only through a grand reformation would redemption be reached. And if they accepted the rabbis' definition for substantial parts of the needed reformation, or at least, conformed to it, the reason may well have been that they hoped that by so doing, they would see the realization of the ancient hope of Israel, the time their lips would tire from saying 'Enough.'

FURTHER EXEGESES ON EXODUS AND ESTHER

In Chapter Two section v, are cited exegeses on Exodus and the Esther-Scroll relevant to early Sasanian times. For the sake of completeness, I shall cite further extant comments to indicate the character of the continuous commentary on Ex. 1-3 and parts of Esther, which Rav and Samuel produced.

On Exodus we have the following comments:

'Now there arose a new king' (Ex. 1.8). Rav and Samuel, one said, Really *new*, and the other said, his decrees were new. And they built for Pharoah store cities [Miskenot (Ex. 1.10)]. Rav and Samuel, One said, They endangered (mesaknot) their owners, the other, they impoverished (memaskenot) their owners.

(Ex. R. 1.10)

'Pithom and Ramses '(Exodus 1.11). Rav and Samuel, The real name was Pithom, and it was called Ramses because one building after another collapsed. The other said, the real name was Ramses, and it was called Pithom because the mouth of the deep swallowed up one building after the other.

(b. Sotah 11a, compare on Ex. 1.8. b. 'Eruv. 53a, Ex. R. 1.8, 9)

'And the king of Egypt spoke to the Hebrew midwives' (Exodus 1.15). Rav and Samuel, One said, mother and daughter, the other, mother-in-law and daughter-in-law, either Yoḥebed and Miriam, or Yoḥebed and Elisheva.

(b. Sotah 11b)

'And it came to pass because the midwives feared God that he made them houses' (Exodus 1.21). Rav and Samuel, One said, priestly and Levitical houses, the other said, Royal houses, thus, either Aaron and Moses, or David.

(b. Sotah 11b)

With reference to Exodus 2.4, 'And his sister stood afar off to know', we have the following additional comment:

'And Miriam the prophetess, sister of Aaron' (Exodus 15.20). Then was she only sister of Aaron and not of Moses? R. Naḥman said in the name of Rav, Because she prophesied when she was sister of Aaron only [before the birth of Moses], and said, My mother is destined to bear a son who will save Israel. When he was born, the whole house filled with light, and her father arose and kissed her on the head, saying, My daughter, thy prophecy has been fulfilled. But when they threw him into the river, her father arose and tapped her on the head saying, Daughter, where is thy prophecy? So it is written, 'and his sister stood afar off *to know*', to know what would be the fate of her prophecy.

(b. Sotah 12b=Meg. 14a)

A similar form occurs in passages which otherwise stand by themselves.

'And Jethro rejoiced' (Ex. 18.10). Rav and Samuel, Rav held, He caused a sharp knife to pass over his flesh [circumcized himself], and Samuel said, His flesh crept [with horror at the destruction of the Egyptians].

(b. Pes. 117a)

This form is identical with that exhibited by the continuous commentaries, though having no other relevant material, we cannot reconstruct what Rav and Samuel said regarding the Story of Jethro.

Additional comments on the Esther Scroll include the following:

'And when these days were fulfilled'. The word *ubimloth* (and when . . . were fulfilled) is written *plene*. 'The king made a feast unto all the people that were present . . . seven days'. (1.5) Rav and Samuel joined issue here. Rav said: It means seven besides the hundred and eighty, whereas Samuel said: It means seven included in the hundred and eighty.

(Esther R. 2.5)

'And when these days were fulfilled (1.5)' Rav and Samuel, one said he was a clever king and the other, he was a foolish king. The one who held he was clever said that he did well in entertaining his distant subjects first, because he could win over the inhabitants of his own city any time he wished. The one who held that he was foolish says that he ought to have entertained the inhabitants of his metropolis first, so that if others rebelled against him, these would have supported him.

'In the court of the garden of the king's palace' (1.5)'. Rav and Samuel, one said that those who had the entrée of the court were entertained in the court, and those who had the entrée of the garden were entertained in the garden, and those of the palace in the palace. The other said, he first put them in court and it did not hold them, then in garden, finally in the palace. 'There were white cotton curtains and blue hangings' (1.6) What is *hur*? Rav said, fine lace work. Samuel said, carpets of white silk. [Compare Esther R. 2.8] 'And shell (dar) and onyx marble (soharet) (1.6)' Rav said, this means rows upon rows [=mosaics?]. Samuel said, There is a precious stone in the seaports called 'darah'. He put it in the midst of the guests and it lit up the place as at midday.

(b. Meg. 12a)

'And royal wine in abundance' (1.7) Rav said, this teaches that each one was given to drink wine older than himself.

(b. Meg. 12b)

For the following chapters, the comments are sparser, yet exhibit the same marks of a connected commentary, verse by verse:

'And he changed her and her maidens' (2.9). Rav said, He gave her Jewish food to eat. Samuel said, It means he gave her chines of pork.

(b. Meg. 13a)

'And the king loved Esther above all the women, and she obtained grace and favor in his sight more than all the virgins' (Esther 2.17), Rav said, if he wanted to find in her the taste of a virgin, he found it; of a married women, he found it.

(b. Meg. 13a)

'Like as when she was brought up with him' (Esther 2.20), Rabba b. Lema in the name of Rav said, 'This means that she used to rise up from the lap of Ahasueros and bathe and sit in the lap of Mordecai.'

(b. Meg. 13b)

'Now when Mordecai knew all that was done, Mordecai rent his clothes and put on sackcloth and ashes and went out into the midst of the city, wailing with a loud and bitter cry' (4.1). What [was his cry]? Rav said, 'Ha-

man has raised himself above Ahasueros.' Samuel said, 'The upper king has
prevailed over the lower king.'

'When Esther's maids . . . came and told her, the queen was deeply dis-
tressed' (4.4). Rav said, This means that she became menstruous.

(b. Meg. 15a)

R. Phineḥas and R. Ḥama b. Guria in the name of Rav said: She asked
permission to wear at least as much as a girdle, like a harlot, but they would
not allow her. He said to her: You must be naked. She said, I will come in
without a crown. [He said]: 'If so, they will say, She is a maid-servant. Then
she [a maidservant] might put on royal garments and enter? R. Huna said:
A subject must not put on royal garments.

(Esther R. 3.13)

SUPPLEMENTARY BIBLIOGRAPHY

N.B.: Items listed in Vol. I, pp. 191-213, have not been reproduced here.

A.P., "Shmuʾel veShitato b'khol HaShass", review of D. Hoffman, *Mar Samuel*, signed by initial only, He'Assif 2, 1885, 263-74.

Abelson, J., *The Immanence of God in Rabbinical Literature*, London, 1912.

———, *Jewish Mysticism*, London, 1913.

Abrahams, Israel, "The lost 'Confession' of Samuel", *HUCA* I, 1924, 377-87.

Adam, Alfred, "Manichäismus", *Handbuch der Orientalistik*, VIII, ii, 102-19.

Adams, Robert McC., *Land Behind Baghdad. A History of Settlement on the Diyala Plains*, Chicago, 1965.

Albeck, Chanoch, "Aus der neuesten Mischnaliteratur", *MGWJ* 73, 1929, 4-25.

———, *Mehkarim baBeraita veTosefta veYahasan laTalmud*, Jerusalem, 1940.

Alfaric, Prosper, *Les Écritures Manichéennes*, Paris, 1918, I-II.

Alföldi, Andreas, "The Crisis of the Empire (A.D. 249-270)", *CAH* XII, 167-232.

———, "Der iranische Weltreise auf archäologischen Denkmälern", *Jahrbuch der Schweizerischen Gesellschaft für Urgeschichte* XL, 1949-50.

———, "Die Römische Münzprägung und die historischen Ereignisse im Osten zwischen 260 und 270", *Berytus* 5, 1938, 47-89.

Allan, John, and Trever, Camilla, "Coinage of the Sasanians", Pope, I, 816-30.

Allgeier, A., "Untersuchungen zur ältesten Kirchengeschichte in Persien", *Der Katholik*, 22, 294f.

Altheim, Franz, *Niedergang der alten Welt*, Frankfurt a/M., 1952, I-II.

———, *Utopie und Wirtschaft*, Frankfurt a/M., 1957.

———, and Stiehl, Ruth, *Ein Asiatischer Staat. Feudalismus unter den Sasaniden und Ihren Nachbarn*, Wiesbaden, 1954.

———, *Asien und Rom: Neue Urkunden aus Sasanidischer Frühzeit*, Tübingen, 1952.

Altmann, Alexander, "The Gnostic Background of the Rabbinic Adam Legends", *JQR*, n.s., 35, 371-91.

———, "Gnostic Themes in Rabbinic Cosmology", in I. Epstein, et al., editor, *Essays in Honour of . . . J. H. Hertz*, London, 1942, 19-32.

———, "A Note on the Rabbinic Doctrine of Creation", *JJS* 7, 1956, 195f.

———, "Shirei Qedushah b'Sifrut HaHekhalot HaQedumah", *Melilah* 2, 1946, 1-24.

Aptowitzer, V., "The Heavenly Temple in the Agada" (in Hebrew), *Tarbiz* 2, 1931, 137-53.

Ashkenazi, Moshe Yizḥak, "Maʿaseh Bereʾshit", *HaKarmei* 2, 1873, 90-92.

Bacher, Wilhelm, "Abba Arika (Rab)", *JE* I, 29-31.

———, *Die Agada der Babylonischen Amoräer*, Frankfurt a/M., 1913.

———, *Die Exegetische Terminologie der jüdischen Traditionsliteratur*, repr., Darmstadt, 1965.

———, "Exilarch", *JE* V, 289.

———, "Die Gelehrten von Caesarea", *MGWJ* 45, 1901, 298-310.

———, "Zur Geschichte der Schulen Palästina's im 3 und 4 Jahrhundert, Die Genossen", *MGWJ* 43, 1899, 345-60.

———, "Der Massoret Hamnuna", *MWJ* 18, 1891, 58-9.

———, "Le mot 'minim' dans le Talmud, désigne-t-il quelquefois des Chrétiens", *REJ* 38, 1899, 38-45.

————, "Le Schem Hammephorasch et le nom de quarante-deux lettres", *REJ* 18, 1899, 290-293.

————, "Vortragende Tradenten Tannaitischer Lehrsätze in den Amoräischen Schulen", *Festschrift zu Israel Lewy's Siebzigsten Geburtstag*, Breslau, 1911.

Bank, L., "Une agada provenant de l'entourage du Resh Galouta Houna bar Nathan", *REJ* 32, 51f.

————, "Rabbi Zeira et Rab Zeira", *REJ* 38, 1899, 47-63.

Bartholomae, C., *Über ein sasanidischen Rechtsbuch. Sitz. d. Heidel. Ak.*, 1910.

————, *Zum Sasanidischen Recht. Sitzungsberichte der Heidelberger Akademie der Wissenschaften*, I, 1918, II, 1920, III, 1922, IV, 1922, V, 1923.

————, "Notes on Sasanian Law", translated by L. Bogdanov, *Journal of the K. R. Cama Oriental Institute* 18, 1931 et seq.

Bauer, Walter, *Rechtgläubigkeit und Ketzerei im ältesten Christentum*, Tübingen 1934.

Beer, Moshe, "LeShe'elat Shihruram shel 'Amora'e Bavel miTashlum Misim uMekhes" *Tarbiz* 33, 1964, 248-58.

————, *Ma'amadam HaKalkali vehaHevrati shel 'Amora'e Bavel*, Ramat Gan. 1963.

————, "Rivo shel Geniva b'Mar'Ukba", *Tarbiz*, 31, 1962, 281-6.

————, "Talmud Torah veDerekh 'Erez", *Bar Ilan Annual* 2, 1964, 134-62.

Beloch, Julius, *Die Bevölkerung der griechisch-römischen Welt*, Leipzig, 1886.

Ben Dor, Shabtai, "Dina' deMalkhuta' Dina'", *Talpioth* 9, 1964, 230-7.

Benveniste, E., *The Persian Religion according to the Chief Greek Texts*, Paris, 1929.

Bergmann, J., "Zwei talmudische Notizen", *MGWJ* 46, 1902, 531-3.

Bianchi, Ugo, *Zaman i Ohrmazd*, Rome, 1958.

Blau, Ludwig, "Gnosticism", *JE* V, 681-6.

————, "Tossefta, Mischna, et Baraita dans leurs rapports réciproques, ou Halacha palestinienne et babylonienne", *REJ* 67, 1914, 1-23.

Bloch, Renée, "Écriture et Tradition dans le Judaisme. Aperçus sur l'origine du Midrash", *Cahiers Sioniens* 8, 1954, 9-34.

————, "Note Methodologique pour l'étude de la littérature rabbinique", *Recherches de Science Religieuse* 43, 1955, 194-225.

Boulnois, L., *La Route de la Soie*, Paris ,1963.

Brandt, W., *Die Mandäische Religion*, Leipzig, 1889.

Brill, Haim Yizhak, *Life of R. Simeon b. Lakish*, St. Louis, Missouri, 1921.

Brüll, N., "Papa b. Nazar", *Ben Chananja* 2, 1866, 62.

Büchler, A., *'Am Ha' Arez HaGalili* (trans. to Hebrew by I. Eldad), Jerusalem, 1964.

Bulsara, Sohrab J., *The Laws of the Ancient Persians as Found in the Mâtîkân Ê Hazâr Dâtastân*, Bombay, 1937.

Burkitt, F. C., "The Christian Church in the East", *CAH* XII, 476-515.

————, *The Religion of the Manichees*, Cambridge, 1925.

————, "The Religion of the Manichees", *Journal of Religion* 2, 1922, 263-76.

Casanowicz, Immanuel, "Non-Jewish Religious Ceremonies in the Talmud", *JAOS* (Proceedings), 16, 1895, 76-82.

Casartelli, L. C., "An Inscribed Sassanian Gem", *BOR* 8, 1895, 211.

————, *The Philosophy of the Mazdayasnian Religion under the Sassanids*, translated by Jamasp Asa, Bombay, 1889.

Charlesworth, M. P., "Roman Trade with India, a resurvey", in *Studies in Roman Economic and Social History*, ed. P. R. Coleman-Norton et al, Princeton, 1951.

Chaumont, M.-L., "Le Culte d'Anāhitā à Staxr et les Premiers Sassanides", *RHR* 153, 2, 1958, 154-75.

————, "Recherches sur les Institutions de l'Iran Ancien et de l'Arménie", *JA*, 249, 1961, 297-320, and 250, 1962, 11-22.

Chesney, F. R., *The Expedition for the Survey of the Rivers Euphrates and Tigris*, London, 1850, I-III.

Childs, B. S., "The Birth of Moses", *JBL* 84, 1965, 109-22.

Christensen, Arthur, "Abarsam et Tansar", *AO* 10, 1932, 43-55.

————, *L'Empire des Sassanides, Le Peuple, L'État, La Cour*. Copenhagen, 1907.

————, "Qui Est l'Auteur de l'Inscription du Ka'ba de Zoroastre", *Professor A. V. W. Jackson Memorial Volume*, Bombay, 1954, 25-9.

————, "Sassanid Persia", *CAH* XII, 109-37.

Cohon, S. S., "Pharisaism, A Definition", *Joshua Bloch Memorial Volume*, N.Y., 1960, 65-74.

Cook, S. A., Adcock, F. E., Charlesworth, M. P., Baynes, N. H., *Cambridge Ancient History XII, The Imperial Crisis and Recovery*, Cambridge, 1939.

Coulborn, Rushton, "The State and Religion: Iran, India, and China", *Comparative Studies in Society and History* 1, 1958, 44-57.

Cumont, Franz, *The Oriental Religions in Roman Paganism*, N.Y. repr. 1956.

————, *Recherches sur le Manichéisme*, Brussels, I, 1908, II, 1912.

Darmesteter, James, "Lettre de Tansar au Roi de Tabaristan", *JA* 9th series, 3, 1894 185-250, 502-555.

De Menasce, Jean Pierre, "La Conquête de l'Iranisme et la récupération des mages hellénisés", *École Pratique des Hautes Études*, Paris, 1956, Annuaire, 1956-7.

————, "Les données géographiques dans le Mātigān-i Hazār Dātistan", in *Indo-Iranica*, Wiesbaden, 1964, 149-54.

————, *Une encyclopédie mazdéenne, Le Denkart*, Paris, 1958.

————, "Les mystères et la religion de l'Iran", *Eranos Jahrbuch*, 1944, 167-87.

de Meynard, C. B. and de Courteille, P., *Maçoudi, Les Prairies d'Or, Texte et Traduction*. Paris, 1863, II.

Doresse, Jean, *Secret Books of the Egyptian Gnostics*, N.Y. 1960.

Downey, Glanville, *A History of Antioch in Syria from Seleucus to the Arab Conquest*, Princeton, 1961.

Drower, E. S., editor, *The Haran Gawaita and the Baptism of Hibil-Ziwa*, Vatican City, 1953.

E. S. Drower, *The Mandaeans of Iraq and Iran*, Leiden, 1962.

————, *The Secret Adam. A Study of Nasoraean Gnosis*, Oxford, 1960.

————, and Macuch, R., *A Mandaic Dictionary*, Oxford, 1963.

Duchesne-Guillemin, J., "Rituel et eschatologie dans le Mazdéisme", *Numen* 8, 1, 46-51.

————, *The Western Response to Zoroaster*, Oxford, 1958.

Duncan, Edward J., *Baptism in the Demonstrations of Aphraates the Persian Sage*, Washington, 1945.

Dussaud, R., *Les Arabes en Syrie avant l'Islam*, Paris, 1907.

Echols, Edward C., translator, *Herodian of Antioch's History of the Roman Empire*, Berkeley, 1961.

Ehrmann, Daniel, "Zur Sprache des Talmud", *Ben Chananja* 5, 1862, 43-7, 51-4.

Elbogen, Ismar, "Geschichte des Achtzehngebetes", *MGWJ* 46, 1902, 330-57, 427-39, 513-30.

————, *Der jüdische Gottesdienst in seiner geschichtlichen Entwicklung*, 4th ed., repr. Hildesheim, 1962.

Ensslin, Wilhelm, "Zu den Kriegen des Sassaniden Schapur I", *Sitzungsberichte der Bayerischen Akademie der Wissenschaften. Phil.-Hist. Kl.*, 1947, 5, Munich, 1949.

Epstein, J. N., "Gloses babylo-araméennes", *REJ*, 73, 1921, 27-58; 74, 1922, 40-72.

————, *Mavo leNusaḥ HaMishnah*, Jerusalem, 1948, I-II.

Federbush, Simon, *Bin'tivot HaTalmud*, Jerusalem, 1957.

Feldman, W. M., *Rabbinical Mathematics and Astronomy*, N.Y. repr., 1965.

Ferguson, Everett, "Jewish and Christian Ordination", *HTR* 56, 1963, 13-19.

Feuchtwang, D., Review of S. Funk, *Juden in Babylonien*, *MGWJ* 47, 371-5.

Fiebig, Paul, "Talmud babli, Traktat Götzendienst, *ZDMG* 57, 1903, 581-604.

Finkelstein, Jacob J., "Mesopotamia", *JNES* 21, 1962, 73-92.

Frank, Edgar, *Talmudic and Rabbinical Chronology*, N.Y. 1956.

Frankel, Zechariah, "Geist der palästinischen und babylonischen Hagada", *MGWJ* 2, 1853, 388-98.

————, *Mavo HaYerushalmi*, Breslau, 1870.

————, "Zur Geschichte der jüdischen Religionsgespräche", *MGWJ* 4, 1855, 161-81, 205-18, 241-50, 410-13, 447-54.

Freund, L., "Über genealogien und familien-reinheit in biblischer und talmudischer Zeit", *Festschrift Adolf Schwarz*, Berlin & Vienna, 1917.

Friedlander, M., *Der vorchristliche jüdische Gnosticismus*, Göttingen, 1898.

Friedman, M., "Netivot HaAgadah" (On Samuel on Esther), *Bet Talmud* 1, 1871, 39-44, 71-5, 102-6.

Frye, Richard N., "The Charisma of Kingship in Ancient Iran", *IA* 4, 36-54.

————, Review of E. Honigmann and A. Maricq, *Recherches sur les Res Gestae Divi Saporis*, *JAOS* 74, 1954, 183-5.

Funk, Salomon, "Beiträge zur Geographie des Landes Babel", *JaJLG* 9, 1911, 198-214.

————, "Beiträge zur Geschichte Persiens zur Zeit der Sasaniden", *Festschrift Adolf Schwarz*, Berlin & Vienna, 1917, 425-36.

————, *Die haggadischen Elemente in den Homilien des Aphraates*, Vienna, 1891.

————, "Die Stadt Nehardea und ihre Hochschule", *Festschrift David Hoffman*, Berlin, 1914, 97-104.

————, *Talmudproben*, Leipzig, 1912.

Furlani, Giuseppe, "I pianeti e lo zodiaco nella religione dei Mandei", *Atti della Academia Nazionale dei Lincei*, Rome, 1948, *Classe di Scienze Morali, Storiche, e Filologiche* VIII, ii, 3, 119-187.

Fürst, Julius, "Geschichte der jüdischen Literatur in Babylonien," *Literaturblatt des Orients* 7, 1846, 51, cols. 801-6, 819-26, etc.

Gagé, Jean, *La Montée des Sassanides et l'Heure de Palmyre*, Paris, 1964.

Gandz, S., "The Robeh, Or the Official Memorizer of the Palestinian Schools", *PAAJR* 7, 1935-6, 5-12.

Ganneau, Clermont, "Odeinat et Vaballat, rois de Palmyre, et leur titre romain de corrector", *Revue Biblique* 29, 1920, 382f.

Gaster, Moses, *The Exempla of the Rabbis*, London, 1924.

Getzav, Naḥman Ẓvi, *ʿAl Neharot Bavel*, Warsaw, 1878.

Ghirshman, R., *Iran, From the Earliest Times to the Islamic Conquest*, Baltimore, 1954.

Ginzberg, Louis, *Perushim veHiddushim baYerushalmi*, N.Y. I-III, 1941, IV, ed. by David HaLivni Weiss, 1961.

————, *On Jewish Law and Lore*, Philadelphia, 1955.

Glatzer, Nahum N., "The Attitude toward Rome in Third-Century Judaism", in Alois Dempf et al., eds., *Politische Ordnung und Menschliche Existenz*, Munich, 1962, 243-57.

Goldberg, Ber, "Shem miShmuʾel", *HaMevaser* 2, 1862, 6, 41-2, 7, 49-50.

Gordon, Cyrus H., "Aramaic Incantation Bowls", *Orientalia* 10, 1941, 116-41, 272-84, 339-60; see also *AO* 6, 1934, 319-34, 446-74.

Graetz, Heinrich, "Die talmudische Chronologie und Topographie", *MGWJ* 1, 1852, 509-21.

————, "Zur Chronologie des talmudischen Zeit", *MGWJ* 34, 1885, 17-34, 193-209, 289-302, 433-53, 481-96.

Grant, Robert M., *Gnosticism*, N.Y. 1961.

Gray, Louis H., *The Foundations of the Iranian Religions*, Bombay, 1926.

————, "Some Recent Studies in the Iranian Religions", *HTR* 15, 1922, 87-95.

Grousset, R., Massignon, L., and Massé, H., eds., *L'Âme de l'Iran*, Paris, 1951.

Grünhut, L., "Sifra veShaʾar Sifré deve Rav", *Festschrift David Hoffmann*, Berlin, 1914, 1-11.

Guey, Julien, "Les 'res gestae divi Saporis'," *Revue des Études Anciennes*, 57, 1955, 116-22.

————, and Pekáry, Thomas, "Autour des 'res gestae divi Saporis' ", *Syria* 38, 1961.

Gutman, Y., "Milhemet HaYehudim bimei Trayanus", *Sefer . . . Assaf*, ed. M. D. Cassuto, J. Klausner, et al., Jerusalem, 1953, 149-84.

Haase, Felix, *Altchristliche Kirchengeschichte nach orientalischen Quellen*, Leipzig, 1925.

Heichelheim, F. M., "The Influence of Hellenistic Financial Administration in the Near East and India", *Economic History* 4, 1938, 1-13.

Heinemann, Joseph, *Prayer in the Period of the Tannaʾim and the Amoraʾim, Its Nature and its Patterns*, Jerusalem, 1964 (in Hebrew with English summary).

Heller, Bernhard, "Persische Königsnamen in einem halachischen Merkspruch", *MGWJ* 69, 1925, 448-9.

Henning, W. B., "The Dates of Mani's Life", *Asia Major* 6, 1957, 106-21.

————, "The Manichaean Fasts", *JRAS* 1945, 146-64.

————, "Mani's Last Journey", *BSOS* 10, 1940-42, 141-53.

————, "Neue Materialien zur Geschichte des Manichaeismus", *ZDMG* n.f. 15, 1936, 1-19.

————, and G. Haloun, "The Compendium of the Doctrines and Styles of the Teaching of Mani, the Buddha of Light", *Asia Major* 3, 184-212.

Heschel, A. J., *Theology of Ancient Judaism*, London ,1962, I. (in Hebrew).

Higgins, Martin J., *The Persian War of the Emperor Maurice (582-602). Part One: The Chronology, with a Brief History of the Persian Calendar*, Washington, 1939.

Hölscher, Gustav, "Les origines de la communauté juive à l'époque perse", *Révue d'Histoire et de Philosophie Religieuses* 6, 1926, 105-26.

Horovitz, J., "Hebrew-Iranian Synchronisms", *Oriental Studies in Honour of C. E. Pavry*, London, 1933, 151-5.

————, "Mar Samuel und Schabur I", *MGWJ* 30, 215-31.

Huebsch, "Ḥasinai veḤanilai ʾAḥim", *HaMevaser* 3, 1863, 131-2, 144-5, 154-5.

Hyman, Aaron, *ʾIggeret Rav Sheriraʾ Gaʾon*, London, 1910.

Idelsohn, A. Z., *Jewish Liturgy and its Development*, N.Y. 1932.

Jackson, A. V. W., "Contributions to the Knowledge of Manichaeism", *JAOS* 44, 1924, 61-72.

————, "The Personality of Mani, the Founder of Manichaeism", *JAOS* 58, 1938, 235-40.

————, *Researches in Manichaeism with Special Reference to the Turfan Fragments*, N.Y. 1932.

————, "The so-called Injunctions of Mani", *JRAS* 1924, 213-29.

————, "Traces of Biblical Influence in the Turfan Pahlavi Fragment M. 173", *JAOS* 56, 1936, 198-207.

————, "Zoroastrianism", *JE* 12, 697.

Jackson, F. J. Foakes, "The Influence of Iran upon Early Judaism and Christianity", in *Oriental Studies in Honor of C. E. Pavry*, London, 1933, 172-5.

Jacobs, Louis, "Evidence of Literary Device in the Babylonian Talmud", *JJS* 3, 1952, 157-62.

Jeiteles, Berthold, *Oẓar Tanna'im ve'Amora'im. Konkordanẓia Talmudit. I. Rav.* Manchester, 1961.

Joffe, A. J., "Beiträge zur Geschichte der Amoraim", *MWJ* 12, 1885, 217-24.

Jonas, Hans, *The Gnostic Religion*, Boston, 1958.

Jones, A. H. M., *The Later Roman Empire, 284-602*, Oxford, 1964, I-III.

Jordan, Samuel Alexander, *Rabbi Jochanan bar Nappacha*, Budapest, 1895.

Judelowitz, M., *Ha'Ir Pumbedita bimei ha'Amora' im*, Jerusalem, 1939.

Kahana, K., *Seder Tanna'im ve'Amora'im*, Wurzburg, 1932.

Kahle, Paul, and Weinberg, T., "The Mishna Text in Babylonia", *HUCA* 10, 1935, 185-221; 12-13, 1937-8, 275-325.

Kanter, Felix, *Beiträge zur Kenntnis des Rechtssystems und der Ethik Mar Samuels*, Bern, 1895.

Kaplan, Julius, *The Redaction of the Babylonian Talmud*, N.Y. 1933.

Kirchheim, Rafael, "Die Talmud in seinen Beziehungen zu den ... persischen Gesetzbüchern nach Schorr", *Ben Chananja* 8, 1865, 719-20, 737, 782, 800-1, 829-30, 861, 875.

Klein, Samuel, "Aus den Lehrhausern Ereẓ Israels im 2-3 Jahrhundert". *MGWJ* 73. n.s. 42, 1934, 164-9.

Klima, Otakar, "PĀQĪD - Didaskalos", *ArcO* 23, 1955, 481f.

———, *Manis Zeit und Leben*, Prague, 1962.

———, "Zur Chronologie von Manis Leben", *ArcO* 19, 1951, 393-403.

Knox, Wilfred L., *St. Paul and the Church of the Gentiles*, Cambridge, 1951.

Kohut, Alexander, "Ist das Schachenspiel im Talmud genannt, und unter welchem Namen", *ZDMG* 46, 1892, 130-5.

———, "The Talmudic Records of Persian and Babylonian Festivals Critically Illustrated", *AJSLL* 14, 1897, 183-94.

Kraeling, Carl H., "Mandaic Bibliography", *JAOS* 46, 1926, 49-55.

———, "The Origin and Antiquity of the Mandeans", *JAOS* 49, 1929, 195-218.

Kramers, J. H., "The Military Colonization of the Caucasus and Armenia under the Sassanids", *BSOS* 8, 1935-7, 613-8.

Kraus, Heinrich, *Begriff und Form der Haeresie nach Talmud und Midrasch*, Hamburg, 1896.

Krauskopf, Joseph, Influence of Mazdeism upon Talmudism. Unpublished Dissertation, Hebrew Union College-Jewish Institute of Religion Library, Cincinnati, no date.

Krauss, Samuel, "Études sur la Mischna", *REJ* 67, 1914, 24-39.

———, "Notizen zur 'Kleinen Chronik' ", *MGWJ* 61, 1917, 7-25.

———, "R. Eleazar b. R. Simeon als Römischer Befehlshaber", *MGWJ* 38, 1894, 151-6.

———, "Talitam shel Talmidei Ḥakhamim", *Bloch Jubilee Volume*, Budapest, 1905, 83-97.

———, "Talmudische Nachrichten über Arabien", *ZDMG* 70, 1916, 321-53.

Krochmal, Avraham, "Toldot Sh'mu'el Yarhina'i", *HeḤaluẓ* 5, 1852, 66-89.

Kronberg, N., "Die Amoräer in neuer Beleuchtung", *MGWJ* 46, 1902, 439-48, review of HaLevi, *Dorot HaRishonim*.

Kuk, S. H., "She'ar Sifrei deVe Rav", *Sefer Zikaron A. Z. Rabinowitz*, Tel Aviv, 1924, 121-2.

Landersdorfer, S. "Schule und Unterricht im alten Babylonien", *Blätter für Gymnasialschulwesen*, 45, 1909, 577-624.

Langlois, Victor, *Collection des Historiens Anciens et Modernes de l'Arménie*, Paris, 1867.

Lauterbach, Jacob Z., "Samuel Yarhina'ah", *JE* X 29-31.

———, "Ze'era", *JE* 12, 651-2.

Lebreton, J., *Gnosticism, Marcionism, and Manichaeism*, London, 1934.

Lechtmann, A., "LeToldot Rav Huna Bavla'ah", *K'nesset Yisrael* 3, 1888, 297-303.

Leszynsky, Rudolf, "Isaak Halevis Zitate", *MGWJ* 58, 567-80, 690-99.

Lévi, Israel, "Le mot 'minim', désigne-t-il jamais une secte juive de gnostiques antinomistes?" *REJ* 38, 1899, 204-10.

———, "Notes de grammaire judéo-babylonienne", *REJ* 1, 1880, 212-21.

Lewy, Hans, *Chaldaean Oracles and Theurgy. Mysticism, Magic, and Platonism in the Later Roman Empire*, Cairo, 1956.

Lewy, Hildegard, "Le calendrier perse", *Orientalia*, 9th series, 10, 1941, 1-64.

———, "Genesis of the Faulty Persian Chronology", *JAOS* 64, 1944, 211f.

Levinsohn, Aharon, "Korot Tanna'im ve'Amora'im", *Jeschurun*, 1, 1856, 81-6.

———, "Toldot R. Yehoshu'a ben Hananiah", *Bikkurim* 1, 1864, 26-35.

Lewysohn, Avraham, "Toldot Rav", *Jeschurun* 4, 1864, 114-24, 7, 1871, 6-16.

Lidzbarski, Mark, *Das Johannesbuch der Mandäer*, Giessen, 1915, part II.

Lieberman, Saul, *Shki'in*, Jerusalem, 1939.

———, "Talmudah shel Kisrin", *Musaf LaTarbiz* 2, Jerusalem, 1931.

———, *HaYerushalmi Kifshuto*, I, Jerusalem, 1935.

Liebreich, Leon J., "Aspects of the New Year Liturgy", *HUCA* 34, 1963, 159-63.

———, "Insertions in the Third Benediction of the 'Amidoth", *HUCA* 35, 1964, 79-101.

L'Orange, H. P., *Studies on the Iconography of Cosmic Kingship in the Ancient World*, Oslo, 1953.

Löwenmayer, M., "R. Jochanan ben Napcha", *MGWJ* 4, 1855, 285-94, 231-28.

Löwy, Josef, "Andeutungen auf die Pehlevischrift im Talmud", *Ben Chananja* 2, 1866, 42

MacDermont, B. C., "Roman Emperors in the Sassanian Reliefs", *Journal of Roman Studies* 44, 1954, 76-80.

Magie, David, "Roman Policy in Armenia and Transcaucasia and its Significance", *Annual Report of the American Historical Association* 1, 1919, 295-304.

———, trans., *The Scriptores Historiae Augustae*, N.Y. 1924, I-III.

Mann, Jacob, "S'kirah Historit'al Dinei N'fashot b'Zman HaZeh", *HaZofeh leHokhmat Yisrael* 10, 1926, 200-8.

Mantel, Hugo, "Toldot HaHinukh b'Erez Yisrael b'Tekufat HaTanna'im veHa'Amora'im", *Enziklopedyah Hinukhit*, 147-57.

Margoliot, Re'uven, *Yesod HaMishnah ve'Arikhatah*, Tel Aviv, 1956.

Maricq, André, "Res Gestae divi Saporis, Le Texte grec." *Syria*, 35, 1958, 295-360.

Marmorstein, Arthur, "The Confession of Sins for the Day of Atonement", *Essays in Honour of . . . J. H. Hertz*, London, 1942, 293-306.

———, *The Old Rabbinic Doctrine of Nod*, London, I, 1927, II, 1937.

———, "On Certain Spiritual Movements in the Generation of R. Joshua b. Levi", *Lévi Volume*, Hebrew section, 1-16 (=*REJ* 82).

———, "L'Opposition contre le Patriarche R. Judah II", *REJ* 64, 1912, 59-66.

———, "Les persécutions religieuses à l'époque de R. Johanan b. Nappacha", *REJ* 67, 1923, 166-76.

———, "La Réorganisation du Doctorat en Palestine au IIIe siècle", *REJ* 66, 1913, 44-53.

———, *Studies in Jewish Theology*, edited by J. Rabbinowits and M. S. Lew, London, 1950.

————, "The Unity of God in Rabbinic Literature", *HUCA* 1, 1924, 467-99.

Marquardt, J., "Beiträge zur Geschichte und Sage von Eran", *ZDMG* 49, 1895, 628-72.

————, *Südarmenien und die Tigrisquellen*, Vienna, 1930.

Mason, K., ed., *Iraq and the Persian Gulf*, London, 1944 (Naval Intelligence Division, The Royal Navy).

Mayer, Joseph, "Mar Samuel als Arzt", *Festschrift Salomon Carlebach*, Berlin, 1910., 190-5.

Millar, Fergus, *A Study of Cassius Dio*, Oxford, 1964.

Minovi, M., *Letter of Tansar*, Tehran, 1932.

Montgomery, James A., *Aramaic Incantation Texts from Nippur*, Philadelphia, 1913.

Moore, George F., "Zoroastrianism", *HTR* 5, 1912, 180-225.

Mordtmann, A. D., "Die Chronologie der Sassaniden", *Sitz. b. Königl. Bayer. Ak. d. Wiss. zu München, phil.-philol. Kl.*, Munich, 1871, 3-30.

Morgenstierne, Georg, *Indo-Iranica: Mélanges Présentés à Georg Morgenstierne, à l'Occasion de son soixante-dixieme anniversaire*, Wiesbaden, 1964.

Morrison, G., "The Sassanian Genealogy in Mas'ūdī", in S. M. Ahmad and A. Rahman, eds., *Al-Mas'ūdī Millenary Commemoration Volume*, Calcutta, 1960.

Neusner, Jacob, "Barukh b. Neriah and Zoroaster", *JBR* 32, 1964, 359-60.

————, "The Conversion of Adiabene to Christianity", *Numen* 13, 2, 1966, 144-50.

————, "The Conversion of Adiabene to Judaism", *JBL* 83, 1, 1964, 60-6.

————, *A History of the Jews in Babylonia, I. The Parthian Period*, Leiden, 1965: Studia Post-biblica IX.

————, "Jews in Pagan Armenia", *JAOS* 84, 1964, 230-40.

————, "Judaism in Late Antiquity", *Judaism*, 15, 2, 1966, 230-240.

————, "New Perspectives on Babylonian Jewry in the Tannaitic Period", *Judaica*, 22, 2. 1966, 82-112.

————, "Škand Miscellanies", *JAOS*.

————, "A Zoroastrian Critique of Judaism: Translation and Exposition of the XIII and XIV Chapters of the Škand Gumanik Vičar", *JAOS* 83, 1963. 283-94.

Nock, Arthur D., "Development of Paganism in the Roman Empire", *CAH* XII, 409-49.

————, "Genius of Mithraism", *Journal of Roman Studies*, 27, 1937, 108-13.

Norden, Eduard, *Agnostos Theos*, repr. Darmstadt, 1956.

Obermann, Julian, "Two Magic Bowls", *AJSLL* 57, 1940, 1-29.

Ochser, S., "Samuel ben Nahman", *JE* XI, 25-6.

————, "Ze'iri", *JE* XII, 652.

Odeberg, Hugo, *III Enoch, or The Hebrew Book of Enoch*, Cambridge, 1928.

Oppenheim, A. Leo, *Ancient Mesopotamia*, Chicago, 1964.

Parker, H. M. D., *A History of the Roman World from A.D. 138 to 337*, London, 1935, Revised ed., edited by B. H. Warmington, London, 1957.

Paruck, D. J., *Sassanian Coins*, Bombay, 1924. Review, *JRAS* 1926, 740-2.

Patkanian, M. K., *Essai d'une histoire de la dynastie des Sassanides d'après les renseignements fournis pas les historiens arméniens*, *JA* 6th series 7, 1866, 101-238, translated by E. Prud'homme.

Pavry, J. D. C., "Manichaeism — A Rival of Zoroastrianism and Christianity", *JR* 17, 1937, 161-9.

Pedersen, J., "The Ṣābians", in *A Volume of Oriental Studies Presented to Edward G. Browne*, ed. by T. W. Arnold and R. A. Nicholson, Cambridge, 1922, 383-91.

Pedersen, V. S., "Le Mandéisme et les origines chrétiennes", *Revue d'Histoire et de Philosophie des Religions* 16, 1937, 378-84.

Peeters, P., "Le 'Passionnaire d'Adiabène'", *Analecta Bollandiana* 43, 1925, 261-304.

Peterson, Eric, "Urchristentum und Mandäismus", *ZNW* 27, 1928, 55-97.

Pfister, R., "Les premieres soies Sassanides", *Études d'Orientalisme (Mélanges Linossier)*, Paris, 1932, 461-79.

Pigulevskaja, N., *Les Villes de l'État Iranien aux Époques Parthe et Sassanide*, Paris, 1963.

Pilchik, Ely E., *Judaism outside the Holy Land*, N.Y. 1964.

Polotsky, H. J., "Manichäismus", *Pauly-Wissowa Real-Encyclopaedie der Classischen Altertumswissenschaft*, Stuttgart, 1935, Supplement Vol VI, cols. 240-71.

Preuss, Julius, *Biblisch-Talmudische Medizin*, Berlin, 1923.

Puech, Henri C., *Le Manichéisme, Son Fondateur, Sa Doctrine*, Paris, 1949.

Pugliese-Carratelli, Giovanni, "La Crisi dell'impero nell'età di Gallieno", *La Parola del Passato* 4, 1947, 48-73.

———, "Ancora sulle 'Res Gestae Divi Saporis' ", *La Parola del Passato* 5, 1947, 209-239.

Quispel, Gilles, "Gnosticism and the New Testament", *Vigilae Christianae*, 19, 1965, 65-85.

Ratner, Baer, *Ahavat Ziyyon Virushalayim*, Vilna, 1901f., I-XIII [Variant Readings in the Palestinian Talmud].

———, "Die Mischna des Levi ben Sisi", *Festschrift A. Harkavy*, St. Petersburg, 1908, 117-22.

Rawlinson, George, *The Seventh Great Oriental Monarchy*, London, 1876.

Reifman, Jacob, "Resh Galuta", *Bikkurim* 1, 1864, 36-49.

Reinach, Theodore, "Le calendrier des Grècs de Babylonie et les origines du calendrier juif", *REJ* 18, 1889, 90-94.

Reines, C. W., "The Terms 'Yoshbei Kranoth' and 'Am Ha-ʾaretz' ", *Joshua Bloch Memorial Volume*, N.Y. 1961, 75-81.

Reuther, Oscar, "Sasanian Architecture", Pope, 493-578.

Rosenthal, Franz, *Die Aramaistische Forschung*, Leiden, 1964.

Rossell, William H., *Handbook of Aramaic Magical Texts*, Ringwood Borough, N.J., 1953.

Rudolph, Kurt, *Die Mandäer*, Göttingen, 1960, I-II.

Sachau, Eduard, "Vom Christentum in der Persis", *Sitz. d. Königl. Preuss. Ak. d. Wiss.*, Berlin, 1916, 958-80.

Salim, S. M., *Marsh Dwellers of the Euphrates Delta*, London, 1962.

Sarre, F., "Sasanian Stone Sculpture", Pope, 601-30.

Schachter, M., "Babylonian-Palestinian Variations in the Mishnah", *JQR* n.s. 42, 1951, 1-36.

Schaeder, Hans Heinrich, *Esra der Schreiber*, Tübingen, 1930.

Schechter, Solomon, "Seder 'Olam Suta", *MGWJ* 39, 23-8.

Scheftelowitz, J., "Gleichklangzauber in Indien und im jüdischen Volksglauben", *ZDMG* 78, 1924, 106-10.

———, "Die mandäische Religion und das Judentum," *MGWJ* 73, 1929, 211-32.

Scholem, Gershom, G., *On the Kabbalah and its Symbolism*, translated by Ralph Manheim, N.Y. 1965.

———, *Ursprung und Anfänge der Kabbala*, Berlin, 1962.

Schwab, Moise, *Répertoire des Articles relatifs à l'histoire et à la litterature juives parus dans les Périodiques de 1665 à 1900*, Paris, 1914-1923.

Seston, W., "Roi sassanide Narsès, les Arabes, et la Manichéisme", *Mélanges Dussaud* I, 227-34.

Seyrig, Henri, "L'incorporation de Palmyre à l'empire Romain", *Syria* 13, 1932, 266-74.

Sheikovitz, Nahum Meir, "Tadmor", *HaMeliz* 10, 1870, 55-6.

Shurin, Aharon Benzion, "Z'ev Yavetz, The Orthodox Historian", *Talpioth* 9, 1964, 410-14.

Smith, Morton, "Observations on Hekhalot Rabbati", *Biblical and Other Studies*, ed. Alexander Altmann, Cambridge, 1963, 142-60.

———, Review of Zaehner, *Dawn, Anglican Theological Review*, 1962, 231-4.

Smith, V. A., "Invasion of the Panjab by Ardashir Papakan, First Sasanian King of Persia, A. D. 226-241", *JRAS* 1920, 221f.

Snowman, Jacob, *Short History of Talmudic Medicine*, London, 1935.

Starcky, Jean, *Palmyre, La Fiancée du Desert*, Damascus, 1948.

Steinsaltz, E., "Links between Palestine and the Land of Israel", *Talpioth* 9, 1964, 294-306 (in Hebrew).

Talmon, Shmaryahu, "'Wisdom' in the Book of Esther", *Vetus Testamentum* 13, 1963, 419-55.

Taqizadeh, S. H., "Dates of Mani's Life", translated with commentary by W. B. Henning, *Asia Major* 6, 106-21.

———, "Some Chronological Data Relating to the Sasanian Period", *BSOS* 9, 1939, 125-40.

———, "Zur Chronologie der Sassaniden", *ZDMG* 91, n.f. 16, 673-80.

Thompson, E. A., *The Historical Work of Ammianus Marcellinus*, Cambridge, 1947.

Trachtenberg, Joshua, *Jewish Magic and Superstition*, Philadelphia, 1961.

Turner, H. E. W., *The Pattern of Christian Truth*, London, 1954.

Urbach, E. E., "Rabbinical Laws of Idolatry in the Second and Third Centuries in the Light of Archaeological and Historical Facts", *IEJ* 9, 1959, 149f.

van der Waerden, B. L., "History of the Zodiac", *Archiv für Orientforschung* 16, 1952-3, 216-30.

Venetianer, L., "Hashpa'at Sippurei Bavli-im 'al Darkhei HaPerush BaTalmud", *Sefer HaYovel Rabbi M. A. Bloch*, Budapest, 1905, 56-63.

von Wesendonk, O. G., "Bardesanes und Mani", *AO* 10, 1932, 336-63.

———, *Das Weltbild der Iranier*, Munich, 1933.

Vööbus, Arthur, *History of Asceticism in the Syrian Orient*, Louvain, I, 1958, II, 1960.

———, "Manichaeism and Christianity in Persia under the Sassanids", *Yearbook of the Estonian Learned Society in America*, I, 1951-3, 7-13.

———, "The Origins of Monasticism in Mesopotamia", *Church History*, 20, 1951, 27-37.

———, "The Significance of the Dead Sea Scrolls for the History of Early Christianity", *Yearbook of the Estonian Learned Society in America*, II, 1954-8, 54-62.

Walser, Gerold, and Pekáry, Thomas, *Die Krise des Römischen Reiches*, Berlin, 1962.

Watelin, L. C., "Sasanian Buildings near Kish", Pope, 584-600.

Waxman, Meyer, "Rav", *HaDoar*, 1962, i, 8-9, ii, 24-5.

Weis, P. R., "The Controversies of Rab and Samuel and the Tosefta", *JSS* 3, 1958, 288-97.

Weiss, A. H., "Rabanan d'Agadata' uMorei HaKenesiah", *Bet Talmud* 1, 1870.

Weiss, Abraham, *'Al HaYeẓirah HaSifrutit shel Ha'Amora'im*, N.Y. 1962.

———, "Haza'at HaḤomer b'Masekhet Qiddushin, Mishnah veTosefta", *Ḥorev* 12, 1957, 70-148.

———, "He'Arot l'Berakhot Perek VI", *Ḥorev*1948, 1-26.

———, *Hithavut HaTalmud b'Shlemuto*, N.Y. 1943.

———, *LeḤeker HaTalmud*, N.Y. 1956.

———, "Perushim veHe'arot baMishnah uvaTalmud", *Ḥorev* 11, 1951, 85-122; 14-15, 1960, 127-156, etc.

———, "Studien zur Redaktion des babylonischen Talmuds", *MGWJ* 73, 1929, 131-43, 184-211.

Welles, C. Bradford, "The Population of Roman Dura", *Studies in Roman Economic and Social History*, ed. P. R. Coleman-Norton, et al., Princeton, 1951, 251-74.

Widengren, Geo, "Die Mandäer", *Handbuch der Orientalistik*, VIII, ii, 83-101.

———, *Mani und der Manichäismus*, Stuttgart, 1961.

———, *Mesopotamian Elements in Manichaeism*, Uppsala, 1946.

———, *Die Religionen Irans*, Stuttgart, 1965.

Wilson, R. McL., *The Gnostic Problem, A Study of the Relations between Hellenistic Judaism and the Gnostic Heresy*, London, 1958.

Yamauchi, Edwin Masao, *Mandaean Incantation Texts*, Brandeis University Dissertation, Microfilm, Ann Arbor, 1964.

Zeida, Ya'akov, "Shmu'el Yarhina'ah HaRofé", *Sinai* 8, 1941.

Zeitlin, Solomon, "Mar Samuel and Manumission of Slaves", *JQR* n.s. 55, 1965, 267-9.

Ziegler, Karl-Heinz, *Die Beziehungen zwischen Rom und dem Partherreich*, Wiesbaden, 1964.

Ziemlich, Bernhard, Review of Bacher, *Agada*, *MWJ* 5, 1878, 190-7.

Zimmels, B., "Zur Geschichte der Exegese über den vers Gen. 49.10", *MWJ* 17, 1890, 1-27, 145-65, 177-97, 261-79.

Zimmern, H., "Babylonische Vorstufen der vorderasiatischen Mysterienreligionen", *ZDMG* 76, 1922, 36-54.

Zotenberg, Hermann, trans., *Tabari, Chronique*, repr. Paris, 1958.

Zuckermandel, M., *Tosefta, Mischna, und Boraitha in ihrem Verhältnis zu einander, oder, palestinensische und babylonische Halacha*, Frankfurt, I-II, 1908-9, III, 1910.

———, "Über dem Seder Tana'im v'Amora'im," *MGWJ* 22, 1873, 228-9.

Zulay, Menahem, *Zur Liturgie der Babylonischen Juden. Bonner Orientalistische Studien*, Stuttgart, 1933.

Zuri, J. S. (Sheshak), *Hok HaMita'sek shelo b'reshut, Negotiorum Gestor*, London, 1941.

———, *Rab, Sein Leben und seine Anschauungen*, Zürich, 1918.

———, *Rabbi 'Akiva*, Jerusalem, 1924.

———, *Rabbi Jochanan, der erste Amoräer Galiläas*, Berlin, 1918.

———, *Rabbi Yosi bar Hanina mikisrin*, Jerusalem, 1926.

———, *Tarbut HaDeromim*, Warsaw, 1924.

———, "Tefilat HaGalili-im", *Sefer Zikaron l'A. Z. Rabbinowitz*, Tel Aviv, 1924, 50-55.

———, *Toldot Darkhei HaLimud b'Yeshivot Darom, Galil, Sura, veNeharde'a'*, Jerusalem, 1914.

———, *Toldot HaD'romim b'Yahasehem 'el haGalilim*, Paris, 1913.

———, *Torat HaMishpat Ha'Ezrahi Ha'Ivri. Shitat HaTa'anot*, London, 1933.

ADDENDA ET CORRIGENDA AD VOLUMEN I

Page 26, second line from the top: "on which a Parthian delegation". *Add*:
(or perhaps, Jewish agents of the Parthian government, for familiarity with the teachings of a 'certain old man' suggests they may have been Jews, as Professor Smith points out)

P. 29. Thus the Parthians restored an independent, Hasmonean government in Jerusalem. *Add.*:
though it might not be entirely accurate to call it 'independent' by comparison with one put in by the Romans, Professor Smith points out.

Page 57, At the end of the second paragraph, ". . . the Parthian imperial interest would greatly benefit". *Add.*:
One cannot, moreover, ignore the meaning of the destruction of the Temple, and its agency of autonomous Jewish government, in Palestine, which would have required the Parthian government to take measures to ensure that its local Jewish community was not subject to the decrees of a Jewish regime subservient to Rome (see vol. II, pages 92-96).

Page 61 note 3: "and compare Graetz." *Add*:
"Zur der Anwesenheit der Adiabenischen Königin in Jerusalem und des Apostel Paulus", *MGWJ* 26, 1877,

Page 65 Note 3. Add:
See also Karl-Heinz Ziegler, *Die Beziehungen zwischen Rom und dem Partherreich* (Wiesbaden, 1964), 77 n. 237.

To Page 72 note 1.
Dr. Moshe Beer kindly calls my attention to the excellent article of Joshua Gutman, "Milhemet HaYehudim bimei Trayanus", *Sefer . . . Assaf*, ed. M. D. Cassuto, J. Klausner, *et al.*, Jerusalem, 1953, 149-84. In that article, Gutman provides a defiinitive account of the messianic overtones of the Jewish war against Trajan in the Roman orient. The evidence dealing with Mesopotamia and Babylonia is so slight, however, that we cannot be certain whether the Jews' revolt in occupied Parthia was similarly motivated or not.

Page 77 note 1. *Add*:
See also Ziegler, *op. cit.*, 103 n. 50, and L. Motta, "La tradizione sulla rivolta ebraica al tempo di Traiano", *Aegyptus* 32, 1952, 474f. Compare the view of E. S. Bouchier, cited below, p. 87 n. 2.

Page 111, 7th line from the bottom:
". . . and authorized" ADD "by him".

To Page 134, at the end of the Footnote:
W. Bacher, ("Der Massoret Hamnuna", *MWJ* 18, 1891, 58-9, and see also his article in *MWJ* 17, 1890, 169-72) proves that there was still another refugee at the time of the Hadrianic persecutions, a teacher of R. Hamnuna and R. Ada, by the name of Nakai.

To page 135, line 1.
". . . deliberations at Usha or elsewhere;" *Add:* Nor, of course, was R. Ishmael himself included, see Y. N. Epstein, *Introductions to Amoraic Literature*, 251-3.

Page 152-153, Note 5, Add:

Professor Lieberman comments, "Bet Din Shaveh" can *only* mean "a court of one mind." In rabbinic literature, the expression "shavin" in this meaning is very frequent, as Mishnah Shabbat I, 9, "veshavin ᵓelu veᵓelu" which means that Bet Shammai and Bet Hillel are "shavin" [in agreement] in this respect. In the very same text you refer to, you find the expression "ᵓilu ᵓashve ⁽imi," i.e. "if he had agreed with me", compare translation on p. 94, last line.

Page 153-3, n. 4.

Professor Morton Smith points out that it is hardly surprising that different Jewish communities should have had similar forms for grace after meal, in this instance Jewish-Christians and other Jews, especially since the similarity does not go beyond thanking God for creating food for men. The really surprising thing in the Dura fragment is that it presuppose a meat meal. It must, therefore, be a festival prayer.

Page 169, Add to Note:

See also H. E. T. Turner, *Pattern of Christian Truth* (London, 1954) for a penetrating critique of W. Bauer, *Rechtgläubigkeit und Ketzerei im ältesten Christentum* (2nd ed. Tübingen, 1964).

ii. Corrigenda

Page 102.

Dr. Moshe Beer kindly points out that the source referred to in n. 3 does not indicate *direct* contact between R. Ḥiyya and the exilarch, but rather, that R. Ḥiyya was disturbed at prayer because he was wondering who would take precedence at the emperor's court, the exilarch or the arkapat. Such a theoretical problem would not, Dr. Beer rightly points out, prove that R. Ḥiyya actually was with the exilarch when the latter was at court. In the same note, the last line should read, "Rav's daughter married the exilarch's son".

p. xvi		1. 24	*instead of*:	abent	*read*:	agent
1		24	„	ficed	„	fixed
3	n. 1	4	„	*Wélanges ffapart*	„	*Mélanges Capart*
5		3	„	ni	„	in
	n. 1	3	„	post-Biblical data	„	post-Biblical data"
7		10	„	Bacchanate	„	Bacchanates
10		25	„	many Jews knew little	„	many Jews knew a little
		27	„	there may have been	„	there must have been
12		19	„	oiwing to the aid	„	owing to the aid
13		8	„	veery reason	„	every reason
16	n. 1	3	„	(Tubingen, 188)	„	(Tuebingen, 1888)
20		15	„	geographical limits	„	g.l., except for Thrace and Egypt
21		17	„	compaign	„	campaign
22		28	„	adverse	„	averse
25	n. 2	1	*instead of*:	94-95.	*read*:	94-95. See also Koh. R. 7. 12. 1
30		13	*delete*:	independently and legitimately		
42		12	*instead of*:	but were	„	but the correspondence was
42		12	„	event	„	one
43		12	„	(in part)	„	(partially)

				instead of:		*read*:	
	n. 1	7		"Die Jüdischem Apostel"		"Die Jüdischen Apostel"	
47		3	,,	prevent	,,	require	
49		30	,,	heard	,,	learned	
50		1	,,	as it was by	,,	as by	
52		4	,,	Artabanus	,,	The Artabanus	
52	n. 1		,,	New York	,,	Baltimore	
54		32	,,	he added	,,	he added to it	
		36	,,	rule, according	,,	rule. According	
57		1	,,	Semites	,,	also the native Semites	
57		19	,,	Greek, Semitic	,,	Greek, Syrian and Se-mitic	
59		19	,,	Monobazus	,,	Monobazes	
60	n. 1	13	,,	Monobases	,,	Monobazes	
62		20	,,	Monobases	,,	Monobazes	
63		10	,,	noble	,,	royal	
65	note	1	,,	Monobazus	,,	Monobazes	
68		3	,,	Nonetheless, it is	,,	Nonetheless, on the basis of three evi-dences, it is	
		21	,,	and co-incidentally assist		a.c. have assisted	
73		32	,,	and connections with	,,	a. the reported c. of R. Nathan's father with	
77		14	,,	relationships	,,	relationships	
p. 80		1. 5	,,	the death of Marcus Aurelius.	,,	the death of Pertinax	
81		14-15	,,	unrest in the year	,,	unrest in the second year of	
82	n. 2	10	,,	or permitted	,,	or have permitted	
83		21	,,	It would have been...	,,	To send a gem to R. Judah would h.b. a h.i.m.o.i.J.B.w.h. philo-Judaism.	
87		1	,,	Antonines	,,	Antoninus	
		10	,,	most likely in the gift	,,	m.l. in connection with the gift	
90		13	,,	There was a large	,,	From Hellenistic times, there w. a l.	
92		37	,,	That patriarch's	,,	That the patriarch's	
93		7	,,	lest		least	
93	n. 1	3	,,	Arabia was led	,,	Arabia led	
94	n. 1	1	,,	*Jews in B*	,,	*Jews of B.*	
98		22	,,	and death, and who	,,	and death,	
99		30	,,	(below), Hezekiah	,,	(below), with Hezekiah	

Page		Line		instead of	read
104	n.	24	*instead of*:	and taught the sons of	*read*: and taught Rav and Rabbah b. Hana, the sons of
104	n. 2	2	,,	Galilean accent)	,, Galilean)
105		19	,,	Rabbi has	,, Rabbi had
106		32	,,	But it should . . . . . even calling him	,, But R. Hiyya is also reported to have had great respect for R. Judah, even applying to him the quotation,
107		19	,,	agency	,, agent
108		12	,,	reminded him	,, reminded Rabbi Judah
		26	,,	helds	,, holds
109		10	,,	While this was	,, While this is
110		22	,,	inhabitants . . . . . R. Judah.	,, inhabitants of a certain village were so angry about a ruling . . . of R. Judah that they renounced Judaism.
		30	,,	a formality, which the Palestinian	,, act a formality, or an of courtesy to R. Judah the Prince, since they had been his pupils. It may be that the Palestinian patriarchate consistently accorded it to some of
112		15	,,	seems to have had	,, seems to have had at first
115	n. 2	21	,,	heirs	,, the heirs
122		11	,,	One source . . . more reasonable	,, One source may make it seem more likely that there was a Judah b. Bathyra II.
p. 122		1. 16	,,	If the source is contemporary	,, If the source represents the men as contemporary
123		25	*delete*:	Hence it appears . . . approximately 100 and 160 c. e.	,,
124	n. 1	1	,,	The evidence. . . is not extensive.	
125		23	*instead of*:	with them also.)	,, with them.)
127	n. 1	22	,,	epoch,	,, epoch?
	n. 1	24	,,	And also, the	,, And also, The
128		7	,,	c.e. circa 80/100	,, circa 95-105
		10	,,	c.e. circa 90/100	,, circa 100/110
129		7	,,	was given to the colleagues of	,, was given to his colleagues in
131		8	,,	migrated toward	,, migrated during
		15	,,	He spent	,, R. Ahai spent
133		5	,,	have lived to study	,, have studied

133		32	*instead of:*	there and also in Babylonia	*read:* in Babylonia
137		3	,,	form	,, from
138		1	,,	He was, therefore	,, He is, therefore
139		2	,,	patronymic	,, patronymics
		11	,,	scroll" as follows	,, scroll' beginning ,, as follows
140		1	,,	Eli^cezar b. Shamua	,, Eli^cezar b. Shammu^ca
141		9	,,	the latter	,, Jonathan
		11	,,	Benjaminitic (Davidic)	,, Davidic
	n. 1	3	,,	Kafri	,, Ḳafri
142	n. 3	4 .	,,	*HaNesiut vehaBaad*	,, *HaNesiut veha Vaad*
143		14	,,	and for	,, and forth
144		1	,,	the same exegesis	,, an interpretation
		21	,,	medicine, educated	,, medicine, and educated
145		5	,,	of Rav, he	,, of Rav. He
147		3	,,	patriarchate	,, patriarchate often
149		10	,,	synagogue	,, synagogues
151	n. 1		,,	34. 9.	,, 34. 9. See Tanhuma Mishpat im 8, ed. Buber II, 85
152	n. 4	3	,,	that R. Judah the Prince	,, that R. Judah the Prince (who died. . . . before 226),
153		2	,,	involved	,, was
		9	,,	Such a legal principle	,, Such awareness of legal liability
153	n. 3		,,	of inquiry	,, of inquiry. But it is more likely anti-Zoroastrian, insisting that cattle are to be used for food.
154		13	,,	in academies there called,	,, in academies, and was called,
155	n. 2	1	,,	in the middle century	,, in the middle of the third century
157		10	,,	an axiom for	,, claimed by at least one of
159		17	,,	Haninah	,, Ḥananiah
		20	,,	Ḥaninah	,, Ḥananiah
160	n. 1	6	,,	status	,, strata
160	n. 4		,,	volume	,, volume. On Merkavah preaching in Babylonian, see also b. Shabbat 80 b.
162		17	,,	were in contact	,, was in contact
163	n. 1	2	,,	planetary influence was	,, planetary influence was effective on Israelites
169		10	,,	influence	,, influence gained ground

169		21 *instead of*: progress.		*read*: progress. Professor Smith comments, "This looks like the penetration of an undifferentiated "Jewish" population by rival, organized parties at pretty much the same time. I do not think it was so much a matter of Christianity's failing to make headway where Pharisaism was already established, as of each party's shutting out the other from the areas it came to control. If this can be so, the Christian acquisition of Adiabee suggests that the royal family there had been converted to the older Yahwism of the Temple rather than to Pharisaism"	
170-171 n. 1	7	,,	they survived,	,,	they survived, they
172	1	,,	oral law	,,	Oral Law
174	15	,,	authority	,,	rulings
p. 175	1. 27	,,	indicate	,,	claim, (and this is in fact most unlikely)
179	29	,,	probability table	,,	table of references
180	43	,,	Yohai	,,	Gamaliel
188	28	,,	for 'secret	,,	for his 'secret
189	25	,,	Gamaliel	,,	Yohai
220	4	,,	130 n.	,,	130 n. 179, 186

INDEX OF BIBLICAL AND TALMUDIC PASSAGES [1])

I. Hebrew Bible

[1]) Indices were prepared by Mr. David Goodblatt, Jewish Theological Seminary of America, under a grant from the Dartmouth College Faculty Fellowship Expense Fund.

VI. Babylonian Talmud

IX. Ge'onic Literature

GENERAL INDEX

A

Abaye, xiv, 69n., 135n., 159
Abba, R., 229
Abba, Father of Jeremiah b. Abba, 98
Abba, Father of R. Simlai, 141, 144
Abba Afrika (Rav, q.v.), 127, 134n.
Abba b. Abba, Father of Samuel, 42-44, 49, 78, 79, 80n., 103, 104, 105, 134, 137, 176, 178, 244, 260, 278n., 279, 281
Abba b. Kahana, R., 155n.
Abbahu, R., 44, 73, 126
Abbuha b. Ihi, 265
Abgar V, 93n.
Abgar IX, 93n.
Abidarma, 82
Abin of Toran (Abitoran), 79n.
Abitol the Hairdresser, 59
Ablat (Avlat), 26n.; contact with Levi, 86; contact with Samuel, 85n., 86, 139
Abrahams, Israel, 162, 163
Abu Othman al Gahiz, 90n.
Achemenids, xiv, 3, 7, 30, 246; treatment of Jews by, 65
Adam, literature of, 136n., 158, 185, 187
Adam, Alfred, 20n.
Adams, Robert McC., 11, 245, 146, 247, 248
Adda the Fisherman, 132
Adda b. Ahava, R., 133, 134, 146, 212, 282
Adda b. Mattenah, R., 218
Adiabene, 40, 241, 257; Jews in, 241-242
Advenpat, 4n.
Afes, R., 129, 138
Afsatia, 247, 278n.
Agathias, 13, 148
Agoranomos, 107, 112-113, 114n.
Agricultural offerings, application in Babylonia of, 259-261
Aḥa, R., 207, 282
Aḥa, Brother of Abba the father of Jeremiah b. Abba, 98
Aḥa b. Huna, R., 270
Aḥadebui, R., 177
Aḥai b. R. Josiah, R., 254n., 274, 278, 286
Ahriman, 18
Ahuramazda, 19
Aibu, Son of Rav, 14, 130
Akiba, R., 37, 53, 98n., 99, 158n., 180n., 187, 230, 233, 238; cited more by Rav than by Samuel, 234; methodology of study, 235; Rav studies with disciples of in Palestine, 234; school of, 180, 229, 239; support of Bar Kokhba by, 66; theology of, 180n.
Aknaya, 88, 89n.
ʿAkov, 96, 104. See Ukba, Mar
Akra di Agma, 146, 262
Albeck, Ḥ., x, 96n., 97n., 161n., 163n., 166n.
Alemanni, 9

G

Gagé, Jean, 4n., 5n., 6n., 49, 51n.
Galileans, 183n.; methodology of exegesis of, 233-234
Gallienus, xix, 9
Gamaliel II, R., 94
Gaster, Moses, 105n.
Gazaca/Ginzak, 98, 99, 101n., 104, 137n., 241, 242
Geiger, B. xi, xii, 32n., 54n., 59n., 89n.
Genealogy, Jewish concern for purity of, 229, 256-259
Genivah, 178; quarrel with Mar Ukba, 106n.
Geniza, 162
Gentiles, Jewish influence on, 81
Geonim, Geonic, 36, 47, 98; traditions of, 38, 54, 96-97, 104, 106, 155n.,
Gezirpati (see Hazarpat), 54
Ghirshman, R., 2n., 4n., 5n., 14n., 15n., 20n.
Giddal, R., 171, 173, 177, 206, 228, 255, 270
Giddal b. Minyumi, R., 179, 282
Ginzak. See Gazaca
Ginzberg, Louis, X, 41n., 52n., 73n., 136n., 142n., 157, 161n., 166n., 169n.,
    177n., 179n., 180n., 183n., 186n., 276n.
Glatzer, N. N., 52n.
Gnostics, Gnosticism, 91, 182, 186n., 187n.,; Christian, 183; Jewish, 183, 186;
    Mandean, 158; Pagan, 183; rabbinic, 184; speculation on Adam, 136n.
God, rabbinic ideas on. See Theology
Goodenough, E. R., 59
Gordian, 9
Gotarzes, 40, 92, 93n.
Goths, 9
Graetz, H., xi, 46n., 50, 51n., 105, 106, 126n., 134n., 242n
Greece, 113
Greek, 77; Knowledge of Rav of, 133
Greeks, 1, 30, 31, 38, 88, 93, 239
Gutman, Y., 40n.

H

Haase, Felix, 22n.
Hadji-Abad, xiv
Hadrianic period, 88
Hagrunia, 247
Ḥairan, 29n.
Halevi, Y. I., xii, 51, 97n., 105n., 109, 126n., 128n., 136n., 147n., 259
Ḥaliẓah, 271
Ḥama b. Guria, R., 11, 37, 192, 228, 291.
Ḥama b. R. Ḥanina, R., 193, 196
Hamadan, 241, 242
Hamnuna, R., 145, 162
Ḥanan, R., 276
Ḥanan of Baghdad, R., 263
Ḥanan, R., Son-in-law of Rav, 130
Ḥanan b. Rava, R., 76n., 190, 198
Ḥananel, R., 96, 97, 154, 171, 211, 212, 241
Ḥananiah, R., Nephew of R. Joshua b. Ḥananiah, 123, 141, 184

L

Labourt, J., 22n., 29n.
Laodicea, 45, 46n.
Lauterbach, J. Z., 194n.
Law, Jewish in Babylonia, civil, 109-112; of damages, 110, 117, 264-267; escha-
    tological significance of observance, 285; of Kashrut, 274-276; of marriage
    and divorce, 115-116, 252, 256-257, 267-272; on minim, 74; on menstrual
    separation, 274, 276-277; of mourning, 279-280; on pagan artifacts, 82-84;
    of personal status, 267-273; popular observance of, 253-255, 273-281,
    283; on prayer, 170-178; rabbinic enforcement of, 250-251, 253, 259-281;
    on relations with pagans, 73-74 78-82; of Sabbath, 274, 277-278; on transfer
    of property, 261-267
Lazarus, Felix, 97n., 105n., 121, 122
Legitimacy, rabbinic views on, 2, 251-252, 256, 267, 268-269
Leipoldt, Johannes, 22n.
Levi b. Sisi, xii, 37, 73n., 108, 129, 137, 138, 146, 162, 218, 221n., 263, 278;
    contact with Ablat, 85-86
Levin, B., 49n., 96, 126n.
Levine, Baruch, 32n.
Levy, J., 28n., 59n., 115n., 135n.
Lewy, Hans, 154n.
Lewy, Hildegard, 1n., 15n., 92n., 93n.
Lidzbarski, Mark, 24n.
Lieberman, Saul, xi, xiv, xvii, 5n., 25n., 27n., 44, 46n., 49n., 84n., 87, 90n.,
    111n., 112n., 133n., 159n., 162n., 165n., 166, 174n., 214n.
Liebreich, Leon J., 165n., 166
Liturgy, contributions of Rav to, 159-168, 187; contributions of Samuel to,
    159-168, 181; daily, 159-160; Days of Awe, 161-162, See Tekiata deve Rav;
    Festivals, 161; messianic element of emphasized by Samuel, 159-160, 167;
    popular practice, 280-281; rabbinic influence on, 280-281. See Blessings.
Lucius Verus, 6, 7
Lud, 144
Ludi Saeculares, Jewish Knowledge of, 87-88

M

Ma'aseh Bere'shit (Works of Creation), 153, 181, 182
Ma'aseh Merkavah (Works of the Chariot), 153, 154, 181, 182. See Merkavah.
Macrianus, xiv, 9, 51
Magic, 182; bowls (incantation bowls), 90-91; Jewish, 25; Jewish influence on
    magical literature, 91n.; knowledge of Rav, of 131
Magie, David, 5n., 46n.
Magus, Magi (Mogh), 2, 4n., 13, 15, 16-19, 28, 29, 36, 37, 54, 56n., 57, 59, 73,
    85, 133, 149n., 151, 168, 228; attitude of Rav and Samuel toward, 85; com-
    pared to rabbis, 148-149; functions of in Sasanian times, 148-149; Jewish
    hatred of, 90
Mahoza, 246, 247, 248; academy of, 232
Maktak/Maktik, Maktiks, 18, 19
Mandean, Mandeans, Mandaeism, 15, 18n, 19, 20, 23-25, 73n., 91; anti-Jewish
    climate of, 22, 24-25, 90; faith in Jesus, 72; influence on Jews and Judaism,
    25, 91n.; Jewish conversion to, 25; origins of, 24n.; source of Jewish magic,
    25; syncretism of Jews of Mesene with, 26n.
Mandelbaum, B., 162n.

Qumran, 60

R

Rabba b. Lema, 290
Rabbah, xiv, 271
Rabbah b. R. Adda, 216
Rabbah b. bar Ḥanah, 28, 129, 144, 252, 279n.
Rabbah b. R. Huna, 175, 275
Rabbah b. Samuel, 35
Rabbinovicz, R., 28n., 74n.
Rabbis, as holy men, 147-149; authority and influence of on people, 251-254, 266, 281-286; authority in civil litigation, 110-111; compared to Magi, 148-150; replace priests as religious leaders, 148
Rabin, 244
Ramram, R., 174
Rashi, 71n., 74n., 87
Rav, Son of Samuel, 135n.
Rava, xiv, 110, 255
Rava b. Ḥinena the Elder, 178
Rava b. Meḥassia, 11, 37, 192, 228
Rawlinson, George, 2n., 5n., 14n.
Redemption, views of Rav and Samuel on, 67
Resh Galuta (Exilarch, q.v.), 98, 107, 108
Resh Lakish, 230, 231
Resh Sidra/Resha derabbanan, 109, 127n.
Reuven b. Iẓtrobili, R., 153
Roifman, Jacob, 92n.
Rome, Roman, Romans, xix, 1, 2, 3, 4, 5n., 6n., 49, 67, 70, 87, 88, 122, 228; approval of Pharisaic party by, 94; attempt to win Jewish support, 94; benevolence of rule of in third century Palestine, 44; collapse of power in Middle East, 47; concern for Jewish opinion in Parthia, 94; condition of Jews under, 27, 37; destruction of Temple by 44; devastation of Judea by, 44; hostility of Samuel toward, 68; Jewish attitude toward, 27, 44, 52-53, 65-66; Jewish revolts against, 95; Jewish support for in Roman Orient, 48; policy toward Jews, 27n.; relationship with House of Judah the Prince, 28n.
Rosenthal, Franz, 135n.
Rostovtzeff, M., 4n., 5n.
Rudolph, Kurt, 24
Rumki, 241

S

Sabbath, popular observance of, 274, 277-278
Sachau, Eduard, 21n., 29n.
Salome Alexandra, 229, 232n.
Samuel, R., 241
Samuel b. Isaac, R., 166n.
Samuel b. Marta, R., 223
Samuel b. Shilat, R., 133, 144, 224
Samuel b. Unia, R., 213, 223
Samuel Yarḥinaʾah, 135-136
Sar Mushad, inscription of, 19
Sasan, 3

Shiʿur Qomah, 63, 184
Shustar/Shuster, xix, 242
Siegel, Seymour, xvii
Sikara, 247
Simai, R., 160
Simeon b. Gamaliel, R., 208, 230
Simeon b. Koziba. See bar Kokhba
Simeon b. Yehozadak, R., 184
Simeon b. Yohai, R., 53
Simlai, R., 141
Simlai of Lud, R., 144
Simon, R., 151
Simon, Maurice, xvii
Sis/Sisin, 21
Škand Gumanik Vičar, 154n.
Smith Morton, xvii
Sons of Aibu, beraita of, 109
Southerners, methodology of exegesis, 233-234
Spandarmad, 88
Spicehandler, Ezra, xvi, 113, 114n., 126n.
Sprengling, Martin, 4n., 6n., 17n., 18n., 54n., 113n.
Spuler, B., 20n., 22n., 24n.
Sramans, 18
Starcky, J., 51n.
Strabo, 245
Stube, 24n.
Sura, 50n., 78, 98, 144, 145, 247, 253, 263; academy of, 232-234; court of, 261;
    synagogue of, 78-79
Susa, 242
Sybilline Oracles, 237, 238
Synagogue, art of, 78-79. See Dura-Europos; practices in, 274-275
Syrians, in Babylonia, 38; under Parthians, 30
Szold, H., 186n.

T

Tabari, 3n., 11, 21n., 29n., 73n.
Tacitus, 92n.
Tadmor, Tadmorites (Palmyra, Palmyrenes, q.v.), 51n., 52n.
Talmon, S., 58n.
Talmud, xiv, xv, 25, 78, 170, 228, 233, 254; Babylonian, xiv, 161n.; Palestinian,
    xiv, 160, 161n.; editors of, 28
Tannaim, Tannaitic, 229, 233; beraita, 152; court, 64n.; Judaism, 151; times,
    171, 173; traditions, 55, 109, 251; traditions in Babylonia, 23
Tansar. See Tosar
Taqizadeh, S. H., 1n., 3, 4n., 16n., 20n., 88, 89
Tarfon, R., 64n., 73n., 74
Tarsus, xix
Tatlafus/Tatlefush, 247, 275
Taurus, passes of, xix
Taxes, 13, 122, 259
Tekiʿata deve Rav, 163-166
Temple of Jerusalem, 44n., 194, 206, 232n.; construction of, 193; destruction
    of, 53, 63, 64, 66, 74, 93, 153, 168, 238; reconstruction of, 223

X

Xosroes, xix 7

Y

Yamauchi, Edwin Masao, 91n.
Yannai, R., 82
Yavetz, Z., XII, 51n., 69n., 95n., 104n., 109n., 110n., 162n., 166n.
Yavneh, 93, 94
Yoḥanan, R., 8, 28, 32, 46n., 51n., 52n., 53, 54, 65, 97, 127, 129, 137, 141, 144,
    145, 148, 162, 168, 200, 210, 212, 217, 218, 223n., 231, 232 231.242n., 259, 266
Yoḥanan b. Zakkai, R., 37n., 53, 63, 67, 107, 184, 187, 194n., 238, 239; agreement
    with Rome, 66; political policy of, 66; recognition of by Rome, 94
Yosi, R., 100, 169, 171, 218
Yosi of Ḥuzal, 85

Z

Zabdi b. Levi, 188
Zaehner, R. C., 16n., 17, 18n., 148, 149n.
Zakkai, R., 100n.
Zamaris, 35
Zandik, Zandiks, 18, 19, 21
Zaradusht, 20
Zeʿiri, R., 145, 147n.
Zeitlin, S., 135n.
Zenobia, 10, 51
Zera, R., 55, 103n., 173, 228, 250
Zeugma, 242
Ziegler, Karl-Heinz, 6n., 51n.
Zoroaster, 20
Zoroastrian, Zoroastrianism. See Mazdean, Mazdaism
Zunz, Y. L., 96n., 97, 161n., 163n., 164, 165n., 166n.
Ẓuri, Y. S., xvi, 52n., 56n., 96n., 105n., 114n., 126n., 127n., 129n., 134n., 146n.,
    167n., 183n., 232-234, 236
Zurvan, 73n.
Zurvanism, xiii
Zutra, Mar, 162
Zutra b. Tobiah, R., 152, 154, 156, 171, 175, 213, 219